Sacral Revolutions

Sacral Revolutions is a unique project reflecting the contribution that Andrew Samuels has made to the general field of psychoanalysis and Jungian analysis in both clinical and academic contexts.

Gottfried Heuer has brought together an international array of authors – friends and colleagues of Samuels – to honour his 60th birthday. As a result, the collection provides a creative and cutting-edge overview of a fragmented field. The chapters demonstrate the profound sense of social responsibility of these analysts and academics, whose concerns include the mysteries and hidden meanings in social and political life.

This open and engaging volume includes a previously unpublished interview with C. G. Jung, adding to its usefulness as an essential companion for academics, analysts, therapists, students and candidates.

Gottfried Heuer, Ph.D. is a Jungian Training Analyst and Supervisor, and a Bodypsychotherapist and Trainer in private practice in West London. He has 35 years of experience in clinical practice and has published widely on the links between analysis, radical politics, bodypsychotherapy and spirituality. He is Co-founder and Chairman of the International Otto Gross Society.

Sacral Revolutions

Reflecting on the work of Andrew Samuels
– Cutting Edges in Psychoanalysis and
Jungian Analysis

Edited by Gottfried Heuer

Routledge
Taylor & Francis Group

LONDON AND NEW YORK

First published 2010
by Routledge
27 Church Road, Hove, East Sussex BN3 2FA

Simultaneously published in the USA and Canada
by Routledge
270 Madison Avenue, New York, NY 10016

Routledge is an imprint of the Taylor & Francis Group, an Informa business

© 2010 Selection and editorial matter, Gottfried Heuer; individual chapters, the contributors.

Typeset in Times by Garfield Morgan, Swansea, West Glamorgan
Printed and bound in Great Britain by TJ International Ltd, Padstow, Cornwall
Paperback cover design by Gottfried Heuer

This publication has been produced with paper manufactured to strict environmental standards and with pulp derived from sustainable forests.

British Library Cataloguing in Publication Data
A catalogue record for this book is available from the British Library

Library of Congress Cataloging-in-Publication Data
Sacral revolutions : reflecting on the work of Andrew Samuels : cutting edges in psychoanalysis and Jungian analysis / edited By Gottfried Heuer.
    p. cm.
  Festschrift for celebration honoring Andrew Samuels.
  Includes bibliographical references and index.
  ISBN 978-0-415-48172-4 (hardback) – ISBN 978-0-415-55461-9 (pbk.) 1.
Samuels, Andrew. 2. Jungian psychology–Congresses. 3. Psychoanalysis–
Congresses. I. Heuer, Gottfried, 1944-
  BF173.S252 2009
  150.19'54–dc22

                                                            2009019718

ISBN: 978-0-415-48172-4 (hbk)
ISBN: 978-0-415-55461-9 (pbk)

"The psychology of the unconscious
is the philosophy of the revolution"

Otto Gross, 1913

"Like fishermen, we scientists sit on the banks
of the stream of life and cast our hooks
more or less at random.
Sometimes one of us pulls out mud and weeds,
another fishes out a piece of gold,
but a third one comes up with something
that will change part of the world"

Wilhelm Reich, 1934

Contents

Figures

Contributors

Michael Vannoy Adams, DPhil, LCSW, is a Jungian psychoanalyst in New York City. He is a Clinical Associate Professor at the New York University Postdoctoral Program in Psychotherapy and Psychoanalysis and a faculty member at the Jungian Psychoanalytic Association, the Object Relations Institute, and the New School, where he was previously Associate Provost. He is the author of three books – *The Fantasy Principle*, *The Mythological Unconscious*, and *The Multicultural Imagination*. He is the recipient of three Gradiva Awards from the National Association for the Advancement of Psychoanalysis. He has been a Marshall scholar in England and a Fulbright senior lecturer in India.

Neil Altman is Adjunct Clinical Professor in the Postdoctoral Program in Psychotherapy and Psychoanalysis at New York University, and Emeritus Editor of *Psychoanalytic Dialogues: The International Journal of Relational Perspectives*. He is author of *The Analyst in the Inner City: Race, Class and Culture through a Psychoanalytic Lens* and co-author of *Relational Child Psychotherapy*.

Sue Austin, PhD, Sydney University, trained with the Australian and New Zealand Society of Jungian Analysts. A book based on her PhD was published by Brunner-Routledge in 2005, entitled *Women's Aggressive Fantasies: An Exploration of Self-Hatred, Love and Agency*. Sue's private practise comprises general analytic work, but she also specialises in working with eating disordered adults (especially those who have been severely and chronically ill). She has run numerous clinical workshops and seminars in the public and private health sectors in Australia, New Zealand, the UK and the USA and has published a number of clinical and theoretical papers.

Deirdre Bair wrote *Jung: A Biography* (NAAP Gradiva Award, LA Times Book Prize finalist), and biographies of Samuel Beckett (National Book Award), Simone de Beauvoir (New York Times Best Books, LA Times Book Prize finalist), and Anaïs Nin (New York Times Notable Books).

She also wrote a cultural study of late-life divorce: *Calling it Quits*. Her current project is a biography of the artist Saul Steinberg. She holds fellowships at the Bunting, Guggenheim, and Rockefeller Foundations, the van Waaveren Foundation and the C. G. Jung Institute of New York. She has been a literary journalist and university professor of comparative literature.

John Beebe, a psychiatrist, was certified as a Jungian analyst by the C. G. Jung Institute of San Francisco in 1978; he first met Andrew Samuels at the IAAP Congress in San Francisco in 1980. Like Andrew, he lectures frequently in different parts of the world and has published papers in numerous journals and books. As sole author, co-author, or editor he has published *Psychiatric Treatment: Crisis, Clinic and Consultation* (written with C. Peter Rosenbaum), *Jung's Aspects of the Masculine*, *Integrity in Depth, Terror, Violence and the Impulse to Destroy*, and *The Presence of the Feminine in Film*.

Jessica Benjamin is a psychoanalyst in private practice in New York City; a faculty member at the New York University Postdoctoral Psychology Program; and author of *The Bonds of Love, Like Subjects, Love Objects: Essays on Recognition and Sexual Difference* and *Shadow of the Other: Intersubjectivity and Gender in Psychoanalysis*. She has lectured and supervised all over the world, and is Associate Editor of *Psychoanalytic Dialogues*, Co-founder of the International Association for Relational Psychoanalysis and Psychotherapy, and the Director of the Acknowledgment Project, a series of dialogues between Israeli and Palestinian mental health practitioners, initiated with Dr. Eyad el Sarraj of Gaza and sponsored by the Norwegian Foreign Ministry.

Paula Pantoja Boechat is a medical doctor from Brazil. After having lived in Zürich (1974–1979), where she attended the Jung Institute, she did her training in Jungian Analysis and in Systemic Family Therapy in Brazil, and in 1991 was one of the founding members of The Jungian Association of Brazil (AJB). She did an MA in Clinical Psychology at the Pontifical Catholic University of Rio de Janeiro, has published in Brazil and abroad, and wrote *Family Therapy: Myths, Symbols and Archetypes*. She is the Director of Studies of the Jungian Institute of Rio de Janeiro. She is married and has two daughters.

Walter Boechat, AJB, IAAP, is a medical doctor from Brazil who did his training at the C.G. Jung Institute, Zürich, from 1974 to 1979. He is a founding member of the Jungian Association of Brazil. He coordinates a Post-Graduation Course on Analytical Psychology at the University of Rio de Janeiro. He has numerous scientific publications in Brazil and abroad. He wrote a comprehensive study on myth: *Mythopoieses of the Psyche: Myth and Individuation*. His main interests are: Brazilian and

Latin American cultural identity, race and inter-racial problems, psycho-somatics and body–mind totality. Walter Boechat is married, has two daughters and holds a private practice in Rio de Janeiro.

Joe Cambray, PhD, IAAP, is currently the President-elect of the International Association of Analytical Psychology. He is also the American Consulting Editor of the *Journal of Analytical Psychology* and an editor on several journal boards. He teaches internationally and is on the faculty of the Center for Psychoanalytic Studies at Harvard Medical School. Joe has published numerous articles, co-edited a book, *Analytical Psychology: Contemporary Perspectives in Jungian Psychology*, and delivered the 2008 Fay Lectures (*Synchronicity: Nature & Psyche in an Interconnected World*). Joe is a practising Jungian analyst with offices in Boston, MA, and Providence, RI.

Linda Carter, MSN, CS, IAAP, is a graduate of Georgetown and Yale universities and of the C. G. Jung Institute, Boston. She maintains private practices in Boston and in Providence, RI, where she also lives. With Joe Cambray, PhD, IAAP, she co-edited *Analytical Psychology: Contemporary Perspectives in Jungian Psychology* (2004). For the *Journal of Analytical Psychology*, she is the US Book Review Editor. As a member of the Art and Psyche Working Group, she helped develop, organize and produce an interdisciplinary conference revolving around art and depth psychology. She presents and teaches internationally.

Giles Clark has been practising as an analyst for over 30 years, from 1975 to 1994 in London and since 1995 in Sydney. He has taught and run seminars for analytic training groups in England, Europe and Australia. He taught the History of Ideas Pertaining to the Emergence of Depth Psychology on the MA course in Analytical Psychology at the University of Western Sydney. He is particularly interested in psychosomatic (mind-body) issues as manifest and experienced in transferential relations with personality disorders. His current work includes research on the use of neo-Spinozan thinking to inform analytic theory and practice.

Professor **Petruska Clarkson** († 2006), DLitt et Phil, PhD, FBPS, FBACP, was a philosopher, a chartered psychologist, a UKCP-registered psycho-therapist, and a management consultant. She contributed an acclaimed 30 years to the psychotherapy professions and is author of over 200 publications in the field. She wrote several seminal books including the celebrated *The Therapeutic Relationship* and *The Transpersonal Relationship in Psychotherapy*. Petruska's chapter contains excerpts from 'The archetype of Physis: the soul of nature – our nature', *Harvest Journal of Jungian Studies*, Vol. 42 (1), 1996, and *Physis*, her unfinished PhD thesis, 2003.

Muriel Dimen, PhD, is Adjunct Clinical Professor of Psychology, Professor Postdoctoral Program in Psychotherapy and Psychoanalysis, New York University, and Professor Emerita, Anthropology, Lehman College, the City University of New York. She is Editor of *Studies in Gender and Sexuality* and Associate Editor of *Psychoanalytic Dialogues*; Founding board member of the International Association for Psychoanalysis and Psychotherapy; and author of *Sexuality, Intimacy, Power* (Hillsdale, NJ: Analytic Press, 2003; Goethe Award, Canadian Psychological Association), *Surviving Sexual Contradictions* (NY: Macmillan, 1986), *The Anthropological Imagination* (NY: McGraw-Hill, 1977). She is Co-editor of *Gender in Psychoanalytic Space* (NY: Other Press, 2002), *Storms in Her Head* (NY: Other Press, 2001), and *Regional Variation in Modern Greece and Cyprus* (Annals, NY Academy of Sciences 263, 1976). She is a Fellow of the New York Institute for the Humanities.

Moira Duckworth is a training analyst, supervisor and past Chair of the Association of Jungian Analysts, London, and is in private practice in North London. She is an honorary and professional member of the Foundation of Psychotherapy and Counselling (FPC), teaches and supervises for several counselling and psychotherapy trainings and travels regularly to Moscow to supervise IAAP training. With Martin Stone, she has researched outcomes of therapy related to frequency of analytic sessions. Her interests include working with older people, endings, and assessment. She sings with the London Philharmonic Choir and her publications include a chapter on 'Fours in Supervision' (2001 IAAP Congress proceedings), and (with Martin Stone) a chapter on 'Frequency and the Analytic Framework', in *Controversies in Analytical Psychology*.

Maria Gilbert is a UKCP registered Integrative Psychotherapist, a Chartered Clinical Psychologist and a BACP-accredited supervisor. She is currently joint head of department, with Vanja Orlans, of the Integrative Psychotherapy, Integrative Counselling Psychology and Psychotherapy, Coaching Psychology and Supervision Department at Metanoia Institute in West London. She has co-authored two books on supervision and integrative psychotherapy with Ken Evans, a manual for supervisees with Michael Carroll and more recently, a manual for the beginning coachee, with Michael Carroll.

Christopher Hauke is a Jungian analyst in London, a writer, a film-maker, and a Senior Lecturer at Goldsmiths, University of London. His films include the documentaries *One Colour Red* and *Green Ray*. A new short drama, *Again*, is awaiting its Film Festival premiere. He is the author of *Human Being Human: Culture and the Soul* (2005) and *Jung and the Postmodern: The Interpretation of Realities* (2000), and he co-edited *Jung and Film: Post-Jungian Takes on the Moving Image* (2001) and

Contemporary Jungian Analysis: Post-Jungian Perspectives from the Society of Analytical Psychology (1998). He is co-editing a new book *Jung and Film – The Return* and writing a new introduction to Jung's psychology for Routledge (www.christopherhauke.com).

Birgit Heuer is a Jungian Analyst with the British Association of Psychotherapists. With a previous training in body-oriented psychotherapy, she has 30 years of clinical experience in private practice. She has worked as clinical supervisor at Kingston University and served on the Jungian Training Committee at the BAP. She has lectured widely and published on the themes of the body in analysis, the role of clinical paradigm in analytical discourse, the experience of the numinous in the consulting room and on forgiveness. She is currently writing a doctoral thesis on the theme of sanatology, a clinical theory of health and healing.

Gottfried Heuer, PhD, is a Jungian Training Analyst and Supervisor with the Association of Jungian Analysts, and a Biodynamic Bodypsychotherapist and Trainer, in private practice in West London. With 35 years of experience in clinical practice, he has published widely on the links between analysis, radical politics, bodypsychotherapy and spirituality, and on the history of analysis in English, German, Finnish, French, Portuguese and Serbo-Croat. He has contributed papers to *The Journal of Analytical Psychology*, *The International Journal of Psychoanalysis*, *Harvest*, *Spring* and others, and for the International Otto Gross Society (www.ottogross.org), which he co-founded and chairs, he has (co-) edited five volumes of Congress Proceedings (www.literaturwissenschaft.de) for the society.

Jean Kirsch, MD, is a Jungian analyst practising in Palo Alto, California. A graduate of Stanford University Medical School, she is a member and past president of the C. G. Jung Institute of San Francisco, where she was instrumental in establishing a program (International Student for Analytical Psychology) through which mental health professionals from countries with no formal training opportunities may spend two years at the San Francisco Institute studying Analytical Psychology. She is part of the training faculty at the C. G. Jung Institute.

Thomas B. Kirsch, MD, was born in London, England, and moved to Los Angeles at the age of four. He graduated from the Yale MD Program in 1961 and did a psychiatric residency at Stanford. He graduated from the CG Jung Institute of San Francisco in 1968 and was its President from 1976 to 1978. He was Vice President and then president of the IAAP, 1977–1995. He is Co-editor of the Jungians section of the *International Dictionary of Psychoanalysis* (Callman-Levy, edited by Alain de Mijolla, 2002), Co-editor of *Initiation: The Reality of an Archetype* (Routledge, 2007) and author of *The Jungians* (Routledge, 2000).

Lynne Layton, PhD, is Assistant Clinical Professor of Psychology, Harvard Medical School. She has taught courses on women and popular culture and on culture and psychoanalysis at Harvard College. Currently, she teaches at the Massachusetts Institute for Psychoanalysis. She is the author of *Who's That Girl? Who's That Boy? Clinical Practice Meets Postmodern Gender Theory*, co-editor of *Bringing the Plague: Toward a Postmodern Psychoanalysis*, and co-editor of *Psychoanalysis, Class and Politics: Encounters in the Clinical Setting*. She is editor of *Psychoanalysis, Culture & Society* and associate editor of *Studies in Gender and Sexuality*. Her private practice is in Brookline, Massachusetts.

Roderick Main, PhD, is Director of the Centre for Psychoanalytic Studies, University of Essex, UK. He is the editor of *Jung on Synchronicity and the Paranormal* (Routledge, 1997), and author of *The Rupture of Time: Synchronicity and Jung's Critique of Modern Western Culture* (Brunner-Routledge, 2004) and *Revelations of Chance: Synchronicity as Spiritual Experience* (SUNY, 2007).

Konoyu Nakamura, PhD, is Professor, Chair of the Department of Psychology at Otemon Gakuin University in Osaka, Japan, and is working in Kyoto as a Jungian-oriented psychotherapist. Recent publications include: 'The image emerging: the therapist's vision at a crucial point of therapy', in Huskinson, L. (ed.), *Dreaming the Myth Onwards: New Directions in Jungian Therapy and Thought* (Routledge, 2008); 'No-self' initiating the transcendent – the image of *Mahavairocana-tatha-gata* emerging from the therapist on a crucial point of therapy, in Mather, D., Miller, M., Ando, O. (eds.), *Self and No-self: Continuing the Dialogue between Buddhism and Psychotherapy* (Routledge, 2009).

John Nuttall, PhD, MA, ADip Psy, Dip Couns, is Principal Lecturer and Director of the Professional Doctorate programme at Regent's College and Lecturer at the University of Greenwich. He is Chair of the West London Centre for Counselling, a UKCP and BACP-accredited psychotherapist, a Certified Management Consultant, and a Chartered Marketer. He has written widely on management and psychotherapy and his PhD focused on the process of personal psychotherapy integration. As a scholar and colleague of Petruska Clarkson, John has produced and edited her work for the purpose of this commemoration.

Susie Orbach co-founded The Women's Therapy Centre, London, in 1976 and The Women's Therapy Centre Institute, a training institute in New York, in 1981. Her interests have centred around feminism, psychoanalysis, countertransference, the public sphere, the construction of femininity, globalization, body image and emotional literacy. Publications include *Fat is a Feminist Issue*, *Hunger Strike* and *The Impossibility of Sex*. Her latest book, *Bodies*, was published in 2009. Susie is Visiting

Scholar at The New School in New York, and has consulted to the World Bank, the NHS and Unilever. She is a board member of The International Association for Relational Psychoanalysis and Psychotherapy (IARPP), is chair of the Relational School in the UK and has a clinical practice where she sees individuals and couples.

Renos Papadopoulos, PhD, is Professor of Analytical Psychology at the Centre for Psychoanalytic Studies, Director of the Centre for Trauma, Asylum and Refugees, and a member of the Human Rights Centre, all at the University of Essex. He is a Consultant Clinical Psychologist at the Tavistock Clinic and a training and supervising systemic family psychotherapist and Jungian psychoanalyst in private practice. As consultant to the United Nations and other organizations, he has worked with refugees and other survivors of political violence in many countries. He is the founder and director of the Masters and PhD programmes in Refugee Care, offered jointly by the University of Essex and the Tavistock Clinic.

Rozsika Parker is a writer and psychoanalytic psychotherapist in private practice in London. She is a professional member of the Foundation for Psychotherapy and Counselling. Her publications in art history, gardening and psychoanalysis include *Old Mistresses: Women, Art and Ideology* (co-authored with Griselda Pollock), *The Subversive Stitch: Embroidery and the Making of the Feminine* and, more recently, *Torn in Two: The Experience of Maternal Ambivalence*.

Dr **Henrique Pereira** is a Clinical Psychologist in private practice in Rio de Janeiro and Niterói, Brazil. He earned his doctorate in Social Psychology from the University of the State of Rio de Janeiro. In his doctoral thesis he examined Analytical Psychology from the sociological perspective of Bruno Latour's Actor-Network Theory. He teaches Jungian Psychology at the University Estácio de Sá, Rio de Janeiro, in both undergraduate and post-graduate programs. Currently, he and Marcus Quintaes offer seminars on *Jung and the Post-Jungians* in Rio de Janeiro.

Fred Plaut (1913–2009) was a Training Analyst at the Society of Analytical Psychology and a Lehranalytiker of the Deutsche Gesellschaft für Analytische Psychologie. Previously he was a Consultant Child Psychiatrist, at Middlesex Hospital, London. He was a former Editor of the *Journal of Analytical Psychology* and since 1939 published over 90 papers and two books: *Analysis Analysed: When the Map Becomes the Territory* and *Between Losing and Finding: The Life of an Analyst*. His most recent paper is entitled 'The roots of intuitive interpretation – or, what case reports omit'.

Marcus Quintaes is an Jungian psychoanalyst living in Rio de Janeiro, Brazil. He did his postgraduate work in mental health at the Federal University of Rio de Janeiro. He is one of the coordinators of the group Himma: Studies in Imaginal Psychology (www.himma.psc.br). He is a member of the International Association for Jungian Studies (IAJS). He has been dedicating himself to the study of the works of Andrew Samuels and Post-Jungian ideas for the last 17 years and has been trying to disseminate these ideas to the Brazilian Jungian community, and to coordinate seminars on Archetypal Psychology and Post-Jungian thought in Rio de Janeiro and São Paulo.

Denise Gimenez Ramos, PhD, is a Clinical Psychologist and has a private clinic in São Paulo, Brazil. She is a professor at the Pontifícia Universidade Católica de São Paulo, where she coordinates the Center of Jungian Studies at the Graduation Program in Clinical Psychology. She is a member of the Academy of Psychology of São Paulo (27th Chair). She was Vice-President of the IAAP and director of the Brazilian Society for Analytical Psychology. For the last 12 years she has been the editor in chief of the "Junguiana" – a Jungian journal edited in three languages – and author of several articles and books.

Dr. **John Rowan** is the author of a number of books, including *Healing the Male Psyche: Therapy as Initiation* (Routledge, 1997); *Ordinary Ecstasy: The Dialectics of Humanistic Psychology* (3rd edition) (Routledge, 2001); *The Future of Training in Psychotherapy and Counselling* (Routledge, 2005); *A Guide to Humanistic Psychology* (AHPP, 2005); and *The Transpersonal: Spirituality in Psychotherapy and Counselling* (Routledge, 2005). He is a Fellow of the British Psychological Society, a qualified individual and group psychotherapist (UKAHPP and UKCP), a chartered counselling psychologist (BPS), a senior accredited counsellor and supervisor (BACP) and a personal coach (AC).

Susan Rowland, PhD, is Professor of English and Jungian Studies at the University of Greenwich, UK. She publishes on Jung, literature and gender and also detective fiction. Her book on Jung's creativity in writing and theory is *Jung as a Writer* (Routledge, 2005). Other monographs include, *Jung: A Feminist Revision* (2002). Recently published is an edited collection, *Psyche and the Arts* (Routledge, 2008) and a book on *Jung and the Humanities* will be published in 2009. She was founding Chair of the International Association for Jungian Studies (2003–6).

Christine Shearman is an Assistant Teaching and Supervising Member of The Gestalt Psychotherapy Training Institute, a Certified Transactional Analyst with Clinical Speciality, and has a Diploma in Integrative Psychotherapy. She is a Primary Supervisor for the Integrative department of the Metanoia Institute, West London. She co-edited a journal dedicated to the transpersonal, and published an article on the transpersonal from a Jungian perspective in this edition of the journal.

Thomas Singer, MD is a Jungian analyst and a psychiatrist. After studying religion and European literature at Princeton, he graduated from Yale Medical School and later trained at Dartmouth Medical Center and the C.G. Jung Institute of San Francisco. His writing includes articles on Jungian theory, politics and psychology and he has written and/or edited the following books: *Who's the Patient Here? Portraits of the Young Psychotherapist*; *A Fan's Guide to Baseball Fever: The Official Medical Reference*; *The Vision Thing: Myth, Politics and Psyche in the World*; *The Cultural Complex: Contemporary Jungian Perspectives on Psyche and Society*; and *Initiation: The Living Reality of an Archetype*. Dr. Singer lives and practises in the San Francisco Bay Area.

Martin Stanton is a psychoanalyst, artist and writer. He founded the first Centre for Psychoanalytic Studies at the University of Kent in 1986, and has been active since developing Psychoanalytic Studies in the UK and internationally. He is an Associate Research Fellow at the University of Cambridge, Visiting Professor at Roehampton University, Consultant Staff Counsellor at University College London, and Employee Support Consultant at Birmingham University, where he has pioneered his own form of psychoanalytic employee support (Confidential Assessment). He is the author of numerous books and articles. Further details of his work are available on his website (www.martinstanton.co.uk).

Martin Stone is a Training Supervisor and past Chair of the Association of Jungian Analysts, London, and is in private practice in North London. He travels regularly to Moscow as liaison person and supervisor for an IAAP programme training Russian mental health professionals to be Jungian analysts. With Moira Duckworth he has researched qualitative and quantitative outcomes of therapy related to frequency of analytic sessions. Other theoretical interests include the body–mind interface, synchronicity and relational psychology. Publications include papers on splits between Jungian groups, embodied countertransference, individuation and supervision, and (with Moira Duckworth) frequency and the analytic framework.

Dr **David Tacey** is Associate Professor in the School of Critical Enquiry, La Trobe University, Melbourne. He teaches courses on spirituality, religious studies, analytical psychology and literary studies. He is the author of eight books, including *The Spirituality Revolution: The Emergence of Contemporary Spirituality* (Routledge, 2004) and *Jung and the New Age* (Routledge, 2001). His most recent book is *How to Read Jung* (Granta, 2006). With Ann Casement, he co-edited *The Idea of the Numinous*

(Routledge, 2006). His main research topic is the recovery of meaning in the contemporary world.

Nick Totton is a body psychotherapist, supervisor and trainer in private practice in Calderdale, West Yorkshire. He is the author of several books, including *Psychotherapy and Politics* (Sage), *The Water in the Glass: Body and Mind in Psychoanalysis* (Rebus/Karnac), *Body Psychotherapy: An Introduction* (Open University Press), and *Press When Illuminated: New and Selected Poems* (Salt), and has edited several others, including *The Politics of Psychotherapy* and *New Dimensions in Body Psychotherapy* (both Open University Press). He is the editor of *Psychotherapy and Politics International*. Current interests include ecopsychology, and he is working on the concept of 'Wild Mind'. There is an extensive website at www.erthworks.co.uk

Liliana Liviano Wahba, PhD, is a psychologist and a Professor at the Pontifical Catholic University of São Paulo. She is President of the Brazilian Society for Analytical Psychology (SBrPA), a Co-Editor of *Junguiana* and a Former Honorary Secretary of the Ethics Committee of the IAAP.

Polly Young-Eisendrath, PhD, is a Jungian analyst and psychologist. She is Consultant for Leadership Development at Norwich University and Clinical Associate Professor of Psychology and Psychiatry at the University of Vermont. She is in full-time practice in central Vermont and has published 13 books that have been translated into more than 20 languages, including *The Resilient Spirit: Transforming Suffering into Insight and Renewal*, and *Women and Desire: Beyond Wanting to Be Wanted*. Her newest book is *The Self-Esteem Trap: Raising Confident and Compassionate Kids in an Age of Self-Importance* (Little, Brown).

Luigi Zoja, PhD, is a former Training Analyst of the C.G. Jung Institute, Zürich, a Past President of Centro Italiano di Psicologia Analitica (CIPA), and a former President of IAAP (when he chose Andrew Samuels as Honorary Secretary). He has taught at the Universities of Palermo and Insubria and has clinical practices in Zürich, New York and Milan. He has a Diploma in Analytical Psychology from the C.G. Jung Institute, Zürich, and has published in Italian, German, French, Spanish, Portuguese, Greek, Russian, Polish, Czech, Lithuanian, Slovenian, Chinese and Korean. Publications in English include: *Drugs, Addiction and Initiation* (1989/2000); *Growth and Guilt* (1995); *The Father* (2001) (Gradiva Award 2001); *The Global Nightmare* (ed.) (2002); *Cultivating the Soul* (2005); and *Ethics and Analysis* (2007) (Gradiva Award 2008).

Acknowledgements

In deepest gratitude to all contributors and my editors at Routledge, Kate Hawes and Jane Harris, as well as Dawn Harris of the production team and Sally Mesner for her careful and caring copy editing.

My grateful acknowledgement of the permission to publish, for the first time, the interview with C. G. Jung (see editorial note, p 11). I also gratefully acknowledge permission to publish previously published materials from Dr Joseph Cambray, representing the IAAP, for Michael Vannoy Adams' text; from Professor Dr Renos Papadopoulos, former editor of *Harvest*, for Sue Austin's text; from Taylor and Francis for Muriel Dimen's interview with Andrew Samuels; from Nancy Cater, editor of *Spring*, for Gottfried Heuer's text; and from Routledge for Lynne Layton's text, which is a reworking, with some new material of "Attacks on Linking: The Unconscious Pull to Dissociate Individuals from their Social Context", pp. 107–117, in Lynne Layton, Nancy Caro Hollander, and Susan Gutwill (eds.) (2006) *Psychoanalysis, Class and Politics: Encounters in the Clinical Setting*, New York: Routledge. Every effort has been made to trace Map Collector Publications, the copyright holders of an earlier, different version of Fred Plaut's text, to no avail.

Gottfried Heuer, London, June 2009.

Introduction

A plural bouquet for a birthday celebration in print

Gottfried Heuer

The two quotes from Gross (1913: 384) and Reich (1994: 6) which precede this introduction hint at the particular *other* tradition of Andrew Samuels' original, innovative and creative thinking and working – the main tradition being, of course, Jungian (this is represented by the interview with Jung that follows this introduction, published here for the first time). Already some 100 years ago, the psychoanalyst Otto Gross took the first steps towards an integration of the personal and the political, the analytical with both radical politics and the sacral, and a generation later Wilhelm Reich continued this work. What distinguishes Andrew from both of them is the fact that in both instances their work was so radically new for their times that they became outcasts in the analytical world: to this day, neither is really being quoted in conventionally serious texts. By contrast, Andrew has managed to walk the tightrope path to the peak of the profession *without* betraying any of his humane, innovative and radical ideas: in the mercurial manner of a messenger of the Gods he has achieved a worldwide dissemination of and engagement with his ideas: hardly any texts that deserve to be taken seriously in the field can be said not to be directly or indirectly influenced by his work. From the four corners of the world, Jungian and psychoanalytic, academic and clinical, the authors of the present volume are testimony to this fact. My heartfelt thanks to all of them for their contributions!

This book is a plural bouquet, a birthday celebration in print, in honour of my dear friend Andrew Samuels' 60th birthday. My original idea for this firework of ideas was to make the Festschrift a total surprise. Yet when I discussed this just over a year ago with Andrew's beloved Anna Price, it became almost immediately clear that this was unrealistic: nobody but Andrew himself would be able to know whom he would want to be invited to this celebration! So, to the extent of adding to my original ad hoc list of invited guests from all over the world, he was "in" on the secret. It speaks of Andrew's charisma that, *without exception*, every one of the "guests" invited – some 40 in all – responded with enthusiasm: *nobody* wanted "to stay at home"!

At the same time, having been drawn in, Andrew was adamant that the contributors should not feel they had to do more than consider writing in a manner that actively related to his main areas of interest; they should not be asked for a series of responses to his work, nor to write personal encomia. In the event, many contributors did either take off from Andrew's *oeuvre* or write in part of their personal connection to and appreciation of Andrew. I took the editorial decision to allow such naughty diversity to flourish.

This introduction would be incomplete without at least an attempt to summarise the multi-faceted achievements – gifts towards "changing part of the world" (in Reich's words, above) – that Andrew has so generously given to us. To do this, I am going to draw on a previous mark of esteem for him. Some years ago, a biennial Andrew Samuels Lecture was created by the Confederation for Analytical Psychology. Both of the speakers to date (Jessica Benjamin and Polly Young-Eisendrath) are represented in this volume. As the lecture is a public event (with the stipulation that the topic should link analytical psychology to another discipline or to other disciplines), it was necessary to produce a sort of introduction to Andrew, and what follows is largely based on that document.

Andrew is Professor of Analytical Psychology, University of Essex; Visiting Professor of Psychoanalytic Studies, Goldsmiths College, University of London; Honorary Professor of Psychology and Therapeutic Studies, Roehampton University; and Visiting Adjunct Clinical Professor, Postdoctoral Program in Psychoanalysis, New York University.

He was elected one of the initial group of six Honorary Fellows of the United Kingdom Council for Psychotherapy (the national multi-modality umbrella organisation with over 7,000 registrants). He is a Training Analyst and Supervisor at the Society of Analytical Psychology, London. He served on the Committee of the International Association for Analytical Psychology for 12 years and, particularly when working as its Honorary Secretary, performed a generally acknowledged uniquely hermetic role in linking and developing analytical psychology around the globe. Since the early 1980s, Andrew has been a pioneer in introducing Jungian psychology and therapy in countries where there were not only no psychotherapy structures but the very activity itself was illegal.

He is currently a Board Member of the International Association for Relational Psychoanalysis, and, as a declaration of his belief in psychotherapy integration, he remains a member of the Association for Humanistic Psychology (GB). He is in private practice in London and also works internationally as a political consultant. He was a main co-founder of Psychotherapists and Counsellors for Social Responsibility and Antidote, the campaign for emotional literacy. He is Consultant Editor of *Psychotherapy and Politics International*.

His many books have been translated into 19 languages and he is the author of *Jung and the Post-Jungians* (1985), *The Plural Psyche* (1989), *The Political*

Psyche (1993), and the award-winning *Politics on the Couch: Citizenship and the Internal Life* (2001). He has co-written and edited a number of volumes including *A Critical Dictionary of Jungian Analysis* (1986), *The Father* (1986) and *Psychopathology* (1989). He has published over 100 papers.

Andrew was the key founding member of the Confederation for Analytical Psychology, which was created in response to a stormy episode in the UK psychotherapy scene when the British psychoanalysts decided to part company with the United Kingdom Council for Psychotherapy, taking two major Jungian Societies with them. Andrew's initiative in creating CAP meant that those members of the Society of Analytical Psychology and the British Association of Psychotherapists (Jungian Section) who wished to retain registration with UKCP and its principles could do so. As a result, there are approximately 60 'Jungians' registered with the UKCP today who, without Andrew's intervention, would not be registered.

At the same time as representing analytical psychology, Andrew has contributed to the inclusive and relational spirit and structure of the UKCP from its very beginnings. He has done this with a passion for sustaining professional working relationships between differing groups, networking and advising – all with his own brand of energy and political intelligence. He has served on UKCP's committees and working groups for 20 years – from 1989 until the present day.

With other 'Jungian' academics, Andrew was instrumental in founding the International Association for Jungian Studies, a multi-disciplinary group with over 400 members in many countries worldwide.

Andrew is a Patron of Counselling in Prisons, a Trustee of the Refugee Therapy Centre, a Trustee of the Work/Life Balance Trust, and a Consultant to Immigrant Counselling and Psychotherapy (which is the lead agency of Irish Government-sponsored work with survivors of institutional abuse in Ireland who are living in the UK).

Developing his specific blend of post-Jungian, relational psychoanalytic and humanistic approaches, Andrew has been involved in the education and training of psychotherapists for over 30 years. He has functioned as a training analyst/psychotherapist, supervisor, lecturer and seminar leader for virtually all the depth psychological organisations in the UKCP (and, indeed, within the British Psychoanalytic Council as well). In addition, he has participated significantly in the training activities of numerous humanistic and integrative organisations, as well as keynoting humanistic and integrative conferences.

Andrew's leadership role in psychotherapy education was recognised in 2003 when he was awarded the Hans W. Loewald Award for Distinguished Services of the International Federation for Psychoanalytic Education.

In terms of raising awareness of the profession, Andrew is a frequent broadcaster in both radio and television, and a contributor to national newspapers.

He has worked closely with the British Association for Counselling and Psychotherapy as a judge for their awards programme. As a keynote conference speaker, Andrew has an international reputation and is invited to speak all over the world. He was, for example, a keynote speaker at the World Congress for Psychotherapy in Buenos Aires, Argentina, in 2006.

As far as clinical excellence is concerned, Andrew has made many contributions. We would like to underscore his commitment to combating racism, sexism, homophobia and other prejudices in clinical practice as well as in the theoretical domain. This was recognised by the UKCP Equal Opportunities Committee and also by the Ethics Committee when they invited Andrew to their 2004 conference at which he outlined his argument that equal opportunities and the whole inclusive/diversity agenda are very much ethical and spiritual as well as political matters.

Concluding on a personal note: putting this volume together over the past year has been a labour of love for me – with the emphasis, clearly, on *love*: "A friend is a gift of God, and He only who made hearts can unite them."[1] For almost 20 years now I have been blessed with the loving and caring generosity of your friendship, dear Andrew. Editing the present volume cannot be but a small expression of my gratitude: Thank you, from the depths of my heart! And: to your *next* 60 years! – Enjoy!

Gottfried Heuer, London, January 2009.

Bibliography

Gross, O. (1913) Zur Ueberwindung der kulturellen Krise. *Die Aktion*, III: 14, col. 384–387.

Reich, W. (1994) *Beyond Psychology*, New York: Farrar, Straus and Giroux.

Note

1 Robert Southey.

Chapter 1

"The hope that we might find a way . . ."

A birthday interview with C.G. Jung in his 80th year

Carl Gustav Jung and Ingaret Giffard

Editorial Note

For the first time ever in print, I am happy to present the transcript of the complete interview of C.G. Jung by Ingaret Giffard (1902–1997), commissioned by the British Broadcasting Corporation, London, and recorded by her husband, Sir Laurens van der Post (1906–1996) in Ascona, Switzerland, on 24 March 1955. The program was to mark Jung's 80th birthday, on 26 July 1955. Parts of the interview were used in a broadcast by the BBC Home Service on 20 July 1955, 8.20–9.00p.m. The present transcript is based on three sources:

1 The sound recording of the interview, held at the National Sound Archive under Catalogue No. 885525, Reference No. 21852–21854 (3), is on five sides of three shellac records. These records, or "discs" are numbered 9CL0032031, 9CL0032043 and 9CL0032041. Each of the five parts is indicated in the text with "[Pt.1], [Pt.2]" etc., respectively.

2 A transcript of the broadcast (the only known copy, it seems, as there is none known in the BBC Archives nor at the National Sound Archive), held at the ETH Bibliothek, Zürich, under No. Hs 1055: 1007. On the first page, this carries a notice, "This script is for your private information only and should not be published or quoted in published material or used in any way without permission first having been obtained from the BBC." Also, there is the seal of the BBC ("Nation Shall Speak Peace Unto Nation") with the typewritten notice, "From Mrs. Helen Rapp's Office", as well as a printed one, "With the Compliments of the British Broadcasting Corporation."

3 Another copy of what appears to be the original complete interview on a reel-to-reel tape I discovered in 1998 in that part of the estate of the late Dr. Sasha Duddington (1921–1998), a dear colleague of mine, that he had left to the Association of Jungian Analysts, London, of which he had been a longtime member and previous Chair.

In the transcript that follows, passages in italics were not part of the BBC broadcast but have been supplemented from the Duddington copy of the original interview and the copy in the National Sound Archive. Minor corrections, like insertions into or omissions from the recorded interview in the BBC transcript, have been made unmarked, as have obvious corrections of audio-mistakes, e.g. the BBC transcript says "metanschainen" instead of "*Weltanschauung*". In all instances, the spoken word on the sound recording has been followed.

In the BBC broadcast, the Introduction was followed by a eulogy, "The Eightieth Birthday of Carl Gustav Jung", by Sir Laurens van der Post, which is about as long as the actual interview itself. This I have omitted from my presentation.

Sometimes, in the BBC transcript, Ingaret Giffard summarises a question or gives a brief introduction to a new topic. In this present transcript I have followed, instead, the recording of what appears to be the original interview from the sound copies.

It is impossible to ascertain whether the "Opening Announcement" actually ended where the text presented here stops, as this first page is unnumbered.

I am most grateful to Ms. Vicky Mitchell of BBC Rights & Business Affairs, London, the actual copyright holder, for not only giving me permission to publish this text – under the condition that I obtained also permission from the Jung heirs – but also for most generously waiving the copyright fees normally due. I am equally grateful to Herrn Ulrich Hoerni of the Stiftung der Werke von C.G. Jung (successor in interest of the Erbengemeinschaft C.G. Jung), Zürich, for not only giving me permission to publish this text – under the condition that I obtained permission from the BBC – but also for helping me to secure the official permission from the Agentur Paul & Peter Fritz AG, Zürich. Of course, my thanks go also to Frau Dr. Yvonne Voegeli of the ETH Archiv, Zürich, for sending me a copy of the transcript of the BBC broadcast.

Gottfried Heuer, London, October 2008

Carl Gustav Jung – An interview with Ingaret Giffard

OPENING ANNOUNCEMENT: This is the BBC Home Service.

Carl Gustav Jung.
Tuesday next is the eightieth birthday of the distinguished Swiss psychologist, Dr. Jung, and to-night we present a program in his honour. We do not propose to try and give a resumé of Dr. Jung's work or attempt to assess his contribution to the study of the human mind. His best testimonial is to be found in his books and it is still too soon to assess finally his contribution to psychology, except to say that it has been

very great indeed. The program you will hear, in which Dr. Jung himself speaks, has not therefore been compiled by a psychologist but by two of Dr. Jung's personal friends: Laurens van der Post, the African explorer, and his wife Ingaret Giffard recently visited Dr. Jung at his home [sic] in Ascona, taking with them a tape recording machine. The first half of the program we now present consists of a recorded talk by Laurens van der Post on his personal impressions of the man himself, and the second half consists of a recorded conversation.

[. . .] ?

[PT.1]

INGARET GIFFARD [INTRODUCTION]: We spent some time with Dr. and Mrs. Jung at Ascona and in the afternoons I would sit with Dr. Jung in the lounge of his hotel by a window which looked on to the lovely lake. I would ask him some questions and discuss the answers with him. Both the questions and the answers were spontaneous and unrehearsed. The only factor of premeditation in the situation was a tape recorder which my husband had brought with him, and he sat in a chair not far away and recorded our conversation.

I.G. [QUESTION]: Dr. Jung, could you tell me what it was that first made you take up psychology as your life's work? Was it something that you always wanted to do from childhood, or was it something that came to you later in life?

CARL GUSTAV JUNG: Oh well, you know the real reason why I took up psychology was that when I was a child, I already noticed that I didn't understand people – they were *always* incomprehensible to me, for a certain reason, and that – well, that came from the fact that they'd say certain things and did other things and there didn't seem consequence in all that. I saw so many inadequate emotions, because the people were excited over things which were not a bit exciting, or they made a fuss about something – why should one make a fuss about it?

I.G.: I know the feeling.

C.G.J.: Well, for instance, once an aunt of mine took me to a museum, a zoological museum, and of course I was enchanted looking at all these stuffed animals, and then suddenly the bell rang, and the time was up and we had to hurry to the exit and – we had to cross another part of the museum, and that was a gallery of sculptures, of antique sculpture. I never had seen such a thing. It was marvellous! It was a revelation! And my aunt said, "You horrible boy! Shut your eyes! Shut your eyes! Don't look at the things! Come along!" And I said, "Why, it is so beautiful? Why shouldn't I?" I had to turn round – hanging back now, you know, looking at these wonderful . . .

I.G.: Wonderful figures . . .

C.G.J.: And then I thought, "Now why did she say such a thing? They are so beautiful." And then I discovered they were naked – see? Then I discovered something, you see? That is what my aunt couldn't stand, you know, because they were naked, *horrible – and I am the horrible boy, you know that?* [laughs]

I.G.: *I think if you could tell us about your early association with Sigmund Freud, it would be very, very interesting and very helpful to people.*

C.G.J.: *Well, that was in about 1907. In 1906 I had written a book about the psychology of what one called* dementia praecox *then,*[1] *nowadays it's called schizophrenia, you know. And I went to Vienna to pay a visit to him and there our discussion began. The first day we were talking for thirteen solid hours. And, I could not agree with him with everything he said, with all of his theories, but I said, "Well, you understand more than I do", and so I worked with him for seven years, and I'm afraid that I was a terrible disillusion* [sic] *to him, because he thought I would take up and continue his work.*

I.G.: *Yes, I understand that. – Well then, now really we've reached the point when you're standing by yourself, alone. It brings me, although it's rather a jump, to something that's always moved me personally very much about your work, and that is your clear recognition of the importance of religion in the life of the individual.* I've always felt that you see religion, Dr. Jung, in essence as a great process of healing that which [sic] is torn and tattered in man. And I think if I remember rightly, you speak of the Churches as the great therapeutic establishments of mankind. Do you feel that one of the gravest aspects of our time is the increasing failure of the Churches to maintain this function? And why do you think they are failing in this way?

C.G.J.: Well obviously, there is some trouble along that line. It is quite visible to everybody that in [sic] – just with educated people – the confessions of religions don't fulfil that role any more which we *would* expect of them. [Pt.2] You know the – for instance, Christianity speaks of *salus*, I mean the salvation, and the healing, and that is making man whole.

I.G.: Quite, yes.

C.G.J.: And – but when I look at all my educated patients, they hardly know what Christianity is really. People don't even read the Bible, they don't know what there is in the Bible, and they don't understand the symbols of the Church. They don't know what that should mean, that Christ is a Redeemer, or that we are purified from our sin, or redeemed from our sin. These things have become words that don't work any more.

I.G.: The meaning has – emptied of meaning in some way.

C.G.J.: They don't function any more, because they don't fulfil what they promise. *And, therefore, oh, I have many patients that were just confused and lost because they had no orientation of a spiritual kind. Now, since times immemorial all old peoples and tribes and so on they had their form, their religious form, which makes them whole. And that has disappeared in our times.*

I.G.: Could you tell us something of what your work has revealed to you about the nature of God?

C.G.J.: *Well, I wouldn't be able to tell you anything about that because* I could never claim that any kind of human work could reveal something about the nature of God, or about His existence. I only know that the idea of God is a pattern, an age-old pattern, a primitive pattern that always has been and never lost its – *what we call* numinosity, that means its emotional significance and importance. It is always there, and it still plays the same role as it always did, and it is therefore by no means indifferent [sic] whether somebody knows about that image of God or not. Our human mind is *so narrow*, and restricted that it wouldn't be able to understand or to formulate such an entity as God. That is an absolutely transcendent idea. But we can establish the existence of that pattern, and that is for our practical purposes enough, because when we can integrate such an idea in our mind, the idea of such a being, then that gives an entirely different scope to things.

I.G.: Yes, that is extremely interesting *and very important.*

C.G.J.: And it is exceedingly short-sighted when people say, "Well, you cannot prove the existence of God." One cannot prove the existence of God as you cannot prove the existence of immortality or eternity or anything like that. *Because all that is a matter of concepts.* But you can prove the existence of the pattern, there is no doubt about that, and the pattern is something that demands its way. It's like an instinctual pattern without which the bird cannot build its nest. I was deeply impressed hearing the Pueblo Indians telling me once, "A man in the mountains, being quite alone, cannot even build his fire without Him that walks over the hills."[2]

I.G.: Ah yes, that puts us in our place a little bit. – *Thank you, Dr. Jung.*

[Pt.3] What you know of human nature, Dr. Jung, does it make you despair of our chances of avoiding another world war? And in particular, what do you think is going to come out of this discovery of the atom bomb, and these latest developments of nuclear physics?

C.G.J.: Well, I'm not certain at all that we are making for a third world war. There might be a war, but I don't know, it can be avoided, perhaps. Yet the problems that lead to the actual situation, namely that enormous split that goes through the whole world, that exists and everything that has led up to it, can lead up to a war; and even if the war doesn't happen, the split is there.

I.G.: When you say split, Dr. Jung, you mean the split in human beings?

C.G.J.: The split between the East and the West, which is the split in every human being, because we are all human.

I.G.: *Yes, that's very to the point.*

C.G.J.: So you see there is a certain hope that man can understand something about the split in himself, and then it is no more necessary to represent that split politically outside.

I.G.: Yes, that answers it completely.

C.G.J.: But it means a complete change of our mental and spiritual outlook.

I.G.: Which perhaps has started. Do you feel that?

C.G.J.: Well, it is difficult to say whether it has started or not, at least I do my best to start it [laughs].

I.G.: *Yes, yes!* Dr. Jung, I'm now going to ask you, if I may, a few specific questions, in order to try and get into focus the outline of your work and its entirely new approach to the being of man. As we sit here talking, I can see the mountains opposite, one snowy side brilliant in sunshine, and the other side always in shadow; and I wonder, isn't that something of the way in which you see the nature of man? Could you tell us, therefore, something of what you have called the shadow side of mankind?

C.G.J.: The simile that you use of the sunny side of a mountain and the dark side, the shadowy side of a mountain, it's quite apt in a way. Where one's – our consciousness shines, there everything is bright and apparently in order, but there is another side where we are inferior and not so good, and not so brilliant, and that side obviously is not welcome, one doesn't like to be there, or to look at it, but occasionally it becomes unavoidable and that [sic] you fall into that side, and then you are quite astonished. You can see that phenomenon on a grand scale in history. For instance, take what happened to the Germans. The German nation has certainly appeared wholly transformed. They got into the shadow side of the human nature, and look at the horrors that are there. Now, that is the shadow in everybody, every individual has such a dark side where there are things lurking we don't know of, often what is called just horrors, sometimes it is not so bad.

I.G.: [Pt.4] Yes, quite, yes. Thank you, Dr. Jung. – Then it would perhaps be correct to say that the whole purpose of your work has been to achieve the integration of man's personality, his inner wholeness? In other words, to make sure that the unknown shadow side of each individual becomes known to him?

C.G.J.: Well, it is always, nearly always so because it's the rule that when you begin to work with an individual that the question of the shadow begins to play a role. One discovers one thing after the other, and one has to try to fit that in, into the total of human consciousness, so that the individual doesn't look at himself as an ideal figure or what he wants to be, but what he really is, and that thing has its dark sides. Now, that is the way in which every work with an individual begins.

I.G.: *Dr. Jung, your work seems to me to emphasise, in such a very marked degree, that it's the individual that is the only carrier of life, and existence, and therefore of paramount importance in human society. Why therefore, do you think, do* all the current developments of science, sociology and philosophy, for instance, tend to discourage the individual and substitute for him mass and group values?

C.G.J.: Well, that is, of course, one of the consequences of our modern science, which is chiefly based upon the average, the statistical average. Now, the statistical average produces a picture of man which is utterly unimportant. It is a mere abstraction, it is not a real man. Our Weltanschauung that is based upon the statistical average is an abstraction. It is not the real world. And therefore the individual is a sort of random phenomenon. But in reality the individual is the only reality. And if you follow the idea of the statistical average, then you have only the idea of the so-called "normal man", and the normal man does not exist. He is a mere abstraction. We have to deal with individuals only. So, anything that can happen in the way of development or results or so on, happens to the individual, and not to an average man. *And you cannot do it with masses, with numbers. It must be the concrete, individual man that has to do it, or that has to develop. There is no prescription that would heal 10,000 on one stroke.*

I.G.: [Pt.5] *And now, Dr. Jung, I was going to ask you, as we are drawing to the end of this talk, could you please tell us something of what you are working on at the moment?*

C.G.J.: That is a most indiscrete question.

I.G.: I know it is, I know it is [laughs]. You must side-step it.

C.G.J.: You force me to make my confession: I am working at nothing, I am enjoying my old age, I am glad I had for the time being no new ideas at all. My last ideas have been so difficult that apparently I reached the ceiling.

I.G.: You reached the ceiling, yes, and you've got to absorb them.

C.G.J.: I mean, I couldn't say that I'm working at something. I have still certain ideas, but I couldn't possibly explain to you what they are.

I.G.: I imagine that when you have an idea of this sort, or whenever you have an idea, it has to go through a period of incubation, it has to be absorbed.

C.G.J.: Oh yes, you know, my time has become short for these incubations. I went through quite a number of incubations [laughs], but I don't know whether the time is still granted to me to continue in the same way.

I.G.: One final question, please, Dr. Jung: Looking back on these long years of your great research into the nature and the soul of man, what would you say is the main lesson for us?

C.G.J.: The main lesson would be to learn more about the subject "man". We have discovered many things, but we know very little about man himself. We are afraid, for instance, nowadays, of these awful inventions of uranium fission, and the hydrogen bomb, but it is man that is manipulating these things, and we should know more about man, or how to manipulate man's psyche, because now it is really the question, "What is man going to do with these new inventions?" It all depends upon human decision. Our greatest danger is man himself, and therefore, I think, it is of the utmost importance that we begin with a serious study of what man is and means, and that is my whole program. I don't consider myself a redeemer, I only want to understand, as I said in the beginning, what man is doing, and why he is doing things, and I want to learn about his nature, of course, with the hope that we might find a way with man so that he doesn't need to destroy himself by such terrible devices like the hydrogen bomb, etcetera, or cobalt bomb.

I.G. [CONCLUDING COMMENT]: As Dr. Jung finished speaking, I remember that his daughter and his grandchildren entered the room, and the last picture I have of him is setting off on an evening walk by the side of Lago Maggiore with his family round him.

Notes

1 *Über die Psychologie der Dementia Praecox: Ein Versuch* (Halle: 1907); The Psychology of Dementia Praecox, CW 3.
2 Ochwiay Biano (Mountain Lake), chief of the Taos Pueblos. (Cf. Jung, C.G., 1963, *Memories, Dreams, Reflections*, London: Collins, pp. 275–282, esp. p. 279.)

Chapter 2

The Sable Venus on the Middle Passage

Images of the transatlantic slave trade[1]

Michael Vannoy Adams

Among all archetypes, the journey is perhaps the most universal. Of course, there are always variations on themes. There is the external journey, and there is the internal journey. There are personal journeys, and there are collective journeys. There is the journey as quest, but there is also the journey as conquest. There are journeys of heroes, journeys of villains, journeys of victims, and journeys of survivors. There are journeys of exploration and journeys of exploitation. Not every journey is a journey of individuation.

There is the journey to Africa – for example, the journeys of Jung to North Africa in 1920 and to East Africa in 1925–26, as well as the journey of Jungians to South Africa in 2007. There is also the journey from Africa. Of journeys from Africa, the most universal is the journey of all humanity from Africa, as the evidence of mitochondrial DNA has conclusively proved, but there is also another journey from Africa, not of all humanity, but the journey of Africans in the transatlantic slave trade – the 'night sea journey' of the Middle Passage to the Americas.

The passengers on the ships of the Middle Passage were not immigrants but 'imports'. They were slaves. As James A. Rawley says, a slave was a 'commodity', and the slave trade was a 'business' (1981: 7). Rawley estimates the imports of slaves into the Americas, 1451–1870, at 11,345,000 (1981: 428).

The most notorious image of those ships is the diagram of the *Brookes* (Fig. 2.1). Abolitionists published the diagram in 1788, when a law that would restrict that ship to 454 slaves was under consideration in the British Parliament. One witness testified that in 1783 the ship had carried approximately 600 slaves, of whom 70, or 11.6 per cent, had died on the journey. 'It was calculated,' Rawley says,

> that if every man slave was allowed six feet by one foot, four inches, platform space, every woman five feet ten by one foot four, every boy five feet by one foot two, and every girl four feet six by one foot, the *Brookes* could hold 451 slaves.

> (1981: 283)

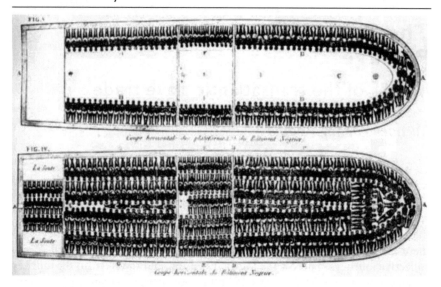

Figure 2.1 The *Brookes* Diagram, **1788**.

These are, of course, merely the physical dimensions of the journey – not the psychic dimensions, which Rawley aptly calls the 'trauma of the Middle Passage'. It was not just that Africans were traumatized when they were enslaved. They were also traumatized when they were, as Rawley says, 'confined on a ship that would sail into the alien sea for an unknown destination and unknown purposes' (1981: 290).

Hardly any personal accounts of the journey exist, but one by Olaudah Equiano describes an initial experience of the ship. 'I was now,' he says, 'persuaded that I had gotten into a world of bad spirits and that they were going to kill me.' On the ship he saw 'a large furnace or copper', and he had a fantasy that the white men on the ship were going to boil him. He fainted. When he recovered, he asked other slaves on the ship 'if we were not to be eaten by those white men with horrible looks, red faces, and long hair' (Gates 1987: 33). There is, of course, a certain irony to all this, for one of the fantasies of Europeans was that Africans were cannibals who would boil them and eat them. Equiano was reassured that he was not going to be boiled and eaten, that he was not going to be killed, but he was still convinced that the world of white men that he had gotten into on the ship was a world of 'bad spirits' – and that was, in fact, an accurate description of the psychic reality of the situation. The white men *were* bad spirits.

'The psychological impact,' Rawley says, 'of the Middle Passage upon the involuntary passengers was noted by contemporaries.' For example, a doctor reported that one ship had carried 602 slaves, of whom 155, or 25.7 per cent, had died on the journey. He estimated that two-thirds of those

Figure 2.2 The "Night-Sea-Journey" of the Middle Passage.

deaths had been the result of melancholy. The doctor, Rawley says, 'could cure none who had the melancholy' (1981: 291). Diagnostically, the trauma of the transatlantic slave trade was an incurable depression.

The archetype of the journey comprises three stages: separation, initiation, and return (Campbell 1968: 30). As a journey, however, the transatlantic slave trade included only two stages: separation and initiation – or separation and trauma. In a sense, of course, every initiation is a trauma, and every trauma is an initiation. Also, every journey is a journey toward an unknown destination for unknown purposes. The slave trade was hardly exceptional in that respect. Every journey is a journey of the ego into the unconscious (Figure 2.2).

As an initiatory experience, however, the slave trade was especially traumatic. It was a journey with no return. On a beach in Dahomey, there is the 'Gate of No Return'. It symbolizes, Henry Louis Gates, Jr., says, that 'the spirits of slaves, the dead, are welcome home through this gate' (1999: 226). Of course, it is one thing to return dead and in spirit, quite another thing to return alive and in body.

What so depressed Equiano was the realization that 'I now saw myself deprived of all chance of returning to my native country' (Gates 1987: 33). The result was often, if not insanity, suicide. The captain of one ship reported that slaves committed suicide because ''tis their belief that when they die they return home to their own country and friends again' (Mannix 1962: 117–18). A doctor on another ship also reported that slaves 'wished to die on an idea that they should then get back to their own country'. The captain of that ship devised an ingenious solution to the problem – to behead the dead in order to prevent any idea of suicide. 'The captain in order to obviate this idea,' the doctor said, 'thought of an expedient viz. to cut off the heads of those who died intimating to them [that is, to the slaves] that if determined to go, they must return without heads' (Mannix 1962: 118). From a psychoanalytic perspective, decapitation is dissociation. To return without a head would be to return without spirit – or without psyche. To sever the head from the body was to sever the slave from Africa spiritually or psychically.

Of course, some contemporary descendants of slaves do return to Africa – for example, to Goree Island off the coast of Senegal. This is not just the slave trade, in an ironic reversal, as a tourist trade, a mere exercise in nostalgia or sentimentality. It is a return to the scene of the trauma, as if such a journey might be a curative experience.

Perhaps the most egregiously perverse image of the transatlantic slave trade is the Sable Venus. 'Venus' is, of course, the proper name of a goddess, but it is also a generic name, or epithet, for a woman. The most famous 'Venus' from Africa is not the Sable Venus but the Hottentot Venus.

The Hottentot Venus was a real woman, Saartjie Baartman (cf. Figure 2.4). In 1810, she was transported from South Africa to Europe, where she was exhibited as a curiosity in England and France. Europeans were fascinated by her body, which was caricatured with a Cupid on her buttocks (cf. Figure 2.3.) After her death in 1815, her body was dissected by Cuvier, and her skeleton, brain, and genitals were preserved and displayed at the Musée de l'Homme in Paris until 1974. Her remains were finally interred in South Africa in 2002.

In contrast to the Hottentot Venus, the Sable Venus was not a real woman but an imaginal woman. A book, *The History, Civil and Commercial, of the British Colonies in the West Indies* (1801), by Bryan Edwards includes a poem, 'The Sable Venus: An Ode', by Isaac Teale. The poem compares the Sable Venus to the Venus of Botticelli:

> The loveliest limbs her form compose,
> Such as her sister VENUS chose,
> In FLORENCE, where she's seen;
> Both just alike, except the white,
> No difference, no – none at night,
> The beauteous dames between.

(Edwards 1801: 34–5)

The second volume of the third edition of the book includes both the poem and an image. The image is 'The Voyage of the Sable Venus from Angola to the West Indies' by Thomas Stothard, Esquire, of the Royal Academy (cf. Figure 2.5). If any image is obscene, this is it. It is iconography as pornography. 'No more preposterous misinterpretation was ever perpetrated of the

Figure 2.3 The Hottentot Venus, caricature, early nineteenth century.

"Middle Passage",' Hugh Honour says, than the Sable Venus. Honour remarks that neither the poem nor the image 'so much as alludes to slavery: the theme of both is the physical charm of the black woman' (1989: 33).

Daniel P. Mannix notes that 'a wealth of classical details' embellishes the image (1962: 113). In this image, there is no African goddess, and there are no African gods. The goddess and the gods are all Roman – and although the goddess is black, all the gods are white. The image 'Romanizes' and 'whitens' the slave trade. There are twelve figures in the image. Eleven of the figures are white – only one of the figures is black. The Sable Venus rides on a scallop shell and sits on a velvet throne. In the sky are six cherubs. Two cherubs fan the Sable Venus with ostrich plumes while one cherub holds peacock feathers. In the sea, two dolphins, with two cherubs, pull the scallop shell, while to the right Triton blows a horn. On the left Cupid draws a bow and aims an arrow at Neptune, who holds not a trident but a flag, the Union Jack. The Sable Venus eyes the reins and holds them as she guides the

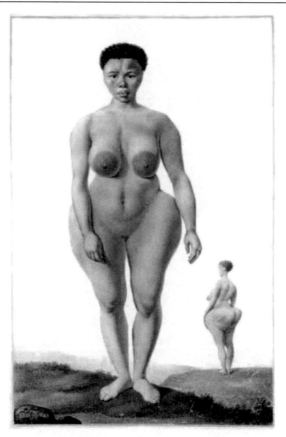

Figure 2.4 Saartjie Baartman, 1810.

dolphins, as if the journey from Africa to the Americas were entirely voluntary – as if it were not a journey by force but a journey by choice.

The Sable Venus is virtually nude. 'Except for bracelets, anklets, and a collar of pearls,' Mannix says, 'she wears nothing but a narrow embroidered girdle' (1962: 112). The obscenity of the image is not the virtual nudity. The perversity of the image is the audacity of the mythological amplification. Roman myth is utterly inappropriate and inapplicable as a parallel to the slave trade. This is not just an incompetent amplification – a comparison for which there is no basis. It is a radically disingenuous amplification. The amplification is a euphemism that represses the enormity of the slave trade and conveniently excuses it.

The image reveals even as it conceals. It is obviously not an image that accurately depicts the psychic reality of black African men and women in the transatlantic slave trade. The value of the image is that it accurately depicts the psychic reality of white European men. The image is not a slave

Figure 2.5 *The Sable Venus*, engraving by W. Grainger after a painting by Thomas Stothard for Bryan Edwards, *The History, Civil and Commercial, of the British Colonies in the West Indies*, 1801.

narrative but a master narrative. It is a projection, a cultural imposition that serves a quite specific purpose for white European men. The image is an example of how Africa has provided Europe with an opportunity for what Gates calls 'the projection of fantasies from its collective unconscious' (1999: 16–17) – or, more accurately, from its cultural unconscious.

The image is not so much a cultural complex as it is a cultural duplex. It is a duplicitous image, an image that, even as it represses what Hugh Thomas calls the 'iniquity' of the slave trade (1997: 11), expresses the duplicity of white European men. The image is a certain variety of anima that a certain variety of ego imposes culturally on a scene. It is the exotic, erotic anima of an imperialistic, psychopathic ego. In this image, which is both racist and sexist, the slave is a woman – and not just any woman but a woman no man coerces because she always consents. As a woman, the slave never resists.

The function of the image is aesthetic. The image stylizes an ugly, coercive experience, the slave trade, and revises it into a beautiful, consensual – and sensual – experience. Slavery is lovely. In this stylization and revision, Britain waves the flag, and, like Neptune, rules the waves – and, by Cupid, loves the slave as a woman. The image implies that slaves are like women who, like Venus, just love it. Slaves, however, were not goddesses enthroned on shells. They were women and men, girls and boys, confined on ships. They did not wear bracelets, anklets, and collars of pearls. They wore chains. In the slave trade there were flags – among them the Union Jack and the Stars and Stripes – but there were no cherubs, dolphins, Triton, Cupid, and Neptune, and there was no Venus. What Marcus Wood calls 'the ludicrous panoply of Gods and putti' (2000: 54) is not just the use of an image. It is the abuse of an image.

On the journey of the Sable Venus, there are no white men with horrible looks, red faces, and long hair. There are no bad spirits. There are only white gods. There are no black slaves – much less 600 black slaves. There is only one black goddess – and she is not a black African goddess but a black European goddess. The wealth of classical details does not just embellish the image to demonstrate the erudition of the artist. The mythological amplification converts an atrocity into art. It does not just normalize the slave trade. It idealizes it. It is all royally academic. This is not truth and reconciliation. It is lie and rationalization.

Bibliography

Campbell, J. (1968) *The Hero with a Thousand Faces*, Princeton, NJ: Princeton University Press.

Edwards, B. (1801) *The History, Civil and Commercial, of the British West Indies*, 3rd edn., London: John Stockdale, vol. 2.

Gates, Jr., H.L. (ed.) (1987) *The Classic Slave Narratives*, New York: Mentor.

—— (1999) *Wonders of the African World*, New York: Alfred A. Knopf.

Honour, H. (1989) *The Image of the Black in Western Art*, Cambridge, MA, and London: Oxford University Press, vol. 4, pt. 1.

Mannix, D.P., with Cowley, M. (1962) *Black Cargoes: A History of the Atlantic Slave Trade, 1518–1865*, New York: Viking Press.

Rawley, J.A. (1981) *The Transatlantic Slave Trade: A History*, New York and London: W.W. Norton.

Thomas, H. (1997) *The Slave Trade: The Story of the Atlantic Slave Trade: 1440–1870*, New York: Simon & Schuster.

Wood, M. (2000) *Blind Memory: Visual Representations of Slavery in England and America, 1780–1865*, New York: Routledge.

Notes

1 This chapter is based on a paper presented at a plenary session of the Congress of the International Association for Analytical Psychology, Cape Town, South Africa, 15 August 2007, and is included in the proceedings of that conference.

Chapter 3

Repetition and repair

Commentary on the film *Love and Diane* by Jennifer Dworkin[1]

Neil Altman

The film *Love and Diane*, by Jennifer Dworkin, follows the lives of Diane Hazzard, her daughter, Love Hazzard, and Love's son Donyaeh. Diane had previously lost custody of her six children due to her drug abuse. At the time of the filming, which extended over a period of five years, Diane is attempting reunification with some of her children. Jennifer Dworkin, the filmmaker, virtually lived with the family during this period capturing many of the crucial events in real time as Donyaeh is placed in foster care due to alleged neglect on Love's part, followed by the eventual reunification of the family. This chapter pursues the themes of trauma, repetition and repair as they occur in the events documented in the film.

So much has already happened by the time we meet Love and Diane at the beginning of the extraordinary film that bears their names. So much of it is unthinkable, unbearably painful if we stop to reflect on it, and making us stop to reflect on it is certainly one function of the film. In the case of African-Americans, we must start with being kidnapped into slavery, the Middle Passage, and life, if you can call it that, in slavery in the United States. As Gump (2000) has pointed out, slavery, and then life in the Jim Crow South, created a legacy of trauma, transmitted across the generations, with which African-American families have had to cope and still have to cope. In the case of Diane, we know that she was abandoned in a car, along with her siblings, by her parents at age three, that she used drugs and alcohol perhaps at first in a misguided effort to cope with the untold pain in her life, could not take care of her children and lost custody of them. One of her sons, Charles, committed suicide. One of her children, Love, kept running away from home, got placed in a group home, contracted the HIV virus and got pregnant. As the film opens all of this has already happened. Beyond shame and guilt, the horror of this situation is such that one wonders how Love and Diane were able to bear it. The question I would like to raise in this chapter is how people do bear such pain. The question in the background for me as a psychoanalyst is repetition. Unprocessed trauma tends to be repeated. The proximal trauma in this case is that of having a child with high hopes, only to lose that child, to have that child taken away. There are more distal, unknown traumas to be sure, going back to slavery, when children were taken away, when whole families were torn apart. For how many generations has that been repeated? Much recent work in psychoanalysis has been done around the question of how the cycle of repetition can be interrupted. Freud (1914) counterposed repetition, clinically, to remembering. What is not remembered is repeated. Selma Fraiberg (1975) amended this formulation, using the word 'remember' in an emotional sense – emotions that are not remembered lead to repetition. More recently, Fonagy *et al.* (2002) and Main and Hesse (1990) have put another variation on this theme with their concept of mentalization. What cannot be thought about tends to be repeated. Flashbacks become repetition in the absence of the ability to think *about* trauma. So one way the cycle of repetition can be interrupted is to foster the capacity to think about trauma, to think about the unthinkable, to somehow render the unthinkable thinkable.

This way of formulating the question as to how the cycle of repetition can be interrupted has to do with what goes on within the person, with her capacity to think. Although another person, a therapist or someone else, may be instrumental in fostering this capacity, the crucial change takes place within the psyche. Another line of thought about interrupting repetition has to do with how trauma tends to be repeated within relationships, and specifically within the relationship of a psychoanalytic treatment. One way to define a psychoanalytic treatment is as a relationship specifically designed to elicit repetitions of trauma within a sort of transitional space that creates space both to think about what is happening as it occurs, and to work together to fashion a new ending to an old story. The patient comes to treatment expecting to be traumatized in the same old way, often abandoned or exploited in one way or another. There is also, except in the most extreme destructive situations, some hope that this time it can work out differently. The therapist's job is to participate in an enactment of trauma that will often play out around some real/perceived abandonment or exploitation, around money, in private practice, or a failure to understand something, for example, while remaining curious in collaboration with the patient about how meaning is made of the events. In the traumatic script that is pre-written, the therapist's role is to retaliate or abandon the patient further when the patient, enraged or deeply discouraged, reacts to the first hint of abandonment or exploitation. The unthinkable becomes thinkable as it is relived with another person whose job it is to keep thinking about what is unfolding, rather than engage in knee-jerk defensive reactions as people often do in real life. This process may fail for a number of reasons. The balance of destructive and hopeful forces within the patient may be too unfavorable, and/or the therapist may be unable to resist being drawn into the vortex of defensive or retaliatory reactions because of past trauma in *her* life, for example. In this sense, interruption of the cycle of repetition depends on an interpersonal situation, on the capacity of two people, working together to fashion a different ending to an old story. And we should always keep in mind that there is no guarantee that the unthinkable can be rendered thinkable. In a situation such as that encountered in this film, we, and all those in the film, are working at the edge of what is bearable for human beings.

Sometimes there seems to be an uncanny similarity between the way in which a person was traumatized early in life, and the traumatic situations that arise later in his or her life. The woman who was sexually abused has a daughter then forms a relationship with a husband or boyfriend who sexually abuses her daughter, for example. Therapists are familiar with ways in which they, horrified, start to realize that they are upsetting their patients in ways uncannily similar to ways in which the patient was traumatized in the past. The person who was abused and neglected in early life may come to feel that the therapist's quiet listening stance is unconscionably neglectful. How can you just sit there while such horrible things are happening in my life? How can you be so intent on ending sessions on time when I am pouring out my heart to you? The question that comes up at such moments is, to what extent is past trauma being repeated as a function of subtle ways the patient *makes* it happen, and to what extent does the outside world, other people, you and I as therapists or caseworkers, somehow keep failing the patient in the same ways? Relational psychoanalysts have been grappling with this question in recent years, trying to give substance to the general idea that *both* must always be happening, i.e. the patient is inducing from the therapist the very behavior they fear, but at the same time, the therapist can be plausibly seen as fostering the repetition. My experience was that the situation with Love and Diane seemed to move inexorably toward Love losing her baby, as she had been lost to her mother. Is there some way in which Love and Diane were setting up this repetition? Is there some way in which those involved with them in the human services system colluded with the repetition? And how do we imagine how this repetition could be interrupted, in part was interrupted, so that the cycle of trauma and repetition could be broken?

Whatever Diane's life was like up to that point, it is most striking that she named her child 'Love'. There is, of course, hope in that name, hope that is reflected again in Love's anticipation of love from her baby. As Love makes explicit, for a person who has been deprived of love, a baby is born with the obligation to make good on that broken promise to her mother. If I had been there at the time, I would have worried about whether Diane was taking account of how difficult it is to take care of a baby and to raise a child and an adolescent, how much hate as well as love gets evoked in this relationship. I would have worried about what would happen when Love did not live up to her name. Diane comments on how Love, and all her children, were meant, but failed, to repair the 'hole in my heart' from not having had a mother and father herself, indeed that the more children she had the more she felt that hole in her heart.

There is also the question of rivalry among the siblings when there may not be enough parental nurturance to go around and when there is the potential for idealizing, and thus denigrating, the children. It is significant, in that connection, that the outburst of rage that resulted in Love initially losing her child grew out of an incident of being teased by a sibling. One must also wonder what are the factors that led Love to her violent outburst, given that at some level she must have known that she was under scrutiny as to her ability to be a competent parent. Love, with characteristic insight in her better moments, explains it like this: 'Nobody understands that I'm hurting but all they do is push me away and when they teased me I didn't know what to do so I reacted and threw things.' We can also wonder whether in the background was some ambivalence about the burdens of parenting, given that she had not yet been parented, or whether success as a parent was threatening to her in some way, or whether living a life too different from the one she had known was unimaginable at the time, or whether she felt like such a bad person that she was not entitled to happiness as a mother or as a person. We must wonder what was going on when Love did not attend sessions with her therapist even though she knew that would be the crucial factor in determining whether she would get her baby back. To me, there always seems to be more at play than is suggested by what a person in the grip of a traumatic repetition can explain. It often seems that there is some powerful and nearly inexorable destructive force at work.

In the film, for all that, Love and Diane bring many assets to their lives, to the effort to avoid the repetition of the family trauma. They do tolerate the co-existence of love and hate in relation to each other. First of all, Diane is able to bear feeling guilt about having abandoned her child. How difficult must that be, especially given the guilt she must already feel about her son's suicide? The alternative could have been to demonize Love, to try to convince herself, Love, and the rest of the world that Love deserves whatever bad things happen to her, not that she, Diane, had set a chain of events in motion that led to Love's life situation. I was struck with how little of that demonization there was, and how strong Diane was to put into words how badly she felt about the mistakes she had made in her life and how her children had been made to suffer. The capacity to bear guilt arises from the integration of love and destructiveness, from the recognition that one has hurt someone that one also loves. Those who can't bear guilt need to make those whom one has hurt all bad, so that guilt doesn't arise. For her part, Love shows the ability both to love and to hate her mother. She gives full voice to her anger and hatred about her mother's failures. Yet, in one of the film's most touching scenes, she acknowledges how much she needed, and, by implication, still needs, her mother, how when she ran away from foster placements, it was always to look for her mother. Love says: 'I'd do anything to get my mother's attention – I thought they thought I was the worst because I said my mother's smoking crack – I had a lot of guilt so I went my separate way.' There is a vulnerability that shows how deeply Diane and Love touch each other, how much love has survived between them. Given what has gone down in their lives, it is very impressive to me that they could be so open to each other. This is where the film gave me the most cause for hope.

So, in that way, the film shows how Love and Diane survived and found a way to bear the pain of their lives. I also note that Donyaeh appears to bring a great deal of strength to the stressful circumstances of his life. He maintains his equilibrium and his *joie de vivre* as he is moved from care-taker to caretaker, without meltdowns and without appearing to dissociate. At times of transition he seemed to me understandably and appropriately sober. The only hint of his stress appears in the form of very mild opposi-tionalism as he is returned to Love and very deliberately puts her book in the fish bowl. Also, parenthetically, I was very struck by the extraordinary attachment the baby's foster mother developed to him, to the point where she could not be present when he was returned to Love. She had fallen in love with him. This speaks, perhaps, both to her personal qualities, and the baby's appeal. It also spoke to how much love can develop and be sustained in the temporary foster placements that are all too common in the system. Finally, I was struck with the quiet, reassuring presence of Love's boy-friend, Courtney, who, until nearly the end, seemed to provide another witnessing, containing presence at Love's side. These are all factors that promoted a relatively positive outcome to the story as far as we are made privy to it, so that as the film ends we can hope that the cycle of trauma and repetition might be interrupted. There is, of course, the wild card of Love's HIV infection and how she manages to cope with being attached to her son knowing that her time with him could be cut short. It is possible that the die had been cast in some respect before the film begins in such a way that certain outcomes are inescapable, but within those constraints the film shows us how human intervention and human strength can give people in some of the most extremely unfavorable circumstances a degree of freedom to author their destiny.

Bibliography

Fonagy, P., Gergely, G., Jurist, E. and Target, M. (2000) *Affect Regulation, Mentalization, and the Development of the Self*, New York: Other Press.

Fraiberg, S., Adelson, E. and Shapiro, V. (1975) Ghosts in the nursery: A psycho-analytic approach to the problems of impaired mother-infant relationships. *Journal of the American Academy of Child Psychiatry* 14: 387–421.

Freud, S. (1914) Remembering, repeating and working through. In *Standard Edition of the Complete Psychological Works of Sigmund Freud* 12: 145–156.

Gump, J. (2000) A white therapist, an African-American patient. *Psychoanalytic Dialogues* 10: 619–632.

Jaques, E. (1955) Social systems as a defense against persecutory and depressive anxiety. In *New Directions in Psychoanalysis*. New York: Basic Books.

Main, M. and Hesse, E. (1990) Parents' unresolved traumatic experiences are related to infants' disorganized attachment status: Is frightened and/or frightening parental behavior the linking mechanism? In M. Greenberg, D. Cicchetti, and E.M. Cummings (eds.) *Attachment in the Preschool Years: Theory, Research, and Intervention*, pp. 161–182. Chicago: University of Chicago Press.

Menzies, I.E.P. (1975) A case study in the functioning of social systems as a defense against anxiety. In *Group Relations Reader I*, A.D. Colman and W.H. Bexton (eds). Jupiter, FL: A.K. Rice Institute, pp. 281–312.

Note

1 This chapter is based on a paper that was originally given at a conference on the film *Love and Diane*, directed by Jennifer Dworkin, at Cornell University, September 9, 2005.

Chapter 4

Women's aggressive energies, agency and psychological change

Sue Austin

Aggressive energies in relationship

In this short piece I want to suggest that aggressive energies and fantasies can be the conduits of important changes in the realms of relationship and agency for women. Of specific interest to me is the point where relationship and agency appear to clash, leaving women with what appears to be a choice between two irreconcilable alternatives. The capacity to attain a third position, from which aggressive energies can be held and directed for the good of relationship, is a significant human achievement, and an increasing capacity to do so correlates with an increasing capacity to build and sustain lively relationships without compromising oneself or one's values.

A short story by Helen Garner ('The Feel of Steel 1', 2001) illustrates. The author recalls an early encounter with the sport of fencing at age 15, describing her teacher in the following terms:

> What Mr Fadgyas had at his disposal was a way of focusing and directing aggression: of making fighting beautiful. The aggression in me, however, was deeply buried. Though I was quick on my feet, I was scared – not of getting hurt, but of attacking.
>
> (2001: 173)

Garner went on to flirt with fencing, but eventually lost interest through 'a couple of inglorious competition bouts'. Her interest was, however, re-aroused in her 50s, through her sister Judi (who had also been involved in fencing as a young woman), who faxed her an advertisement for 'Fencing for Older Adults'. Garner describes her second lesson:

> Judi and I pulled on masks and breastplates, stepped on to the piste and crossed swords. I went for her. She blocked me. I went again. It was thrilling. Adrenalin streamed through me. I wanted to attack, to be attacked, to have to fight back. I remember the lunges, the sliding clash of metal, how the sword hand rises as the foil-tip hits the target. It was

glorious. We both burst out laughing. We only stopped because she didn't have a glove: I almost struck her hand and she flinched back. We lowered the blades. She pulled off her mask. Her eyes were bright, but I saw with a shock how gentle her face was, how feminine, under the cloud of hair.

(2001: 174)

What is being described here is more than the pleasure of physical exertion, or even the thrill of fighting. Garner is exploring the edges of her identity as a woman and, in particular, the places where that identity breaks down in interesting and enlivening ways. The breakthrough that she is pointing to is that the disciplined, aggressive tussle of fencing connects her to her sister's gentleness and, I would suggest, not only her sister's beauty and humanity, but also to something important in herself. Through the shocking recognition of the immediacy of her sister's aliveness Garner is connected to her own aliveness.

This kind of heightened apperception of the Other (and of oneself through the splendour of the other) is a moment of passionate love. That it can come through the disciplined and focused use of aggressive energy is the point that interests me. Garner recognizes the rarity and value of what her aggression offers and concludes:

That's what I want. I want to learn to fight, but not in the ordinary wretched way of the worst of my personal life – desperate, ragged, emotional. I want to learn an ancient discipline, with formal control and purpose. Will my body hold out? I hope it's not too late.

(2001: 175)

Garner's short story was brought to my attention by an analysand – a woman in her 60s who felt that Garner's description echoed a crucial aspect of her own struggle. My analysand, whom I shall call Amy, had brought up her children more or less single-handedly, having been left by her partner when the children were young. Amy had structured her career around her responsibilities to her children and came into analysis saying that she had been angry all her life, and felt that now, for the first time ever, she had space to explore that. When, some time into analysis, she came across Garner's story, she was very drawn to the idea of learning to fight, but, as Garner says, not in the ordinary, desperate, ragged, emotional way, but in some other way, for which she had no language or images. Like Garner's, Amy's aggression was buried, and she was scared of her desire to attack. Amy could see, however, that something about her buried, unmapped aggression might provide a link to the sense of aliveness and capacity for greater intimacy with others that she sought, and Garner's short story seemed to be gesturing towards these links too.

Amy's concerns echoed the many conversations I have had with women analysands who describe themselves as having always been angry, or having been angry for decades. Her comments also resonated with something from my work with women with long-term, severe eating disorders, which is my area of clinical specialisation.

What are aggressive energies for?

As I reflected on this material, I found myself asking a very Jungian question: what are these aggressive energies *for*? Andrew Samuels' reading of aggressive fantasy provided a crucial point of departure:

> Aggressive fantasy promotes a vital style of consciousness . . . Aggressive fantasy has much to do with our desire to know; it is not, in itself, completely bloodstained and unreflective . . . Aggressive fantasy can bring into play that interpersonal separation without which the word 'relationship' would have no meaning. In this sense, aggressive fantasy may want to make contact, get in touch, relate . . . Aggressive fantasy forces an individual to consider the conduct of personal relations. When one fantasizes an aggressive response to one's desires on the part of the other, one is learning something about that other as a being with a different but similar existence to one's own. Without aggressive fantasy, there would simply be no cause for concern about other people and so aggressive fantasy points beyond ruthlessness to discover the reality and mystery of persons. 'It is only when intense aggressiveness exists between two individuals that love can arise'. (1989: 208–209, quoting Storr)

A follow-on story by Garner ('The Feel of Steel 2', 2001a), resonates strongly with this understanding of aggressive fantasies and energies. The author finds out that she is expected to fence in the Inaugural Veteran's Section of a State fencing competition. She tries to get out of it, but her coach will not let her. The day of the competition arrives with muggy, 30°C weather, and she pulls on the mask – heavier than her practice one, with darker wires, smaller holes and a more spongily padded bib than she is used to. Garner describes sweat trickling through her hair, and dripping off her as she dons the layers of competition clothing. She faces a Sherman tank-like man from the country, who swats her blows like she is a mosquito. Just as we expect her to start to withdraw in the face of anticipation of a humiliating, ugly defeat, she writes: '[h]e wiped me out. I shook his hand in bliss' (2001a: 205).

Then, as the tournament went on:

The longer we fenced in the awful heat, the cooler my head became. I felt *daring*. I didn't care if I lost but I went all out to win. My mind, normally so scattered and fleeting, tuned itself to my body. I grasped for the first time in my life what tactical thinking might be, how I could vary my attacks, feint and wait and spring a surprise. I saw in a series of bright flashes what was required, what I might one day be capable of, if I stuck at this.

(2001a: 205–206; original italics)

Garner's text points to the extraordinary transformation which comes from being able to play over her own aggressive desires again and again, until there is a shift in her capacity to think. Garner's commitment to exploring her own aggressive energies and the outer edges of her capacity to stay with them enables her to keep going without being overcome by shame, humiliation, a sense of helplessness, frustration or despair. Through this, I would suggest that she is able to be totally absorbed in the moment – without self-judgement or self-criticism. She simply no longer cares what the Other thinks of her. Garner has forged an amalgam of aggression and curiosity – a passionate desire to learn about herself, which she is exploring relationally. Hence, perhaps, her bliss while shaking hands with the man who has beaten her, and has provided her with the opportunity to learn something vital (in both senses) about herself.

Most importantly, Garner is not interested in winning – simple notions of competition and power are not her focus. Instead, she is after a different kind of power: genuine power 'within', rather than power 'over'. Thus she describes getting a bronze medal for her participation as a moment of 'radiant companionship'. Garner is not exploring aggression in order to beat others (or to beat them up), but to come closer, to know herself and others better.

Vivienne's story

Garner explores the limits of her aggressive capacities in a place where the gradients are favourable: a fencing class is much safer than being a female teacher dealing with violent adolescents, or being a woman in a violent domestic situation. I suggest, however, that 'ordinary' women explore their own aggressive energies and fantasies in less apparent ways all the time, and often in unfavourable circumstances. While circumstances may vary, there is an area of overlap, which is the frame of mind in which aggressive energies are most likely to flip over into a vehicle for breakthrough. This emotional space is often arrived at through some form of disciplined psychological work and Radical Buddhist nun Robina Courtin sketches a Buddhist perspective on the kind of emotional framework in which such a breakthrough is possible.

While being interviewed on Australian national radio, Courtin explains that the Buddhist emphasis is on learning to distinguish between the negative, neurotic, I-based use of energy and other potential uses of the kind of strong energy which can manifest as anger, or, if configured differently, as compassion. She lists the characteristics of energy coming from such a negative state of mind as: 'it comes from a huge sense of I, it comes from fear, it's narrow, it's a sense of separateness, and it wants to harm' (Courtin, interviewed by Rachel Kohn, 2003). Garner's story describes the non-neurotic, positive use of strong energy – her aggression is expressed with a minimal sense of I, very little fear, great breadth of vision and willingness to engage as fully as possible, and without the desire to harm herself or the Other. One of the women who contributed material to my Ph.D. thesis and book (2005) provides an example of how, from this psychological place, aggression can become a point of connection and expansion.

> Vivienne: Some time during our 'courtship', when Geoffrey and I had been going out regularly for a considerable amount of time, I began to have the feeling that he had lost enthusiasm for our relationship. One night, as he was about to leave, I found the courage to ask him about it. I actually asked him whether he really still cared about me, or whether he needed someone to accompany him socially. Or something like that. I assumed he would assure me about his continuing affection (why else really would he have continued the relationship). He looked uncomfortable, but replied that what I had feared was true – he said, quite simply, that I was filling a need for him. I felt as if I was cracking into a hundred pieces, but managed to stay together long enough to ask him to leave – which he did, very quickly – before the messy combination of shock, rage, humiliation and loss overflowed as I integrated his simple admission. Somewhere in the mess, though, I registered that he had given me an honest answer to my question. Much later, together after a long break, planning marriage, and later still, married to Geoff, I was to assign to this quality of unambivalent honesty a greater value. Somehow I could trust someone who was willing to express such an unpalatable truth.
>
> Before marriage I had come to know Geoff in a particular way. We had found deep resonances between us of a particular combination of spiritual, altruistic dreams and hopes. It was as if I was privy to an inner potential in him which was invisible to the casual observer.
>
> Upon marriage, the experience changed – mystifyingly, sharply. I found myself thrown into a world where Geoff's primary focus was (apparently always had been, had I been able to see it) the lived outer reality of a male camaraderie which completely overshadowed the commitment to home, relationship and shared dream. Attempted conversations. Promises. Recriminations. Occasional apologies. My

attempts to discuss what felt to me like a betrayal of our previous intimacy, were repudiated on the grounds that 'it always turns into an argument'. And we couldn't have that. I felt emptier and lonelier as the months passed. Nothing worked. I experienced incredible impotence and mounting rage.

Then one night, 18 months into the marriage, something changed in me. Impotent rage coalesced into a penetrating focus. If this is life with Geoff then I'm out of it. Over some hours I observed this idea – tossing it, turning it, challenging it, digesting the possibilities, feeling the fear of it, until I felt absolutely clear. I realised I did, after all, have some power in this situation. I steeled myself to face the consequences, whichever way he responded – and I had absolutely no way of knowing – and allowed my feelings of disappointment and betrayal to flow into a letter which basically set out why I was leaving and what would have to change if I were to reconsider life together. If he even cared. It was very clear, and I felt very strong. I did not know the outcome, but trusted I could manage, whichever way the cards fell. I left no contact number, and went to stay with a friend.

Suffice it to say, 30 years later, we are still together. Geoff refers to 'the letter' each year, on our anniversary. Apparently, that letter gave him the necessary strength to do what he wanted to do anyway, which was to reconnect with that part of him that I had known first, and disconnect from some pretty unhealthy people and practices. He was able to acknowledge them as such. Marriage is not perfect, but we muddle onwards, with a level of mutual respect for each other's differences and individual needs.

While trying to sort out her relationship with Geoff, Vivienne accesses what Courtin calls 'strong energy', and like Garner in her fencing match, she brings it into an amalgam of compassion, generosity and commitment to relationship. She gets into a fight with Geoff but she is not fighting *against* him: she is inviting him to *fight with her*, for the relationship, knowing that if she does not fight there will be no relationship, even if the marriage lasts for 60 years.

Vivienne conducts her fight 'cleanly', with her fears having been explored and then largely put to one side. She writes of impotent rage coalescing into a penetrating force, an image which parallels Garner's discovery that while fencing in 30° heat and high humidity, something coalesced inside her that could think strategically. Vivienne's tossing, turning, challenging and digesting of the possibility of leaving Geoff echo a fencer's manoeuvres, and she writes of 'steeling herself' to face the consequences of her decision.

Part of what enables Vivienne's stand to work is that she is not coming from a small, fear-dominated, blaming, or vengeful place. She does not blame Geoff for her disappointment, or demonise him. She arrives at a place of clarity about his limitations and makes her own decisions in relation to what she sees. This combination of razor-sharp, unsentimental clarity of vision combined with compassion can be seen as a distillation of what lies at the heart of aggressive energies. It is as if Vivienne boiled her rage down to a sharp point where it could be used to cut away the layers of rationalisation for both parties, exposing the unpalatable truth, and opening that up as solid ground from which decisions could be made.

Aggression as the very stuff of relationship

This trusting, respectful, but demanding and determined move is love in the sense that Samuels describes above. Once this level of vulnerability and honesty had been achieved, Geoff was able to move on in his own life, cutting free from his own destructive habits and sorting out his real priorities. This is what Garner seems to be gesturing towards too – the sense that if aggressive energies can be boiled down, focused and explored, significant changes can occur, provided that the longings for connection and learning which dwell within the aggressive energies can be kept in mind.

Clearly, I am discussing states of psychological being which can take many years of hard psychological, emotional and (in the case of Courtin's use of Buddhist understandings) spiritual work to even glimpse, let alone achieve with any consistency. Nonetheless, aggression need not be the blood-stained threat to relationship it is so often assumed to be. Approached in right way, it can be the very stuff of lively and enlivening relationships and the basis of women's psychological growth.

Bibliography

Austin, S. (2005) *Women's Aggressive Fantasies – A Post-Jungian Exploration of Self-Hatred, Love and Agency*, London: Routledge.[1]

Courtin, R. (2003) 'Chasing Robina', transcript of interview with Rachel Kohn on *The Spirit of Things*, Sydney: ABC Radio 13/07/2003. Online at http://www.abc.net.au/rn/relig/spirit/stories/s897932.html (accessed 19 July 2003).

Garner, H. (2001) 'The Feel of Steel 1' in *The Feel of Steel*, Sydney: Picador.

Garner, H. (2001a) 'The Feel of Steel 2' in *The Feel of Steel*, Sydney: Picador.

Samuels, A. (1989) *The Plural Psyche*, London: Routledge.

Storr, A. (1970) *Human Aggression*, Harmondsworth: Penguin.

Note

1 I would like to thank Routledge for permission to use sections of my 2005 book as the basis of this chapter.

Chapter 5

Faintclews and indirections
Jung and biography

Deirdre Bair

Most of this chapter was presented as a lecture to the Millennium Conference organised by the Society of Analytical Psychology in London in February 1999. The invitation to speak came from Andrew Samuels whose brainchild the conference was. Given the nature of the present book, it felt appropriate to include this material pretty much in the way in which I first wrote it back then, four years before the publication of my Jung biography. For Andrew was a very significant and early supporter of my Jung project and I wanted to acknowledge that alongside his many other professional achievements, not to mention years of personal friendship. Readers seeking the relevant academic apparatus may refer to C.G. Jung: A Biography. (Bair, 2003).

Walt Whitman wondered rhetorically in *Leaves of Grass* (1947, p. 54) if someone might be inspired to write about him after his death. His words resonated throughout the long years it took me to write a biography of C. G. Jung:

> As if any man really knew aught of my life,
> Why even I myself I often think know little or nothing of my
> real life. Only a few hints, a few diffused faintclews and indirections
> I seek for my own use to trace out here.

It might seem unlikely to pair an American poet with a Swiss psychologist, but each man knew in his lifetime that he would be the subject of biography and that the re-telling would be controversial. I sought 'faintclews and indirections' as I wrote the biography, just as Jung did in writing *Memories, Dreams, Reflections* (1989). This essay will explain how his autobiography influenced some decisions I made while writing his biography.

In the last decade of his long life (1875–1961), Jung thought a great deal about what it had been and whether it deserved preservation as auto-biography, memoir, or biography. Jung made the distinction (as I and others do) that autobiography is a factual recitation of the external events of one's life, as full, complete, and objective as the subject can make it. A memoir is more elusive and can take many forms. It can be one's internal memories, random and chosen at whim; a written account of selected events that carry particular meaning and resonance; or, simply, the written recall of a particular person who mattered in one's life.

As for biography, the idea had been afloat since the 1930s, when several persons approached Jung about becoming his official biographer. Jung reluctantly tried to cooperate but these attempts eventually came to naught. The pressure intensified by the 1950s, when Emma Jung and Toni Wolff were dead and Jung's health became impaired. Concern arose that his thesis of analytical psychology and his version of its tenets and history might perish with him. No matter how much those closest to him differed over the form it might take, Jung's friends, followers, and family, all wanted his life and work to be captured for posterity.

I told the full story of the original would-be biographers in my book, so I will move quickly from the first to the third. Lucy Heyer-Grote envisioned a neat and tidy work that Jung's trusted associate Cary F. Baynes, described as 'the Little Red Hen writing about Fafnir the Dragon' (letter from Cary Baynes to C. G. Jung, November 19, 1953, Archives of Eidgenössische Technische Hochschule, Zurich). British theologian H. L. Philp wanted to write a biography focused entirely on Jung's attitude toward religion, and Jung's friend, Dr. E. A. Bennet, proposed himself as the '[Ernest] Jones' to Jung's 'Freud' (letter from E. A. Bennett to C. G. Jung, December 10, 1956, Archives of ETH, Zurich).

Initially, Jung told both men that theirs was 'a very interesting proposition,' but he was 'a somewhat complicated phenomenon which can hardly be covered by one biographer only.' He suggested they convene a 'committee of experts' to listen to his version of his life and then write it accordingly (letter from C. G. Jung to E. A. Bennett, December 10, 1956, Archives of ETH, Zurich). Otherwise, he cautioned,

> a biography of me can never be comprehensive because I have more than two aspects. The specifical [sic] psychological synthesis would demand somebody equally at home in primitive psychology, mythology, history, parapsychology, and science – and even in the field of artistic expression.
>
> (letter from C. G. Jung to E. A. Bennett, December 10, 1956,
> Archives of ETH, Zurich)

Philp found it too daunting and withdrew but Bennet sent Jung a list of questions he called 'moments of illumination.' What was Jung's attitude toward school? Were his talents stimulated or hindered there? What role did each of his parents play in his life? Was he a healthy boy in a healthy family, or were he and they frequently ill? And, did he have boyhood friends?

Jung was staggered by these simple questions. Readers of *Memories, Dreams, Reflections* (1989) recognize what resonance such questions bear, but they were too overwhelming for Jung to deal with in the early 1950s. He told Bennet they were 'complicated, confusing topics,' and he was eighty-one and did not want to spend his remaining years composing written responses to complex questions. Jung said the false starts of previous biographers created 'misunderstandings' that left him 'rather scared to tell the truth about my biography as I see it' (letter from C. G. Jung to E. A. Bennett, December 10, 1956, Archives of ETH, Zurich).

Bennet abandoned the project with the excuse that he did not want to 'clash with Aniela Jaffé,' who was working on behalf of the esteemed publishing couple, Helen and Kurt Wolff. They had appeared at the right moment to channel all this biographical ferment into the hybrid of auto-biography and memoir that eventually became *Memories, Dreams, Reflections* (op. cit.). Kurt attended the Eranos conferences for years, hoping to persuade Jung to write his autobiography, and by the 1950s, appeared to have succeeded. But as soon as Jung began to write, he was stymied: how was it that words flowed so easily when he wrote about ideas, but when he wrote about himself, he needed the prodding of an outsider? Various persons were asked to collaborate, and through a series of happenstances, his secretary, Aniela Jaffé, was chosen.

Jung still had serious reservations about his 'so-called autobiography' and was 'continuously disturbed by a most peculiar and unexpected fact, the degree of subjectivity that colors my earliest memories.' He wrote to several friends that he was

> struggling in solitude to work out the history of my childhood and youth. Seen as I have seen it; as it was in my youth without my then knowing what it meant, and unable then to express it in words.
> (letter from C. G. Jung to E. A. Bennett, December 10, 1956,
> Archives of ETH, Zurich)

Now, as an elderly man trying to relive those earlier moments, he was struck by 'how one has an absolutely certain feeling of value on the one side and on the other, an equally certain doubt about its value.' (ibid.)

His question became: how could he mine these memories? He thought one possible way would be to write 'Improvised Memories' (letter from C. G. Jung to Kurt Wolff, May 30, 1959, private archive) that would not to try to perceive every moment from the vantage point of age and wisdom, but rather, from the perspective of the age he had been when he experienced them: 'I am trying to think of what I thought when I was a child. Not what I think of that child who was myself now that I am an old man.' (ibid.) He told Wolff even this technique was not working:

> I regret that my biography, or what I take to be it, is unlike other biographies in many respects . . . for me, life was something that had to be lived, not spoken . . . I am as I am, an ungrateful autobiographer, to be exact.
>
> (ibid.)

Jung told Wolff he was too old and weak to organize the material of his life. Desperate to salvage the project, Wolff urged Jung to talk to Mrs. Jaffé about any subject at all, whatever came to mind. Her role was to take dictation, occasionally to suggest further questions or propose possible subjects such as his genealogy, or how he came to study medicine, or works of literature that had lasting influence. Jung agreed, and for the next several years, they met in regular sessions each week.

Questions about *what* Jung initially envisioned a unified biographical work should be, and *how* these conversations eventually became *Memories, Dreams, Reflections*, have long intrigued readers who tried to use the text as the basis for explicating the principal facts of Jung's life. Gerhard Adler, one of the first to address the question, concluded that 'strictly speaking, it is no autobiography at all, but the report of encounters with the inner world of the psyche' (Adler, 1964, p. 139). Jung's first sentence verified Adler's contention. His earliest known draft began with this sentence, which he retained throughout the long process ending in publication. His life was 'the story of the self-realization of the unconscious,' and was based on his own 'personal myth.' He would not make 'direct statements' but would only 'tell stories' (Jung, 1989, pp. 3–5). Whether or not they were true was not his problem because his aim was to tell '*my* fable, *my* truth' (ibid.). And yet, through telling his fable and truth, Jung inadvertently created the problems and confusions with which scholars, most particularly biographers, have had to grapple.

Early on, I decided that anyone who intended to write an objective and impartial biography of Jung must begin with a close reading of every extant version of the 'Protocols,' the working title for Jung's conversations with Jaffé and the segments of his own writing that were melded to became *Memories, Dreams, Reflections*. My intention was to 'de-privilege' Jung's final published version because I believed total reliance upon the book gave rise to serious misunderstandings and false interpretations that were frequently touted as statements of fact.

Unwittingly and unintentionally, Jung created such a situation. Here follows a brief explanation of the genesis of his text along with some of the decisions that were made about its final form. Currently, there are between four and six known 'Protocols' of Jung's 'reconstructed' life, this being a term literary scholars have borrowed from psychoanalysts to describe techniques for recovering past experiences, emotions, and events. Neuroscientists tell us that no matter how sincerely – even desperately – a writer of autobiography and memoir strives to discover the 'real' reality and the literal truth of the 'self,' it is almost impossible to do so. Indeed, Jung offered self-revelation as he and Jaffé revisited so many aspects of his life in their conversations, many of which did not survive in publication.

There were no tape recordings, only Mrs. Jaffé's written account in a combination of German shorthand and script. These were typed by trusted associates and corrected by Jung and Mrs. Jaffé, thus creating another script to be re-typed by secretaries so that each successive text thus became further removed from the original. In some cases – childhood being one example – Jung wrote a great many pages by hand that were later inserted into various, constantly changing Protocols. All this was in German, even though Jung insisted from the beginning that the book be translated and published first in English. Naturally, when the English-language editors received the translation, they made more changes, many of which unintentionally changed Jung's original meaning.

Thus, at every step throughout, others were also reading, editing, and in some instances re-writing. Sometimes the changes were as mundane as Jung's children's objection to his memory of walking to school in winter snow without socks and in shoes with large holes. They permitted the editors to say that Jung walked in snow with wet shoes but references to his being sockless were removed because in Switzerland, revealing dire poverty embarrasses descendants. There were serious changes, as illustrated by Kurt Wolff's anguish over the incident of the Basel Cathedral: 'why can't they let the old man say "God *shits* on his cathedral" if he wants to!' (letter from Kurt Worff to Cary Baynes, January 19, 1961, Helen Wolff Archives, Beinecke Library, Yale University). The entire passage was eventually sanitized to diminish the powerful emotion of the original.

I wrestled with such information throughout my biography. My editors insisted that biography must begin with birth and end with death, but I argued that I needed several more chapters and an epilogue after Jung died because it was the only way to explain the posthumous publication of *Memories, Dreams, Reflections.* One of the most important clarifications I had to make concerned Aniela Jaffé's role throughout this difficult, fractious process. She was frequently accused of 'tantefiziering' or 'auntifying' the text, which I discovered was an unjust charge. There were always too many others intent on sanitizing it, while Jaffé most often tried to follow Jung's original wording and intention, which was to rearrange for coherence without changing content. I think she was correct to revise the first three or four Protocols because from an editorial perspective, none was publishable and none fully honored Jung's intentions.

Jung's remarks were sometimes garbled and discursive, as he veered from one subject and period to another without any indication that he was making a leap in time, space, and subject matter. Sometimes in a single German sentence he used Latin maxims or Greek words, English slang and

French idioms. Correspondence among the editors shows frequent argument over how to turn convoluted thought patterns into passages that expressed Jung's meaning. I marvel at how they created a luminous text that corresponds so closely to the rowdy, breezy, quirky, opinionated, and sometimes poignant remarks and brilliant insights that this old man then in his eighties wanted posterity to have.

People often ask why a biography takes so long to write, and Jung's provides both insight into the process and explanation of the difficulties. From the previous discussion, the reader can see how much sifting, sorting, and deconstructing had to be done before actual writing could begin. Concurrently, textual research had to be bolstered with interviews and conversations with Jung's family, friends, followers, and in some cases, his analysands. Because most of his archives are in the Swiss Federal Institute of Technology (ETH), I made bi-annual visits to Zurich during the six years it took to do the research.

Being there became a way of integrating myself into the local culture and society. Marie-Louise von Franz and C. A. Meier, two of Jung's last remaining colleagues during his lifetime, gave me important interviews. Other clinicians explained the divergence of various theoretical orientations. Swiss scholars introduced me to the fables and folklore of the Lake Constanz area. Jung's children and grandchildren took me to the places where he lived and to settings where important events happened. They showed me the famous breakfront where the knife cracked, and let me soak in the atmosphere of his study and library.

I was able to add important information through an American woman who was married to a Swiss man and who introduced me to her friends in various social classes and cultures. Through them, I learned much about Jung's standing in the community and how others regarded his practice as they made the letters, diaries, and analytic journals of their parents and grandparents available. This allowed me to describe how Jung worked in a clinical setting but it raised concerns about the concept of privacy and became one of the most sensitive areas of the biography.

My access to personal documents was always granted with the stringent caveat that I must list their provenance as 'private source, private archive.' When I explained that my three previous biographies had named every source and document with scrupulous specificity, the donors became agitated and threatened to withdraw permission. They would not allow me to deposit a document in a restricted archive for fifty years because even that would cause their descendants distress of epic proportions. They insisted that an American might not understand such Swiss cultural behavior but if I wanted to use the documents I had to respect it, and so I did.

This led directly to the question of doctor–patient confidentiality. The Jung heirs insisted that Jung kept no analytic records, but many of his patients kept detailed accounts of their sessions. Certainly, an analytic encounter presented only from the patient's perspective is one-sided, but I still thought it would be useful to show how patients viewed Jung's treatment. In some cases, they or their descendants permitted individual recollections but in others, they asked me to create a composite or 'case study.' I share James Hillman's (1983) opinion of the case study as 'the ultimate fiction,' but here again I had to comply. Sometimes I had to so disguise the person(s) that my account was devoid of pronouns that might reveal gender.

I had Jung's version of the analytic encounter in a single instance, a diary kept by Mary Briner over the several decades she consulted him. He was anguished when she asked to publish it, saying she could not possibly convey 'the overtones and undertones' of all that transpired in the analytic hour. Briner honored Jung's wishes and destroyed the diary, so I was fortunate to have their correspondence discussing its content (personal communication from the Briner family).

Since publication, my biography has raised differing opinions among clinicians and scholars about confidentiality. A large faction favors the traditional view that doctor and patient are eternally bound by confidentiality and death does not sever the pact. Another faction argues that doctors frequently present the material of an analytic session either alone or as a case history, which constitutes a partial transgression of the ethical boundary of permanent silence. We think of the anguish and outrage of persons who believed they were recognized, from Bertha Pappenheim as Anna O., to Michael Fordham, still angry half a century later because of H. G. Bayne's thinly disguised case study (Fordham, 1993, pp. 70ff.). This faction asks how clinical students will learn if there is no prior analytic history to guide them.

A particularly Swiss attitude toward surviving documents arose when Marie-Louise von Franz told me of the 1,000 extant letters Carl and Emma Jung wrote to each other. Their heirs were shocked when I asked permission to read them. They will keep the letters but will not invade their grandparents' privacy by reading or allowing others to read them. This was yet another instance where I had to convey Swiss-German sensitivities to an international audience and to honor the obligation to present Jung first and foremost as a Swiss man deeply imbued with the cultural underpinnings of his background.

My ultimate aim in writing Jung's life was to inspire my readers to read his writings. My intention was not to paraphrase Jung's work but to present it so tantalizingly that readers would want to read it. 'Where does simplicity become simplistic?' I asked Andrew Samuels, whose reply I respected: 'The writer should not make the work as simple as possible, but rather, as simple as it needs to be' (personal communication, 1999).

I spoke earlier of 'de-privileging' both written text and oral testimony. I have given careful consideration to the memories of others but I have not accepted them as an ultimate truth. If we rely on what Jung told us of his life, we must remember that he was old and wise when he wrote about it. So, too, was his boyhood friend, Albert Oeri, when he wrote a memoir of Jung's early years (1935). We must ask from what age and vantage point did Oeri write? Did he have an agenda, theory, or thesis into which he wanted to fit Jung's life and work? With every commentator at every stage of Jung's long life, a biographer must ask these questions before permitting ultimate authority to any testimony. We must be mindful of the ongoing debate between objective truth and any narrative truth we seek to impose. The story told by everyone from family friends to the most impartial biographer is still a narrative truth. It always contains what might be called a violation of the subject's objective truth, even though these commentators have told no actual lies.

To return to *Memories, Dreams, Reflections*, we are all dependent on these narrative truths because they bring order and coherence to the raw truths of so-called 'real life,' which are often messy and muddled. Perhaps it is hubris to think that we can provide definitive answers about a protean figure such as Jung when we can't possibly conceive the questions future generations will raise. Still, the contemporary biographer, and indeed, all other scholars, have the obligation to try.

References

Adler, G. (1964) The memoirs of CGJ. *Spring*.

Bair, D. (2003) *C.G. Jung: A Biography*. New York: Little, Brown & Co.

Fordham, M. (1993) *The Making of an Analyst: A Memoir*. London: Free Association Books.

Hillman, J. (1983) *Healing Fictions*. Barrytown, NY: Station Hill.

Jung, C.G. (1989) *Memories, Dreams, Reflections* (recorded and edited by Aniela Jaffé, trans. Richard and Clara Winston). New York: Vintage Books.

Oeri, A. (1935) Ein paar Jugenderinnerungen. In *Festschrift zum 60. Geburtstag von C. G. J. herausgegeben vom Psychologischen Club Zürich*. Berlin: Springer Verlag.

Whitman, W. (1947) *Leaves of Grass*. New York: Modern Library Paperback.

Chapter 6

The integrity of the supervisor and the sins of psychotherapy supervision

John Beebe

The supervisor of someone learning to do depth psychotherapy is expected to share more than just a complement of skills. The supervisor is also required to embody what he or she would be like if acting in the role of therapist. Enacting the part of a role model, however, has a tendency to bring out not only the virtues, but also the sins of the supervisor.

Like its contrasting term 'virtue', 'sin', a seemingly outdated word, has taken on new currency in the contemporary discourse of moral philosophy, which like depth psychology has strongly emphasized the relationship between self and other. Moral psychology understands 'self and other' as most frequently a relationship between persons, and so sin has been described as 'a violation of a particular relationship between two persons' (Kellenberger 1995: 271). According to this philosopher, 'Sin against persons, violating a relationship we have with persons, is not so much something we do as it is something we do to persons' (ibid.: 272). 'Virtues', by contrast, though serving well the relationships we have with others, are most often conceived by contemporary moral psychologists as supporting the integrity of the self (MacIntyre 1984). With regard to the internal consequences of the exercise of virtue, one's own self becomes the other whose integrity one must take pains to protect (Ricoeur 1992).

The protection of the virtues

I first became aware of the role the virtues play in preserving integrity when I was invited to lecture on integrity in Anaheim, California, home to Disneyland. I decided to reread the Grimms' fairy tale *Snow White* (Grimm 1857/1977), the basis of Disney's first animated cartoon. As I did so, it dawned on me that the famous Seven Dwarfs, with their Protestant work ethic, are lingering images of the seven cardinal virtues. (The cartoon renders them with just the right touch of 1930s American irreverence, to convey the persistence of the shadow in any attempt at moral superiority.) Just as integrity, for the medieval churchman, was watched over by the exercise of the virtues, the pure Snow White is protected in the story by the hard-working dwarfs. To be sure, Snow White herself does not represent a mature integrity, in the sense of a 'developed sensitivity to the needs of the whole' (Beebe 1992: 125), possessed of the 'reflective purity' that is 'the fruit of having achieved objectivity, breadth, and depth in morality' (Kekes 1989: 235), but she does personify an earlier root of that integrity, the native 'pre-reflective purity' (ibid.: 232) of the original self. She epitomizes what a philosopher of virtue has recently called 'natural goodness' (Foot 2001), a quality associated with 'moral luck' (Williams 1981; Nussbaum 2001) that under fortunate circumstances can mature into an ethical sense, but has nevertheless not yet had enough experience of life and of relationship to know how to function unaided on its own in morally ambiguous situations. For that reason, Snow White, her natural beauty signifying a kind of nascent integrity, needs to be protected and kept alive by the dwarfs, that is, by the exercise of virtues.

The meaning of the story is that the virtues support our integrity during the tenderest stages of its development. They also counteract the damage arising out of our desire to develop a consensually validated persona (the Queen/Witch) that everyone might take for integrity but which actually threatens to destroy the moral purity of our native goodness.

The envious stepmother Queen in the story, with her excessive concern for the approval of others, represents the danger that a too-collectively oriented moral thinking can pose to the more self-motivated (and therefore finally more attractive) ethical consciousness that Snow White promises. Walt Disney offered this familiar story in such compelling form at a time when fascism was consolidating its power in backlash to the free-thinking morality of democratic modernity (Disney 1937). A little over a decade later, the Jungian analyst Erich Neumann (1949/1990) defined the problem that Disney's cartoon had already shown us in the unforgettable figure of the envious, persecutory Queen: the 'old ethic' of established collective morality distrusts and seeks to destroy the 'new ethic' of a developing individual consciousness. Snow White represents the potential for moral individuation,[1] as shown by her hair, her skin, and her lips carrying the three alchemical colors (black as ebony, white as snow, and red as blood), as a kind of living legacy from, and promise to, her mother, who died just after seeing her, but not before having wished for a child such as this. The corset that the envious stepmother later tries to put on Snow White (which nearly suffocates the child when the Queen, disguised as a peddler woman, laces it up) would be the tight, straight-laced moral strictures that crimp the style of natural goodness. The comb that introduces poison as she combs the child's hair suggests the moral philosophies that would arrange our natural moral ideas (thoughts that, like hairs, grow naturally out of our heads) schematically, and thus kill our individual moral reasoning at its root. The apple would represent the central theological doctrine of medieval Christianity that an 'original sinfulness' inheres in our very disposition to make our own moral choices. This is a doctrine that, if sustained, would absolutely kill off any possibility of trusting our natural goodness to ground our conscience. When Snow White eats the apple, she falls to the earth as if dead, only to be revived by the Prince, possibly an allegory of Christ, but in the heretical sense of a restored integrity's capacity to function on its own, apart from collective morality.

Read in this allegorical way, the story tells us that for a mind that is naturally disposed to be moral (Snow White), a knowledge and practice of the virtues (the Seven Dwarfs) has the capacity to forestall threats to the individuation of its integrity, understood as the maturation of a free mind's ability to achieve its own discernment in moral matters.

The renaissance of virtue theory in contemporary moral philosophy (Foot 1978) has reminded us that the virtues provide a practical set of guidelines to support our integrity when it is threatened. Consciously exercising the seven cardinal virtues – justice, temperance, fortitude, prudence, faith, hope, and charity – in the presence of another person protects them and enables their native moral integrity to thrive. The psychological objection that can be raised to this approach to fostering integrity in supervision is obvious: by appealing only to the natural goodness of the supervisor, it leaves out the supervisor's shadow, which also has a role to play in the process of supervision.

Superego in supervision

To survey Pride, Envy, Gluttony, Lust, Anger, Greed, and Sloth – the names that, following a very old tradition, I will give the deadly sins here – may seem a highly arbitrary, even musty, way to get at the shadow that can undermine the integrity of supervision. I invite the reader to embrace the irony of having to fall back on such a model. We have so little in our own psychology to accommodate the grossness of the types of shadow we can fall into in supervision.

The idea that a helping professional can harm a client who comes for help is well enough accepted within the practice of psychotherapy. The last three decades have been rife with the discovery of the ways a therapist can hurt a patient. Without assuming that all the lessons have been learned, I find myself these day less worried about the potential to do harm in therapy and more concerned with what goes on in supervision. Psychotherapy, after all, is much more adequately protected by the professional superego. Few dynamic psychotherapists practicing today ignore the problem of boundaries. Despite their openness to a somewhat freer way of working, most psychotherapists are quite leery about going very far in the direction of a free-for-all. Freud's rule of abstinence is still a collective value for psychotherapists, who frequently say in supervision, 'I don't know if I'm allowed to say that.' Their emphasis on self-restraint is well-reinforced by contemporary codes of ethics and the threat of legal and civil action and loss of license, reputation, and even the right to earn an income for the psychotherapist who becomes too free in the use of self.

But in supervision, a much more reckless attitude reigns, and here the license that attends any unbalanced freedom in human endeavors is more frequently enacted. To understand what threatens the integrity of the supervisor, we have to develop a capacity to imagine how the relative freedom of the supervisor can be misused in ways that would be unthinkable within a psychotherapy relationship. In what follows, then, the Seven Deadly Sins of traditional Catholicism will be used as signposts to identify the moral pitfalls into which a supervisor may fall (Maguire 2004). For each of these integrity-compromising stations of the shadow, I will suggest a Cardinal Virtue that may enable the supervisor to recover the moral balance that has been lost.

Confronting the sins of supervision

Pride: The first of our sins – and for medieval Catholics the deadliest – is Pride. When I enact this sin in supervision, my pride in my own product extends to the supervisee him or herself. I have ambition for the supervisee, who, by becoming a credit to me, will demonstrate my own prowess as clinician and teacher to everyone else.

Cure: The cardinal virtue that has most often saved me from the sin of pride is *Prudence*. Prudence means not allowing a present desire to make one neglect future consequences for oneself or the other. I exhibit prudence when I show appropriate concern for my supervisee's future. Few people get very far as someone else's man or woman. My supervisees are best positioned for good careers if they learn to do psychotherapy properly and develop theoretical and clinical habits that are organic to them. I shouldn't make them feel that they owe more to me.

Envy: In modern psychotherapeutic practice, Envy is usually considered the deadliest sin, i.e. the most unconscious one, the one we attribute to 'primitive' and 'borderline' patients, a sure sign that we don't want to look at it in ourselves. But it comes up frequently, and at quite a conscious level, when one has a talented psychotherapist as a supervisee, someone who fits into the field naturally. Envy surfaces when there is a fantasy of scarcity (Sullivan 1986). Supervisors who fall victim to this sin assume that all of the goods of psychotherapy, including access to patients and colleagues, are available only to the supervisee. Naturally, if I feel that way, I'm going to resent the supervisee and am going to try to rectify that state of affairs, Iago-like, by taking the supervisee down a peg. When I enact my envy by inspiring an unwarranted lack of self-confidence in the supervisee, I betray a secret anxiety about my own scarce access to the supplies of goods available to the supervisee, who will eventually pay me back by going elsewhere and thriving. But not before I've done damage by trying to position myself as the only authority the supervisee can trust. Along the way, I will have depreciated the supervisee's own sources of information and understanding and undermined the supervisee's trust in him or herself. Upon recovery from my interventions, the supervisee will not look upon me kindly, and I will envy him or her all the more because that which did not kill made him or her strong.

Cure: The cardinal virtue that I have found to make a big difference when envy surfaces is *Hope*. When I allow myself to trust that my own efforts will be rewarded in time, the fact that someone else got to some of the goods first will not matter as much to me. It's important for a supervisor to engage with activities that renew hope, to break down the isolation that breeds envy. A good activity for the supervisor who envies is to go into supervision or therapy him or herself, or even to take a course that brings the goods of psychotherapy nearer.

Gluttony: When I enact the sin of Gluttony in supervision, I seek to enlarge my role in the supervisee's life. I want to monopolize his or her learning. I become touchy about the supervisee getting any significant mentoring from others. I'm even tempted to get my supervisee to see me for individual psychotherapy. I may act this wish out indirectly by referring patients to the supervisee.

Cure: The virtue whose practice most rescues us from gluttony is *Temperance* (in analytic circles this is sometimes called the rule of abstinence). Temperance demands due proportion in all things, including frequency of sessions, limitation of dual and triple relationships, and avoidance of contacts beyond those required for the work we've already set out to do. As Bernard Gert's discussion of temperance suggests, practicing this virtue involves avoiding trying to take control of the present in an irrational way (Gert 1998: 277–309). A supervisor who lets him or herself be guided by temperance trusts the present, already agreed-upon, arrangements with the supervisee to be satisfying.

Lust: The cardinal sin of Lust is even more direct in its designs on the supervisee. In the grip of lust, I want to directly appropriate the supervisee. Mentoring relationships are often highly eroticized, so it is not surprising that a supervisor in the grip of lust wants to make the supervisee a lover, a spouse, a best friend, or all of the above. The main way to recognize lust before it takes possession is to see that I don't want to let go of the supervisee. When I enact my lust in a shadowy way, I find ways to keep holding the supervisee back so that he or she has to have more contact with me.

Cure: The only real cure for lust is love, which in the language of the cardinal virtues is called *Charity*. Charity loves the person with sympathy for his or her situation, which never includes a need to possess the person. One lets the lusted-after supervisee go because it is the most charitable thing to do.

Anger: Psychotherapists have all but forgotten that Anger is a deadly sin. But scrutinizing the supervisee through the spectrum of reactions that range from irritation and resentment to hostility and hatred is a common way for a supervisor not to hear or work at caring for the person being supervised. Aside from direct expressions of anger at supervisees, which are rare, supervisors frequently enact their rejection of a supervisee in passive aggressive ways – by coming late, forgetting the appointment, rudely interrupting the supervisee, and so on. When I start doing these things, I have to examine my countertransference to the supervisee.

Cure: The virtue that has most helped me to get past the thoughtless enactment of anger is *Justice*. All anger carries the shadow of doing an injustice to another person. Justice demands that I look, on the one hand, more exactly at what I'm finding difficult to tolerate in the supervisee, and on the other, at why that particular thing is so hard for me to address. In adjudicating the problem, I must confront my own failure to communicate what I found problematic when the issue first surfaced for me. Then I have to find a constructive way to communicate my criticism or concern. If I trust the supervisee with my negative feelings, the supervisee may in turn confess a resistance that has been setting off counter-resistance in me. With these psychological facts on the table, our work together goes forward in a spirit of doing justice to the issue that is germane to the supervision.

Greed: When I enact the deadly sin of Greed, I start to actually steal from the supervisee. I steal *ideas, energy,* and even *time* and *money*. The easiest way to do the last is to decrease the time I spend with the supervisee by coming late or stopping early and doing nothing to rectify the matter financially. Ideas from the supervisee are treated as if my own, to appear in my lectures and papers. And I take from the supervisee by bringing my problems as a therapist and even as a person to him and to her. Only a really talented supervisee is likely to be the target of this kind of greed. But when such a one is identified by a needy supervisor, the demands on the supervisee can be insatiable.

Cure: The cardinal virtue that enables one to avoid succumbing to greed (and perhaps this is why so many capitalists insist on going to church) is *Faith*. Faith implies a belief in the stable provision of goods, and that what is provided is enough. It is akin to Hope, except it is a more comfortable sense that one already has what one needs. Frieda Fromm-Reichmann (1950: 9–24) has stressed the importance of the psychotherapist meeting basic needs for satisfaction and security outside the therapeutic situation. Faith figures into this in giving us a confidence that we don't need to turn to the supervisee for gratification since we will be gratified in adequate measure during the times we are not with the supervisee. Faith is a trust in one's own ability to provide for oneself, a confidence in our access to a suprapersonal source that will provide the energy to get what we need and that it will be there when we remember to ask for it.

Sloth: When I enact the sin of Sloth, I'm going through the motions of being present to the supervisee, but without really engaging with the material. A sure sign that I am succumbing to sloth is that I go into a daze that I rationalize as following the affect, not the content of what's being communicated. With a supervisee, it's easy to fall into a countertransference funk that is reactive to the supervisee's own frustration, confusion, and despair in the face of disconcerting clinical situations.

Cure: The virtue that gets me through my bouts of Sloth is *Fortitude*. This is perhaps the most important of all virtues for the supervisor. One should work as hard at understanding the supervisee's case as one would a case one is treating directly. Being a supervisor is hard work, and Fortitude enables one not to allow the continuing hardship of being a supervisor, needing to understand the case through the filter of someone else's difficulty in understanding it, to make one fall into irrational despair. I have to rouse myself to ask questions, learn more, get aboard with the case, and eventually risk saying how I might handle the difficulty at hand. When, I do, the daze disappears and the energy to remain present to the entire situation, content *and* affect, returns.

The effect of the supervisor's integrity on the supervisee

The supervisee who is able to experience a supervisor's integrity in confronting temptations within their relationship is helped to realize how powerfully psychotherapy itself is enhanced when the ethical dimension of the healing transaction is addressed. For this reason, even though the supervisee's transference is not usually interpreted, it is frequently advisable for a supervisor to find ways of signaling to the supervisee that the supervisor's countertransference is being attended to.

Inevitably, the supervisee is the beneficiary of the supervisor's moral process. To the degree that the supervisor mobilizes virtues to stay responsible for the sins that emerge in supervision, integrity is not only protected but also established as a value in professional psychotherapeutic work.

Bibliography

Beebe, J. (1992) *Integrity in Depth*, College Station, Texas: Texas A & M University Press.
—— (1998) "Toward a Jungian Analysis of Character," in Ann Casement (ed.) *The Post-Jungians Today: Key Papers in Contemporary Analytical Psychology*, London and New York: Routledge.
Disney, Walt (producer) (1937) *Snow White and the Seven Dwarfs*.
Foot, P. (1978) *Virtues and Vices, and Other Essays in Moral Philosophy*, Oxford: Blackwell and Berkeley; University of California Press.
—— (2001) *Natural Goodness*, Oxford and New York: Oxford University Press.
Fromm-Reichmann, F. (1950) *Principles of Intensive Psychotherapy*, Chicago and London: University of Chicago Press.
Gert, B. (1998) "Virtues and Vices," in *Morality: Its Nature and Justification*, New York and Oxford: Oxford University Press, Chapter 11, pp. 277–309.
Grimm, J. and Grimm, W. (1857/1977), Ralph Manheim (trans.), *Grimms' Tales for Young and Old: The Complete Stories*, New York: Doubleday.
Kekes, J. (1989) *Moral Tradition and Individuality*, Princeton: Princeton University Press.
Kellenberger, J. (1995) *Relationship Morality*, University Park, PA: Pennsylvania University Press.
MacIntyre, A. (1984) *After Virtue*, 2nd edn, Notre Dame, IN: University of Notre Dame Press.
Maguire, A. (2004) *Seven Deadly Sins: The Dark Companions of the Soul*, London: Free Association Books.
Neumann, E. (1949/1990) *Depth Psychology and a New Ethic*, Eugene Rolfe (trans.), Boston & Shaftesbury: Shambhala.
Nussbaum, M. C. (2001) *The Fragility of Goodness: Luck and Ethics in Greek Tragedy and Philosophy*, 2nd edn, Cambridge: Cambridge University Press.
Ricoeur, P. (1992) *Oneself as Another*, Kathleen Blamey (trans.), Chicago: The University of Chicago Press.
Sullivan, B. S. (1986) Personal communication, in response to Louis B. Stewart's paper, "Affect and Archetype in Analysis," at the Ghost Ranch Conference for Jungian Analysts and Candidates, Abiquiu, New Mexico.
Williams, B. (1981) *Moral Luck: Philosophical Papers 1973–1980*, Cambridge: Cambridge University Press.

Note

1 I have elsewhere given my reasons for regarding individuation as the maturation of moral integrity (Beebe 1998).

Chapter 7

Mutual acknowledgement?

Obstacles and possibilities for recognition in the face of asymmetry and injury[1]

Jessica Benjamin

Three days after September 11 in New York City. I walked the streets – empty of all traffic like a ghost town – downtown to Union Square on Friday to the unofficial memorial meeting. I knew that for three days and nights already hundreds of people at a time gathered there, lighting candles and writing on the pavement. What I saw was something one never saw during the Vietnam War: the people who wanted to bomb everybody and anybody and the people against all bombing were gathered together in grief. On the sidewalk in chalk in large letters: 'Let's bomb them, let's show them they can't do this to us!' and right below it 'NO! that will only cause more injury, we must find another way!' The larger We of grief encompassed all the different voices as part of the human response to tragedy, the voice of 'Us against Them' and the voice of 'Them and Us, we are all one.' These conflicting voices were integrated in the symphonic power of loss, each a single instrument against the backdrop of the entire string section carrying the main theme: Nothing left to lose, our consolation lies in our compassion and tolerance for one another. This overarching sense of a lawful community that could hold contradictions and antagonisms represented the Third as I use the term – the space that holds and contains relational tension and growth. The ethical third, in my usage, is the lawful principle or principles that the group is committed to, which sustain the possibility of recognition among ourselves, and allows for renewal of that recognition when it breaks down (Benjamin, 2004).

A few weeks later I found myself in a quite altered state. Panic in the media about future attacks began to affect me, I went through a brief post-traumatic reaction, finding myself imagining what would be the least harmful form of violence that could render helpless those who might infect all our children with smallpox. While I had always assumed I would react like the Bereaved Parents circle, people who devote themselves to reconciliation and preventing further violence, I could recognize in myself the existence of more paranoid responses. The fantasies of revenge were, I felt quite clearly, a reaction to terror and the inability to tolerate the helplessness of such things actually happening.

In psychoanalytic thinking of the Kleinian tradition the acceptance of loss is supposed to promote a reality-based, depressive solution which aims to repair and prevent suffering, while the fear-driven aim of preventing loss or retroactively undoing it feeds on manic, vengeful, paranoid solutions. In North American relational or selfpsychological theorizing, more emphasis is placed on restoring the self after frightening or shameful fragmentation. But, to put this back into my theoretical framework, we need to ask how a third is created that provides the relational conditions for going beyond normal responses of fight, flight or shutdown in the face of traumatic injury. What kind of group experience, collective embodiment of the ethical third, allows the attachment system to be repaired? How to deal with fear-driven, shame-filled or hateful parts, rather than suppressing them with politically correct efforts to be good? How do we find our way back to the world of meaningful engagement with others so as to find consolation and recognition by a connection with a witnessing person or world, to use our attachment system (P. Ogden *et al.*, 2007).

Recent trauma theory confirms the importance of recognition in overcoming trauma. At the same time, we know that it is often very difficult to gain access to past trauma in a way that loosens their grip. In the clinical dyad we often see how the fear response is more likely to trigger behavioral enactments that repeat the past than overcome it in the form of prevention of recurrence. We observe how collectively victimized groups believe the suffering of ancestors and families experienced in the past – what Volkan has called the 'chosen trauma' – can be 're-dressed' with dignity and honor by present active aggression.

In brief, the idea is that traumatic experience of helplessness generates the wish to reverse positions. The reversal is based on the perception that the powerful other who has injured or humiliated us/those we identify with represents the only alternative position to the one of being injured, tortured, humiliated. In my theorizing, I propose that the structure of split complementarity characterizes individual and collective enactments of the doer–done to dynamic.

The basic 'doer–done to' positions, the see-saw structure that Lacan first called our attention to, is associated with the imaginary position of kill or be killed that can only be transcended by the third (for Lacan, the third of speech). In my view, the experience of breakdown into split opposition and the struggle to find a way back to a recognizing third is related to surrender. The acceptance of helplessness, that is, the surrender to our ultimate lack of power, which is a precondition of finding and claiming the power that we do have, relies on the perceived real existence of a witness, an Other who could recognize our suffering. Conversely, the perpetuation of the complementary position occurs because of the 'failed witness,' the collapse of the moral third, often in the world at large. For those who feel entirely abandoned by the world, left to suffer with complete indifference, there is no such third and there is no way out of powerlessness except to engage in violent reversal.

I suggest that we call reconciliation the effort to use the third position based on the witness to create a paradoxical form of power. The third space – the one which stands between the two poles of annihilation, self or other – in which some form of witnessing is possible, is not based on extinguishing the clashing aspects of reaction to loss and violence, but on holding them as part of a larger picture – for instance, outraged anger at injustice can coexist with the desire to be released from anger through reliance on lawful redress. Transformational movements create a form of this witnessing as well as an attachment to a group and to a set of ideals that provide a safe enough context for relying on one's own agency and the recognition of others.

Conversely, the absence of refusal of social recognition for injury generates behavior associated with the complementary structure. When two parties are involved, a negative symmetry takes over based on escalating reactivity, such that impasse is created. Based on internal splitting, ejecting responsibility into the other in the form of blame, a structure of mutual accusation takes hold where neither party can truly recognize the pain or the struggles of the other. Even when the relationship is asymmetrical – even when one side has power over the other – each side has the symmetrical experience of being helpless to change it. Complementary relations are characterized by loss of agency and responsibility on both sides, depletion of the capacity for empathy, and belief that one's own reaction can be legitimated as caused by the other.

The collapsed third cannot be recreated, in part because to do so would require accepting one's own guilt, one's own losses. But this seems impossible in the moment where one is being accused, facing one's own weakness, hatefulness, responsibility for causing damage or denying the other's humanity not as an understandable reaction but a reprehensible failure that evokes hate, blame and aggression in the other. The escalating reactivity, based on states of hyperarousal and traumatic reactions that have deep historical grooves, cancels the space of the third wherein it is possible to hold knowledge of human fears and compassion for loss as truths that apply to both self and other. The higher the trauma-based hyper-arousal and the greater the sense of threat, the more the complementary positions sharpen and mutual accusation takes over – unless there are lawful structures or third forces in place to hold that common knowledge and allow recovery from reactivity.

The hallmark of such reactivity is that blame can be shifted simply by punctuating differently the line of cause and effect: either 'A causes B causes A causes B' or, to the contrary, 'B causes A causes B causes A' etc. Whereas in the space of the third – the position of the witness – it is apparent that A and B are co-determining and co-determined, part of a dynamic with a life of its own. But this can be observed only from a third outside the system, not within it.

In psychoanalytic therapy such impasses also occur, wherein the therapist, despite her or his seemingly greater knowledge and authority, feels rendered helpless by this dynamic. Relational therapists have come to think that a necessary if not sufficient condition of transforming or loosening the grip of such impasses is to 'surrender' in the Buddhist sense – to accept what is. In this case, to accept our failure to live up to an ideal of never harming, being right, being ideally self-regulating rather than reactive or defensive in response to the other's sense of our badness, their aggression or submission, accusations, despair or plain old failure to be helped by us (see Bromberg 2007, Benjamin 2006). We need to recognize instead our own tendencies to protect ourselves or hold onto our own sense of injury at the expense of the other, to dissociate in response to their pain or experience of us as inadequate, or to insist on the rightness of our own view of reality. Indeed, more globally, to accept that we are likely to become disregulated in such a way that we hold on to a position that we know, even in the moment, is untenable. It is because of these tendencies that we have come to understand that the therapist must change (Slavin & Kriegman, 1998), that is, in tandem with the patient they must come to grips with their own traumas and dissociations, their self-protectiveness and failures to live up to their own ideals.

Further, from this point of view we recognize that even within the asymmetrical relation of therapy where the focus is on the patient, it is this willingness to accommodate and adjust, to explore openly how each contributes to enactments and impasses, to take responsibility for one's own contribution, that furthers the patient's confidence that taking responsibility for her own difficulties can be done freely, not as the stigmatized one who is ill or the one assuming all burden of badness for the other. It allows for the absolutely vital distinction, the one so hard to hold onto, between blame and responsibility. Since, at a deep level, often unconscious or unformulated, each partner responds symmetrically to the other, the analyst's self-forgiveness can be mirrored by the patient. It is thus that our own forgiveness and responsibility can inspire a symmetrical response on the part of the other even under asymmetrical conditions.

Reconciliation is a third that specifically requires holding two very different positions, not exactly opposite but certainly with different vectors: forgiveness and responsibility. It is impossible to forgive oneself for actions that one refuses responsibility for – that would be not forgiveness but evasion and excuses. On the other side, without the premise that forgiveness is possible, the sense of being blamed and accused will produce only a simulacrum of responsibility. The ability to forgive the other and forgive the self relate to the same psycho-emotional constellation – if one tries to do one without the other, one only perpetuates the splitting into good and bad, blamed and blaming that underlies cycles of violence. Frequently forgiveness is conflated with forgetting or accepting excuses or justifications: in the sense I am using it, forgiveness relates to surrender, accepting what has happened without demanding magical efforts to redress, but rather seeking a matching form of remorse and acknowledgment that confirm rather than exculpate the injury – perhaps going further to take responsibility for repair.

Andrew Samuels has written about self-forgiveness as a vital element of the moral imagination. Forgiveness requires moving beyond blame into acceptance of suffering, which I think is an essential point – not imagining that rectitude, righteousness, undoes suffering but rather that it embraces it. He contrasted the moral imagination with the black and whiteness of what he called 'original morality,' based on the judgmentally flavored split of superior/inferior which 'has helped to create our divided world, slouching towards apocalypse.' Forgiveness based on original morality, he suggests, would consist of 'reducing the other to nothing but a blob of contemptible and penitential stuff – hence easily pardonable from on high' (Samuels 1989: 203f).

As Andrew makes clear in his discussion of the Kol Nidre prayer spoken yearly at Yom Kippur, which specifically releases us from all prior vows and oaths, forgiveness begins with recognizing our own inability to fulfill. More deeply, he suggests that the release from vows – those given, those we will give and perhaps fail to honor – that is, the canceling of all contracts based on original morality, leaves us free to contract with God (that is to say, in my terms, with the lawful third). I find this connection between freedom and forgiveness very compelling. Forgiveness begins with ourselves, with relinquishing omnipotence and accepting loss, failure, inadequacy – and it is through this act of surrender that we are *free* to return to the third, whether conceived as God or truth or love or integrity.

One of the main functions of forgiveness, understood in this way, is that it tries to make room for an acceptance of our own fragility and fear such that we can cease to deny our own suffering, and instead lift the dissociation regarding it. What has to be accepted is what the relational analyst Sue Grand (2002) calls 'the bestial gesture of survival,' the action taken to escape death and inflict suffering rather than bear it oneself. This can never be a fully conscious act, but when it does come to consciousness, it requires forgiveness. To forgive it requires us in certain situations to recognize that the traumas and fears that motivate those gestures were real – but in the past rather than the present. To have defended ourselves when we didn't need to is one of the first things for which we need to forgive ourselves – as well as others. But we can do this only if we find a way to create a different kind of awareness of past suffering, of traumas that are collectively transmitted, which reads as felt awareness rather than attempts to claim the mantle of victim. In the dissociated world of the media appeals may be made to historical events like war or genocide to legitimate more bestial gestures while the felt connection both to past suffering, helplessness and violence is as unreal as the sense of the present.

Even while claiming victimhood, the victim who defends his right to retaliate or climb over the other is usually severely dissociated from, unable to contain and know his own pain, driven by fear. From the standpoint that identifies victimhood with righteousness – a standpoint that has been quite popular in the era of anti-colonial and post-colonial consciousness – a parallel dissociation is expressed in the calculus of moral indignation whereby only the victim is, or can be, forgiven for such gestures. This has gone along with the mentality of reversal in which universalist leftists have generally participated. The defense of one's own survival cannot be owned or forgiven because it is not permitted to us; we cannot be so bestial. 'We' the 'Subject' are always supposed to put righteousness before survival while the 'Other' or Victim is allowed to fight for survival. That is because of an odd doubling: we believe we are powerful, that we are the ones capable of doing injury, and yet aspire to champion the side of the victims and the oppressed; we try to be righteously good by admitting our side's badness precisely in order to disown it, to perpetuate denial that we could ever actually be 'the bad ones,' on the side of those who harm or exploit.

However problematic this position has proven to be, I do not believe it invalidates the difference in suffering between the powerful and the oppressed. It does not invalidate the facts of colonial oppression, class oppression, racism or patriarchal domination. However, it means that we have to take a more complicated view of the resistance to such domination, i.e., whether it occurs in the name of reversal of domination and dehumanizing acts on behalf of survival, or whether it remains conscious of the need to strive for the lawful third and affirm a more complex morality of responsibility.

The issue for those who would create transformation is whether we are acting in the name of, and striving to fulfill, an ethical third, and to provide the recognition and witnessing that reduces the existential fear of annihilation or annihilating humiliation which drives violence. Without the lawful third, reparative actions become destructive reversals; without the recognizing, witnessing third, there is no support for such action because the law is vitiated of its real meaning – it becomes a moralistic demand for self-sacrifice. Particularly in situations where recognition or surrender of power have not been forthcoming – where transformation takes place violently – it is most difficult for the oppressed or victims to consciously avoid a retaliatory reversal, imitating the power of the perpetrator, thus in many cases perpetuating violence. The renunciation of violence and efforts at reconciliation, which Mandela came to espouse during his years of imprisonment, have often seemed exemplary for a vision of resistance that takes responsibility for maintaining a third.

I suggest that in part such assumption of responsibility depends upon social recognition. But in many cases – and this relates to the need for non-violence – the ability to receive recognition from the witnessing world is compromised by any admission that one has retaliated or reacted unjustly; therefore one cannot expect to be recognized and protected by anyone. The stuck place around blame, I suspect, is the one in which a person or group feels that having been in the wrong, having done damage, one loses the right to have one's own suffering validated and recognized – you must be right to be recognized. This fear of badness impedes acknowledging responsibility for suffering. Indeed, as we can recognize in the Middle East, on both sides of the conflicts it brings the parties' need for recognition of the historical injuries and pain they have been subject to into opposition to the fear they feel in regard to being wrong, hurtful, indeed perpetrators of the very same hateful actions that they themselves were victims of. The conflict exemplifies the predicament when the paramount issue becomes blame and right-eousness: If one is to blame, then one's suffering is somehow deserved, whereas if one's suffering is greater, one cannot be blamed. Thus we enter the economy in which the moral capital of suffering rules.

As we would expect psychoanalytically, it is not simple fear of injury or the Other's aggression that leads to intractable cycles of violence and inability to reconcile, even though fear and trauma underlie the mutual escalation of many reactions. Rather it is the link that is made uncon-sciously between the right to survive and the need to be in the right. The discourse of blame has been central in relation to the Middle East but I believe that despite continual references to the Holocaust, dissociation remains regarding the fear of annihilation. My colleague Eyad el Sarraj, with whom I initiated a project for acknowledgment between Israelis and Palestinians, has consistently argued that the problem is that Israelis think that if they admit to something by apologizing for it, they delegitimize themselves and their right to exist; they feel they will invite annihilation because they will no longer have the right to protect themselves.

Let us return then to the problem of 'original morality,' the belief that only blamelessness can guarantee one's own right to exist, can allow one's own suffering to be acknowledged. I have tried to show how the primitive form of blame rather than responsibility perpetuates the expectation of denial of one's own suffering in return. The 'original morality' of blame and punishment thus actually undermines the ability to take responsibility and requires projecting all the Badness into the other, maintaining all the Goodness and Righteous Suffering on one's own side. When responsibility for causing suffering, or damage done in one's own name, is repudiated, the actual consequence is helplessness, as ameliorative action, reparation, and thus the connection to a lawful third is broken. There is no longer any secure attachment to a third, and thus to the imagining of a lawful world in which protection is possible. For this reason social recognition of trauma, the defense of a witnessing function that upholds lawful behavior, may be more crucial to cessation of violence than has heretofore been realized. Not the simulacrum of justice – justification and blame – but the actuality of recognizing suffering is essential. In this, the psychoanalytic understanding of morality on the one side, of dissociation and trauma on the other, have much to contribute.

Bibliography

Benjamin, J. (2004) Beyond doer and done–to: an intersubjective view of thirdness. *Psychoanalytic Quarterly* 73(1): 5–46.

Benjamin, J. (2006) Our Appointment in Thebes: The Analyst's Acknowledgment and the Fear of Doing Harm. Delivered at IARPP conference, Boston, January 2006.

Bromberg, P. (2007) Potholes on the royal road – or is it an abyss. In *Awakening the Dreamer*. Hillsdale, NJ: The Analytic Press.

Grand, S. (2002) *The Reproduction of Evil*. Hillsdale, NJ: The Analytic Press.

Ogden, P., Minton, K. and Pain, C. (2006) *Trauma and the Body: A Sensorimotor Approach to Psychotherapy*. New York: Norton.

Gobodo-Madikizela, P. (2006) *A Human Being Died that Night*. London: Portobello.

Samuels, A. (1989) *The Plural Psyche*. New Haven and London: Routledge.

Slavin, M. and Kriegman, D. (1998) Why the analyst needs to change. *Psychoanalytic Dialogues* 8: 247–285.

Note

1 Originally given as a Lecture in Honor of Andrew Samuels, World in Transition Conference, London, October 2006.

This chapter is from an originally much longer paper, prepared in gratitude to Andrew for his *friendship* as well as all his pioneering work in putting psycho-analysis into service understanding the social and political realm, always taking positions out there and ahead of the pack. As I finished this paper the Israelis began their attack on Gaza, reminding me once again how much destruction against innocent civilians can occur in the name of defending oneself against an experience of victimization that derives from events in the past.

Chapter 8

Violence in the family

Challenges to the fantasy of shelter and protection

Paula Pantoja Boechat

To you, Andrew, who are part of my soul family.
My warm wishes for your sixtieth anniversary.

The destruction of nature brings forth a considerable amount of stress to human beings, as it is by contemplating and experiencing nature that we are able to reach what is most healthy and transcendent in our own selves. Stress also causes us to look for the wrong forms of relief, and by adopting these we place ourselves increasingly more distant from nature, which results in our ignoring, abandoning or destroying nature even more. The nature we refer to here is that of the rivers, seas, plants and animals and especially human nature and everything that relates thereto.

We are all worried about rivalry, anxiety and the growing violence in contemporary society. The space of the family, whether it is that of our blood relations (parents, children, grandparents, grandchildren, etc.) or of our soul family (good friends) is diminishing, especially in terms of affective exchanges.

By this I do not mean that feelings must always be positive; this would be hypocritical. Within a family, the relationships should be as clear as possible.

> It is not enough for parents to say that they love their children. They often manage to love them, and they have all types of other feelings. Children need more from their parents than just being loved. They need something that is still there even when they are hated or hateful.
>
> (Winnicott 1966: 43)

Jung says: "For those people who are looking for theory, the essential fact behind everything is that the things which have the most powerful effect on children do not come from the conscious state of parents but rather from their unconscious" (Jung 1927 par. 84).

The problem of family violence is hence a *hamartia*, or rather, a type of family curse, which tends to be handed down from grandparents to parents, sons and daughters, similar to the curse of the House of Atreus in Greece, according to the *Orestia* of Aeschylus (Jung 1927).

More than 50 per cent of the men who commit some kind of family violence have a previous history of ill-treatment or have been witnesses of ill-treatment inside their families. We can thus understand that violence is a problem which does not come about as a result of the family situation or the system at that specific moment but has deeper roots in the life stories of the persons participating in that relationship.

In our practice, we are often faced with the *Hamartia* which manifests itself in the suffering of the patients who have been imprisoned in the inability to understand and change their legacies (Paiva and Gomes 2008).

A clear example of this *"hamartia"* is the recent assassination of the teenager Eloá, 15, by her former fiancé, Lindemberg, 22, in October 2008, in a suburb of São Paulo. Eloá had been kept hostage by Lindemberg for 100 hours in the apartment of her parents. The police authorities and her parents stood outside the building, on the sidewalk, trying to negotiate her freedom. Eloá appeared several times at the window of the apartment to talk to her parents and to the police, always trying to calm them down. Upon hearing a shot, the police invaded the apartment to arrest Lindemberg, to find that he had shot Eloá in the head, killing her.

Surprisingly, in the course of the subsequent days, the newspapers revealed the news that Eloá's father was a hired gunman, and had been consistently sought out by the police authorities of the state of Alagoas, in the northeast of Brazil, for various murders committed there. Eloá was probably unable to metabolize her legacy, and she repeated the *hamartia*, choosing a violent man to be her fiancé, like her mother chose her father as a husband.

Focusing on the question of violence in family relations, according to Jung:

> When someone complains that they cannot deal with their wife or people whom they like, there are always awful quarrels and reactions; so you can realize, in the analysis of this person, that they actually had an attack of hatred. They lived in a *Participation Mystique* with those they loved. They extended themselves over the others until they became identical to them, and this is a transgression of the principle of individuality. . . . So I say: *It is quite naturally unfortunate that you always have problems, but can't you see what you are doing? You love someone, identify with them, and then you naturally turn against the object of your affection and oppress them through your excessively obvious identity. You treat them as if they were yourself, and so naturally there will be reactions. It is an offence to the individuality of the other person and a sin against your own individuality.*
>
> (Jung 1932: 64)

When referring to *participation mystique*, a term coined by the anthropologist Lévy-Bruhl, Jung is speaking of a type of relationship between two or more people in which the subjects see themselves as identical or indistinguishable. It can be said that this concept is similar to the psychoanalytical concept of projective identification: a part of the personality is projected onto an object, and the object is then experienced as if it were the projected contents (Samuels 1989: 169–70).

Minuchin *et al.* (1967) qualify as enmeshed or fused the type of relationship which is characteristic of a family structure in which there are disturbances in the formation of the frontiers of interpersonal relationships. Family members are unable to establish frontiers between themselves and their ancestral or original families. Roles inside the family are not clearly established, and a hierarchy and more especially a clearer differentiation between its members is lacking. It is as if there were an undifferentiated egoic mass, a fusion.

For example: A couple sought therapy. They were in the following situation. Successful professionals, they had been married for seven years and had small children. Both reported that they were professionally very independent from one another, but when they told me about their lives, I understood that they were from the same field and that neither of them did anything without obtaining the opinion of the other. In the beginning of their relationship this was a factor that helped to create a strong bond between them. In time, however, it led them to a destructive competition. I could note that each time that one of them made a movement towards being creative, the other severely criticized him or her.

When I asked them when and how they felt that their relationship was getting worse, they told me that it had been so since he had decided to try a new job. This didn't affect her work as it was just something concerning him, an attempt to innovate. She accused him of betrayal and was very hurt. (She probably felt less creative and that he was breaking the symbiotic pact, whereby one could only develop together with the other.) In his new job he was temporarily earning less and she accused him of wasting her money on his luxuries. He then criticized her as a mother and housewife, telling her she was incompetent as a woman. (For him the new professional experience was also a frightening challenge, and he realized that he would never be forgiven if he wasn't successful.)

Jung wrote:

> Logically, the opposite of love is hate . . . But, psychologically, it is the will for power. Where love rules, there is no will for power, and where power has precedence, there is a lack of love. One is the shadow of the other.
>
> (Jung 1917: par. 78)

Uncontrolled aggression, both verbal and physical, became more and more frequent. The misunderstandings reached their peak with an epileptic fit of their six-year-old elder son.

For Perrone (1997), in families where there is violence there is a person who will act as a "safety fuse" whenever there is the threat of a conflict. The role of the fuse is to lower the electrical phase or turn off the power whenever there is an overload of the system.

There is another kind of safety fuse which I have observed in my clinic: that which has the same behavior as that of the pacifier but without victimizing himself directly. As a result of very specific family conditions, he has a special place and manages to change the violent environment by taking over power within the family.

For example: a three-year-old boy, B. His parents are separated, and he is jointly looked after (even before this could legally take place in Brazil). Whenever they meet, the parents still quarrel. B then shouts out loud, making his parents shut up immediately.

Recently, the paternal grandfather, who lived with the father, died after a long illness. The paternal grandmother and B's aunt, who lived in another country, came to the funeral. B's grandmother and father quarrel a lot, which resulted in B adopting the same shouting in order to make them all shut up. This grandmother had divorced B's grandfather when B's father was ten years old. After therapy the father understood that he had had the same task of calming down the rows of his parents when he was small, with the difference that, instead of shouting, as his son does, he used to attract attention by playing up or breaking things accidentally. This role of the safety fuse ends up by giving enormous power to the child, thereby confusing the family hierarchy, in addition to increasing the stress within the family. B's father is now 33 years old, anxious and suffers from arterial hypertension. Despite their separation, the couple was recommended for divorce therapy, so that B could be relieved of his role as a safety fuse.

People who have been victims of childhood abuse may keep their secret hidden and never mention it, believing that this will rid them of the past. However, in their lives they tend to repeat the role of the aggressor.

For example, a man came to me for therapy complaining about difficulties in his affective relationships, both with his wife and children, and with friends and colleagues at work. He felt that for reasons which at times were unimportant he lost his mind, or became totally paralyzed (when he was with a superior), or reacted with violence, only to soon afterwards regret his shouting, threats and hitting the wall. These situations were more frequent at home. He ended up by hurting himself in order not to hit his wife and children, but at critical moments he was unable to contain himself.

On one occasion during therapy he talked about his anger when his 14-year-old son insisted on going alone to the house of a friend who lived nearby. The boy's insistence led the father to hurt himself by shouting and banging on the table. This situation left him very uncomfortable and he could hardly sleep that night. In the session we talked a lot about what had happened, and he remembered an armed attack he had suffered when he was 12 years old, walking home from school. In the attack an armed man had taken him to a piece of waste ground, taken his belongings and raped him. As soon as he managed to get away from the attacker, he ran home. His mother opened the door, and he told her he had been robbed and needed to have a shower. He went into the shower and threw his clothes onto the bathroom floor. His mother came into the bathroom, and, on seeing his clothes dirty with feces, laughed at him saying: "You were so scared that you dirtied yourself!" After this comment, he could never find the courage to tell her, or anyone else, what had really happened.

This revelation during analysis brought him great relief and a much wider understanding of his problems. It is clear that his mother's lack of understanding and his father's lack of presence were factors that had been there for a long time before the attack. However, after the attack, things became different, and he felt as if the blame for the rape had been his own, and thus he needed to react with so much anger every time he felt that he was not being accepted. When he told his wife what he had recollected in the therapy she was able to get closer to him and understand his pain. She told him that every time he got violent she became very afraid and distant from him (inadvertently repeating his father's lack of contact). She had not understood that what he most needed at that time was her physical proximity, affection and support. He needed to be helped to understand what was really happening in his relationships; he had still not developed the ability to perceive the difference between a constructive critique and a total rejection.

The treatment of those who have been victims of violence lies in the possibilities of reconstructing the history of their lives. We must clarify the fear, blame and shame with all the family so that the person can recover their self-esteem. It is only in this way that the role that they were obliged to live and still live may be clarified and changed.

The importance of non-violent relationships is decisive for both our psychic and physical health. In an article by the psychoanalyst and psychiatrist Contardo Calligaris, published in the *Folha de São Paulo* newspaper, he comments on a study published in the December 2005 issue of *Archives of General Psychiatry* (vol. 62, no. 12). This study was directed by Janice Kiecolt-Glaser, of the Institute for Behavioral Medicine Research at Ohio State University. The main points of the article are as follows:

The theme of the study is: "Hostile Marital Interaction and Wound Healing." In all, 42 couples (between 22 and 77 years old) were selected, and small wounds were made in all of their arms. These wounds were covered so as to measure the variation in the fluids which the body produces in order to help healing. They then took part in two discussion sessions. The first was directed to pleasant subjects, and the second was designed for the couples to argue. It was discovered that the healing was always slower after the couples had been arguing, and the healing of the most quarrelsome couples was 40 per cent worse than that of the others. Conclusion: quarrels have an effect on the body and are bad for health.

Belmont, in the introduction to *Violence and Suffering in Children and Teenagers*, puts this very clearly and poetically:

> The small river is born as a brook, pure, with a crystalline appearance like that of the source of rivers. It flows and receives tributaries, people, care or lack of care, rubbish. Even when it is polluted, when it is near death, both rivers and men can find through devotion and love the hope of living, or re-living, discovering a crystalline purity which it was often difficult to maintain. This happens both with rivers and men, when they discover in the world an ethical being to which they can devote themselves.
>
> (Belmont 2008: 15–16)

What is here called ethical being could either mean the ability to be ethical, or that ethical human being who can help someone recover from violence wounds.

Bibliography

Belmont, S.A. (2008) Introdução. In Rosa, J.T., Motta, I.F., *Violência e Sofrimento de Crianças e Adolescentes na perspectiva winnicottiana*. São Paulo: Idéias e Letras.

Brandão, J.S. (1986) *Mitologia grega*, vol. 1, Petrópolis: Vozes.

Calligaris, C. (2006) Crônica: Corpo e Mente, *Jornal Folha de São Paulo*, 6 April, Notebook E, fl.10.

Elkaim, M. (ed.) (1998) *Panorama de Terapias Familiares* vols. 1 and 2. São Paulo: Summus.

Jung, C.G. (1917) *The Psychology of the Unconscious. CW* VII. London: Routledge and Kegan Paul.

—— (1927) *The Development of Personality: CW* vol. XVII. NY: Bollingen Series XX, Princeton University Press.

—— (1932) *Psychology of Kundalini Yoga*. The Notes of the Seminar Given in 1932. Princeton: Princeton University Press (1999).

Kiecolt-Glaser, J., Loving, T.J., Stowell, J.R., Malarkey, W.B., Lemeshow, S., Dickinson, S. and Glaser R. (2005) Hostile Marital Interactions, Proinflammatory Cytokine Production, and Wound Healing. *Archives of General Psychiatry*, 62: 1377–1384.

Minuchin, S., Montalvo, B., Guerney, B., Rosman, B.L. and Schumer, F. (1967) *Families of the Slums: an exploration of their structure and treatment*. New York: Basic Books.

Paiva, Maria Lúcia; Gomes, Isabel (2008) Violência Familiar: Transgeracionalidade e Pacto Denegativo. In Rosa, J.T. and Motta, I.F. *Violência e Sofrimento de Crianças e Adolescentes na perspectiva winnicottiana*. São Paulo: Idéias e Letras.

Perrone, R., Nannini, M. (1997) Violencia y abusos sexuales en la familia. Un abordaje sistémico y communicacional. Buenos Aires: Paidós.

Samuels, A. (1989) *The Plural Psyche*. London and New York: Routledge.

Samuels, A., Shorter, B., Plaut, F. (1991) *Dicionário Crítico de Análise Junguiana*. Rio de Janeiro: Imago.

Sluzki, C. (1996) *Violência Familiar*. In Schnitman, Dora F. (ed.) *Novos Paradigmas, Cultura e Subjetividade*. Porto Alegre: Artes Médicas.

Winnicott, D. (1966) *The Family and Individual Development*. London: Tavistock Publications.

Chapter 9

The dream in psychosomatic patients

Walter Boechat

To a soul, to die is to change into water;
to water, to die is to change into earth.
However, earth gives birth to water,
and water to the soul.

Heraclitus of Hephaesus, Frag. 36 (*apud* Bornheim, 1992)

I dedicate this chapter to my very dear and inspiring friend, Andrew Samuels. With his rich and creative mind, Andrew has always suggested new ways to direct my thoughts and writings. Above all, Andrew has opened up new attitudes to social reality both internationally as well as in relation to Latin America's complex identity. My recent research on racism in Brazil and the problem of fundamentalism in Latin America was based on some of his ideas and suggestions. The present chapter deals with another interest for me, psychosomatics. The clinical case studied here, which looks at the importance of racial prejudice in the developing of tensions and aggressions within a middle-class Brazilian family, also shows some influence of Andrew's.

I would like to demonstrate the function of dreams in somatic patients, showing this with a clinical situation of autoimmune disease accompanied by an initial dream with major symbolic elements. Client M, 35, female, came to consult me afflicted by *primary Sjögren's syndrome*. As the therapy evolved, a depressive pattern emerged, possibly a *unipolar depressive disorder*.

Sjögren's syndrome is an autoimmune disease that leads to the malfunctioning of the *exocrine glands*[1] in the human body. My patient had the constant feeling of a dried body, deprived of water due to the glandular malfunction. Ocular alterations were very typical: without tears, her eyes became dry, easily exposed to ulcerations of the cornea and infections caused by irritating agents in general; she did not produce saliva, and therefore she underwent several alterations in the oral mucosa; the health of her mouth was affected, with adverse consequences to the eventual teeth prosthesis, diet, taste, speech and nutrition. Mouth dryness could even lead to difficulties in swallowing (dysphagia).

As M arrived for her sessions, her attitude was very regressed, typical of patients with an apparently incurable chronic pathology. Given the prolonged, excessive use of cortisone medications, she was all swollen and appeared to be above her ideal weight. She spoke slowly and looked downwards, evidencing strong signs of depression. She constantly carried drinking water to use during the sessions in order to minimize the adverse effects of the lack of salivation. Her skin was dry and shiny. As to the diagnosis of affective depression disorder, she was using medication prescribed in a public hospital: lithium, 30 mg/day, plus fluoxetine hydrochloride, 60 mg/day.

Her family history was extremely complicated and would perhaps endorse the associate diagnosis of affective unipolar depressive disorder, given the fact that in her family there were several such cases. M was the third daughter in a family of four siblings, and she had two elder sisters and a much younger brother; her parents had a marital situation rather common in lower middle class Brazilian homes: her father was a depressive alcoholic, and her mother was aggressive, very domineering and narcissistic. The father does not come up too often in her reports, but the mother is constantly referred to because of her sadism and control. Hence the absence of the depressive father was compensated by the dominating, authoritarian image of the mother. Being a third daughter, M always felt rejected, since she was taken care of by third parties, such as aunts and domestic maids.

In her grandparents' generation, a deep conflict came up: her grandfather developed an uncontrollable passion for a domestic maid and became sexually involved with her. He was of European descent and she was black. His wife, M's grandmother, felt abandoned and became very depressed. The grandfather had several children with the maid. As a result, his original family suffered a severe loss of financial means. When the maid left the grandfather, he forced the presence of his other children on M's mother, who felt very humiliated by this. Mutual attacks and quarrels ensued, and M's mother was very adamant in considering her father's other children as inferiors, due to their darker skin. Racial hatred then appeared in all its symbolic power, the darker skin symbolizing the illegitimate wedlock, on one hand, but also epitomizing the force of authentic love, on the other.

There was hence the birth of this great destructive hatred in the bosom of the macro-family, contaminating all the rest, and sieving through the generations. The grandmother hated the grandfather for having been abandoned for a socially inferior woman, her own domestic maid. M's mother, as a child, traumatized by the scenes, identifies herself with her own mother and hereby hates all men, *for all men are the same. She will never marry, or if she does marry, it will be to a weaker man, whom she can control.*

The following generation is contaminated by this hatred: the half-sisters hate each other and compete intensely, as do the subsequent generations of cousins. In this environment of hatred and rejection, M is born, rejected by a mother who cannot love her because she is herself emotionally injured. The relationship existing between M and her mother is so deficient that she reports having spent many of her childhood years in the company of her aunts – the dark-skinned daughters of the maid and her grandfather – who by then had no financial status any longer, and thus hated her mother and her side of the family due to their possessions and their access to studies. This situation of continuous hatred and rejection led M to a state of low self-esteem and depression. She however managed, with much difficulty, to finish her Psychology studies, although she had very low marks. Her interests in History, Politics, Arts and culture in general showed me that she, however, had a good level of intelligence. As she was about to end her studies, her depression set in more significantly, and she felt unable to exercise her profession as a psychologist. She finally decided to take a job as a public employee as an elementary school teacher, receiving very low wages.

This is when the initial symptoms of Sjögren syndrome manifested themselves: dryness of the lachrymal glands, the saliva glands, the sweat glands, the Bartholin glands, with consequent vaginal dryness.

In the course of the therapy, transference was marked by what Luchina (1977) describes as *bodily autism*, which is a form of transference very common in hospitalized patients: the patient is intensely regressed and transferred to his or her own body initially; the therapist is always referred in connection with the physical symptoms of the disease, due to their intensity. Thus, M would first initiate by speaking of her body symptoms, the ever-encompassing dryness, accompanied by a general tiredness, a tendency to lie down all day long and a lack of disposition to do anything.

But she also had frequent feelings of being unworthy. When I said I could assist her she showed immense surprise and gratitude, as if she did not deserve a more differentiated treatment. And yet, her transference of permanent and huge gratitude towards me constellated itself in an idealized transference. This was not solely due to the price charged for the session, but also because I was there, available to assist her. Of course, this idealization did not only occur in her analysis, but also in other parts of her life, due to her regression and the lack of structure of her ego.

She made repeated attempts at finding maternal protection in the figure of the analyst: she would call me several times, and send me many e-mails. Her slow way of expressing herself, her demands for help, her insistent praise, her great idealization and a rational, apparently forced attempt to seduce me would provide a colorful backdrop for the transference. Such a prolonged emotional charge finally took its toll on me, by causing me to become a bit irritated and impatient towards the patient. At times I had the impulse to end the session somewhat earlier, when there was no interesting material to be discussed, or when she was too tired or depressed. In certain sessions, my own psychosoma was influenced, for I felt some tiredness myself, and even became sleepy on certain occasions. Indeed, I felt rather impatient with her repeated telephone calls and e-mails. Such impatience came as a surprise to me, mainly because of the suddenness with which it would appear.

The answer to the problem of the *interactive field*[2] being so filled with hostility came up when M reported her recent therapeutic relationship with two other professionals, a general practitioner and a psychologist. The first one, a seasoned medical doctor, despite the breadth of his own professional experience, ended up *expelling her* from his consulting room, not being able to stand the transferential burden. My own experience with M showed that she carried such an amount of hatred and destructiveness in her psyche that she was capable of contaminating her therapeutic relationships with an *interactive field of destruction*. However, I did not approach this phenomenon as a case of dissociative disorder or character disorder. I tended to value instead the *enormous amount of destructive energy* that was present in her dissociated shadow, the same hatred that had ultimately caused her disease, in my evaluation.

As her therapy evolved the patient started to develop feelings of thankfulness and deep respect towards me. The transference progressed once she revealed her most confidential family secrets, something which was difficult in view of the very aggressive mother she had. Meanwhile, M received a medication, pilocorpine, which induced the functioning of the exocrine glands. She also continued to receive adequate dosages of cortisone medication. She started to take better care of herself, and her physical appearance evidenced this.

At the start of her therapy, M brought to my attention a dream which I consider the initial dream in her analysis:

> I find a myself at the bottom of the ocean; the waters are very deep. I see myself as a big whale. I have the feeling that I have been there at the bottom for a very long time, and I must come up to the surface, in order to breathe, for the lack of air has started to annoy me. I wish to have the means to be able to come up to the surface and breathe. I also have the strange sensation that this whale has been a stone at some point in the past, and has thus lain at the bottom of the sea.

The dream emphasizes her deep isolation, which had prolonged itself for some years. The analysis had the task of elaborating that isolation and the deep regression. I also believe that the dream provides the perfect image of *how the self sees the body* or, as Jung put it, how *dreams can compensate for the conscious situation*. There are various images for solitude; the most frequent and repeated one is the desert, as well as vast, uninhabited distances; and even the emptiness of any given room. It was hence very suggestive for the self *to have chosen the watery image* of the deep ocean, *to reflect the solitude of a dried body.* It is as if the self had also taken into consideration the biological reality of the disease, in its compensation. This could not evidently have been otherwise, given the fact that *the archetype is always psychoid.*

In M's dream, *water* stands for the unconscious. One should remind oneself that *in alchemy,* one of the basic representations of *mercury – the acqua mercurialis, or acqua vitae –* or the unconscious, is water.[3] If on the one hand in her body there was a lack of water, a dryness, and on the other hand in her psyche there was excess water, she was overwhelmed by water in her self-destructive thoughts and in the *petrifying* depression she had.

Another aspect of her dream, a very important one, is the fact that *the whale had earlier been a stone.* Petrification is a well-known motif in myths and tales of psychotic processes, for it stands for the stagnation of the libido in the unconscious, the impossibility of a creative flow of energy. The reason for the petrification seemed to be the great depression that gained control of M, insulated her in deep waters and deprived her of creative relationships and a productive life.

Air is the missing element, but the patient feels that she has to come up to the surface in order to breathe. The air is hence the positive element, the social interchange, the adapting conscious life, a better structuring of the ego and the persona. But M's need to come to the surface is already a good sign, in the midst of graver elements such as her isolation and petrification.

Indeed, after the first year, the patient had another dream that illustrated her improvement: 'I run beside a fish, which moves close to the floor. I run a lot, then I become a bird and fly.'

Here one can remark how very gradually the identification with the waters gives way to the pursuit of wider spaces, higher flights, a closer contact with her own capabilities and hence a clearer view of her problems. M had an overall improvement, as she became more closely connected to her own personal issues in several aspects.

One should hence remark that once again *aggression* plays its role in psychosomatic diseases. The level of aggression in this case was enormous, involving a three-generation time span.

I wish to emphasize therefore that Sjögren's syndrome affected M in moments of great despair, due to the incertitude and depression inherent to that specific period of life. One must remember the frequent association between depression and unexpressed aggressiveness, or vice versa, aggressiveness as a response to depression. In her case, her intensive aggressiveness, not having been elaborated on a psychological level, expressed itself in the body/mind totality as an autoimmune disease.

M's family environment was extremely negative for her psychological development. What happened to M is, in fact, quite common when the patient has very adverse parental complexes – in her case, an absent, alcoholic father; and a very destructive mother – a strong and compensatory bond to a sibling occurs. In M's case, there was a merger with her younger sister, who was a registered nurse who specialized in providing nutrition to hospitals (a motherly function!). This sister also suffered from a unipolar depressive disorder, interrupted by frustrated suicide attempts. I wish to emphasize further that *the body is a deintegrate of the self* (Fordham, 1976, 2001). It is possible that the primary self may have dissociated itself at a bodily level, thereby bringing forth the autoimmune disease, in order to protect the totality from an even larger psychological dissociation, or even death. When dreaming, imagination and fantasizing are not sufficient to contain the symbolic processes the self must *disintegrate* on a bodily level (Sidoli, 2000, pp. 106, 107). We thus have an autoimmune (i.e., auto-aggressive) disease and its analogous dream symbols as the last defense of the body/mind totality against fragmentation and not-being.

Bibliography

Bornheim, G. (ed.) (1992) *Os filósofos pré-socráticos*. S. Paulo: Cultrix.

Fordham, M. (2001) *Children as Individuals*. London: Routledge.

Fordham, M. (1976) *The Self and Autism*. London: Karnac.

Jung, C. G. (1946/1972) *The Psychology of the Transference*. C.W. vol. 16. London: Routledge.

Jacoby, M. (2008). *Empathy and interpretation within the interactive field of analysis*. Seminar at the Jungian Association of Brazil (AJB), Rio de Janeiro, March, 2008.

Luchina, N.; Luchina, I.; Ferrara, H. (1977) *La interconsulta médico-psicológica en el marco hospitalario*. Buenos Aires: Nueva Vision.

Schwartz-Salant, N. (1992) *Borderline Personality*. Illinois: Chiron.

Schwartz-Salant, N. (1995) On the interactive field as the analytic object. In Murray Stein (ed.) *The Interactive Field in Analysis* vol. 1: 1–36. Wilmette, Illinois: Chiron.

Sidoli, M. (2000) *When the Body Speaks*. London: Routledge.

Notes

1 *Exocrine glands* secrete substances – such as saliva, tears and vaginal secretions externally to the blood current, either to the cavities (or orifices) in the body or to its external surface, contrary to what is done by the *endocrine glands.*

2 The *Interactive Field* is the subtle field that forms between patient and analyst, containing objects that pertain both to analyst and patient. The interactive field may strongly affect the therapist in his or her reactions and interventions. See Jacoby (2008) and Schwartz-Salant (1995).

3 See watery homonyms for mercury, in Jung (1946/1972), *The Psychology of Transference*, C.W. vol. 16, paras 453, 454, 455.

Chapter 10

How they see us now

Joe Cambray

By the end of the 1990s an exciting set of exchanges between analytical psychologists and psychoanalysts had begun. Theoretical and clinical materials from each side were put forth for purposes of comparison in several professional journals and at conferences. Thus in 1996 *The Psychoanalytic Review* published a 'Symposium: post-Jungian Thought' guest edited by Andrew Samuels. During that same year the *Journal of Analytical Psychology (JAP)* held the first of a series of conferences bringing together analytical psychologists, psychoanalysts, and historians of the field. The primary focus of these conferences was to broaden and enhance dialogue among analytic schools. Then *Psychoanalytic Dialogues* in 2000 published a group of prominent Jungians responding to a questionnaire designed in part by Andrew Samuels, who served as liaison editor for the issue (volume 10, number 3).

In 2001 at the XVth IAAP International Congress in Cambridge, England, I gave a presentation on a day devoted to 'analytical psychology and psychoanalysis.' The talk, 'How They See Us Now,' came from discussions I had with James Fosshage the co-editor of *Psychoanalytic Dialogues*, who had been active in publishing the issue on contemporary Jungian thought. As US editor for the *JAP* at the time, I wished to further the dialogue and to generate a response in kind. Andrew kindly lent his support and advice to me on this project in which I engaged a group of eight psychoanalysts representing a spectrum of differing theoretical perspectives. Fosshage together with Coline Covington and Barbara Wharton, my co-editors of the *JAP*, helped with the design of my questionnaire. The questionnaire and responses were eventually published in the *JAP* (volume 47, number 1) in 2002. In honor of Andrew and as a contribution to this Festschrift for him, I am offering excerpts from my analysis of the responses, which I presented in Cambridge.

The topic of how the Jungian community is perceived in various psychoanalytic circles was of general interest but complicated at times with discomfort on both sides. The urge to juxtapose these two approaches to human psychological experience arose out of the relatively brief but intense relationship between the founders, Jung and Freud. While their failure to sustain mutual engagement had numerous causes, the resulting legacy of alienation has persisted for many through several generations of followers despite various modifications of theory and practice and the diversification of schools within each tradition.

Some historians, in detailed examination of Jung's sources and mentors, have questioned the 'dissident' status often assigned to him and, with cause, have counseled Jungians to detach from psychoanalytic identifications. Nevertheless, many analytical psychologists find concepts and methods from the psychoanalytic literature to be of considerable assistance in their work – personally, I have found selected psychoanalytic formulations and handling of clinical issues related to primitive mental states to be useful. There has been an obvious asymmetry in our borrowings, which I think acts as an irritant to Jungians' collective self-esteem as our contributions to understanding the psyche are often unacknowledged outside our own community and the Jungian-oriented public, and the asymmetry itself has unwelcome overtones regarding authority. Our relative isolation has also impoverished the psychoanalytic world; many otherwise erudite psychoanalysts have only a fleeting, often stereotyped acquaintance with Jung's writings despite its relevance to their work, not to mention the contributions of generations of Jungians. Our marginalization within the broader analytic community, however, has not been wholly negative. As an independent tradition we have been able to cultivate a set of attitudes, ideas, and methods whose transformative potentials may well have been lost or diluted by premature exposure to other traditions with different roots. However, this is not a question that can easily be settled once and for all.

In the past most efforts at bridging within the English-speaking world have been initiated from the Jungian side. While a certain amount of rapport has developed between individuals, sustained dialogue between schools has not generally resulted nor has the psychoanalytic literature been much impacted by Jungian or post-Jungian thinking regardless of the various personal relationships and occasional publication of Jungian articles or chapters in psychoanalytic books or journals. Thus, as late as 1992 with the publication of *The Common Ground of Psychoanalysis*, edited by Robert Wallerstein (a former president of both the American Psychoanalytic Association and the International Psycho-Analytical Association), the Jungian approach to analysis is mentioned almost solely in terms of the extrusion of early 'dissidents' (Adler, Stekel, and Jung) from Freud's psychoanalysis. Wallerstein's denial of the legitimacy of analytical psychology as a form of analysis contrasts with his usual open, ecumenical stance towards divergent viewpoints.

Recently the increasing integration of intersubjective models of the mind and reassessment of the impact of the inescapable nature of the analyst's subjectivity on the analytic process has produced a fundamental broadening of the conception of analysis and the role of the analyst. These shifts have occurred within the larger post-modern zeitgeist, with its pluralistic bent, so that those who have embraced them have tended to become more attentive to those people and ideas on the margins. Thus, many innovative psycho-analysts have been drawn to re-examine the edges of their discipline and in doing so have begun to venture into areas, such as the role of spirituality in analysis, that would have been dismissed summarily by most of their colleagues in the past. Some current psychoanalytic thinkers and students are therefore poised for engagement with Jung and analytical psychology. A concern of this study was to locate and assess analytic orientations and subjects that may lead to further productive encounters and to note where our views may be outside current limits of diversity in psychoanalysis. It is time for another assessment of our relative lack of dialogue.

Questionnaire and respondents

The questionnaire is given in the appendix. The first two questions are intended to draw out the respondents on their orientation and understand-ing of the therapeutic process. Questions 3, 4, and 5 focus on subject matter anticipated to be of mutual interest for psychoanalysts and analytical psychologists, while also attempting to gauge the influence of cultural trends valuing diversity. Then, questions 6 and 7 look more directly at the inclusion or exclusion of several key Jungian concepts in the thinking of the psychoanalytic respondents. Finally, the last two questions seek to discern future directions both for the kinds of emerging dialogues of which this questionnaire is a part and more broadly for the field itself. Implicit in the final two questions is a qualitative assessment of the tendencies towards convergence and/or divergences between analytic communities. The pro-posal for this chapter was made after the *JAP* project was under way and so the focus of the questions was not specifically designed for the present study but results had to be extracted from the responses.

In the letter that accompanied this questionnaire emphasis was placed on the mutual interest and benefit of the study with a request for respondents to seriously engage and reflect on the similarities and differences between analytical psychology and their area of expertise in psychoanalysis. We explicitly stated our desire to offer our readers an external view of analyti-cal psychology as well as providing a range of contemporary perspectives on subjects of interest to all analysts.

The appendix also provides the names of the eight respondents together with their primary orientation or theoretical allegiance – an oversimplifica-tion used for purposes of categorization. The attempt was to find represen-tative voices of different schools but is not meant to appear comprehensive. Each respondent has had some contact with members of the Jungian community; they have differing degrees of familiarity with basic tenets of

Jungian psychology – to assist those who wished for brief statements of selected Jungian concepts definitions from *CW 6* (for self, para. 789–791, and individuation, para. 757–762) and from *A Critical Dictionary of Jungian Analysis* (entries for self, individuation and dreams) were provided.

Highlights of results and discussion

An analysis of the responses was organized along several axes including the degree of familiarity with Jungian ideas, willingness to engage in dialogue, and tone of disagreements; an attempt was also made to assess the quality of misreading when they were perceived. Grids were constructed to condense and represent the data (Cambray, 2003). Through examination of the data it became evident that among the respondents analytic orientation is the single most important factor in determining receptivity to dialogue. Thus the more classically Freudian authors display the greatest caution and are best engaged through carefully reasoned debate. More surprising on the surface is the contentious, rather dark view of Jungians taken by the Kleinian, especially given stated theoretical overlaps. He is at pains to differentiate a Kleinian approach from what he believes is a Jungian idealization of the unconscious. In contrast, the Bionian's views include a role for positive aspects of the personality that are mobilized by analytic interventions; her stance is correspondingly less critical. Due to overlaps in thinking about the radical otherness of the unconscious, and a stance on subjectivity that is inclusive of conscious and unconscious processes, the Lacanian displays openness to selected Jungian themes. The greatest potential for ready engagement clearly comes from the self-psychological/relational school hybrid, though a blurring of concepts was noted at times. The contemporary movement to include an interpersonal dimension in analytic considerations seems to be bringing an increased valuing of diversity relative to that found in those who maintain a strictly intrapsychic focus – theoretically a shift from conflict/repression models to those including trauma and dissociation in the etiology of psychogenic suffering, which is closer to Jung's model of the psyche based on complexes.

In brief, several overall observations and recommendations with regard to engagement are:

- Consideration of theoretical orientation is primary but not absolute
- Inclusion of subjective/intersubjective perspectives increases receptivity
- Evaluation of fluency with basic concepts, paying particular attention to tone and possible misperceptions.

On specific topics some surprising similarities to Jungian views were discovered. For example, despite a conservative Freudian stance, the respondent's 'multiple functions' perspective on dreams had real parallels with a self-function operating unconsciously lending shape to analyses, and including: 'anticipations of psychic events not yet organized as secondary process'. The implication of a prospective quality to dreams would be an especially important point for future comparative explorations with this school. Similarly the moderate Freudian's use of countertransference responses to dreams was close to Davidson's view of 'Transference as form of active imagination' (1969). A larger gulf was found in all the discussions of the value of an archetypal perspective; most of the psychoanalysts were focused exclusively on the danger of loss of contact with the emotional realities of the patient. More details can be found in the Congress Proceedings paper (Cambray, 2003).

Future directions and conclusions

From the study a list of potential future collaborations and cautions includes:

- Dream theory and practice are well suited for comparative work.
- The impact of culture on clinical practice may be treated with suspicion.
- Archetypal theory will not easily be given credence in psychoanalysis.
- Gender and sexuality studies are not yet fully integrated into psychoanalysis; Jungian contributions are possible.
- The clinical significance of the numinous offers opportunities for dialogue.
- Detailed, comparative analysis of major concepts is needed, especially with regard to their comprehensiveness and motivational dynamics.
- The understanding of symbolic expression, in terms of origins, pathologies, overt content and processes, needs clinical comparisons.
- Comparative evaluation of limitations and problems with various analytical models is needed (archetypal theory is the area of greatest divergence).

No attempt was made in this study to explore the value and application of the cognitive and neurosciences, which hold much interest and promise for various analytic orientations.

While the small, somewhat idiosyncratic sample of psychoanalysts chosen for this project precludes any definitive, general conclusions, their reflections on possible future directions for dialogue are useful to those who may be seeking to extend engagement. The single most important area identified by the majority of respondents is in-depth exploration of shared clinical experience, focusing on the specifics of how we work analytically, what interventions we employ, when, and to what ends. This, of course, requires a measure of trust that what is revealed as we disclose our work will be received with an attitude of mutual respect. At present this may exist with select individuals to varying degrees but it cannot be presumed.

Respondents also offered several additional approaches for engagement, e.g., the Kleinian, despite previous sharp criticisms, suggests three avenues: empirical comparisons; pluralism, exploring 'diverse positions across the analytic field as comparable to the unintegrated parts of an individual's psyche'; and historically informed study of 'the evolution of the ideas . . . and under what influences, conceptual, emotional and economic . . . divergence has happened'. The moderate Freudian offered a list of eleven areas for comparative examination, from various topics in theory and technique to the kinds of research question we each believe should be studied. These proposals deserve serious consideration and reply.

My own conclusion from this study is that a focus on the relational aspects inherent in Jung's theory, as have been and are continuing to be elaborated by a number of analytical psychologists, will yield the greatest possibilities for engagement with contemporary psychoanalysts, especially those who have been impacted by the relational turn in the field generally. In this, I have no hopes of rapid, immediate success but believe that sustained efforts demonstrating a capacity to listen analytically as well as to cogently present ideas clinically can have a cumulative influence.

There are two interrelated projects that I believe may help foster such engagement. The first is a multi-level assessment of the relationship and interests of Jung and Ferenczi; as a start, at the second History Symposium, co-sponsored by the *JAP* and the San Francisco Jung Institute, I chaired a panel on Jung and Ferenczi. Second, following up on the liberal Freudian's contribution, I have been examining how our conception of synchronicity can be extended and employed more fully in the clinical setting; how it can be used to more deeply understand seemingly mundane daily exchanges in the specific ways in which we engage unconscious processes, intrapsychically and intersubjectively, in the consulting room. However, I do not think the relational focus is the only direction open to Jungian theory and practice. Examining the limits and possible extensions of our own unique heritage and traditions from within provides parallel pathways for our development and appears to also be bringing us into dialogue with numerous other fields of study. In this, I believe that the challenges of engagement ultimately force us to continue the unending process of discerning who we really are.

Bibliography

Cambray, J. (2003). How They See Us Now (Cambridge 2001). In *Proceedings of the Fifteenth International Congress for Analytical Psychology*. Einsiedeln, Switzerland: Daimon Verlag, pp. 141–162.

Davidson, D. (1966). Transference as a form of active imagination. *JAP* 11, 3, 135–146.

Jung, C. G. (1971). *Psychological Types*. CW 6.

Samuels, A. (ed.) (1996). Symposium: Post-Jungian Thought. *Psychoanalytic Review*, 83, 469–587.

Samuels, A., Shorter, B. and Plaut, F. (1986). *A Critical Dictionary of Jungian Analysis*. London and New York: Routledge.

Wallerstein, R. S. (ed.) (1992). *The Common Ground of Psychoanalysis*. Northvale, NJ: Jason Aronson.

Appendix:

Questionnaire

1   What in your opinion brings about or facilitates therapeutic change? How has your perspective on this evolved in your practice? Could you offer a clinical example?

2   How do you conceive the role of the analyst in the treatment experience? What, if any, changes in your conceptions of this role have occurred? How has this manifested in clinical encounters? Could you offer a vignette?

3   What role do dreams play in your analytic practice? What approaches to dreams do you find most helpful? Do you consider cultural aspects of dream material to be a valuable source of information? How do you handle dreams clinically?

4   The Oedipus myth is one that has been employed extensively by psychoanalysts for its psychological and developmental value. What place does the Oedipus complex currently hold in your thought? How do you view the role of the Oedipus complex in female development and psychology? Have you employed other myths to enhance your understanding of human behavior? If so, what role or function does myth have in the clinical setting?

5   Do you see a place for discussion of religious attitudes or spiritual seeking of analysands within the context of analysis? Have your views of these kinds of concerns altered over time?

6   Various contemporary analytic theories of personality include the concept of a self; which if any of these do you find useful? In the practice of analysis which of these models do you deem the most clinically applicable? How do your choices overlap, if at all, with Jung's conception of the Self (a succinct statement of Jung's formulation can be supplied if it would be helpful)?

7   What is your theoretical perspective on adult development, of psychological growth and maturation? Can this be compared with Jung's model of a lifelong potential for unfolding of the personality (what he

termed "individuation" – again, a lexicon of Jungian terms can be provided)?

8   What do you consider the central paradigm shifts occurring in psycho-analysis today? If possible could you comment on how they are related to developments in other fields?

9   What topics do you feel would generate the liveliest response from psychoanalysts interested in furthering dialogue between our communities?

Table 10.1   Questionnaire respondents

Respondent	Theoretical orientation	Society affiliation	Area(s) of specialization
Ana-Maria Rizzuto	Freudian (conservative)	Psychoanalytic Institute of New England	Psychodynamics of Religious Belief
Theodore J. Jacobs	Freudian (moderate)	New York Psychoanalytic Institute	Countertransference; Enactments
Elizabeth Lloyd Mayer	Freudian (liberal)	San Francisco Psychoanalytic Institute	Gender; Intersubjectivity of Knowledge
Robert D. Hinshelwood	Kleinian	British Psychoanalytic Society	Groups; Communities; Kleinian Theory
Judith L. Mitrani	Bionian	Psychoanalytic Center of California in Los Angeles	Primitive Mental States
Ross Skelton	Lacanian	Irish Forum Psychoanalytic Psychotherapy	Matte-Blanco's Theories
James L. Fosshage	Self-psychology	Institute for the Psychoanalytic Study of Subjectivity	Dreams
Stephen A. Mitchell	Relational	William Alanson White Institute	Relational Theories

Chapter 11

Night terrors

A titanic experience considered from science, art and psychology

Linda Carter

I am honored to offer this chapter as a contribution to this volume celebrating the creativity and life work of my dear friend and colleague Andrew Samuels.

Clinical vignette and scientific background

The Sleeper sits bolt upright, eyes wide open, with a facial look of utter terror, body filled with tension and SCREAMS at grand volume ". . . AAAH . . . HELP ME! . . . HELP ME! AAAH! . . . HELP ME! . . ." His shocked wife, woken from peaceful sleep, has been through this before and is well aware of how frustrating it is to interrupt such an episode and make human contact; her husband in these moments seems otherworldly on the one hand, animal-like on the other. Indeed, he

> almost appears possessed. She tries soothing words, body contact, and finally in sheer frustration and exhaustion says, "Help is on the way." Her husband immediately settles, makes ordinary eye contact with her, and plunges into sleep for the rest of the night. Meanwhile, his poor wife and rescuer lies awake wondering about the daytime and nighttime personalities of her husband.

This vignette attempts to convey a human experience that feels entirely otherwordly to anyone who suffers night terrors, also known as pavor nocturnus and incubus attacks. The patient described above will be known as S.G., a thirty-five-year-old man who has lived with night terrors for his entire life, disrupting his sleep, that of bed partners, and even people in adjoining hotel rooms.

This state of possession was also well known to the Norwegian artist Edvard Munch, whose painting *The Scream* (1893) visually portrays the equivalent of the night terror moment. The experiences of these two men will be used throughout this brief chapter to describe an extraordinary psychosomatic condition which is not documented in the Jungian literature.

S.G. is among a relatively select group as night terrors are rare (Knapp 1987: 183). Kales *et al.* (1980: 116) found that the prevalence of sleepwalking and night terrors in first-degree relatives of an affected individual is at least ten times greater than in the general population. Garland and Smith (1991: 553) claim night terrors occur in about 3 per cent of children, while Hartmann (1984: 221) notes that night terrors are most frequently reported in children between the ages of three and eight. The most common assumption is that night terrors in children are due to delays in central nervous system maturation which resolve with time and development. However, it has been reported in one study, by DeMario and Emery (1987: 505), that 36 per cent of childhood night terror cases persisted into adolescence. In addition, there is a significant group of people whose onset of night terrors can be traced to a specific event. This would include the children of the Chowchilla bus kidnapping, war veterans, and abuse survivors.

Night terrors arise out of slow wave, non-rapid eye movement (NREM), stage four sleep, as opposed to nightmares, which arise out of REM sleep. Broughton (Fisher *et al.* 1973: 76) groups night terrors with enuresis and somnambulism, calling them "disorders of arousal" – meaning that they do not occur during "dreaming sleep" (REM sleep) as recorded by an EEG. Fisher *et al.* (ibid.: 76) state the following:

> In night terrors and somnambulism, although the attack is initiated out of stage 4 sleep, it takes place in an EEG stage approaching that of light sleep or wakefulness, during which the subject appears to be dissociated, out of contact with the environment, delusional, and/or hallucinating. Although the subject is not asleep when the night terror is enacted, he is not in a fully alert waking state either; the EEG may show an alpha rhythm. In this state there is altered or decreased cortical responsiveness to visual stimulation and incapacity to integrate sensory input.

As a result, in the midst of an "attack," the sufferer is neither awake nor asleep but in a kind of dissociated, liminal state located between the worlds of consciousness and unconsciousness. By EEG standards he is not "dreaming" despite the fact that images and mental contents may be available although not always remembered in the morning. Researchers describe this gap as a "psychological void" and a "physiological vacuum."

What is most astounding about the night terror is its rapid onset with no preparation or warning. Fisher *et al.* (1973: 75) report that: ". . . the night terror arises out of physiologically quiescent sleep as indicated by the normal or slightly less than normal cardio-respiratory rates during the first NREM period and absence of skin resistance changes prior to the attack." Heralded by an intense scream, the heart rate can double or triple from, for example, 64 bpm to 152 bpm and go as high as 170 bpm within 15 to 30 seconds (ibid.: 92). Night terror sufferers are consumed by the "fight-flight" response of *massive* autonomic discharge. In contrast to REM nightmares where there is a build up of heart rate and respiration with no motility, the night terror is extraordinarily sudden and active, plunging its victim into all-consuming fear.

From a Jungian point of view, we could say that consciousness experiences the night terror "as if" it were a nearly "unclothed" archetypal force arising from the primordial collective psyche rather than as a personal complex. It slips through the "psychological void" and "physiological vacuum," coursing through psyche and soma with such extreme power and velocity as to make one speculate that perhaps there has been a temporary rupture in the ego-Self axis. It can be likened to an unmediated "looking on the face of God" or in medical terminology a brief psychotic episode. However, what is most extraordinary in night terror cases is the ego's capacity to reassert its position, making contact again with the Self, allowing return to "normal" sleep, dreaming, and waking life. From another point of view, one could say that night terrors are psychic contents outside conscious awareness seemingly residing in the implicit memory system. The extraordinary fear response with such dramatic, sudden ignition of the autonomic nervous system implies firing of the amygdala without inclusion of the hippocampus, so necessary for the recording of explicit, conscious, factual memory. This rapid but primitive life-saving mechanism is efficient and necessary but fails to lay down retrievable memory of events. That the images, content, and even the experience itself are often forgotten by the dreamer disallows opportunities for metabolization, with consequent generation of meaning and hopefully integration, instead leading only to further retraumatization and wounding to psyche and soma.

Modern neuroscience has a great deal to contribute to psychoanalytic theory and practice, which I discuss in a longer version of this paper. Division of memory into explicit and implicit sectors allows for a neuro-physiological basis for the unconscious and has significant treatment impli-cations. For example, lifting repression will never make implicit memories accessible. The work of Dan Stern involving caregiver–infant observations has been applied to adult analytic work with fascinating possibilities. With his "Boston Change Process Group," Stern proposes a model whereby transference and interpretation are involved but there is a focus on the process of interaction rather than only on internal structures. This dynamic model of "self in relation" looks at the reciprocal interaction in the implicit "real relationship" and attends to highly charged "moments of meeting." The hope is that these significant connections may recontextualize historical experiences and offer new ways of relating (Stern *et al.* 1998: 918). Reson-ance with the transcendent function is notable here.

One could also say that Jung's dissociative model with vertical splits (as opposed to the horizontal splits with repression) fits well with these recent discoveries of the implicit system. Unconscious complexes or splinter psyches could be seen as forming via fear, anxiety, and trauma in outer relationships and registered as emotional memories organized by archetypal scaffolding internally. Jean Knox (1999: 525) argues cogently for a linkage between unconscious complexes and implicit memory in her 1999 paper.

The Titans, a mythological amplification

Just as science and the subjective experience of a night terror sufferer have been used as descriptors, so the mythology of the Titans may offer a poetic understanding of this problem. The Titans are an ancient race of giants said to predate the Olympians, to whom they lost a great battle. Zeus banished his powerful progenitors to Tartarus, the most distant underworld realm, where an anvil could fall for nine days without reaching the bottom. Like the Titans, night terrors spring from seemingly distant regions of implicit psychic life. For the Greeks, the Titans represented nature in the form of earthquakes and volcanoes; similarly, night terrors seem to be hidden forces in the depths of psyche and soma. Analogous to the Titans are night terrors which carry buried memories that burst forward, disrupting the seemingly dominant order of consciousness.

According to Lopez-Pedraza, the psychology of the Titans is one with no laws, no order, no limits (1990: 12). It vacillates between "excess" and "emptiness" in contradistinction to the Olympians, who are anthropomorphized as personifying relationship patterns that are more structured and confined, making them more accessible for our identification with them. The tension of warring opposites – the Titans and the Olympians, emptiness and structure – leads to anxiety in the individual and collective. To move too quickly to structure is relieving but may foreclose on emergent potential arising from the unknown.

The Scream and the life of Edvard Munch

Of his thoughts and perceptions leading up to painting *The Scream*, Edvard Munch (1863–1944) said:

> One evening I was walking along a path . . . on one side lay the city and below me the fjord . . . the sun was setting . . . the clouds were dyed red like blood.

> I felt a scream pass through nature; it seemed to me that I could hear the scream. I painted this picture . . . painted the clouds as real blood. . . . The colors were screaming. . . . This became the picture.
>
> (Messer 1985: 72)

Munch's visual descriptions offer a metaphoric window into an intense affective state of near catastrophic proportions. This gives imaginative representation to the feeling in night terror. Says Messer (ibid.: 72) of the main figure of this painting: "Totally alienated from reality, the victim is overcome by the realization of an *unspeakable* [emphasis mine] terror from within." As is evident here, it is through instinct and extraordinary imagery that the individual experience of terror and, simultaneously, our cultural anxiety, are presented. The Titanic nature of Munch's painting reminds us of the extremes of our human vulnerability.

Munch most certainly suffered early trauma with the death of his mother (1868) when he was five and the death of his sister (1878) when he was fifteen. There existed a history of psychiatric illness in his first-degree relatives (Jamison 1993: 236) and serious depression for which Munch was hospitalized. He probably suffered night terrors as evidenced in the following description:

> A mother who died early gave me the germ of consumption . . . an overly nervous father . . . pietistically religious bordering on fanaticism . . . from an old family . . . gave me the seeds of insanity . . .
>
> From birth . . . they stood by my side . . . the angels of anxiety . . . sorrow . . . death followed me outside when I played . . . followed me in the spring sun . . . in the beauty of summer . . . They stood by my side in the evening when I closed my eyes . . . and threatened me with death hell and eternal punishment . . .
>
> And then it often happened that I woke up at night . . . and stared with wild terror into the room.
>
> (Hall and Wykes 1990: 36)

One could make a good case that Munch suffered under the aegis of the dead mother whose absence is ever present in his prolific artwork. *The Scream* could be seen as a psychological portrait of catastrophic emptiness, a response to the mother who has gone missing and cannot be found.

The Scream and André Green's the "dead mother"

The Scream captures an extraordinary psychological state that I believe is a response to Titanic emptiness, the void, or what the psychoanalyst André Green calls "the dead mother" or the ". . . mother who remains alive but who is, so to speak, psychically dead in the eyes of the young child in her care" (Kohon 1999: 2). The mother's affective unavailability leaves "psychic holes" and areas of "blankness" (ibid.: 3). Missing is the linking function described by Bion or the binding functions of Eros described by Freud (Green 1986: 79). Aphrodite and her son are nowhere to be found. The core problem is emptiness and absence of memory. According to Green (ibid.: 149–150), when facing the loss of mother, the infant fights against anxiety by various active methods amongst which are agitation, insomnia, and nocturnal terrors. The compromised unity of the ego that has a hole in it realizes itself either on the level of fantasy, which gives open expression to artistic

creation, or on the level of knowledge which is the origin of highly productive intellectualization (ibid.: 153). According to Green (ibid.: 152), there
is a frantic need to play and compulsions to think and imagine. Artwork
produced, then, could be seen as both expressive and defensive in the face of
what we have described as the Titanic realm of the psyche.

Mirroring his internal world, Munch liked to be surrounded by his works
(particularly a group of paintings he called the *Frieze of Life*) and often
replicated his pieces in multiple media. Alf Boe (1989: 18) says that, "We
know also that Munch did not like being parted from his paintings. When
one was sold he would often paint a new version for his own collection."
The emotional interrelationships among pictures had apparent deep
meaning and comfort for Munch:

> I have always worked best with my paintings around me. I placed them
> together and felt that some of the pictures related to each other through
> the subject matter. . . . When they were placed together, a sound went
> through them right away and they became quite different than when
> they were separate; they became a symphony.
>
> (Torjuson 1986: 142)

Built into this description of resonance is a kind of relational knowing so
well described in the work of Dan Stern. This implicit knowledge manifest
in *The Frieze of Life* seems to allow Munch a much-needed sense of
coherence, so obviously missing in *The Scream*, where disintegration and
depersonalization are palpable. These ". . . multiple images also freed him
to play with – modify and control – the formal and emotional implications
of the subject, and thereby modulate feelings like longing, guilt and helplessness" (Nahum 2001: 33). Painting traumatic experiences from memory,
Munch said, "I paint not what I see but what I saw" (ibid.: 31).

Through his implicit and explicit memories, Munch was amazingly able
to uncover and paint primal affective states known to us as individuals and
the collective.

It seems important, then, as analysts, that we ponder these primitive
states of mind and learn ways of understanding, working with, and holding
intense affect as it emerges in the consulting room and society. Winnicott's
description of transitional phenomena called our attention to presence in
the absence of the mother; perhaps we can attune to and refine awareness of
absence in the presence of another as a critical aspect of analytic work. One
of Jung's major contributions in this area was to identify the numinous
dimension implicit in all such encounters:

> Whenever, therefore, in an excess of affect, in an emotionally excessive
> situation, I come up against a paradoxical fact or happening, I am in
> the last resort encountering an aspect of God, which I cannot judge
> logically and cannot conquer because it is stronger than me – because,

in other words, it has a numinous quality and I am face to face with what Rudolf Otto calls the *tremendum* and *fascinosum*.

Bibliography

Berman, P.G. and Van Nimmen, J. (1997). *Munch and Women: Image and Myth*. Alexandria, VA: Art Services International.

Boe, A. (1989). *Edvard Munch*. Barcelona: Ediciones Poligrafa.

Broughton, R. (1968). "Sleep disorders: disorders of arousal?" *Science*, 159: 1070–1078.

DeMario, F.J. and Emery, E.S. (1987). "The natural history of night terrors." *Clinical Pediatrics*, 26: 505–511.

Eggum, A. (1978). "The theme of death." *Edvard Munch: Symbol and Image*. Washington: National Gallery of Art.

Fisher, C., Khan, E., Edwards, A., Davis, D.M. (1973). "A psychophysiological study of nightmares and night terrors: Physiological aspects of the stage 4 night terror." *The Journal of Nervous and Mental Disease*, 157, 2: 75–98.

Fisher, C., Khan, E., Edwards, A., Davis, D.M., Fine, J. (1974). "A psychophysiological study of nightmares and night terrors: Mental content and recall of stage 4 night terrors." *The International Journal of Psychoanalysis*, 80: 215–223.

Garland, E.J. and Smith, D.H. (1991). "Simultaneous prepubertal onset of panic disorder, night terror, and somnambulism." *Journal of the American Academy of Child and Adolescent Psychiatry*, 30, 4: 553–555.

Green, A. (1986). *On Private Madness*. London: Hogarth Press and Institute of Psycho-analysis.

Hall, D. and Wykes, P.C. (1990). *Anecdotes of Modern Art: From Rousseau to Warhol*. New York: Oxford University Press.

Hall, S. (February 28, 1999). "Fear itself." *The New York Times Magazine*.

Hartmann, E. (1984). *The Nightmare*. New York: Basic Books.

Heller, R. (1978). "Love as a series of paintings." *Edvard Munch: Symbol and Image*. Washington: The National Gallery of Art.

Howe, J. (2001). "Nocturnes: The music of melancholy, and the mysteries of love and death." *Edvard Munch: Psyche, Symbol and Expression*. Chicago: University of Chicago Press.

Jamison, K.R. (1993). *Touched with Fire*. New York: Free Press.

Jung, C.G. (1964). "Good and evil in analytical psychology." *CW 10*.

Kales, A., Soldatos, C.R., Bixler, E.O., Ladda, R.L., Charney, D.S., Weber, G., Schweitzer, P.K. (1980). "Hereditary factors in sleepwalking and night terrors." *British Journal of Psychiatry*, 137: 111–118.

Keith, P. (1975). "Night terrors: A review of the psychology, neurophysiology, and therapy." *Journal of the American Academy of Child Psychiatry*, 14: 477–489.

Kerenyi, C. (1979). *The Gods of the Greeks*. Guilford: Thames and Hudson.

Knapp, S. (1987). "Night terrors in children and adults: emotional and biological factors." *The Nightmare: Psychological and Biological Foundations*. New York: Columbia University Press.

Knox, J. (1999). "The relevance of attachment theory to a contemporary Jungian view of the internal world: internal working models, implicit memory and internal objects." *The Journal of Analytical Psychology*, 44: 511–530.

Kohon, G. (ed.). (1999). *The Dead Mother*. New York: Routledge.

LeDoux, J. (1996). *The Emotional Brain*. New York: Touchstone.

Lopez-Pedraza, R. (1990). "Moon Madness – Titanic Love." *Cultural Anxiety*. Einsiedeln: Daimon.

Messer, T. (1985). *Munch*. New York: Abrams.

Morford, M.O. and Lenardon, R.J. (1971). *Classical Mythology*. New York: McKay.

Nahum, K. (2001). "In wild embrace: attachment and loss in Edvard Munch." *Edvard Munch: Psyche, Symbol and Expression*. Chicago: University of Chicago Press.

Sandler, J., Sandler, A., and Davies, R. (eds). (2000). *Clinical and Observational Psychoanalytic Research: Roots of a Controversy – André Green and Daniel Stern*. New York: Karnac.

Stern, D.N., Sander, L.W., Nahum, J.P., Harrison, A.M., Lyons-Ruth, K., Morgan, A.C., Bruschweilerstern, N., Tronick, E.Z. (1998). "Non-interpretive mechanisms in psychoanalytic therapy: the something more than interpretation." *The International Journal of Psychoanalysis*, 79, 903–921.

Torjuson, B. (1986). *Words and Images of Edvard Munch*. Chelsea: Chelsea Green.

Tripp, E. (1970). *The Meridian Handbook of Classical Mythology*. New York: Signet.

Winnicott, D.W. (1991). *The Maturational Process and the Facilitating Environment*. Madison, CT: International Universities Press.

Winnicott, D.W. (1999). "Memories Lost and Found – Part II." *The Harvard Mental Health Newsletter*, 16, 4, 1–7.

Chapter 12

The embodied countertransference and recycling the mad matter of symbolic equivalence

Giles Clark

I wish to emphasize from the outset that this chapter is largely theoretical. It has to do with metapsychology and hypothetical models, at times even metaphysics. However, theory here is certainly intended to inter-relate with my analytic positioning and so to my applied reverie, critical clinical reasoning and action, and so can help me to see and interpret my way through and out of conditions of destructive psychosomatic attack. I will later attempt to explicate the field I am considering through a brief phenomenological description of the internal and interpersonal worlds of personality disordered persons and their affective relations.

My starting point is to take up and re-direct Andrew Samuels' (1985) seminal concept of the analytically informative 'embodied counter-transference', primarily to suggest that this experiential realm belongs most evidently in analytic relations with states of severe personality disorder – that is, to oversensitive and defensive narcissistic and destructive borderline conditions, and to chronically and acutely regressed states – and that it is a highly informative analytic lens into these difficult zones.

In his paper 'Countertransference, the *Mundus imaginalis* and a research project' (1985), Samuels distinguishes embodied countertransference experience from a reflective countertransferential attitude although, vitally, both necessarily share an imaginal condition and capacity. This Samuels amplifies through the work of Corbin and the hypothesis of the *mundus imaginalis*, which 'functions as a linking factor between patient and analyst . . . a link between soul and corporeality . . . intellect and sense impressions' (Samuels, 1985, p. 60).

He explains that

> 'embodied' is intended to suggest a physical, actual, material, sensual, expression in the analyst of something in the patient's inner world, a drawing together and solidification of this, an incarnation by the analyst of a part of the patient's psyche.
>
> (ibid., p. 52)

He goes on to suggest that 'it is necessary to see our field of reference in analysis as seamless and continuous' and so to realise that 'the coin is three-sided: to body and image can be added relationship' (ibid., p. 68).

I think that one implication of Samuels' hypothesis is a possible re-visioning and extension of the concept of the psychoid into analytic transference and countertransference interaction. My clinical hypothesis is that this psychoid realm is one of psychosomatic mutuality, a pre-verbal relational field that is a conduit for urgent communication, often sickening or seductive, but demanding internal recycling into a more integrated co-ordination and a separation out of identification into differentiation. Thence what have always been intolerable lacks, losses, limitations and intolerable frustrations can be painfully grieved and perhaps mourned, and meaningful causal links can be made, and so there may emerge a more realistic symbolic functionality.

I find the idea of the psychoid to be one of Jung's most fertile and clinically useful concepts. However, we have to be careful not to fall into fantastic and magical thinking in this realm of 'using the psychoid' as clinical theory and practice: an application of critical reason, healthy scepticism and therapeutic pragmatism are needed. We also need to be clear about the issue of whether to understand the psychoid as an object for scientific investigation or as a symbolic 'as if', a unit of meaning . . . or as both simultaneously.

Ann Addison (2009) has most usefully synthesised, developed and extended Jungian and post-Jungian clinical thinking about 'the psychoid'. Jung conceived his idea of the psychoid based on the teleological orientation of Driesch and the more causal and self-determining approach of Bleuler (who held that psyche and soma act on similar, parallel principles). Jung's (1947) idea of 'psychoid processes' was that they are quasi-psychic and lie somewhere between vitalistic phenomena and psychic processes. Jung wrote that 'deepest down of all is the paradox of the sympathetic and parasympathetic psychoid processes' (ibid., para. 418) . . . and that

> (s)ince psyche and matter are contained in one and the same world, and moreover are in continuous contact with one another and ultimately rest on irrepresentable transcendental factors, it is not only possible but fairly probable even that psyche and matter are two different aspects of the same thing (ibid.) . . . (here Jung is using a double-aspect or double identity theory.)

Addison's own hypothesis is that

> psychosensory phenomena, occurring varyingly along the body–mind axis in the transference/countertransference, may be expected to arise

during periods of regression to early states when issues concerning
separation and bodily integrity are at the forefront . . .

(Addison, 2008)

Furthermore she hypothesizes that 'such experiences represent evidence of
the emergence of psyche from soma', and so have to do with the 'development of mind' (ibid.).

I would say that psychoid processes are not only regressive, but are also a
potentiality and a potency. They can also be understood as a basically
emergent and vital organic force, like a seed with the DNA of its form
inherently or conatively determined to make manifest, realize and develop
in both a species-typical and an individually idiosyncratic way, and thence
be re-formed by environmental (conscious and unconscious) experience. To
put this into a language appropriate to analytic experience: an emergence
through psychoid and psychosomatic identity to symbolization, the separation and creation of meaning (out) of matter. Transferentially/counter-
transferentially the 'double identity' of the psychoid realm makes for
'consubstantial' psyche–soma experience at the level of the antonomic
nervous system, which emerges out of, between, around us both in analysis,
whence it calls out for functional symbolic ordering which can move us to a
more relational state.

Analytic work at the psychoid level or through psyche–soma as a
'bodymind' self (Grotstein 1997) is induced and activated by those pre-
symbolic or anti-symbolic regressive behaviours that belong to the pathological nature of destructive borderline relations. Here there are urgent
attacks on the 'concretely fantasized' maternal/analytic breast–body–mind
that is experienced as feeding and poisoning, loving and hating. This is a
realm of fragmented beta disorder which relentlessly compounds its own
sense of frustration, of concretised emotions expressed through psychosomatically infectious, defensive, projective, urgently communicative and
informative forces, and of archaic symbolic equations.

I would further suggest that when such strong affects are experienced
countertransferentially with persons with over-sensitive, thin-skinned (and
secretively grandiose and righteous) narcissistic defences, then they could be
a signal of the split-off but underlying angry core that has hitherto been so
fearfully avoided by such persons. Furthermore, much embodied countertransferential communication and information that is experienced even with
normally neurotic persons (who are not personality disordered) derives
from pockets of early beta pre-order or disorder.

I must however acknowledge that this sort of openness to analytic work
with embodied psychosomatic countertransferential experience, let alone to
a related interest in the psychoid and in consubstantial body–mind identity
states, can be symptomatic of the analyst's need to co-ordinate, re-order
and integrate his/her own psychosomatic and relational disorder. This

possibility must come into his/her assessment of the relative informative usefulness or degree of personal subjective neurosis in such an equivocal field of experience.

To further adapt Samuels' point I would say that the psychoid is always simultaneously both 'bodily matter and sense' and 'mental image and idea'. In other words, we can say that, at the psychoid level, body, image and idea are a unit, an identity experienced or expressed as a double aspect, as different attributes and modes of 'bodymind' as a 'single substance'.

I have written elsewhere (2006) about how a neo-Spinozan substance monism and double-identity theory helps my psychosomatically responsive analytic position. In brief, I described how the 'conatus' (the innate psychic and organic endeavour for self-preservation and the enhancement of powers to maintain the self) is related to the concept that the mind is the idea of the body, corporeality and embodiment, of bodies, body-bits and bodily relations (Clark, 2006). I then further extend this re-conceptualization of the conatus and the mind-as-idea-of-body into an ideational and practical model of internal and inter-personal emotional (and embodied) relations, 'ideas' of bodies and body relations, and the natural tensions between these affects, tensions which are essential to the ongoing formation of identity. I call this dynamic grid a jouissance of affects and their relations (ibid.): conatus-as-jouissance is the 'passions of the bodymind' and incorporates all psychosomatic forces, affective states and their relations, and simultaneously both joins and keeps apart, unites and separates, incorporating the tension between desire and repulsion, joy and sadness, power and limitation. It is of *both mind and of body, may be represented through either, but must be* conceived as though representing *a double identity* and understood as *substantially univocal*.

(It is important, as I said above concerning the psychoid, to take these Spinozan theoretical concepts as also being simultaneously both practical and 'as if' psychic realities.)

This helps me to understand those analytic states that are psychosensually close to psychoid processes . . . (where emotional images, mental ideation and body matters 'are as one'), where self and other, fantasy and reality are unseparated, where we are pulled back into a pre-symbolic or anti-symbolic world which is often transferentially expressed through psychosomatic contamination and mind–body confusions, through projective identifications, destructive acting out and sexualised pressures that attack our necessary boundaries and frames. This is all regressive, anti-imaginal and maddeningly literalising.

Segal (1957) described how in a mental state in which 'symbolic equations' proliferate, symbolic thoughts (and original objects) are treated not as thoughts but as literal things. In her later papers (1991) she followed Bion, and viewed pathological projective identification as responsible for disturbances in symbol formation. She made connections between her work on symbol formation and Bion's alpha and beta elements: concrete symbolic equations can be understood as beta elements, which have the possibility of becoming alpha functioning. In other words, early concrete equations and pre-symbolized objects belong to a state latent with potential symbolic development.

Britton (1998) explains that 'symbolic equation' arises from

> an arrested development of the symbolic process at the point of relinquishment of the original object. The object is preserved by a sustained projection of the self into the place vacated by the absent object and which denies its disappearance. . . . In such thinking there is no world outside the mind: existence of self and object world are co-terminous.
>
> (Britton, 1998, p. 138)

'Symbolic equation' manifests as a pre-ambivalent or paranoid-schizoid position, a realm of identity confusion and identification, arising out of an attempt to deny the intolerable loss or lack of a needed but also envied and murderously hated loved/loving object. In chronic borderline and acutely regressed states, the psychoid pre-order, psychosomatic disorder and pre-symbolic confusion (of body and mind, of actual body bits and zones of meaning etc.) is desperately evacuated and projected. This is where the psychoid processes feel as if they are the mad matter of symbolic equation. The borderline baby-bomb off-loads and communicates his/her intolerable toxicity, dissociation and fragmentation through projective identification into the countertransferential psycho-sensing 'body' of the analyst . . . which is a needed containing, digesting, processing and 'feeding back' (interpretive) object.

To create a phenomenology of the borderline relational world: such a person may think, feel and angrily express their transferential urgency something like this:

> For me mind and body, fantasy and reality, inner and outer, my mind and your mind, my body and your body, you and me, are and must always be fused as one . . . (but you must and must not simultaneously sort out this confusion).

> My desperate (impotent) need is now to somehow make matters such that your mind is my mind and your body is my body.

> Because I am starved of enough of anything good and have never had the necessary power to get the primary love I should have had . . . you must therefore love me now . . . even though I know that you never shall do so enough; and you must love me forever . . . even though I know that you never shall.

My hurt makes me hate, attack and destroy all that is enviably good and loving . . . everyone (such as you) who gets and gives to others the love that I so desperately want.

Because I love you it is outrageous and intolerable that you do not love me back, and for this I hate you, and because of this I will forcibly affect and infect you; or I will seduce you, arouse and move you irresistibly.

I shall get into and posses your separate body–mind by disturbing and infecting you psychosomatically. I shall confuse your thinking, attack your linking, and somatize your symbolizing function . . . as mine is.

Realize and understand (as I do not) that making war is my way of making love.

My anger knows no bounds.

In this evacuative and sickening attack on or seduction of what I have called the 'concretely fantasized' analytic breast–body–mind (using concrete images as units of thought), 'the part-object relationship is with physiological functions: not only to the breast but to feeding, poisoning, loving, hating' (Bléandonu 1994).

From the other side, my analytic mind might operate from an internal position something like this:

I have received in mind and body your furiously urgent message, namely your absolute, compulsive, angry, hungry, ever-frustrated need and thwarted desire. Your emotionally pained mind has regressed to and become your passionately pained body, craving an impossibly absolute connection. I represent the possibility of a linking and thinking bodymind relation, an analytic relation that here and now represents all loves, limitations and losses, and so a relationship which itself must be mourned.

However, the necessary and ethical law of this human world is: No, you cannot have it all (me, others, parents) as you will; you cannot make me disclose and open my separate private self to your devouring hunger to know and have power over my mind and body, for that would preclude necessarily frustrating fantasies; you cannot make me, by force or seduction, love you the way you wish. There is a limiting frame that others (me now) do and shall embody: a Law of the Fathers, necessary parental and social limits.

Your desires, frustrations and hates are here now for us to understand.

Your hurt makes you hate, attack and destroy the good and the possibility of love that you so desperately need . . . because for you they are never enough.

Indeed, as you say and show, your anger recognizes no bounds . . . no boundaries.

But my boundaries and the world's necessities are actually your truest gain: a free necessity. I shall reflect before I act. I shall use my separate thinking mind. Out of a mass of emotional information I shall find selected facts and interpretations.

Thus borderline persons evacuate and communicate their impotent rage through their affecting/infecting/disturbing the integrity of my embodied analytic self, thereby having their impossible desires and furious passions received. This chronic state of global rage and frustration may then become a slow mourning that taps into the concomitant sadness and depression. However much remains perennially un-mourned, which means an ongoing sense of impotence, loss and destruction: the hungry core of outrage and defiance of the super-ego continues to bite and burn.

This all-devouring destructive hunger is exactly the emotional psychic reality that the narcissistic personality defensively and over-sensitively avoids (makes void) both internally and inter-personally. A grandiose false self is a defensive response to the pain of their losses, failures and doubts; and to a core reality that is too fearfully and angrily depressed to be consciously acknowledged and expressed.

Here the perennially split-off anger is a strenuous and tense manoeuvre, and both the disguised, even reversed, anger and the tactical tension can be evoked and constellated in the other (analyst) through subtle 'passive relational activity'.

Although the adhesive identifications of narcissistic need are not so crudely acted out, they can surely be nearly as psychosomatically infectious as the projective identifications of the borderline person, because they function as a defense against their own hidden destructive rage. Adhesive identifications and extractive introjections do 'get right under my skin', 'make my flesh creep', and often make me 'sick with disgust.'

The whole strategic system of narcissistic defences needs to be analytically challenged by naming the person's secret depressive fear of being an oedipal failure and addressing the primitive anxiety, inter-personal terrors and shames, and the hidden manipulations and cruelties of narcissistic defensiveness. This may lead to a shocking recognition of the lethal anger and resentment that is so fearfully hidden in the righteous disdain. I may thus disturb the narcissistic universe in a way that the whole strategic, secretive defensive system of what Kernberg (2004) calls 'malignant self-love' is recognized as being self-defeating. As Kernberg points out, to challenge and so sometimes enable strong and repetitive narcissistic defences to break down into a realization and even expression of the buried (borderline) murderous hate and anger is actually a healthy development towards a more real self: a real sense of outrage and a real attack or fight is actually analytically enlivening and its energetic truth can be integrated.

Both disordered states are basically driven by toxic envy and resentment. They are defensively and desperately re-constellated through transferential inducements in and communications through the body and mind of the analyst's countertransference: their projective poisons get into my auto-immune self-system, but thence a necessary process of self-preservation is activated.

The 'wounded healer' actually heals through his/her survival, management and recycling of his/her own wounds and madness. This contains and processes the maddening wounds of the other.

I am initially countertransferentially open (at a psychoid level) to psycho-somatic infection, projective identification and psychotic beta confusion, but thereby my analytic bodymind is psycho-sensually used and informed by pre-symbolic and anti-symbolic matters, by forceful projections, by transferentially evacuated pains of intolerable lacks and losses, and the furies of thwarted primary love. But thence, out of my counter-transferential experience of consubstantiating processes, out of psychosomatic infection and contagion, I have to find healthy separateness, related reverie, creative imagination, reflection, critical reason, an eventual emergence of 'intuitive knowledge' or of 'selected facts', and so an transformative interpretation.

Thus, due to their very real passion, and when analytically well-contained, borderline persons may be able to grieve and mourn their impotent desires and frustrations, and so develop a greater degree of agency, a relatively functional symbolic understanding, and a capacity to live more constructively and creatively.

Bibliography

Addison, A. (2008) 'Reframing the unconscious', paper given at *Journal of Analytical Psychology* Conference, Orta, Italy; initial publication under the title 'Jung, vitalism and "the psychoid": an historical reconstruction', *Journal of Analytical Psychology*, vol. 54, no. 1.

Bléandonu, G. (1994) *Wilfred Bion*, London: Free Association.

Britton, R. (1998) *Belief and Imagination*, London: Routledge.

Clark, G. (1996) 'The animating body: Psychoid substance as a mutual experience of psychosomatic disorder', *Journal of Analytical Psychology*, vol. 41, no. 3.

—— (2006) 'A Spinozan lens onto the confusions of borderline relations', *Journal of Analytical Psychology*, vol. 51, no. 1.

Grotstein, J. (1997) 'Sane mentis in corpore sano: Mind and body as an odd couple and an oddly coupled body', *Psychoanalytic Inquiry*, no. 17: 204–223.

Jung, C.G. (1947/1953) *On the Nature of the Psyche*, in *Collected Works*, Vol. 8, London: Routledge.

Kernberg, O. (2004) *Aggressivity, Narcissism and Self-destructiveness in the Psychotherapeutic Relationship*, New Haven: Yale University Press.

Samuels, A. (1985) 'Countertransference, the *mundus imaginalis* and a research project', *Journal of Analytical Psychology*, vol. 30, no. 1: 47–71.

Segal, H. (1957) 'Notes on symbol formation', *International Journal of Psycho-Analysis*, vol. 38, 391–397.

—— (1991) *Dream, Phantasy, and Art*, London: Routledge.

Chapter 13

Physis – archetype of nature's soul

Petruska Clarkson with contributions from John Nuttall

Introduction

Samuels (1985) suggested that Jung sometimes disparaged the psychic, imaginal or soul dimension of the material world – the nature within which psyche has its being. Notwithstanding this, Jung discusses the ancient occidental notion of Physis (as Nature and Life) in at least seven volumes of the *Collected Works*. "Man's connection with physis, with the material world and its demands, is the cause of his anomalous position: on the one hand he has the capacity for enlightenment, on the other he is in thrall to the Lord of this world" (*CW11*, para. 263).

Tacey reviewed Jung's ambivalence; "The task ahead is to free ourselves from Jung's dualism, to realise that psychic depth and meaning can be found both in ourselves and in the so called external world" (1993: 278). Hillman writes of the "anima mundi as that particular soul-spark, that seminal image, which offers itself through each thing in its visible form . . . God-given things of nature and man-made things of the street" (1982: 77). In *The Political Psyche*, Samuels discusses two authors searching for "a more fruitful relation to nature" (1993: 120), and makes a passionate case for dialogue between politics and depth psychology. The case for re-visioning psychotherapy made by these writers attends to our hubristic, over-controlling, over-interpretive insularity, which has divorced us from our root activity of soul-healing. Perhaps some re-assessment is necessary:

> The human psyche is one of the great forces of nature, and what is most frightening about this space–time technology is that it exposes us to this force within us as nothing else ever has. We are standing in a world created not by God (except indirectly) but by our psyches. It is undeniably our fate, so we must face the fact that it may be our natural habitat. We have willy-nilly broken through all the old rigidities, all the limits we thought were nature itself, and we can never go back.
>
> (Hillman and Ventura, 1992: 128)

At the same time, perhaps Physis (Nature) has to be re-discovered and honoured:

> But in care of the soul there is trust that nature heals, that much can be accomplished by not-doing. . . . What the great sixteenth-century physician, Paracelsus, said about healing applies to care of the soul: 'The physician is only the servant of nature, not her master. Therefore, it behoves medicine to follow the will of nature.
>
> (Moore 1992: 12)

A pre-Socratic annunciation

For the pre-Socratics, Physis encompassed the images, ideals, and myths that served the work of being, healing, and creating. "Physics" was given to the science of nature, "Physician" to those who heal, and "Physic" to the medicines they prescribe. Physis includes Nature, but is much more. As a verb, it means "to grow", or "to be" – "what things really are". The concept was lit by Heraclitus, for whom Physis meant,

> change or growth which comes from the spirit within the person . . . its Being, its inner dynamism, the process in which it rises up, by which it surges forth and endures, because of which it emerges as what and how it is. The matter at issue is the physis of all things: their Being, their emergence, their presencing.
>
> (Guerrière 1980: 100)

The later Stoics identified Physis with god and the active principle and conceived Physis as the healing factor in illness, the energetic motive for evolution and creativity. Although considered more biological than psychical, it contained a spiritual dimension since it was thought that nature evolved toward the whole or the good. "In Aristotle, the 'nature' [Physis] of a thing is its 'end' or the good towards which it tends, its final cause, that state in which its 'natural' development culminates" (Lovejoy and Boas, 1973: 450) and, for Plotinus, physis is the "nature of soul".

Physis – the archetype and its characteristics

Jung cautioned that as "units of meaning to be apprehended by the intuition" it is a well-nigh "hopeless undertaking to tear a single archetype out of the living tissue of the psyche" (*CW9i*, para. 302). Here, the term is used in the way analytical psychology refers to concepts like the Great Mother, the Puer, or the Self; as "the inherited part of the psyche; structuring patterns of psychological performance linked to instinct; a hypothetical entity irrepresentable in itself and evident only through its manifestations" (Samuels, Shorter, and Plaut, 1986: 26). Guerrière links this to physis:

> The matter at issue in Heraclitus is physis . . . And correlative to the matter is a self-experience which is as deep as physis is comprehensive. The experience of physis is an experience of self for two reasons: (1) physis comprehends (encompasses) the self as it does everything else; and (2) the self is the locus where (for the human self) physis comprehends (understands) itself. Human experience is, in terms of physis, the self-experience of physis. Hence any discourse on physis must eventually become a discourse on man.
>
> (1980: 129)

Nature often resides beyond our consulting rooms. Extra-therapeutic factors have been studied and it has been noted with surprise that other relationships (outside the transference) and other events (falling in love, religious conversion, tragedy) transform and heal lives. The Life Force rarely appears in mainstream psychotherapy trainings. But it is the élan vital that makes the difference between choosing life or death, between apathy and anaesthesia, between transformation and despair. Medics have known this since Hippocrates. Perhaps the very soul of life itself is hidden, secretly imprisoned in nature – not so much because of its shadow but because of our fears. Ignored, circumnavigated or denied, the archetype of life is re-emerging with its voice, its mythical echoes and its vision. However inadequately, this exploration highlights some of the characteristics, images and work of the neglected archetype of Physis.

Phylocryptia (the love of hiding)

In the words of Heraclitus: "Physis loves to hide" (Kahn, 1981: 105). I have lost it many times – sometimes for years – and it seems to disappear from scholarly investigation – for short periods, decades and even centuries. Following attention from Heraclitus it re-emerged in first-century Greek alchemy, "the divine water is said to effect a transformation by bringing the 'hidden nature' to the surface" (*CW11*, para. 39), which is sometimes imprisoned in "the dark of matter" (*CW9ii*, para. 308). The god that hides in matter also conceals itself in the alchemical symbolism of the loving embrace between Nous and Physis. In the small passage below all the main themes of alchemy are powerfully condensed, although analysis may have to rely on the intuitive grasp and the reader's devotions in making obeisance to the *obscurata*.

> In spite of the not always unintentional obscurity of alchemical language, it is not difficult to see that the divine water or its symbol, the

uroboros, means nothing other than the deus absconditus, the god hidden in matter, the divine Nous that came down to Physis and was lost in her embrace. This mystery of the 'god become physical' underlies not only classical alchemy but also many other spiritual manifestations of Hellenistic syncretism.

(*CW13*, para. 138)

And the goal of alchemy often hides in our own work – it is invisible.

The stone is that thing midway between perfect and imperfect bodies, and that which nature herself begins is brought to perfection through the art. The stone is named the stone of invisibility (*lapis invisibilitatis*).

(*CW12*, para. 243)

Or, as Stern suggests, "the something more resides in interactional inter-subjective process" (1998: 903).

Coincidentia oppositorum (the co-existence of opposites)

"Although physis is wont to hide, it manifests itself in multiple ways. . . all suggest a certain oneness in multiple things, a certain *coincidentia oppositorum*" (Guerrière, 1980:102). Heraclitus said, "The way up and down is one and the same" (Kahn, 1981: 75), and although Physis is concerned with life most fully, it also implies its opposite, and in the midst of living, we are dying. Jung grapples with this tension between the opposites:

we might be tempted by the modern brand of nature philosophy to call energy or the élan vital God, and thus to blend into one spirit and nature. So long as such an undertaking is restricted to the misty heights of speculative philosophy, no great harm is done . . . In practical psychotherapy we strive to fit people for life, and we are not free to set up theories which do not concern our patients and may even injure them. Here we come to a question that is sometimes a matter of life and death – the question whether we base our explanations on 'physis' or spirit. If I recognize only naturalistic values, and explain everything in physical terms, I shall depreciate, hinder, or even destroy the spiritual development of my patients. And if I hold exclusively to a spiritual interpretation, then I shall misunderstand and do violence to the natural man in his right to exist as a physical being . . . Whether energy is God or God is energy concerns me very little, for how, in any case, can I know such things? But to give appropriate psychological explanations – this I must be able to do . . . The conflict between nature and spirit is itself a reflection of the paradox of psychic life.

(*CW8*, para. 678)

And the ancients do not provide a neat and tidy formula.

> It is the primordial settling-of-accounts, the fundamental ordering, the
> primitive bringing-forth. This war is the father and king of all . . . it
> allows [the many] to come forth as what and how they are.
>
> (Heraclitus in Guerrière, 1980: 91)

It is an enantiodromia, a violent and sudden transformation from one thing
into its total opposite that "lets the many emerge".

Opus circulatorium and the uroborus

How can such transformation be understood? Guerrière writes, "The concrete matter at issue in the text of Heraclitus is Being in a uniquely
transitional configuration" (1980: 86). Being (for Heraclitus) is becoming, is
process, is presence, and is essentially of a circular nature. It is as a cycle
moving through manifestations of appearing and disappearing, of coming
into being and dying, that nature finds itself. The circular form of the self-
consuming image suggests a cyclical model of the cosmos and of history.

The alchemists were fond of picturing their opus as a circulatory process,
as a circular distillation or as the uroboros, the snake biting its own tail,
and they made innumerable pictures of this process. Just as the central idea
of the *lapis philosophorum* plainly signifies the self, so the opus with the
countless symbols illustrates the process of individuation, the step-by-step
development of the self from an unconscious state to a conscious one. That
is why the lapis as prima materia stands at the beginning of the process as
well as at the end. According to the sixteenth-century alchemist Michael
Maier, the gold, another synonym for the self, comes from the *opus
circulatorium* of the sun. This circle is "the line that runs back upon itself,
wherein that eternal painter and potter, God, may be discerned" . . . This
circle is a magic circle consisting of the union of opposites, "immune to all
injury" (quoted in *CW9ii*, para. 418).

Hillman suggests that, "by means of the archetypal image, natural phenomena present faces that speak to the imagining soul" (1985: 11). There
are many historical images of Physis (von Franz, 1980), and one that
compellingly articulates the force of nature is the *uroboros* – "the basic
mandala of alchemy" (*CW12*, para. 165). Of course, the nature of *being*
human includes *being* animal; and however we try to deny this we can never
escape it. "All aesthetic reactions of our nostrils, muscles, throat and teeth
are the force of nature through us, nature acting upon nature, speaking
with nature" (Hillman, 1986: 105). The *uroboros* has been one of the most
prevalent and profound intimations of Physis in animal form across time
and culture. Klossowski de Rola writes that the *uroboros* symbolises the
infinite eternal one, representing perfectly the "great Cycle" of the universe

"as well as the Great Work which reflects it: perfect stillness and perfect motion" (1973: 14).

The tree of life is often shown under the guardianship of a serpent, as in the book of Genesis. The snake is also associated with healing, as at the shrines of Aesculapius.

> Perhaps the commonest dream symbol of transcendence is the snake, as represented by the therapeutic symbol of the Roman god of medicine Aesculapius, which has survived to modern times as a sign of the medical profession . . . as we see it, coiled around the staff of the healing god, it seems to embody a kind of mediation between earth and heaven.
>
> (Jung, 1964: 154)

Each one of these images emphasises particularities of the work, development or healing of the soul. It is thought that all of them represent the "central archetype of the collective unconscious and a universal symbol of transformation . . . the most ancient image of the alchemical conjunction" (Adams, 1981: 151).

The work of Physis

The uroboros image encompasses all three essential qualities of Physis – it loves to hide, it reconciles the opposites and it captures circularity. It is a rebus for the alchemical opus in which at least three types of work can be differentiated – healing (*CW9i*; *CW16*; Nuttall, 2000), creativity (*CW9ii*; Nuttall, 2002; Zohar, 1990) and evolution (Adams, 1981; *CW12*). Here, I concentrate on the imaginative repercussions of Physis as evolution. Jung (*CW9i*, para. 393) elaborates:

> The descent of spirit into the sphere of human consciousness is expressed in the myth of the divine 'Nous' caught in the embrace of 'Physis'. This process, continuing over the ages, is probably an unavoidable necessity, and the religions would find themselves in a very forlorn situation if they believed in the attempt to hold up evolution.

However, Jung appears to have been ambivalent toward the work of nature, and some of his comments seem disparaging of the modern *Adept*:

> Once more the Gnostic vision of Nous entangled in the embrace of Physis flashes forth in the work of this latecomer to alchemy. But the philosopher who once descended like a Hercules into the darkness of Acheron to fulfil a divine opus has become a laboratory worker with a taste for speculation; having lost sight of the lofty goal of Hermetic

mysticism, he now labours to discover a tonic potion that will 'keep body and soul together'.

(*CW12*, para. 513)

Jung calls the ninth woodcut of the *Rosarium* "The Return of the Soul", in which "the soul, dives down from heaven to breathe life into the dead body" (*CW16iii*: para. 494) of the hermaphrodite. "The 'soul' which is re-united with the body is the One born of the two, the vinculum common to both" (ibid., para. 504) which, surely, is a metonym for the world soul – Physis. This is confirmed in the *Rosarium* itself, which quotes Morienus: "Despise not the ash, for it is the diadem of thy heart" (ibid., para. 495). In psychotherapy, such a return of the soul is only possible after "the psychologist . . . has succeeded in freeing the ego-consciousness from contamination with the unconscious" (ibid., para. 503). The ancient Greeks had similar beliefs:

> If he is ever to achieve understanding and discernment, one must expect, stand in readiness for, or be open to the inducement of physis. Of course the only place to find it is where it actually is – namely, in all things. [As Heraclitus stressed:] The many [the collective] do not find the logos in what they see and hear.
>
> (Murray, 1955: 119)

Adams introduces doubt, "To Kekulè the uroboros means one thing, benzene. And benzene means plastic. The benzene uroboros is not the beginning, the middle and end of things, the life cycle eternally returning. It is merely the end of things – the death-wish fulfilled" (1981: 159). I would say every image also requires the divine work – which also entails the discrimination of opposites; the search for the hidden god in matter which juxtaposes evil and good, soul and world ensouled – however it may rack our preconceptions. The plastic bag, yes, but also the plastic heart valve that saves a mother's life, and the plastic limb that allows a child to walk. The philosopher architect of the League of Nations, Jan Smuts elucidates this ambiguity (1987: 336):

> This world, in the noble language of Keats, is indeed the valley of soul-making; but it could not be that if the valley itself consisted of nothing but souls. To say this is not to assume that there is anything alien or antagonistic between the human soul and the natural environment in which it finds itself in this world. . .Our physical organs connect us with millions of years of her history; our minds are full of immemorial paths of pre-human experience. . . . The intimate rapport with Nature is one of the most precious things in life. This is a universe of whole-making, not merely of soul-making, which is only its climax phase.

Murray (1915) agrees with this view of evolution as Physis:

> We call it 'Evolution'. The Greeks called it Physis, a word which we translate by 'Nature' but which seems to mean more exactly 'growth', or 'the process of growth'. It is Physis which gradually shapes or tries to shape every living thing into a more perfect form . . . It is like a soul, or a life-force, running through all matter as the 'soul' of a man runs through all his limbs. It is the soul of the world.
>
> (Murray, 1915: 33–5)

Eternal return

There appear to be two different images of the soul in relation to the world that exist side-by-side in archetypal psychology.

> One is full-blooded myth and a well-established presence in the ongoing imaginal life of archetypal psychology. Its theme is that soul can be absent from the world, or ill-treated there, and that this is a great fault. This fantasy will be called here a myth of wronged soul. The other fantasy is rough and half-formed, and it constellates only ephemerally. It imagines. . . that soul is present in the world everywhere and always, that nothing of the world lacks a connection with soul. This second fantasy (that of the omnimorphic world soul) is more a germ or suggestion than it is a fully developed piece of imaginal life.
>
> (Wheeler, 1993: 288)

There are also two ways of thinking about Physis which emerge from ancient literature and this exploration. One view is that Physis is in conflict with Nomos (custom and law). This is the common teaching. The other is that there is nothing that is not Physis – no aspect, peculiarity, thread or moment of life which can be separated from the world soul itself. Physis is the world soul. There is also a somewhat uncomfortable notion that corresponds with this, that Physis may not have a particular end. And so, we come full circle. The alchemical search starts and ends with the stone. However, then the work continues. The archetype of Physis hides again while revealing itself, bringing together irreconcilable but co-existing opposites – a linear evolution and a circular revolution, sacred division and sacred whole, the whole ensouled. Logically impossible. Mythologically and psycho-logically necessary. Physis is also Ananke.

Bibliography

Adams, M.V. (1981). The benzene Uroboros: Plastic and catastrophe in gravity's rainbow. *Annual of Archetypal Psychology and Jungian Thought*. Dallas: Spring.

Guerrière, D. (1980). Physis, Sophia, Psyche. In J. Sallis and K. Maly (eds.), *Heraclitean Fragments: Companion Volume to the Heidegger/Fink Seminar on Heraclitus*. Alabama: University of Alabama Press.

Hillman, J. (1982). *Anima Mundi: The Return of the Soul to the World*. Dallas: Spring.

Hillman, J. (1985). *Archetypal Psychology: A Brief Account*. Dallas: Spring.

Hillman, J. (1986). Bachelards *Lautréamont*, or Psychoanalysis Without a Patient. In G. Bachelard, *Lautréamont*, R.S. Dupree (trans.). Dallas: The Dallas Institute, pp. 103–23.

Hillman, J. and Ventura, M. (1992). *We've Had a Hundred Years of Psychotherapy – and The World's Getting Worse*. San Francisco: Harper Collins.

Jung, C.G. (1953–78). *The Collected Works of C. J. Jung*. H. Read, M. Fordham and G. Adler (eds.), London: Routledge. Sources indicated by volume and paragraph number.

Jung, C.G. (ed.) (1964). *Man and His Symbols*. London: Aldus Books.

Kahn, C.H. (1981). *The Art and Thought of Heraclitus: An Edition of the Fragments with Translation and Commentary*. Cambridge: Cambridge University Press.

Klossowski de Rola, S. (1973). *Alchemy: The Secret Art*. London: Thames & Hudson.

Lovejoy, A. and Boas, G. (1973). *Primitivism and Related Areas in Antiquity*. New York: Farrar, Straus and Givaux.

Maier, M. (1616). *De Circulo Physico Quadrato Oppenheim*. Luca Jennis.

Moore, T. (1992). *Care of the Soul: How to Add Depth and Meaning to your Everyday Life*. London: Piatkus.

Murray, G. (1915). *The Stoic Philosophy*. London: Allen & Unwin.

Murray, G. (1955). *Five Stages of Greek Religion*. Garden City, NY: Doubleday Anchor.

Nuttall, J. (2000). The Rosarium Philosophorum as a universal relational psychology. *Psychodynamic Counselling*, 6(2), 70–100.

Nuttall, J. (2002). On the nature of the psyche and Canary Wharf. *Harvest Journal of Jungian Studies*, 48(2), 7–29.

Tacey, D.J. (1993). Jung's ambivalence toward the world soul. *Sphinx*, 5, 275–282.

Samuels, A. (1985). *Jung and the Post-Jungians*. London: Routledge and Kegan Paul.

Samuels, A. (1993). *The Political Psyche*. London: Routledge.

Samuels, A., Shorter, B. and Plaut, F. (1986). *A Critical Dictionary of Jungian Analysis*. London: Routledge & Kegan Paul.

Smuts, J. (1926). *Holism and Evolution*. New York: Macmillan.

Stern, D. (1998). Non-interpretative mechanisms in psychoanalytic therapy. *International Journal of Psychoanalysis*, 79, 903–921.

von Franz, M.-L. (1980). *Alchemy: An Introduction to the Symbolism and the Psychology*. Toronto: Inner City Books.

Wheeler, C.J. (1993). The lost Atlantis: myths of soul in the modern world. *Sphinx*, 5.

Zohar, D. (1990). *The Quantum Self*. London: Bloomsbury.

Muriel Dimen interviewed by Andrew Samuels in the context of the publication of her book *Sexuality, Intimacy, Power*[1]

(Winner, Goethe Award, Canadian Psychological Association, 2003)

Muriel Dimen and Andrew Samuels

Andrew: I suspect you'd agree that all authors are engaged at some level in polemic, writing with an opponent in mind – 'Do be my enemy for friendship's sake" (William Blake 1783/2004). Who – or what experiences – are you writing about/against?

Muriel: Your raising of this unthought – known lets me own my aggression as well as my cooperativeness. I am, first, writing against patriarchy. Or, you might say, the politics of knowledge, hence the politics of psychoanalytic knowledge. Another target then is whatever splits psychoanalysis and politics.

For me, it's both/and. I want to think mind and society, psyche and culture, interiority and exteriority, heart and politics at once, not in the same language, not reductively but in tension, in a matrix, in a third place between and/or containing them. The tension between mind and matter has always drawn me; perhaps that is one reason I have engaged first anthropology and then psychoanalysis. The Marx/Freud synthesis has been my intellectual home since around 1970, although now I see it as vanishing point, not goal. The Marx/Freud nexus in fact situates debate among varied, conflicting languages and perspectives. Feminism, I argue in the Prologue, now contains that discourse, and as such has enriched many disciplines. Why shouldn't psychoanalysis benefit too?

Fantasizing recently about Bloomsbury while listening to Stephen Fry's account of his film *Bright Young Things* (2003), the 1920s well-to-do children of British industrialist fortunes, I ran into a paradoxical sense of both alienation and nostalgia for something I never had, which illuminated my own mission: if their coming of age meant to foster art and culture as well as have a blast, my coming up meant to do good, if not for, then somehow in relation to the world as inhabited by ordinary people. I am upwardly mobile from an upwardly mobile family, and if I don't earn as much as my father did, I've joined the intelligentsia, the professional–managerial class

(Ehrenreich, 1989). I wish I had learned to see art and culture as the most vital thing in the world; how luxurious and bohemian and so very transgressive. Instead, though, I have often suspected the aestheticized life as a trick played on ordinary (read lower middle-class) people – which I suppose really means my highly intimidatable parents. Although I soon de-idealized the possibly condescending and certainly idealizing left notion of "the people," still the quotidian fascinates me. At the same time, I believe in the life of the mind, the examined life, and theory, which, as I use it, is a living creature.

What I write against stems from my graduate school experience, as my Prologue describes: In 1960s anthropology, I encountered a materialist determinism that fit my longings for certainty as well as my interest in everyday life's concreteness. Many experiences – ethnographic fieldwork, the New Left, feminism, psychoanalysis – unveiled a view more complex than determinism's absolutism. In human affairs, objectivity, I came to see, was an oxymoron – perhaps another vanishing point – and truth perspectival. Structuralism, dialectics, and interiority/exteriority began to replace the historical materialism on which I'd cut my teeth. And as I came to train in psychoanalysis, concurrently with my engagement of feminism, I worked on doing a nonmechanistic both/and, reading Marx's *Grundrisse* and Gramsci, later Althusser and Foucault and, even later, Merleau-Ponty. The personal was political was theoretical, each requiring the other's validation, to riff on Nancy Chodorow. I note feminism's absence from this reading list. At that time, the late 70s, I was already struggling with feminism's orthodoxies, principally the idea that to merely mention psyche or the individual, let alone psychoanalysis, was counterrevolutionary.

Andrew: But doesn't citing patriarchy collapse into a monism? I was surprised to see this target written so frankly right at the top of your answer. Maybe I shouldn't have been. Who operates patriarchy, who benefits from it, and who suffers from it? Also, just a wild question really, can you connect the systemic operation of patriarchy with sexual misery of individuals?

Muriel: Wow. You just scared me: I wasn't supposed to put this target up front? I so often do the emperor's-new-clothes thing. Well, let's just say that patriarchy is right up there with those other monisms, racism and colonialism, and let's note the hydraheadedness of the whole fantastic trio. Each has many manifestations, in psychoanalytic theory, institutions, and so on. In Foucaultian terms, patriarchy, like the others, operates throughout the political body, because it is simultaneously material, social, and discursive. In that sense, it's not monistic. Patriarchy plays on many registers. And as persons, we all operate it, don't we? And we all benefit and suffer from it, right? But some get more of the former and less of the latter, and vice versa. Would Richard Nixon have given up the joys of patriarchal power because it deprived him of a heart? Surprise me, and say 'Yes!'

But what do you mean by 'sexual misery'?

Andrew: Maybe I am extrapolating what happens to me when I take a relativistic approach to sexuality. I am often stumped when opponents say "that's all very well, but what if a patient, in intense sexual misery, desperately needs some help to change the situation, including behaviors?" The underlying accusation is that I am being far too theoretical, if not politically correct (in its negative sense).

Muriel: But still you don't say what you mean by "sexual misery." Are you indicating the difficulties of sexual identity? Certainly patriarchy is implicit in what Freud saw as the precarious if not impossible journey from polymorphous perversity to (what we would call) mature heteronormativity. Classical psychoanalysis equates adulthood and reproductive sexuality, and Lacan added sanity to that string. Now, psychoanalysis didn't exactly invent this definition of mental health, but it did codify – medicalize – certain cultural presumptions, whose narrowness of scope makes for sexual misery, sort of like the way the ever fashionable and, may I say, beautiful stiletto distorts the foot.

Hmm. I have drifted toward naturalism. How in keeping with classical psychoanalytic thought, which indicts the constraints of civilization – read gender and sexual identity – for producing neurosis. But in the classical model, as many have pointed out, the romantic idea of a free sexual nature is alive and well. These days we (think we) know better: there is no natural sexuality, no bedrock of innocence and freedom. Sex is always constructed, which creates a different set of sexual difficulties. The meeting of body, mind, and culture through the arousal of two beings is a potent weather system – someone's always going to be uncomfortable or unhappy or disconcerted sometime. In the 70s, we tried to link sexism and sexual unhappiness directly, but those of us who were psychoanalytically inclined soon saw our mistake. Of course, we were making those links on women's behalf: "Free women's sexuality," a placard might have read. One direction we took was toward cultural feminism: an idealization of women and their sexuality. To the degree to which desire was framed and experienced as the opposite of men's, of course, it contained its opposite. This negation preserves, if not reproduces, whatever ills patriarchy generates in the first place. (Not that all is ill in patriarchal sexuality. At some point, deciding I'd had it with male chauvinism hiding in Alan Alda clothing, I found myself compelled by a very sexy, old-fashioned patriarchal type: at least I knew what I was getting. Although the sex was great, if [or because] a bit part-object-ish, the relationship did not hold for the long, whole-object [whatever that is] run.)

Anyway, is one patriarchal sexual ill the divorce of sex from relationship, even from affect? But replacing lust with emotion remedies nothing, a problem some lesbian feminists identified when the prevalence of lesbian bed death came to light. That desire wanes when women are coupled should no more surprise than its abatement in straight and, yes, gay male couples.

Plus ça change: perhaps the vicissitudes of sex and love, and their different fates and incompatibilities, make up the sexual misery to which you refer.

Would this vanishing of lust be, however, a product of patriarchy? Well, if sex as alpha and omega issues from patriarchy, then so do expectations accompanying such exaltation. But these constructions stem from capitalism as well as gender hierarchy, not to mention race and religion. Does sex have a different place in the psychic economy or fantasy life of different individuals and subject positions, of men and women, straight and gay and trans and so on? If so, these differentiated locations are also going to be inflected by class, race, and other categorical elements.

Andrew: Muriel, throughout your book, you explore the relations between the psychical and sociopolitical dimensions of experience. Clearly, you are aware of the criticism, that those who see the unconscious as having been "filled up" by internalization of the social order, have missed the point about the unconscious, the biologically founded drives and the conflicts they create. Cornelius Castoriadis said to me once that the unconscious was "empty" at birth. When I asked him if he really meant empty, he replied, "except for God and a sense of death!" Comment?

Muriel: When I was an anthropologist, the most fun theorizing you could do was to speculate about the earliest human society. Why? Because there were no data. That's what I think about what's in the mind at birth: you can't possibly know, so you can say anything you want and whatever you say will parade itself as the truth. I tend to distrust the idea of Truth. Truths tend to fit where and when you live, not to mention your personal inclinations and history. Is that a know-nothing position? Many sorts of observations and experiments are made on babies. And babies, unlike our earliest ancestors, are live. Perhaps we can know something. But I am more impressed by how our suppositions about infants change historically.

That said, I do not construe the interior life as filled by the social order, just as I do not contemplate the social order as filled by interiority. Internal life, or psychic reality, is, Chapter 4 [of my book] says, referencing Laplanche, as substantial as material reality. And, of course, in the middle or third region, the divide between internal and external evaporates: intersubjectivity challenges the before and after of a mind empty at birth and full later.

Even so, the interior differs from the exterior. One of the prime signs of that difference is dreamlife, not to mention slips of the tongue. *The Psychopathology of Everyday Life*, in other words, signals the existence of this order of mind that we can never put our finger on, but is with us all the time. Unconsciousness, like sexuality and genitalia and birth and death, is weird, and it's our job as clinicians not to rationalize that unknowability because our patient's need for cure and our need to help incline us to put it all (back) together. So I hold inner life as process rather than as contents – castration, Oedipus, breast, and so on. Or rather I am not faithful to a particular set of contents; I choose rather more promiscuously among models of mind, because any given treatment produces many contexts of meaning in which this or that model of mental contents might work. Does that resemble the dread "eclecticism"?

What if eclecticism is really a strategic hybridity? As you examine a sculpture from multiple angles, so you can helpfully offer someone different perspectives on their own dynamics and meanings. Freud took the idea of the unconscious and ran with it, and then passed the torch to us, and what we do with it, we will find out after the fact, even if we think we know what we're doing. To quote myself here (2003), "Like other disciplines whose data talk back, psychoanalysis is neither art nor science, but a third, still evolving practice, which it is too soon to name." Hybridity works because, in the consulting room, diversity is always already there: two people and what goes on between them, not to mention their internal hybridity, or the psychological and historical and linguistic matrix embedding them.

Andrew: Mention of the analyst's need to help and the patient's need for cure – and I acknowledge a possible irony here – brings us up against the social project of psychoanalysis and the psychological project of (some kinds of) feminism. Could you say something about those social problematics where your own distinctive blend/brand of psychoanalysis and feminism makes a contribution, potential or actual, to pressuring the social order to change? I want to explore the relevance of your thinking for social action, I guess.

Muriel: When someone asks how a theoretical point applies clinically, I think reflexively that the point isn't to put the idea into action, it's to think and let action come where it comes from. It's only after much talk about something else that (sometimes) I find, in a roundabout fashion, the clinical implications of the ideas I am trying to work out. Same goes for politics: organize around your own interests, that's how I think. So if we can help people know what their interests are, around their desire, to be fancy about it, then maybe that will result in a person more at home in their skin. And if at home in their skin, then perhaps they won't avoid the contradictions in their mind or the world. One by one? Not good enough, I know.

Andrew: As I see it, your work engages as deeply as anyone's with the question of moral relativism, with respect to relationships, aesthetics, and politics. To play devil's advocate: if I don't ask this question, someone will. Do you ever feel in danger of losing contact with the psychic pain that the patients bring? Is there a risk of being in a sound intellectual place but cut off from one's compassion?

Muriel: What is the relation between moral relativism and pain (not to mention joy)? Does moral relativism foreclose intimacy and mutuality and empathy? Or is thought deemed to disregard suffering? The question, which you suggest others might ask, shocks me. Do people really see intellect and affect and empathy as mutually exclusive? Reich's healthy character was a sexual intellectual. I'm no Reichian and I don't believe there's a single healthy character. But doesn't that pairing suggest what seems to me the ordinary coupling of mind and passion, thought and heart? Certainly I am not always spot-on when it comes to compassion and empathy. But I take my failures to heart. Some academics are markedly uncomfortable with affect: feelings don't belong in the Ivory Tower. Maybe that's why I couldn't stay there. Feeling walks with us every day, with everything we think, and that's why we do this work. Thanks for letting me find that out.

Andrew: From where you have got to in terms of practice and theory in psychoanalysis, what changes would you wish in the field? A huge open-ended question, but let's see where we get to in dialogue.

Muriel: I first took this question to refer to training institutions. Even though psychoanalytic training institutions differ, I would like them to integrate intellectual and political considerations. On this side of the puddle, a certain anti-intellectualism hides amidst our necessary devotion to clinical work. Likewise a certain anti-politics: I say "political," you say "not psychoanalytical." How can there be more than lip service to these goals? How might there be a psychoanalysis that is intellectually, politically, and culturally engagé? Perhaps each course should weave some such readings and discussions into the fabric of the classwork. A tall order, I know. But that might set the stage for clinicians' greater attention to and awareness of their own historical and social context as they carry out their work. Of course, a national single payer system that included mental health services (as in Germany) would help an awful lot to situate mental suffering as a part of ordinary living that requires constant reflection as a routine, valued dimension of daily life and adult existence. It would also help expand our range of patients; I am paralyzedly aware of the white, upper middle/upper, professional managerial/artists class of my clientele. Any chance on our lobbying for that? (Joke.) You will now, I expect, say something sensible in contrast to the foregoing.

Andrew: Oh, I think it is even worse than you say. There can be extraordinary unreflectiveness in the academic part of psychoanalytic trainings to such basic questions as "Why do I want to be an analyst?" or "What is analysis from a social point of view, what is its function, scope, limitations?" These issues, like the contextual, social, and historical ones, are just left to be picked up in the training analysis. But, trying to be sensible, would you agree that what we need to address is candidates' demands for something clinically "solid," "reliable," "effective?" How can we get the candidates to see that the theories we are discussing here truly are highly practical? That good thinking is a part of good relationship? That – unless it is overdry and abstract – the intellect is part of the holism of the human subject?

Muriel: Well, OK, sure, we must address such demands for solid, reliable, effective clinical – what? But surely many other people do so; it can't be that every instructor ignores clinical matters. But, if we eggheads are to give every idea its clinical correlate, then should not every clinical seminar include the social, intellectual, and historical meanings that contextualize its principles and practices? Psychoanalysis began and remains a practice of the intellect as well as of the clinical, and I would want to do all I could to prevent the anti-intellectualism so prevalent in managed care and even doctoral programs from deadening psychoanalysis, our most vital theory of mind.

Bibliography

Blake, W. (1783/2004) 'A Sad Friendship Poem.' In *Poetical Sketches*. Whitefish, MT: Kessinger Publishing.

Dimen, M. (2003) *Sexuality, Intimacy, Power*. Hillsdale, NJ: The Analytic Press.

Ehrenreich, B. (1989) *Fear of Falling: The Inner Life of the Middle Class*. New York: Pantheon.

Note

1 Excerpted from "Muriel Dimen Interviewed by Andrew Samuels in the Context of the Publication of Her Book, "Sexuality, Intimacy, Power," *Studies in Gender and Sexuality* 8 (4): 383–393.

Chapter 15

Between life and death

Weaving the remaining spaces in the tapestry of life[1]

Moira Duckworth

For Andrew. With gratitude and thanks for more than 30 years journeying as friends and colleagues. Moira.

One of the challenges of the 21st century is increasing longevity. Although 25 percent in the European Community are over 60 and average life expectancy approaches 80, our overly negative imagery of old age, 'gerontophobia' (Zoja 1989), adds greatly to the burden of middle age. Some people go through middle age in the shadow of death, as though already very old. Others can grasp new opportunities that arise from the transition into a new stage of life. We need to remind ourselves of the value of ageing as well as the demands on society. Traditionally old people are guardians of the laws, mysteries and memories and thus the cultural life.

Patients in this age group fall broadly into two distinct categories. There are those whose life seems to be falling apart, triggered by some external crisis. They want a quick fix and are wary of long-term work, fearing dependency. They are often narcissistic, inflexible, and not psychologically minded. Others come deeply motivated to pursue an inner path, even if they are not fully conscious of this. It is as if they are trying to complete the tapestry of their lives, to reweave broken and frayed threads, to reclaim or connect to their soul.

The journey towards death begins the moment we are born, but the term ageing usually refers to the later years of the second half of life. It is not the same as being old. It is not reversible nor can it be cured. It is not an illness, it is a process and is always fatal. We rarely ever welcome old age, but unless we die young we cannot ignore it.

In the 2001 BBC Reith Lectures, Professor Tom Kirkwood said

> Dramatic increases in life expectancy are shaking the structure of societies around the world and profoundly altering our perceptions of life and death. Not only are we living longer, but the evidence of recent decades shows that old age itself is being transformed.

For the purposes of this chapter I am taking the older person as being over 60 years, where childhood experiences can feel less relevant and death is more present.

Psychotherapists have traditionally been cautious working with older people. Freud (1905, p. 264) wrote:

> The age should not be above 50 because the elasticity of mental processes is missing. This elasticity, on which treatment depends, is as a rule lacking and the mass of material to be dealt with would prolong the duration of the treatment indefinitely.

Abraham's (1919) clinical work led him to a contrary view that chronological age does not necessarily preclude the intellectual and emotional capacity for analysis.

King (1974) expressed sadness that the gulf between psychoanalysts and Jung had grown so wide that they could not take advantage of Jung's work with older patients. She wondered if psychoanalysts in Britain have divided patients into those below 40 (suitable for psychoanalysis), and older patients 'who would do better with a Jungian'.

Klein (1959), in one of her final works, concentrates on the attenuation of excessive feelings of envy as a requirement for a relatively normal adaptation to old age. She notes that the individual who has identified with the pleasures of other family members in childhood, without excessive envy, can usually identify with the satisfactions of the young in old age. Segal (1958), citing clinical material from work with a man in his mid 70s, confirmed this view. When he was able to mourn loved objects in his life and face his own death, he could enjoy the thought of his children and grandchildren living on and prospering after him.

Kernberg (1987) writes of the tendency of older patients suffering pathological narcissism to devalue objects as a defence against envy, but at the price of a pervasive sense of emptiness. These individuals spoil success with their relentless greed and can never find lasting satisfaction. They envy their children and attempt to maintain their own youth in order to deny the anxieties aroused by ageing, and avoid the mourning involved in the ageing process. The realistic need for support from, and dependence on, others induces shame, failure and a sense of humiliation, leading such people to devalue others (including the therapist) as a defence.

Narcissistic individuals tend to be depressed in later life, and may respond to therapy if they can feel regret, guilt and remorse for wasted time and opportunities. Those who suffer from empty rage and blame their difficulties on others have a more guarded prognosis. Ageing parents are frightening to them; to perceive themselves as ageing, helpless, and dependent has to be denied and fought against. Hypochondriacal reactions and compensatory health fads and rituals may express their fear of ageing and can be seen as an attempt to omnipotently control the body and its functions.

Jung (1933 para. 787) suggested that the tasks for the morning of life are money-making, social achievement, family and posterity and are plain nature, not culture. As culture lies outside the purpose of nature, he wondered if this could provide meaning and purpose to the second half of life.

Focusing on the mid-life crisis and the second half of life Jung (1929 para. 75) wrote:

> It seems to me that the basic facts of the psyche undergo a very marked alteration in the course of a life, so much so that we could almost speak of a psychology of life's morning and a psychology of its afternoon. As a rule, the life of a young person is characterised by a general expansion and a striving towards concrete ends. . . . But the life of an older person is characterized by a contraction of forces . . . The neurosis comes mainly from clinging to a youthful attitude which is now out of season.

A Jungian view of ageing is non-pathological and suggests that the greatest potential for growth and self-realisation exists in the second half of life. The demands of the ego lessen, time is limited, and making contact with the Self is a priority. At this stage, the accent switches from the interpersonal dimension to a conscious relationship with the intrapsychic inner depth processes, and to a concern for spiritual meaning and values. A process has begun whose natural end is death, and ageing is preparation for this. Jung (1933 para.785) wrote, 'For a young person it is almost a sin, or at least a danger, to be too preoccupied with himself; but for the ageing person it is a duty and a necessity to devote serious attention to himself.'

In an interview towards the end of his life (Freeman 1959), Jung spoke of death as a goal: 'Life behaves as if it were going on, and so I think it is better for an old person to live on, to look forward to the next day, as if he had to spend centuries, and then he lives properly.' On my consulting room wall is a poster of a hand holding a tiny tree, with a quotation from Martin Luther, 'If I knew the world would end tomorrow, I would still plant apple trees today.'

Levinson's (1978) developmental system divides the life cycle into 'the major seasons of adulthood' with overlaps between middle adulthood (40–65) and late adulthood (60 onwards). There are parallels with Erikson's (1997) nine life stages, the last having been conceived in his 90's. The last three stages being intimacy versus isolation, generativity versus stagnation, and ego integrity versus despair.

When he stood down from being an MP, Denis Healey (2000) wrote:

> I have lost all my interest in power and position and no longer worry about making money. I still enjoy my work, but only what I want to do

. . . [like] talking to meetings of the National Trust about my favourite countryside. I am now much more sensitive to colours, shapes and sounds . . . I enjoy music even more than I used to because I get greater pleasure out of the sound of different instruments . . . I love my wife, my children and grandchildren more than ever . . . To use Freud's expression – I have lost interest in my ego.

In her journal, published after her 70th birthday, the poet May Sarton (1993) wrote:

What is it like to be seventy? If someone else had lived so long and could remember things 60 years ago with great clarity, she would seem very old to me. But I do not feel old at all, not so much a survivor as a person still on her way. . . . [all things], good or bad, painful or delightful, weave themselves into a rich tapestry.

Jaques (1965) wrote,

I believe that the cause for working too hard too long is the same as what compels most of us to travel faster all the time. There is a control here that we don't teach in our culture. We don't teach a man how to arrive . . . fully and enjoy life. Since people never sufficiently enjoy the things they have on hand, they have to keep moving. Then when they retire they are likely to fall apart because the only thing that kept them in one piece, which was the routine of rushing, is gone.

Gordon (1978) believes that the capacity of the older person to be creative is deeply dependent on their capacity to stare death in the face and to make sense of their lives in spite of or rather because of the reality of death. She reminds us that creativity is not only about artistic creation but also relates to the way we enter into and handle our relationships and nurture our own growth. We could say that the components of the life structure are not a random set of items like things washed up on the seashore. They are rather like threads in a tapestry, woven into an encompassing design.

The focus of my work with older people lies in identifying the recurring themes in the tapestry and in weaving them back into the overall pattern. Usually a small number of components have a central place, with others (though important) being more peripheral. The central components have the greatest significance for the self and the evolving life course, they receive the largest share of one's time and energy and they strongly influence the choices made in other aspects of life. The peripheral components are easier to detach and change, they involve less investment of the self and are less crucial to the fabric of one's life.

During transitional stages in life we are suspended between past and future and struggle to move through the gap that separates them. There may be a reaffirmation of commitment to an existing part of life rather than a change, but the decision to stay put is not always based on a reaffirmed commitment. It may stem more from resignation, inertia, passive acquiescence or controlled despair. This kind of surface stability can herald the beginning of a long decline unless and until new factors intervene. In every life stage we suffer because of the undone developmental work of the previous periods.

Beth was 57 when her husband suddenly left her after 25 years of marriage, with no prior warning. She was numb, and upset, but could hardly believe hearing herself say in our first session, 'the one thing I know is that I do not want him back.' I sensed enormous relief on her part. She had no idea about therapy but she knew she needed help.

The analysis was long, intense, creative and profoundly moving. Initially I thought the heightened intensity was due to her difficult background and pathology, and the fact that she had effectively lived a lie all her married life. Later I came to see that it was because she felt this was her last chance to truly live her life.

Initially I seemed to have all the feelings, and helped her to name her feelings as you teach a child about colours: she had no label for them and could feel very little. Freed from the repression of her husband and marriage, she realised she could do as she wished as her two children were grown up. She read voraciously, started to record her dreams and was fascinated by their rich symbolism. They became her way of keeping in touch with her inner process and she was frightened they would suddenly leave her. I was surprised by the time and energy she put into working on herself between sessions, as if she knew how much she had to do, and how little time there was.

A professional botanist prior to marriage, she would dream of flowers with their botanical names. Sometimes they were names she had no recollection of, but their meaning would invariably directly address what was going on.

She had a difficult relationship with her mother, a witch-like, poisonous person who was nonetheless adored and honoured in her local community. Beth dreamt:

> My mother was very ill. Two visitors reported she had painful legs and a scarf wrapped round her head, cutting her off from people. I was clearing away some shoots of the evergreen shrub euonymus japonica, when I noticed that a freshly cut stem looked as though it was already showing roots.

She had been puzzled for years about the discrepancy between how she felt about her mother and how everyone else seemed to experience her.

Euonymus means 'of good name, fame or honour', probably named ironically as it has poisonous properties! There was her mother encapsulated in this plant, poisonous but with good name, and honoured by the local people.

Beth had achieved a remarkable degree of inner reconciliation with her mother, and was with her in her last days. Soon after her mother died, Beth dreamt: '*A new professor of botany has been appointed locally, and therefore is leaving his post at the university where I studied. I feel excited and then see the very rare blue form of asclepidaceae (more usually seen in orangey-red).*'

The name asclepidaceae is related to Asclepius, the god of healing. After Asclepius was born he was snatched by Apollo from the burning pyre on which his mother's body had just been consumed.

Beth had been a compulsive knitter, and stopped the day her husband left. She had seen knitting as a protection, but I saw it also as a way of trying to knit meaning and pattern into a meaningless life. Half-way through the analysis she started writing poetry, and then to weave. She had never woven before, but aged 64 she became a successful professional weaver. The wool, which had protected her in her married life through knitting, now became the medium for her creativity.

As previously mentioned, work with older people seems to fall into two distinct categories. On the one hand there are patients like Beth, whose energy and commitment to therapeutic work indicate that their survival seems to depend on it. On the other hand, there are those who come with a problem in a crisis and are in a hurry, looking for a quick fix.

From the outset Ben made it clear that he wanted speedy results. He was typical of other highly successful male patients in this age group, who could be described as narcissistic or borderline. They either were or had been married, none had been monogamous, and all appeared never to expect a woman to turn them down. The presenting problem is an excruciating decision to be made. They were struggling with Erikson's last three stages, fearing isolation, stagnation and despair, these fears becoming powerful motivators for change.

Ben was 70, a tall, grey-haired, good-looking man, smartly dressed, with a commanding presence, looking younger than his years. Now past the pinnacle of his successful career, he was still in great demand for his fame and skill. But there was anxiety about the future, which could not meet his narcissistic aspirations, and he had no concept of creative retirement.

He had limited capacity for symbolisation or psychological insight but I warmed to him and felt concern for his psychic pain and inner conflicts. He had been married for 35 years and had left his wife seven years before. For eight years he had been in a relationship with Joy, and could not decide whether to marry her or end the relationship. They spent most weekends and holidays together, but because of their Christian faith did not want to live together.

It was always assumed that they would marry as soon as his divorce was through, but a number of events led him to draw back from Joy. He was especially close to his daughter and her disabled daughter, after her husband died during her pregnancy. Just as Ben filed for divorce his wife collapsed with a terminal illness, and six years later Ben collapsed in the street and needed an emergency operation.

When he told me a friend had just committed suicide I tried to work with the despair this engendered in him, but it was too deep and split-off. 'I hope he doesn't make me ill,' was a recurring thought emerging from the feelings he projected onto me. In the face of the overwhelming material, I focused on helping him to untangle the conflict of the relationship.

There were two turning points. He denied fearing what would happen to Joy if he broke off the relationship. Using my countertransference I said, 'This may not make sense to you, but I think you might feel you are very destructive towards women.' The following session he said that he'd been thinking about it all week and knew it was true. Shortly after this he told me his mother had nearly died when he was born and had not been allowed to have any further children. He had nearly destroyed her.

The second turning point came later. I said I was struck by the fact that he and Joy had never lived together, and he had turned inwards to his family when his wife's tumour was diagnosed, almost as if it was a relief. He never took Joy to see his daughter and grandchild, and I wondered if these were all connected with his guilt. He then said, 'There are two other things you could add. We neither went to church together, nor did we pray together. I have just realised that this means I was ashamed of the relationship. I could not bring it before God. I did not pray about it.' When he realised how guilty he felt, he was able to break off the relationship with Joy.

These two different clinical illustrations show how older people can be worked with if the therapist is mindful of what they really seek. For many people, understanding emerges clearly later in life at the very time we suspect it is too late for us to do anything about it. Another way of looking at this is to say our soul knows better.

Jung (1933 para. 800) said 'From the middle of life onward, only he remains vitally alive who is ready to *die with life*', and 'if you are lucky you will live yourself out of life!' In order to live life fully we must meet and face many tasks, and these become more evident and urgent in the autumn of life. These tasks of ageing are also the tasks of living, for age is not separate from life. It is this finding a place, letting things have their place, weaving the remaining tapestry, which interests me about people in later life with whom I have worked. What is it they have to do to complete their life cycle? There is a need to sum up, make sense, live the life which remains, and then finally let go.

Bibliography

Abraham, K. (1919). The applicability of psycho-analytic treatment to patients at an advanced age. *Selected Papers on Psychoanalysis*. London: Karnac (1988).

Erikson, E. H. and Erikson, J. M. (1997). *The Life Cycle Completed*. London: Norton.

Freeman, J. (1959). Face to Face; Interview, BBC TV. *C. G. Jung Speaking*, eds. McGuire, W. and Hull R. London: Thames & Hudson (1978).

Freud, S. (1905). On psychotherapy, *Standard Edition* (1964) vol. 7.

Gordon, R. (1978). *Dying and Creating*. London: Society of Analytical Psychology.

Healey, D. (2000). And louder sing . . . *Getting a Life: Older People Talking*, ed. Simmons, M. London: Peter Owen.

Jaques, E. (1965). Death and the mid-life crisis. *International Journal of Psycho-analysis*, 46: 502–514.

Jung, C. G. (1929). The aims of psychotherapy. *The Practice of Psychotherapy*. *CW 16*.

Jung, C. G. (1933). The stages of life. *The Structure and Dynamics of the Psyche*. *CW 8*.

Kernberg, O. (1987). Pathological narcissism in middle age. *Internal World and External Reality*. Northvale, NJ: Aronson.

King, P. (1974). Notes on the psychoanalysis of older patients. *Journal of Analytical Psychology*, 19: 27.

Klein, M. (1959). Our adult world and its roots in infancy. *Envy and Gratitude*. London: Hogarth Press (1984).

Kirkwood, T. (2001). *The End of Age: Why everything about ageing is changing*. BBC Radio 4 Reith Lectures. London: Profile.

Levinson, D. (1978). The anatomy of the life cycle. *The Seasons of a Man's Life*. New York: Ballantine.

Sarton, M. (1993). *At Seventy: A Journal*. London: Norton.

Segal, H. (1958). Fear of death. Notes on the analysis of an old man. *International Journal of Psycho-Analysis*, 39: 178–181.

Zoja, L. (1989). Working against Dorian Gray: Analysis and the old. *Psycho-pathology*, ed. Samuels, A. London: Karnac.

Note

1 This chapter is an abbreviated version of a longer paper.

Chapter 16

What's Missing? Death and the Double

Christopher Hauke

What drives us to action? What makes us want to make plans for the next day, the next year? Desires for material things play their part: a new car or plasma TV screen. Or even wishing for a better husband, or a better analyst. What drives us to action is wanting what is Missing. More precisely, wanting what *we* are Missing, because there is a powerful sense of identity in this desire. We form a powerful identity with something that is absent. If this absence gets filled with the Missing element, our sense of self will be satisfied, we believe.

In his novel *Human Traces*, Sebastian Faulks notes how the precondition of all religious faith was 'the physical absence of god . . . there was no need for faith unless there was an absence' (Faulks, 2006: 206). But was god never really there, or was that 'absence' 'a real vacuum that followed a real presence: had someone or something actually vanished?' (ibid.). We derive faith, belief, meaning and activity from the sense of absence. Whether that something ever did exist in the first place is not really the point. As humans we find a vacuum so we may fill it with our surplus of faith, belief and all our symbolic and metaphoric meaning-making. It is when we concretize this presence–absence dynamic that we fall into error and risk a loss for the human spirit. When we seek to correct our feeling-state of incompletion by filling the vacuum we are mistaking metaphor for literal matter. This is the difficulty with late twentieth-century rationalism in every field: intellectual, scientific, political and social. There is a fantasy that we can now find what we have been missing as if that was possible or desirable; it is what Baudrillard calls *The Illusion of the End* (Baudrillard, 1994).

Baudrillard agrees that 'paradoxically. . . . if God exists there is no need to believe in him, but . . . if he does not exist you have to believe in it. Belief is not the reflection of existence, *it is there for existence*, just as language is not the reflection of meaning, it is there in place of meaning' (Baudrillard, 1994: 89). Thus, belief in the Missing is there for our existence, for our being, it is not a reflection of the existence of the Missing. We can also say that such belief in the Missing is not a reflection of its meaning, but it too is there *in place of meaning*!

Free-floating Lack and what we are Missing

According to Jacques Lacan (Felman, 1987), our Desire for Being is recalled time and again through our experience of Lack. Wanting what we are Missing. Put this way, we don't have to wait until something or someone actually goes Missing, Missing is an experience waiting to happen; like free-floating anxiety waits for us to find something to worry about – the anticipation of Lack waits for a Missing Object to be its focus. If something is not missing now, we will discover what is missing soon enough. For forty years, the Cold War gave rise to a fear of Communist infiltration, risking the death of Western Democracy. With the disintegration of the USSR and the Eastern Communist Bloc in 1989, this fear collapsed. This left an anxiety vacuum. With this threat gone, what was to take its place as a global fear? Up until the collapse of the Eastern Bloc, confidence in the security of the Capitalist Nation-States had always been missing. With no threat left to worry about, it is possible that Western governments find their prime role as protector of the people significantly diminished. If you define yourself by identifying what threatens you, when that goes missing it is your own identity that comes under threat. The category of the Missing is a vacuum. Into that vacuum of the Missing, threat is sucked as its replacement.

Global Terrorism gets presented as the new candidate for what is Missing in our Western lives. This new threat can be characterized in two ways which sustain the quality of Missing. On the one hand, there is something that needs to be found and requires a Search. To justify the invasion of Iraq, the British Government insisted Saddam Hussein had Weapons of Mass Destruction. They were, however, missing. So, a search was made and, although they were never found, the war proceeded. The meaning of these Missing weapons persisted while the Missing weapons never materialized. Alternatively, there is The Terrorist – whether conceived as a Hidden Plot, the next 9/11 or 7/7 (not a matter of 'if' but a matter of 'when', we are re-assured) or a Hidden Personality such as Osama Bin Laden. On the other hand, it is not so much the Terrorist that is Missing but the security of our civilized life. So the sense of what is missing, the quality of Lack and the energy of the Search is geared towards finding not only the Terrorist, or the Plot, but also re-finding our missing sense of Security, so we may sleep safely in our beds.

The myth of the Double

To recap: we seem to have an urge to find the Missing; identifying this, and the search activity that follows, creates meaning in our lives and seems to substantiate us as human beings. Whether we have lost our money, our child, our confidence in the safety of civilized national lives, or lost track of those perpetrators who threaten us from the shadows, we find new Meaning as humans when we identify what we are Missing. The development of reflective consciousness, apparently unique in Nature, set us permanently apart from the world, and, crucially, it also set us apart from the part of that world that is actually ourselves. We appear to be the only animals who have any idea of our eventual death. What is Missing is death. The search for the desired Missing objects displaces and postpones the Missing death. This has typically been experienced as the split between our material self and an immortal self or soul and has traditionally expressed itself in images of an afterlife and rituals to ensure the immortality of the soul.

A parallel split resulting from reflective consciousness centers around our sense of identity. Personal identity gets shored up not only through knowing who one *is* but also through the Shadow of this – knowing who you are *not*. As well as the Shadow, we see our own image reflected in water or the mirror. Both reassure us how we appear to others and of who we are to ourselves.

Both experiences – immortality and identity – rely on *the fact there is something missing*. Without knowing of the part that is missing, we cannot be sure of the part that is present. Ironically, the firmer the idea of an immortal soul, the firmer is the notion of our mortality. The greater our awareness of what is Missing and absent – death and other mysteries – the greater our certainty about the presence and who we are.

In private lives, in therapy, and in public and political life, asserting that someone or something is Missing provides the motor energy and the justification for thought and action. Such action is given meaning by the very thing that is *not* present. That which we identify as missing is the very thing that gives meaning to our searching activity. The degree to which something is found meaningful, largely as the result of being perceived as Missing, is vital. In this sense, what is found Missing *'is' this meaning*. In doing so, we conceive our existence as the material aspect of a presence–absence pair. Our existential presence is chained to the Missing absence in a coupling that endorses our sense of identity and meaning. The Missing is an absence that gives meaning to our presence. Without this absence, without an identified Missing, the meaning of our existence, and thus our identity as a self, is profoundly diluted. This is brought home in the myth of the Double, the Identical Other You or Doppelgänger, whose apparent existence – while remaining absent from direct perception – guarantees our full authenticity as a human being. As one psychological writer has put it, this motif expresses the problem that accompanies modern mankind and the evolution of rational, conscious life:

> modern man . . . having created civilization and with it an over-civilized ego, disintegrates by splitting up the latter into two opposing selves. . . . Such dichotomy of conflict, interfering with full living and functioning, is not to be confused with the basic dualism between the natural and

spiritual self which was dynamically balanced in the magic world-view [of the primitive].

(Rank, 1941: 65–6)

And there are two ways to look at this:

the positive evaluation of the Double as the immortal soul leads to the building-up of the prototype of the personality from the self; whereas the negative interpretation of the Double as a symbol of death is symptomatic of the disintegration of the modern personality type.

(Rank, 1941: 65–6)

This sounds like the cultural psychology of Carl Jung. But in fact, the quote comes from the last book written by Otto Rank, *Beyond Psychology* (Rank, 1941), in a chapter titled 'The Double as Immortal Self'.

We know the Double best through the Romantic literature of the nineteenth century – especially in the themes of Dostoevsky, Robert Louis Stevenson, Edgar Allan Poe and de Maupassant. In Dostoevsky's work, 'all his tragic and struggling pairs of real people who appear to themselves as complete entities are presented as two halves of a third divided personality – halves which, like the doubles, seek themselves and pursue themselves' (Rank, 1941: 80–1). One understanding of the appearance of the Double and its popularity in the late nineteenth century is the way in which it represents a protest by the artist against the Rationalism of the time. Once again, human minds became aware of the irrational forces within themselves, but where previous eras looked to spirits and possession, this time around it is *psychology* that offers new tools to explore this motif as a problem of the Self.

Otto Rank refers to an early movie, *The Student of Prague*, dating from before 1920, which was – Luke Hockley tells me (personal communication) – also Carl Jung's favorite film. In the story, a desperate young student sells his reflection in the mirror to the Devil in exchange for a fortune in gold. Trouble ensues: the reflection takes on a life of its own, and, in his attempt to stop this persecution by his alter-ego, our hero is driven to kill it – thus bringing about his own suicide.

From the same Romantic period, the creator of the story of Peter Schlemihl (the man who lost his shadow), when asked what the shadow signifies, reckons, 'It is the health which I lack. The absence of my shadow is my illness' (Rank, 1941: 72). Even earlier than Antiquity, the motif of the Double has been around in many forms 'originally conceived of as a guardian angel, assuring immortality of the self' (ibid.: 76). But the modern use of the Double motif reveals a significant change of emphasis. In a moralistic re-interpretation, the double appears as 'precisely the opposite, a reminder of the individual's mortality, indeed, the announcer of death itself. . . . from a symbol of eternal life in the primitive, the double developed into an omen of death in the self-conscious individual of modern civilization' (ibid.: 75–6).

The Double as Twin

The theme of the Double has an important connection to the rise of religion and civilization, culture and the human individual. The most significant version of this is the mythology of the Twin – with its sense of a Present entity forever shadowed by an identical partner. Sometimes one twin is Missing or murdered, sometimes one twin is exchanged for the other and goes Missing in this way as in the story of *The Prince and the Pauper*.[1]

Myths of interchangeable twins, especially where one dies for the other, appear linked to the formation of human civilizations and the arrival of the heroic character type. In primitive thinking, multiple births seem more animal-like than human, so twin-births offer a symbolic link between our animal past and our sense of being separate from Nature. Famous twins like Romulus and Remus were not only the founders of Rome but also reared by a she-wolf. Castor and Pollux were twins sired by Leda and the Swan (who was Zeus in disguise). The 'rider twins' or heavenly twins who played an important part in ancient Hinduism and are said to be descended from the horse, became tamers of horses and inventors of the yoke. The association of yoked pairs of beasts like oxen and horses, and thus the chariot and the plough, links the pairing motif closely to the agriculturalists who laid the foundations for civilization. The image seems to be one of humans retaining an animal heritage at the same time as the creation of that which seems furthest from Nature: the city – prime symbol of stable civilization.

Prehistoric burials 'indicate that the most primitive idea of a tomb for the dead was a housing for his soul – a replica of the maternal womb from which he was to be reborn' (Rank, 1941: 90). As the concept of the soul – previously referring only to the dead – was extended to the living person, 'the idea of the grave as the house of the soul was ascribed to the human body itself. . . . This development . . . signified a further step towards self-realization impelling the individual to immortalize himself increasingly in personal creation of his own' (ibid.: 91). The twin-tradition is thus an important transition 'between the primitive conception of the Double as immortal self and its creative self-expression as we see in works of art' (ibid.: 91) literature and movies. Twins represent in material form a dualistic concept of the soul and thus the immortality of select individuals.

Death and the Double

In the Hero myths, instead of an actual pair of twins, we note myths of a double or twinned fate where the hero is abandoned and left to die but survives against the odds. This theme of 'certain death yet miraculous survival' supplies us with a metaphorical twin or Double. One is the character who might have died at the start of the narrative, while the other is the 'twin' who survives and lives out the rest of the story. Oedipus, for example, was believed dead, abandoned to a death by exposure by his parents, who feared for their own destiny, but was saved and survived to return and complete the fate of everyone. The same is true of Moses, and even Jesus Christ, whom Herod believed he had slaughtered as a baby, but who survived such attempts to render him Missing and emerged as the adult Christ to complete his mission.[2] As in the earlier myths and in cruel mediaeval customs of burying a living child in a new building to ensure its success, the Missing twin, the Double, is the key to creative culture and self-realization.

> The killing of another infant simultaneously born with the hero and replacing his twin became . . . a true earmark of the heroic type. Mythologically he is constituted by a fusion of the two separate selves, the mortal and the immortal; . . . he has absorbed, so to speak, his original double, be it shadow or twin, into a doubled self which has, as it were, two lives to spare . . . The idea of a doubled self . . . is the essential characteristic of the genuine heroic type.
>
> (Rank, 1941: 95–6)

The myth of the Missing Double or Twin arises as our response to a human desire for immortality and the avoidance of death. Post-Enlightenment, our immortality may be viewed by modern populations as secured through creative human achievement in the arts and sciences – the hero who overcomes death is the creative artist and scientist. Where once we projected fantasies of immortality either as a Shadow, a reflection, the Double or the missing Twin, we now project it into the Missing Truths of our existence. The Missing immortality now gets projected onto our material science – biological truths like the genetic code, onto political truths like the terrorist plot to destroy America and her allies, and onto all the other Universals. These are still metaphorical antidotes to Death, motifs for the Immortal Self of our ancestors that we in our sophistication ridiculed and abandoned. The Missing is back in material form. Now it is the metaphoric and the symbolic that have gone missing.

Bibliography

Baudrillard, J. (1994) *The Illusion of the End*, Stanford: Stanford University Press.
Faulks, S. (2006) *Human Traces*, London: Vintage.
Felman, S. (1987) *Jaques Lacan and the Adventure of Insight. Psychoanalysis in Contemporary Culture*, Cambridge, MA and London: Harvard University Press.
Rank, O. (1941) *Beyond Psychology*, New York: Dover Publications.

Acknowledgement

A longer version of this chapter was first presented at the Brunei Gallery, London October 7th 2006 for the C.A.P. Conference in acknowledgement of Andrew Samuel's work titled: *Worlds in Transition: Prospects for the Political Psyche*

Notes

1 Mark Twain, who wrote this story, not only involved himself in this twinning theme by his choice of *nom de plume*, but once, when talking to a reporter, cried over a fictitious identical twin brother who, he claimed, had drowned when they were having a bath together as babies. 'Then, [Twain said] after some time while everyone was mourning him, it was discovered it was not his brother after all, but he himself who had drowned.' (Rank, 1941: 86).
2 With the story of Christ's resurrection, the death of one and survival of the 'double' is repeated.

Chapter 17

On transformation

The art and the science of forgiveness

Birgit Heuer

This chapter is dedicated to Andrew Samuels on the occasion of his sixtieth birthday. Among the many gifts that Andrew has bestowed on the field of analysis, I would like to acknowledge one contribution in particular that is widely made use of, yet, to my knowledge, has not been sufficiently recognised by the very field it enriches. I have in mind Andrew's unique contribution to the field of clinical discourse. In reflecting on the history of clinical paradigm in the past twenty years, one shift stands out: the axiomatic inclusion of the socio-political dimension in the clinical hour. Due to Andrew's contribution, the very view of reality assumed by clinical discourse has changed to embrace the relevance of human socio-political experience. In my view, the importance of this particular shift will continue to stand out as time passes and will be seen to enable and foster a further shift in the concept of reality underlying clinical paradigm which is currently emerging: the spiritual dimension of the socio-political human being that Andrew Samuels put on the map of clinical discourse in the twentieth century.

Introduction

In this chapter forgiveness will be explored in a variety of ways. Forgiveness can seem extremely personal and intimately bound up with one's own psycho-biography. Yet the ramifications of forgiveness may be highly public and political. In addition, forgiveness is traditionally regarded as a subject of religion and spirituality. Forgiveness has been called an 'art and a science' (Worthington 2005) and its many aspects have also been studied empirically for the past twenty-five years. Here, I shall attempt to convey a flavour of this diversity of approaches.

   In addition, I shall introduce the concept of an essence of forgiveness that interconnects its many facets. I have traced the connection between the mystical experience of grace and what contemporary physicists now term quantum-reality in a previous paper (Heuer 2008). From this perspective 'ordinary reality', including scientific empirical reality, subtly interweaves with a view of reality that usually is mainly accessible through faith. The essence of forgiveness might then involve a mystical place, located in a flow of grace, that is accessible both scientifically and through inner experience.

A further section of this chapter concerns clinical aspects of forgiveness. I shall look into practical, emotional and bodily instances of forgiveness, including its shadow aspects. I shall also give my thoughts on bringing the essence of forgiveness into the clinic.

The final part of this chapter addresses socio-political aspects of forgiveness and their relation to the essence of forgiveness. Here I shall explore relationally oriented ways of resolving conflict. In particular, I shall focus on the work of the Truth and Reconciliation Commission and the socio-political possibilities of forgiveness that restorative justice might enable.

This chapter, then, brings scientific empirical findings as well as mystical quantum knowledge into the psychoanalytic clinic. My overall intention is more illustrative and evocative than critical and I hope to bring depth and texture to the theme of forgiveness.

Forgiveness and empirical science

The empirical exploration of forgiveness started in the mid-1980s and forgiveness is now the subject of a science. No unified definition has come forward – rather, forgiveness has been studied in a multi-faceted way. Thus a multitude of aspects has emerged:

Forgiveness has been studied in relation to conciliatory group behaviour in primates. It has also been examined as individual human behaviour and as related to spirituality/religion, as related to physical health, as related to emotional health, as based on character, vengeful or forgiving; it has been considered from the angle of the victim's experience and their behaviour and/or psychology. There are fewer studies concentrating on the perpetrator. Forgiveness has also been studied in relation to couples, families and larger social groups and from the point of view of social intervention.

Enright and Fitzgibbons (2000) explore forgiveness as a process involving behaviour, cognition and affect, which move through twenty steps in naturally occurring settings, thus contributing hypotheses about the natural occurrence of forgiveness. McCollough, Fincham and Tsang (2003) conceptualise forgiveness as a redirection of conscious motivation, which can change and be measured, with a two-component approach to forgiving, reducing negative motivations and increasing positive ones. Sandage and Williamson (2005) have studied forgiveness in the context of culture, whilst Mahoney, Rye and Pargament (2005) have written about forgiveness and the sacred and the particular challenge of forgiving desecration. There is research into 'anger towards god' by Exline and Martin (2005). Tagney, Boone and Dearing (2005) have written on forgiving the Self. Farrow and Woodruff (2005) have published a paper on the neuro-imaging of forgivability. Wade

(2002) has examined group interventions to promote forgiveness and Armour and Umbreit (2005) have studied the paradox of forgiveness in restorative justice.

The essence of forgiveness

As empirical research highlights the manifold facets of forgiveness, might there be an alternative approach, involving what I shall term the essence of forgiveness? This implies an epistemological discussion about the creative tension between an empirical approach and a paradigm that is informed by the findings of contemporary quantum research. Moreover, it implies a metaphysical shift in what is regarded as the very nature of reality. In a previous paper (Heuer 2008) I have explored how a quantum-scientific and a mystical view of the world interweave in what might be called an integration of reality and eternity. The 'result' is a logical hybrid where two opposing views of reality co-exist simultaneously. From a meta-paradigmatic angle, one might say that mystical experience requires 'making real' in the Winnicottian developmental sense. A similar process is currently unfolding via the socio-cultural reception of contemporary quantum physics. I would like to propose these considerations as a frame for exploring the essence of forgiveness.

The essence of forgiveness emerging from this is best articulated in poetic/ mystical language, inviting resonance to its manifold facets like a song. Such a song might sing of forgiveness as an act of grace, created by the Divine on our behalf, and of forgiveness as inspired by the love of the beauty and goodness of human beings. It reverberates with the essence of forgiveness as the transformative power of the Divine and with human forgiveness as a highly creative and imaginative act. It might sing of forgiveness as the capacity to imagine something better, more wholesome. Another stance might sing of the mystical Divine that is constant in complete forgiveness, at all times, unconditionally. Silently and imperceptibly, continues the song, the mystical Divine always transforms badness into goodness, into grace. Suffering ensues where this flow is seemingly interrupted. Forgiveness is to do with the secret, invisible point at which transformation occurs. Might it flow into us at all times unconsciously and create a capacity which, like any creative talent, can be honed? Is forgiveness a transformation that has already happened, akin to Jones' (2002) view of Jung's teleology? If future forgiveness is already constellated, does it then need 'making real' in the Winnicottian sense?

Forgiveness also links with the Buddhist view of the wheel of karma. The essence of forgiveness brought to the notion of karma means that the wheel is 'halted' and karma voided. If all karma has been transmuted, we are then challenged to 'realise' this, i.e., by softening and unlearning the concept of crime and punishment, the talion law. If we ourselves are forgiven, the talion law ceases to make sense psychologically. As we learn emotionally about Divine forgiveness, we are inspired by its gentle yet extremely powerful ways, enabled by Divine generosity to be generous ourselves. The essence of forgiveness then involves a transformative, generous creative act, inspired by the flow of Divine grace. It involves the unfolding of the holy heart in the human heart, perhaps the development of a heart-mind.

Biochemical empirical research (Pert 1997) now holds that we think and feel with all of our bodies, so that a forgiving heart might be located anywhere in the body or extend to the whole of the body. Broadly speaking, one might consider all instances of non-linearity as a transformation of the talion law, which leads to an abundance of instances of forgiveness. In this way, nature seems designed to be forgiving, as are our bodies. The earth, Gaia, is extremely forgiving in her profound non-linear ability to regenerate in the face of abuse or lack of care and this includes the seasons, the daily rising and setting of the sun, our bodies' ability to rejuvenate and all healing of physical ailments.

Some clinical aspects of forgiveness

In my view, the most important clinical aspect of the essence of forgiveness lies in its potential power of transformation. Conceptually, Jung's transcendent function is closely related to this, as is his idea of an archetypally patterned morality. Clinical instances of forgiveness can be mental, emotional, bodily or spiritual. I consider the most basic – and at the same time profound – instance of forgiveness clinically to lie in the fact of sheer survival of extreme trauma. The fact that the patient who has survived extreme trauma has not killed herself/himself or anybody else seems to me to express forgiveness, in that the talion law is already transcended and continues to be so with every day of survival. Another instance of forgiveness is the release of bodily symptoms related to trauma as in the physical symptoms of post-traumatic stress syndrome, or the release of bodily symptoms that relate to other painful psychic experience. Here it is the body that potentially forgives first. A different example from couple therapy would be the warring couple who have managed to find a degree of peace – without any formal acts of forgiveness – where the forgiveness lies in learning a better way of living together. These are all instances of forgiveness where transformation occurs on a day-to-day level through the way life is lived, rather than any formal acts of forgiveness. It is noticeable that, on this level, there is an abundance of forgiveness everywhere as part of ordinary life. There are untold numbers of everyday ordinary gestures of forgiveness. Yet they link with the deeper, mystical essence of forgiveness and thus have a transcendent, numinous aspect in the midst of seemingly ordinary experience. There is something like perception through the eyes of forgiveness that makes them visible, so that instances of forgiveness seem abundant. When this is realised, particularly clinically, it may create a positive cycle, increasing the potential for forgiveness.

There are, of course, shadow aspects of forgiveness. According to Murphy (2005), these occur when forgiveness becomes 'cheap grace', where it allows an unacceptable situation to continue and constitutes a form of masochistic rage, or where forgiveness is given as a form of manipulation; where forgiveness is an attempt at moral superiority; or where it is given too quickly to defend against resentment, rage or the realisation of trauma. Another shadow aspect of forgiveness arises when we 'play God', by individually attempting to forget and forgive the collectively 'unforgivable', rather than addressing it through socio-political processes of restorative justice.

Forgiveness can also be seen as a creative act. Here its essence inspires the ability to imagine something better and to participate in bringing it about. Unforgiveness, in my view, imprisons a person or an experience in the past. There is usually a traumatic element that serves as unconscious trigger. This area then becomes split off from the psychic blood supply of embracing emotional reality. Here the ordinary work of recovering the repressed is needed, but so, too, is creativity and imagination. Forgiveness can thus be highly individual, like a fingerprint, and include creatively dreaming up, as well as receiving from the essence of forgiveness, an individual way forward that is transformative. As such it needs to be authentically desired (consciously or unconsciously) and then creatively received and brought about. The act of forgiving then is co-terminus with the creative act.

Clinical instances of forgiveness thus range from sheer survival of trauma or the release of bodily symptoms to rituals of forgiveness, from unconscious to conscious expression, and include unilateral or bilateral ways of forgiving. Sometimes it needs atonement from the perpetrator, sometimes this is not possible, yet forgiveness can still be creatively arrived at. Returning to the song of forgiveness, clinical instances of forgiveness are then inspired by the flow of grace from the essence of forgiveness and 'made real' by a creative act.

Social and political aspects of forgiveness

A recent development in the socio-political sphere is the emergence of restorative rather than retributive justice. The concept of restorative justice involves a relational element, as perpetrator and victim are implicitly acknowledged to belong to the same dynamic. This relates to a systemic view (Armour and Umbreit 2005), and also to Jung's idea of the *unus mundus* (Williams 2007). Examples of restorative justice are to be found in the mediation movement and in the Truth and Reconciliation Commission in South Africa. Both approaches transcend the talion law, which links them to the essence of forgiveness. Bishop Tutu writes:

Here the central concern is not retribution or punishment, but [. . .] the healing of breaches, the redressing of imbalances, the restoration of broken relationships. This kind of justice seeks to rehabilitate both the victim and the perpetrator who should be given the opportunity to be re-integrated back into the community he or she has injured by his or her offence as something that has happened to people and whose consequence is a rupture in relationships.

(Tutu 1999: 51–52)

Human interconnectedness and the essence of forgiveness come together in the African concept of *ubuntu*. Bishop Tutu explains:

Ubuntu is very difficult to render into a Western language. It speaks of the very essence of being human. [. . .] We say, 'a person is a person through other people'. It is not 'I think therefore I am'. It says rather: 'I am human because I belong'. I participate, I share. A person with *ubuntu* [. . .] is diminished, when others are humiliated or diminished, when others are tortured or oppressed. [. . .] *Ubuntu* means that in a real sense even the supporters of apartheid were victims of the vicious system which they implemented. [. . .] The humanity of the perpetrator of apartheid's atrocities was caught up and bound up in that of his victim whether he liked it or not. In the process of dehumanising another, in inflicting untold harm and suffering the perpetrator was inexorably being de-humanised as much, if not more than the oppressed.

(Tutu 1999: 34)

In moving beyond the talion law, *ubuntu* brings the essence of forgiveness into the socio-political sphere by connecting it with the very essence of humanity.

Bishop Tutu headed the South African Truth and Reconciliation Commission and gives a moving account of this in his book, *No Future without Forgiveness* (1999). The members of the commission were empowered to grant amnesty to perpetrators of crimes against humanity under apartheid. Several features stand out in this example of restorative justice. Perpetrators could only gain amnesty if they came forward to give full and truthful accounts of their deeds. They had to 'plead guilty' as amnesty would not be granted if they tried to defend their actions. Thus amnesty was given in exchanged for the truth. Wherever possible, perpetrators and victims or their relatives were to be present together. Perpetrators were not required to show remorse or a wish to atone and equally no expectation was made of victims to forgive.

Bishop Tutu's account seems imbued with the spirit of *ubuntu*. He describes occasions where the perpetration of hellish atrocities transforms, as forgiveness is either spontaneously asked for or given and a step is made to restore the humanity of both victim and perpetrator. Armour and Umbreit (2005) define forgiveness as a change in the victim's as well as the perpetrator's attitude, when both are brought together in a restorative justice process. They describe the psychological changes thus: in the victim's eyes, the perpetrator may turn from an inhuman monster into a human being who can be empathised with, and equally, for the perpetrator the victim might become a human being with feelings, rather than a thing that can be abused. Whilst the deed is still completely unacceptable, it becomes subtly differentiated out and neither victim nor perpetrator is completely defined by it any longer. It then seems that with these relational processes which are promoted by the frame of restorative justice, the element of forgiveness lies in re-establishing the humanity of both victim and perpetrator, and in restoring empathy. The restorative justice movement thus carries the essence of forgiveness, adding a particular note, that of humanity shared by us all and that of the basic human right to empathy.

Conclusion

In this chapter, I have inquired into the manifold facets of forgiveness, ranging from empirical study to clinical and socio-political aspect. My inquiry has been in the spirit of exploration, inviting resonance rather than argument. Some emphasis has been given to the idea of an essence of forgiveness which for me, like a song that subtly sounds at all times, is potentially always available, but needs 'making real' creatively. When the perception of what might constitute forgiveness is opened up, it appears more abundantly available and, when set in a relational context, it becomes intertwined with the essence of our humanity. In the words of Bishop Tutu:

> When we had listened to the testimony of people who had suffered grievously, and it all worked itself out to the point where they were able to forgive and embrace the perpetrators, I would frequently say: 'I think we ought to keep quiet now. We are in the presence of something holy. We ought metaphorically to take off our shoes because we are standing on 'holy ground'.
>
> (Tutu 2004: 3)

Bibliography

Armour, M. and Umbreit, M.S. (2005) The paradox of forgiveness in restorative justice, in Worthington Jr., E.L. (ed.) *Handbook of Forgiveness*. New York and Hove: Routledge.

Enright, R.D. and Fitzgibbons, R.P. (2000) *Helping Clients Forgive: An Empirical*

Guide for Resolving Anger and Restoring Hope. Washington, DC: American Psychological Association.

Exline, J.J. and Martin, A. (2005) Anger toward god: A new frontier in forgiveness research, in Worthington Jr., E.L. (ed.) *Handbook of Forgiveness.* New York and Hove: Routledge.

Farrow, T.F.D. and Woodruff, P.W.R. (2005) Neuroimaging of forgivability, in Worthington Jr., E.L. (ed.) *Handbook of Forgiveness.* New York and Hove: Routledge.

Heuer, B. (2004) Buddha in the depressive position. On the healing paradigm. *Proceedings of the XVIth IAAP Congress, Barcelona.* Einsiedeln: Daimon (on disc).

Heuer, B. (2008) Discourse of illness or discourse of health: Towards a paradigm-shift in post-Jungian theory, in Huskinson, L. (ed.) *Dreaming the Myth Onwards. New Directions in Jungian Therapy and Thought.* New York and Hove: Routledge.

Jones, A.M. (2002) Teleology and the hermeneutics of hope: Jungian interpretation in the light of the work of Paul Ricoeur. *Journal of Jungian Theory and Practice,* 4(20): 45–55.

McCollough, M.E., Fincham, F.D. and Tsang, J. (2003) Forgiveness, forbearance and time: The temporal unfolding of transgression-related interpersonal motivations. *Journal of Personality and Social Psychology,* 84: 540–557.

McCollough, M.E. and Root, L.M. (2005) Forgiveness as change, in Worthington Jr., E.L. (ed.) *Handbook of Forgiveness.* New York and Hove: Routledge.

Mahoney, A., Rye, M.S. and Pargament, K.I. (2005) When the sacred is violated: Desecration as a unique challenge to forgiveness, in Worthington Jr., E.L. (ed.) *Handbook of Forgiveness.* New York and Hove: Routledge.

Murphy, J.G. (2005) Forgiveness, self-respect and the value of resentment, in Worthington Jr., E.L. (ed.) *Handbook of Forgiveness.* New York and Hove: Routledge.

Noll, J.G. (2005) Forgiveness in people experiencing trauma, in Worthington Jr., E.L. (ed.) *Handbook of Forgiveness.* New York and Hove: Routledge.

Pert, C. (1997) *Molecules of Emotion.* New York: Scribner.

Sandage, S.J. and Williamson, I. (2005) Forgiveness in cultural context, in Worthington Jr., E.L. (ed.) *Handbook of Forgiveness.* New York and Hove: Routledge.

Tangney, J.P., Boone, A.L. and Dearing, R. (2005) Forgiving the self: Conceptual issues and empirical findings, in Worthington Jr., E.L. (ed.) *Handbook of Forgiveness.* New York and Hove: Routledge.

Tutu, D. (1999) *No Future without Forgiveness.* London: Rider.

Tutu, D. (2004) Heaven can wait. Interview with Desmond Tutu by P. Stanford. *The Independent,* 26 January 2004, pp. 2–3

Van Oyen Witvliet, C. (2005) Unforgiveness, forgiveness and justice: Scientific findings on feelings and physiology, in Worthington Jr., E.L. (ed.) *Handbook of Forgiveness.* New York and Hove: Routledge.

Wade, N.G. (2002) Understanding REACH: A component analysis of a group intervention to promote forgiveness. *Dissertation Abstracts International*: Section B: Sciences and Engineering, 63: 2611.

Williams, R. (2007) *Atonement*. MSc. Thesis, Colchester: University of Essex.

Worthington Jr., E.L. (2005) Initial questions about the art and science of forgiving, in Worthington Jr., E.L. (ed.) *Handbook of Forgiveness*. New York and Hove: Routledge.

Chapter 18

The Gospel of Judas: An emerging potential for world peace?

A post-post-Jungian perspective[1]

Gottfried Heuer

A story told, heard, attended to,
carries with it the possibility of living.

Lisa Appignanesi (2008: 4)

Introduction

In the middle of the previous century C.G. Jung interpreted a change in the valuation of a figure in Christian religion as an important indication of a change in the values of the culture at large, regarding the Church as an important factor in expressing as well as shaping the attitudes of the collective. In this chapter I am applying the same interpretative concept to a more current issue that involves a complete reversal of the view hitherto held for the last two millennia about what is possibly the most despised figure of Christianity. I am concerned with the role of shadow-projection and power in both personal as well as collective relationships. Touching on the role of forgiveness in the process of reconciliation, my considerations also include the religious realm, thus linking politics with spirituality in a way that they each dialectically may enliven the other.

The Gospel of Judas

When the time is fulfilled a new orientation will irresistibly break through.

C.G. Jung (1953/1976: 137)

One of the ways of approaching dreams in clinical practice is to understand them in a teleological sense as speaking of a potential that may be ripe to be realised. Events and enactments may thus sometimes be seen as indicators of future maturational steps. Some sixty years ago, Jung applied this approach to the then-Pope's 'attempts at bringing about the official recognition [. . .] that Mary has been taken up to heaven together with her body' (Jung 1973: 499), attempts that led two years later to the dogma of the *Assumptio Mariae*, which declared the Assumption an article of faith. Jung understood this as 'a spiritual fact which can be formulated as the integration of the female principle into the Christian conception of the Godhead' (Jung 1973: 567). He felt this to be 'the most important religious development for 400 years' (ibid.), because it constituted an important step towards a revaluation of the feminine which had been devalued, if not outright despised, since the beginning of the Christian era – expressing as well as furthering a negative bias in Western culture. He assumed that such a reversal of values regarding the feminine within the Church would have reverberations in the world at large and spoke of a 'feminist revolt' (Jung 1976: 231). Jung did not live long enough to be able to witness the accuracy of his interpretation but I believe that, looking back from today's perspective, it does make sense to link the *Assumptio Mariae* with the powerful upsurge of feminism beginning in the following decade, and as heralding the great changes in feminine values and the transformation of our world by them since then.

It now seems that today, some fifty years later, at the very beginning of the new millennium, a shift in consciousness of at least similar proportions is occurring – unnoticed, as far as I can see, by psychologists. The event that I am referring to is the recent publication of *The Gospel of Judas*. The manuscript was discovered around 1978 in Middle Egypt. It then

> 'vanished into the netherworld of antiquities traders, one of whom abandoned it for 16 years in a bank vault in Hicksville, New York. By the time it reached [the scientists who subsequently prepared the translation and publication], the papyrus was decaying into fragments, its message on the verge of being lost forever'.
>
> (Cockburn 2006: 81)

What is this message and why is it so uniquely important? In *The Gospel of Judas* we find a complete reversal of how Judas has been traditionally seen: far from being the most despised and condemned of Jesus' disciples – in many European languages his very name stands as a synonym for 'traitor' – here Judas is presented as the disciple Jesus feels most close to, the only one he feels truly and profoundly understands him. And it is for this reason that Jesus chooses him to perform the most difficult part to fulfil the purpose of his destiny.

Of course, literary reimaginings of the Judas myth have preceded the publication of *The Gospel of Judas*. De Quincy, Sayers, Borges, Kazantzakis and others come to mind. But this newly found text seems to speak with a different authority, that of preceding the aforementioned by almost 1,700 years: *The Gospel of Judas* is assumed to have been written around 150 CE, some mere 50 years after the gospels of the New Testament. In the language of the New Testament (albeit from a different context) this truly is an instance where 'the stone which the builders rejected the same is become the head of the corner' (Matthew. 21: 42).

The Gospel of Judas purports to be '[t]he secret account of the revelation that Jesus spoke in conversation with Judas Iscariot during a week three days before he celebrated passover' (Kasser *et al.*: 19) At the gathering of the disciples for the eucharist, the disciples 'do not dare to stand before [Jesus], except for Judas Iscariot' (ibid.: 22). 'Judas [says] to him, "I know who you are and where you have come from. You are from the immortal realm"' (ibid.). 'Jesus [says] to him, "Step away from the others and I shall tell you the mysteries of the kingdom. It is possible for you to reach it, but you will grieve a great deal"' (ibid.: 23). And he continues later, '{Come}, that I may teach you about {secrets} no person {has} ever seen. For there exists a great and boundless realm, whose extent no generation of angels has seen' (ibid.: 33; curved brackets indicate words assumed by the editors). Jesus says, 'But you, [Judas], will exceed all of them. For you will sacrifice the man that clothes me' (ibid.: 43). And concludes, 'Look, you have been told everything. Lift up your eyes and look at the cloud and the light within it and the stars surrounding it. The star that leads the way is your star' (ibid.: 43–44). The text ends with Jesus' capture. From this new perspective, Judas kissing Jesus to point him out to his captors can no longer be seen as the epitome of vile treachery. It now becomes an act of loving intimacy – and a farewell: from our traditional perspective a moving example of the Jungian concept of 'embracing the shadow'. The text ends with the words, *The Gospel of Judas*.

We may ask ourselves at this point what the history of Christianity might have looked like if this embrace and kiss of friendship had become the symbol for Christianity instead of the cross, an instrument of torturous execution towards a slow and lonely sacrificial death.[2]

I would also like to mention that *The Gospel of Judas* on several occasions portrays Jesus as *laughing* – not something he has been known for in any of the other gospels! This may well seem not directly relevant to the theme of my contribution, except, maybe, in the sense of the German artist Joseph Beuys' asking, 'Can you *really* conceive of a revolution without laughter?!' (in Schiering 2006).

Potential for Peace?

> We can create such a world as the world has never seen before: a world distinguished by no longer knowing of war, nor of going hungry, and that worldwide. That is our historical potential.
>
> Rudi Dutschke, 1968 (in Faulstich and Hafner 1993)

After two millennia of keeping Jesus and Judas separate as the polar opposites of light and dark, *The Gospel of Judas* presents us suddenly with the mystery of their union, which Jung termed *mysterium coniunctionis*. In this union, the opposites form the same wholeness that is, for example, portrayed in the yin/yang symbol of the East in which, symbolically, light and shadow embrace. 'Judas was always used to represent evil', says the theologian Aaron Saari, 'He is the scapegoat' (in Batty 2008). In what has been called *The Scapegoat Complex* (Brinton Perera 1986), unwanted shadow aspects of the individual are projected onto a shadow-carrier, originally literally a goat that was then ceremoniously sent into the desert to perish. It is the psychological mechanism whereby we 'behold the mote that is in' our 'brother's eye', rather than considering 'the beam that is in' our own (Matthew 7:3). There is no conflict, no war – individually or collectively – without such shadow projection, where the other is being demonised in unconscious acting out. As Eckart Tolle writes, 'violence would be impossible without deep unconsciousness' (1999: 61). Amazingly, for example, Hitler is supposed to have replied, when asked in 1939 whether the removal of Jews from Germany would rid the world of his No.1 enemy,

> We would have to invent them, one needs a visible enemy, one in plain sight. The Jew is always within us, but it is simpler to fight him in bodily form than as an invisible evil.
>
> (in Hardtmann 1982: 244)

Almost unbelievably, at least in the moment of saying this, Hitler was aware of an external splitting that reflects an internal one. The solution to such splitting lies in withdrawing the projection and thus retrieving the projected negative content into oneself. I understand this as being clearly implied in the biblical challenge about 'beholding the mote in our brother's eye'. Splitting and projecting afford the delusion of superiority: for example, in the extreme racism of Nazi-Germany, the conviction of belonging to 'the Master-Race'. Saari sees one of the roots of Anti-Semitism in regarding 'the name Judas as synonymous or equal to "Jewish"' (in Batty 2008). Judaism in English has obvious close links to the name, and in German the word for Jew, *Jude*, is almost synonymous with Judas. Saari continues:

> Jesus and the other eleven disciples become Christians, [. . .] and Judas remains the only Jew. When he becomes associated with the Jewish people, we see an unbelievable rise in anti-Jewish violence. Part of this is owed to the idea that Jews are Christ-killers or God-killers.
>
> (ibid.)

What is called for, at the decisive turning point of radical change, is nothing less than a surrendering of that very delusion, a giving up of that 'power over others' that, in Tolle's words, 'is weakness disguised as strength (1999: 36). In the mid 1970s a London graffiti stated, 'POWER IS LOVE GONE BAD!' What is required in order to reverse this is a re-discovery of love. I am speaking here of healing through love – as Freud did over 100 years ago, when he wrote to Jung, 'Essentially, one might say, the cure is effected by love' (Freud/Jung 1974: 12–13). – As a further illustration of that mysteriously ineffable turning point of change we might also envisage, again from a biblical context, the pivotal moment in which the prodigal son decides to turn around in his wanderings to go back home to facilitate reconciliation by kneeling in front of his father, as in Rembrandt's moving painting.

Otto Gross (1877–1920), the first psychoanalyst to link analysis with the radical political transformation of society, spoke of this process in terms of the necessity to replace 'the will to power' with 'the will to relating' (1919). He conceived of this intrapersonally as well as interpersonally, and individually as well as collectively. Gross understood this transformational step from 'the will to power' to 'the will to relating' as 'the highest goal of the revolution' (ibid.). For him, relationship included a spiritual dimension, he spoke of it in spiritual terms as numinous, as 'the holy third' (1913: 1118). These ideas of his can be understood as the earliest beginnings of relational analysis, of intersubjectivity. In more modern terms, it is the 'Make Love, Not War!' of the 1960s, the idea of reconciliation. Important steps in the process of reconciliation are the withdrawing of projections – and apologising, both of which can form a basis on which forgiveness may be achieved.

Among the examples that come to mind in the collective, I am thinking here first of the spontaneous Christmas truce in 1914, the first winter of the Great War. It began with the joint singing of carols in the trenches – in which the respectively opposing sides joined! German, British and French troops then left their trenches to swap cigarettes, alcohol and personal mementoes and on Christmas Day played football in No Man's Land.

In a further step: is it possible to communicate this transformation any more convincingly than by taking responsibility for past violence and by kneeling to ask for forgiveness? (As the then German Chancellor Willy Brandt did in 1970 at the memorial of the infamous Warsaw ghetto.) More recently, in 2008, the Australian Prime Minister 'opened a new chapter in Australia's tortured relations with its indigenous peoples [. . .] with a comprehensive and moving apology for past wrongs and a call for bipartisan action to improve the lives of Australia's Aborigines' (Johnston 2008).

At the International Congress for Analytical Psychology in Cape Town in 2007, Andrew Samuels suggested in a plenary session that the International Association for Analytical Psychology apologise to black and coloured people for the way they had been treated both theoretically as well as clinically in the past. Sadly, this appeal fell on deaf ears – there was not a single public reaction to it – yet, I do not only hope but trust that eventually it will be heard and lead to the desired result.

We may be still many years away from, for example, a formal apology of the West towards Islam for its defamation of Muslims in the present decades. And, yes, of course, to return to *The Gospel of Judas*, the publication of the text is different from a formal recognition of Judas as a Saint by the Pope. It may well also be argued that with the *Assumptio*, Mary, on her way to heaven, had a shorter distance to cover, so to speak, as she was already highly venerated within the Church, something that can, as yet, certainly not be claimed about Judas. Yet, I believe, we may nevertheless understand the publication of *The Gospel of Judas* as constituting an important stepping stone towards world peace – as a potential ripening that urgently needs to be realised, as there is *No Future Without Forgiveness* (Tutu 1999).

Conclusion

I have applied a Jungian perspective to the contemporary event of the publication of the recently discovered *Gospel of Judas*. I have described how this may be understood as an important milestone in the way we collectively deal with shadow aspects that hitherto have often been projected onto an enemy other, leading to separation and, ultimately, persecution and war. Healing this kind of splitting both intrapersonally as well as interpersonally, both individually as well as collectively, requires a withdrawal of the shadow projection, and possibly apologising in order to further forgiveness on the route towards reconciliation and peaceful, loving relating. I have linked this with the developing theories of clinical practice in terms of intersubjectivity – freely relating as equals – and I have given a few examples from the political sphere to illustrate what these steps might look like.

Almost 40 years ago, Martin Luther King wrote, 'Far from being the pious injunction of an Utopian dreamer, the command to love one's enemy is an absolute necessity for our survival. [. . . It] is the key to the solution of the problems of the world. Jesus is not an impractical idealist; he is a practical realist' (King 1969: 47–48) – 'We have to live together as brothers or perish as fools' (King 1994: 224).

Now, in the words of Nelson Mandela,

> The time for healing the wounds has come. The moment to bridge the chasms that divide us has come. The time to build is upon us. [. . .] We know it well that none of us acting alone can achieve success. We must therefore act together [. . .] for the birth of a new world. [. . .] Let each know that for each the body, the mind and the soul have been freed to fulfill themselves.
>
> (1994)

Bibliography

Appignanesi, L. (2008). All in the mind. *Guardian, Review*, 16 Feb, 4–5.
Batty, D. (Dir.) (2008). *The Secrets of the 12 Disciples*. London: Carbon Media for Channel 4 [TV Documentary].
Brinton Perera, S. (1986). *The Scapegoat Complex*. Toronto: Inner City.

Byrne, R. (2006). The end of Gnosticism? *The Chronicle of Higher Education*, 5 May, A18–A22.

Cockburn, A. (2006). The Judas gospel. *National Geographic*, May, 78–95.

Faulstich, J. and G.M. Hafner (1993). *1968. Aus dem Bilderbuch einer Revolte. Eine Zeitcollage*. Frankfurt, M./Strasbourg: Hessischer Rundfunk, Arte [TV Documentary].

Freud, S. and C.G. Jung (1974). *The Freud/Jung Letters*. W. McGuire (ed.) London: Hogarth & Kegan Paul.

Gross, O. (1913). Notiz über Beziehung. *Die Aktion*, Vol. 3, No. 51, 1180–1181.

Gross, O. (1919). Zur funktionellen Geistesbildung des Revolutionärs. *Räte-Zeitung*. Vol. 1, No. 52, Beilage.

Hardtmann, G. (1982). The shadows of the past. In Bergman, M. and M. E. Jucovy (eds.) *Generations of the Holocaust*. New York: Basic Books, 228–244.

Johnston, T. (2008). Australia Says 'Sorry' to Aborigines for Mistreatment. http://www.nytimes.com/2008/02/13/world/asia/13aborigine.htm (Accessed 2 March 2008).

Jung, C.G. (1953/1976). *Letters, Vol. 2, 1951–1961*. Adler, G. and A. Jaffé (eds.), London: Routledge & Kegan Paul.

Jung, C.G. (1973). *Letters. Vol. 1, 1906–1950*. Adler, G. and A. Jaffé (eds.), London: Routledge & Kegan Paul.

Kasser, M. (2006). The Story of Codex Tchacos and the Gospel of Judas. In Kasser, R., Meyer, M. and Wurst, G. (eds.), *The Gospel of Judas from Codex Tchacos*. Washington: National Geographic, 47–76.

Kasser, R., Meyer, M. and Wurst, G. (eds.) (2006). *The Gospel of Judas from Codex Tchacos*. Washington: National Geographic.

King, M. L. (1969). *Strength to Love*. London: Fontana.

King, M. L. (1994). Remaining awake through a great revolution. Clayborne, C., P.C. Holloran, R. Luker and P.A. Russell (eds.), *The Papers of Martin Luther King, Jr.: Vol II*. Berkeley: University of California Press, 220–239.

Mandela, N. (1994). Statement of the President of the African National Congress Nelson Rohlihlala Mandela at His Inauguration as President of the Democratic Republic of South Africa. Union Buildings, Pretoria, 10 May. http://www.anc.org.za/ancdocs/speeches/inauggpta.html (Accessed 2006).

Meyer, M. (2006). Introduction. In Kasser, R., Meyer, M. and Wurst, G. (eds.), (2006) *The Gospel of Judas from Codex Tchacos*. Washington: National Geographic, 1–16.

Schiering, P. (2006). *Beuys & Beuys*. Mainz: 3sat, Zweites Deutsches Fernsehen [TV Documentary].

Tolle, E. (1999). *The Power of Now*. Novato, CA: New World.

Tutu, D. (1999). *No Future Without Forgiveness*. London: Rider.

Notes

1 Previous versions of this text were presented to the candidates of the Jungian Analytic Training for Qualified Psychotherapists of the Association of Jungian Analysts, London, on 16 March 2008, Palm Sunday; to the students of the Training in Jungian Analytical Psychotherapy of the West Midlands Institute of Psychotherapy, Birmingham, on 28 June 2008; and at the IAAP-IAJS ETH

Conference, Contemporary Symbols of Personal, Cultural and National Identity. Historical and Psychological Perspectives, Zürich, 3–5 July 2008. An extended version has been published in *Spring* 81, Summer, 2009, pp. 265–290.
2 I am grateful to my wife and colleague Birgit Heuer for this idea.

Appendix

The Cape of Good Hope

> We'd booked a tour, somewhat uncertain:
> *other* people?
> We'd much preferred to be by ourselves,
> the two of us on our own –
> at least that's what we'd thought.
>
> The mini bus arrives,
> three Arabs in the back,
> "Mohammed, Awfra, Achmed,"
> the driver introduces them,
> then adds "And I am Bobby,
> originally from Chicago."
>
> Our group complete,
> we leave the city – stunning views:
> the mountains, rocks, the ocean –
> also passing the poor townships
> of "the *other* half" . . .
>
> Rolling along on our way
> to Cape Point and
> the Cape of Good Hope,
> "So, tell me," Bobby asks,
> "where do you come from, Mohammed?"
> And the response is
> "Baghdad." –
> "Oh –"
>
> And everything stops:
> my heart, my breath, all continuity.
> Time stands completely still,
> as if we'd hit a rock
> and crashed the car, and,
> after deafening noise,
> silence

had descended, so that
you could have heard that pin drop. –

When life continues,
after all,
my eyes fill up with tears, "Oh God! –
Baghdad!" – And we:
from London, from the country
that wages war against these very people,
together with the US, Bobby's home.
"I pray for peace every day," he says just then. –

This surely's not what tour guides usually say,
and our meeting – what a gift from God,
what generous grace! –
is not what usually happens either
on a tourist trip:
three Iraqis, one American,
and two of us, from London –
and with each other we can share and voice
how we feel and our awareness
of the symbolic meaning
of us together on our way towards
the Cape of Good Hope.

At Cape Point looking out
into the ocean's vastness – blue infinity,
we pray for peace
and in good hope –
"Insh'allah" – if God will.

Later, we talk more
how daily life in Baghdad is,
how life was hell under Saddam –
Mohammed lost five members of his family,
an aunt was hanged;
how life is even worse now,
argues Achmed, as you can never know
when in the morning you leave home,
that you'll return alive at night.
"No longer any safe zones," Awfra adds.

"It's hell, although a diff'rent one,
right now with the Americans.

But," Achmed says,
"we need them.
We are not able yet on our own
to build democracy."

This makes me choke again,
I think of home, of Germany,
just after I was born,
and after World War II: then
we, too, had not been able to create
democracy on our own . . .

Saying farewell, we embrace,
with tears again in our eyes,
"I pray that you'll be safe," –
"Insh'allah" – if God wills it –, and,
"May God bless you." –

Numinously, the awareness lasts
of both difference and oneness:
that, yes, we do call God by different names,
yet at the same time *know*,
in this moment
as we hold each other, that,
truly,
God
is
all
One.

Gottfried Heuer
Addo Elephant House,
The Eastern Cape, South Africa,
20 August 2007
(London, 11 September 2007)

Chapter 19

Community, *communitas*, and group process seminars in analytic training

Jean Kirsch

'Don't hike alone!' the sign at the trailhead cautions me. I'm entering mountain lion territory. Solitude is what I crave after months of steady engagement. 'Fight back if attacked!' I pass on, picking up a long stick and pocketing some hefty stones as I set off to walk and contemplate what I want to say in honor of my friend, Andrew. A taunting charm of childhood bubbled up in my reverie. 'Sticks and stones may break my bones, but words will never hurt me.' It never worked. Words always wounded and later life revealed their lasting, tender scars. But I entered midlife before I appreciated the vulnerability of a community to damage from careless, intemperate, or self-serving speech from its members. Many colleagues behaved as if they viewed community either as an omnipotent extension of their ideal analyst, who can withstand destructive attacks from an envious analysand, or as benevolent Providence herself, who should provide an ideally nourishing and creative environment. When I witnessed the turmoil and reactive anger expressed by Institute staff, analysts, and candidates alike in the wake of a few boundary-breaking members, I saw firsthand the paradox of the collective: it is both terrible in its power to exile or squelch an individual and his/her creativity; and exceedingly vulnerable to destruction from within as well as from without. Its necessary functions are easily crippled by an individual's or a sub-group's action and speech, whether their destructiveness is conscious or unconsciously motivated. This insight led to a quest for greater understanding of the forces that operate *sub rosa* and motivate individuals from behind the scene whenever they congregate in groups.

Could anything in Jung's work justify my interest in the collective, that theoretical foe of individuation, which was held in such contempt by many loyal first-generation Jungians? After breaking with Freud, in his confrontation with the unconscious, Jung experienced psychic phenomena which he himself had not produced, and which ultimately led to hypotheses that founded his opus. This was a period of ferment and creative chaos. He apprehended that pursuit of these ideas and intuitions would jeopardize fulfillment of the social roles to which he had committed himself – husband

and father, physician and psychiatrist, researcher and scientist, with a family and patients to care for, and a professional reputation to uphold. Society expected him to contribute to its welfare. In 1916 he wrote a little paper, 'Adaptation, Individuation, and Collectivity,' to help sort out this crisis.

When Jung chose individuation and abandoned fulfillment of his roles on the terms in which tradition demanded he fulfill them, he incurred what he called tragic guilt, requiring expiation. Seeing his dilemma in the extreme terms of sin and redemption, he thought that the person who chooses individuation over conformity was thereby obligated to give back to society something equal to the value of that which his choice denies it:

> When, therefore, the demand for individuation appears in analysis under the guise of an exceptionally strong transference, it means farewell to personal conformity with the collective, and stepping over into solitude, into the cloister of the inner self. Only the shadow of the personality remains in the outer world. Hence the contempt and hate that comes from society. But inner adaptation leads to the conquest of inner realities, from which values are won for reparation of the collective. Individuation remains a pose so long as no positive values are created. . . . For the existing society is always of absolute importance as the point of transition through which all world development passes, and it demands the highest collaborative achievement from every individual.
>
> (Jung 1916/1976: 1097–8)

Tension between individuality and group membership is universal, but perhaps Jungian communities have an especially hard time with this dialectic, making it a dichotomy, because in his later work Jung expressed his consistent and unresolved mistrust of collectives. Many Jungian societies were founded by a generation of Jungians who imitated and even extolled his one-sided attitude. Perhaps one-sidedness was required for Jung to develop and realize his intuitive vision of the structure of the psyche. Ultimately, the notion that the individuating individual owes something to the collective was not one of the seed concepts that Jung developed and refined as part of his scientific work, although it appears with informal mention as a necessary element of individuation here and there in his work. The paper itself was published posthumously by Spring Publications in 1970 (Jung 1916/1970).

In the early 1980s when I first read Jung's 1916 paper, his idea that the individual owes something to the collective made sense to me; it influenced the attitudes I adopted toward my own inner development and my subsequent activity as an analyst. I embraced the notion of stewardship for the Jungian community, and I wanted to understand not only what structured and motivated my own psyche but also that of the collective to which I had attached myself. I wanted to understand why, as a group, even analysts could and did behave as Jung predicted. 'Thus a hundred intelligent people together make one hydrocephalus' (Jung 1935/1976: 1314).

W. R. Bion articulates the experience of profound anxiety with which the human mind greets any radical idea, especially one presaging what he calls 'catastrophic change,' toward which anxiety is a natural reaction, since its acceptance and integration leads to deep and lasting psychological change. That is why the mystic and the genius are threatening to the group and why it has such difficulty containing or nurturing them (Bion 1970/1993: 62–71). Something similar to the anxiety and tumult experienced by groups on a collective scale when faced with radical new ideas and intuitions, as described by Bion, might have been experienced by Jung on a personal scale. Could Jung also have intuitively sensed the collective's fundamental antagonism to his ideas, because his ideas threatened the status quo?

Bion sheds light on the underlying dynamics of a group's vulnerability to unconscious forces with his concept of the group unconscious and his observations of the tendency of its constituents to behave as if there were only one group mind determining its nature and purpose – which he called the 'basic assumption group' (Bion 1961/1989). The similarity of basic assumption groups, as collective psychological phenomena, to Jung's personal complex in individual psychology, was readily apparent (Kirsch and Spradlin 2006: 357–80). In Bion's framework, a group that is functioning effectively to accomplish its task is called a work group. Its counterpart in personal psychology is the ego.

Is a group capable of individuation and, if so, what model aids this development? The anthropologist Victor Turner, studying the Ndembu of northwestern Zambia, observed that initiatory rituals serve a social as well as symbolic function, 'generating a "meta"-structural modality of social interrelationship which I call "*communi*tas"' (Turner 1969/1995: xvi). Community is 'a differentiated, culturally structured, segmented, and often hierarchical system of institutional positions,' whereas *communitas* 'presents society as an undifferentiated, homogenous whole, in which individuals confront one another integrally, and not as "segmentalized" into statuses and roles' (ibid.: 96). Parallel to and concurrent with the structures he designated as belonging to community were the rituals that initiated its people into a collective attitude that valued, supported and sustained a socially marginal state which he called liminality, a term borrowed from the anthropologist van Gennep (ibid.: 94).

A colleague introduced Turner's ideas to our local Jungian society (Tresan 2002). Describing and differentiating community and *communitas* according to Turner's classification and outlining how a Jungian society is itself defined by its liminality – since a basic tenet of Analytical Psychology is striving "to know ourselves vis-à-vis universal images, the collective unconscious," hence its dual structure, community and *communitas* – Tresan emphasized the importance of making conscious and cultivating the relationship between these two concurrent psycho-social modalities.

Ideally, a reasonably well-functioning Jungian community – one which dedicates itself to elucidating and making conscious whatever unconscious phenomena are accessible to the grasp of its understanding – might deliberately shelter and value both the individual and groups of individuals who choose to limit their participation in traditional roles in community life and instead, on behalf of the community and in the spirit of *communitas*, surrender to a state of liminality, whereby fresh insight may arise. In theory, a community might even be capable of individuation. Reality, as we well know, often falls short of what is theoretically possible, but still a vision of what might be achieved can serve to inspire and orient us toward behaviors that will promote realization of a goal.

What features, then, constitute community and *communitas*, and how are they related? A Jungian society, in community-mode, establishes a hierarchy that serves both executive and ritual functions. Under the rubric of community come such executive functions as the maintenance of the society's history and records, by-laws, policies and procedures, and the establishment and oversight of its professional standards. It also is responsible for Jungian theory and method, insofar as they are required to meet external standards for professional services or membership. Its ritual functions include designation of elders to oversee executive and teaching activities, the creation of and adherence to the society's mission statement, and expression of its ethos and norms of behavior. Concurrently, the society's members participate in the *communitas*-mode, best described by a term from the *I Ching*, 'holding firm' (Wilhelm [trans.] 1950: 104). 'Holding firm' has three functions: containment; nourishment; and restraint. A society that values *communitas* will embrace and hold firmly both its innocent and its sage, tolerating foolishness and wisdom, making room for both. In a nurturing role, it encourages the generativity of its members and sustains the spirit and soul of the society's mission. *Communitas* restrains by insisting upon respect for the boundaries and rights both of the collective and the individual and by maintaining reciprocity with the genius/mystic. Members of a Jungian *communitas* value subjective meaning, not-knowing, irrationality, and the transcendent function and make use of Jung's synthetic method for heuristic and therapeutic purposes. They strive to further Jung's theory and method, enhancing knowledge about and supporting liminality and its dynamics.

Still, without effective ways to understand and address the ordinary and inevitable disruptions in group life, one is quickly reduced to silence, frustration, discouragement, or cynicism – not that any form of understanding is proof against such unconscious and natural emotional reactions. Jung's psychology offers little practical assistance here. Did he forget or repress his early respectful awe of the just demands of the collective upon the individual? One must look outside Jungian theory for understanding, and once again, W. R. Bion suggests useful models. His observations about the unconscious forces manifesting in group behavior, when translated into and amplified by Jungian language and theory, offer ways to think about community which can further our comprehension of collective life. Also, Bion's thoughts on anxiety and group process contribute to furthering Jungian theory (Kirsch and Spradlin 2006: 366–7).

Since anxiety is a universal of life, a group process facilitator's role is similar to that of the personal analyst, i.e., to make conscious the anxiety which arises within the process and which is unconsciously warded off with stereotyped thinking and behavior, as the individual or group reaches for a firm certainty to reduce anxiety. Jung called this typical and common response a personal complex; Bion, observing the phenomenon in groups, called it a basic assumption; we also might call it a group complex. A similar dynamic applies in the case of the cultural complex (Singer and Kimbles 2004). Often noting the anxiety and describing its character will get the analysis or group process back on track with its analytic work. At the core of each personal complex lies an archetype, wherein lies its growth potential; in addition to acting pathologically (e.g., by co-opting rational ego functions) the complex gives access through the archetypal root to the creative potential of the collective unconscious. Jung's synthetic method of therapy addresses just this edge (Jung 1953: 79–87). Might we not speculate that the same principle applies in group life? Buried in the group's unconscious response to anxiety – a group complex – is a new way to look at the situation with imagination and a chance to generate new adaptations. In this capacity the group can raise its ego-like functioning to a higher level. Where does *communitas* stand in relationship to this formulation?

Tresan (2002) thinks Jungian communities are defined by liminality and believes that 'by the very tenets of our psychology we strive to know ourselves vis-à-vis the backdrop of eternal images.' Might we then learn, in the spirit of *communitas*, to explore the growing edge of our group complexes, to look for the potential of Self in the unconscious assumptions we consistently share as a collective, when faced with incipient change as our community develops? We also need effective language and functional models to recognize and hold firm the boundaries around and between the two social modes. I suggest expanding our Jungian lexicon to include the group ego, the group complex, and the liminal group, with the latter (*communitas*) serving a function for the group ego (community) that is akin to the way we conceptualize anima's function in the ego/Self relationship. These concepts might inspire the Jungian group to separate and link its synchronic social functions, community and *communitas*, in a more conscious and discriminating manner. Their operative value for Jungian group life might be to inspire confidence in the face of the typically confused excitement and/or deadening hopelessness that usually attends the appearance of a group complex, whenever very new ideas or plans for new programs are proposed. Rather than try to eliminate or suppress anxiety and conflict we are advised by Jung to keep them in consciousness. We may remind ourselves that controversy may lead to new or deepened psychological insights and theoretical models, when there is genuine confrontation.

These concepts also might help to demystify analytic training. I have facilitated numerous mandatory group process seminars over the past fifteen years and have observed that candidates were more accepting of and began to apply themselves more effectively in the seminars once group process theory and methods were elucidated and linked to Jungian ideas in our paper (Kirsch and Spradlin 2006: 357–380). Knowing why and wherefore they were meeting was essential to that shift. They began to grasp the ritualistic importance of meeting in a structured way, so as to focus their attention to the study of their own group's unconscious processes. One candidate wrote that after reading the paper, 'I could breathe in a little more deeply, having found an anchor to steady me some as I entered into what seemed like an uncharted deep mysterious sea of analytic training.' For another:

> It reduced my anxiety about participating in the group because it made sense to me that whatever was happening for me in the moment had meaning for the group as a whole . . . and [it] helped me to think about how my experience in the group might in fact relate not only to the immediate group as a whole, but to the larger Jungian community within which we are embedded.

Group process seminars in analytic training might be framed as an initiatory ritual, introducing the candidate to the Jungian community as a place where liminality is valued, both individually and within the context of collective experience. They already offer a container for introducing the behavioral norms of the community, thus preparing the candidate to enter its activities as a necessary participant. In the atmosphere of a learning community candidates as well as analysts might accept personal responsibility for the health and well-being of the whole, of which we are all members.

One candidate is already moving in that direction:

> [My] fleeting experiences of the transcendent function at play in the training setting, when the . . . group is able to . . . listen for the voice, no matter how muted, of the alive collective soul beneath disparate (and at times, desperate) positions of particular individuals and groups [make it] clear to me that there is an ethical imperative to attempt to hold this view, even though I struggle to do so and find that pragmatic

demands often require action before the deeper voice of the group seems audible to me.[1]

Our efforts to understand and articulate what was alive but inchoate in the minds of Jung and our Jungian forebears, whose ideas often sound mystical to the uninitiated, does not weaken the numinous dimension of individual analytic experience or of group life. Nor does deepening our appreciation of what group life might offer us alter the premium we place upon individuals and individuation. Rather, we are strengthened when we have objective terms that also serve as living symbols in the process of coming to know ourselves. Words may also heal. We also might begin to consider the impact of all that we say and do on behalf of and in critical assessment of collective life and Jungian theory, considering our words and actions in light of Jung's perception that '. . . the existing society is always of absolute importance as the point of transition through which all world development passes, and it demands the highest collaborative achievement from every individual' (Jung 1916/1976: 452).

Bibliography

Bion, W. R. (1961/1989) *Experiences in Groups*, London: Tavistock/Routledge.
—— (1970/1993) "The Mystic and the Group," in *Attention and Interpretation*, London: Karnak, 62–71.
Jung, C. G. (1916/1970) *Two Posthumous Papers: 1. Adaptation, 2. Individuation and Collectivity*, New York: Spring Publications.
—— (1916/1976) "Adaptation, Individuation, Collectivity," in *The Symbolic Life*, *CW 18*, para. 1097–1098.
—— (1935/1976) "The Tavistock Lectures (1935)," in *The Symbolic Life*, *CW 18*, para. 1314.
—— (1953) "Two Essays on Analytical Psychology," *CW 7*, pp. 79–87.
Kirsch, J. and Spradlin, S. (2006) "Group Process in Jungian Analytic Training and Institute Life," *Journal of Analytical Psychology*, 51: 3, 357–380.
Singer, T. and Kimbles, S. (eds.) (2004) *The Cultural Complex*, Hove and New York: Brunner-Routledge.
Tresan, D. "Victor Turner," unpublished paper delivered to the Board of Governors of the C. G. Jung Institute of San Francisco on March 14, 2002.
Turner, V. (1969/1995) *The Ritual Process*, New York: Aldine de Gruyter.
Wilhelm, R. (trans.) (1950) *I Ching*, Princeton: Princeton University Press, Bollingen Series XIX, p. 104.

Note

1 I am grateful to the candidates of the C. G. Jung Institute of San Francisco who offered their comments.

Chapter 20

Jung and the world of the fathers

Thomas B. Kirsch

Andrew Samuels has been one of the most prolific and creative Jungian analysts of his generation or for that matter of any generation of analysts. Over the past more than 30 years he has been writing, lecturing, editing, and promoting new ideas on analytical psychology around the world. One of his many areas of interest has been the role of the father in contemporary times. Andrew began his professional interests in the 'father' in order to balance the over-emphasis on the mother-child relationship. His interests have shifted from the personal father relationship to the issue of male authority and to the collective authority of the father as seen in politics. Andrew has been passionately interested in sexuality, gender and how these patterns are expressed in both men and women. I am pleased to present this greatly revised lecture given at the Institute for Humanities in Salado, Texas, in 2001, to honor Andrew as a great friend and colleague on the occasion of his 60th birthday.

The role of the father in psychoanalysis was first prominently discussed in Freud's *Interpretation of Dreams* (Freud 1994). In this book Freud goes through his own self-analysis and discovers the universality of the Oedipus complex. Essentially, the Oedipus complex describes the father–son conflict and how both compete for the love of the mother. In Freud's description the mother remains relatively inert, whereas the main activity takes place between the father and son. Most of the early advocates of psychoanalysis had primary issues related to the father and thus were attracted to Freud's writings. In early classical psychoanalysis the mother issues were generally of secondary importance. This is a gross generalization and, like any generalization, has many exceptions. However, many of the early pioneers in psychoanalysis were attracted to the authority of Freud as a father figure. This was true for Jung, who was looking for a father that he could look up to. Freud gave Jung the image of the father of strong conviction and moral courage, which his own father had lacked.

Jung's father had died while his son was a medical student. They had spent many years fruitlessly arguing about the nature of God, and in Jung's own words:

In the end we abandoned them, each burdened with his own specific feeling of inferiority. Theology had alienated my father and me from one another. I felt that I had once again suffered a fatal defeat, though I sensed I was not alone. He was lonely and had no friend to talk with. He struggled desperately to keep his faith. I was shaken and outraged at once, because I saw how hopelessly he was entrapped by the church and its theological thinking. They had blocked all avenues by which he might have reached God directly, and then faithlessly abandoned him. (Jung 1963: 93)

One can see from this quote that Jung despaired at the emotional distance which existed between himself and his father. He loved and respected his father deeply, but he never felt that he was able to make a real relationship with him. This is in large part why Freud became so important to Jung. Also, Jung's experience with his father influenced his strong desire to connect with theologians of all denominations in an attempt to compensate for the distance that had existed between himself and his father.

Jung increasingly became interested in the role of the mother in psychoanalysis. He began to study the fantasies of a woman, Miss Miller, whose case had been written up by the psychologist Theodore Flournoy in Geneva. Jung studied her fantasies from Flournoy's paper, without ever seeing her, in connection with readings in mythology. He came to the conclusion that regression to the personal mother and then to the world of the archetypal mothers was behind her symptomatology, which he referred to as a 'prelude to schizophrenia.' Jung published this work as 'The Transformation of Libido' in *Symbols of Transformation* (Jung 1967). Freud could not accept two points which Jung described in this work. The first one was the importance of the mother in the development of the child, and the second one was Jung's widening of the meaning of libido. Freud hypothesized libido as sexual and aggressive energy, whereas for Jung the concept of libido was more simply defined as energy or *interest*. According to Jung, primary energy or libido can be directed towards hunger, sex, aggression, culture, religious feelings, and each is seen as primary and not derivative of the other. Where libido is directed depends upon the needs of the individual and the culture. Freud found that in 19th-century Vienna sexual needs had been repressed but that did not mean that in other cultures libido could not flow primarily into other channels. Jung was fond of saying that he had been brought up in a rural area where sexuality was expressed easily, but where the libido flow in other directions could be more problematic.

Much has been written about Jung's relationship to women, but less attention has been paid to his relationship to men. The lore has it that Jung was extremely comfortable with women but that he had difficulty with men.

Let us look at who were some of the men around Jung. On the professional side, the 'crown prince' was Professor C. A. Meier. Meier was a psychiatrist who had trained at the Burghölzli and who had had analysis with Jung in the late 1920s. He became Jung's assistant, and during the 1930s he was Jung's honorary secretary when Jung was president of the International Society for Medical Psychotherapy. This was a stormy time politically, and all the correspondence had both Jung's name and Meier's name on it. Because of the allegations against Jung which were made at that time in relationship to his contact with the Nazis, there has been an eagerness to read this correspondence. This period in Jung's life is now being studied, including the correspondence which Jung and Meier had with the Nazified German section of the International Medical Psychotherapy Association. Jung and by association Meier have been criticized for their connection to this association.

Meier continued to be close to Jung until the time of Jung's retirement in 1941 from the Swiss Federal Technical Institute, also known as the ETH (Eidgenössische Technische Hochschule). The ETH is a prestigious Science and Technology Institute which produced many famous Nobel Prize winners on its faculty. As crown prince it was thought that Meier would take over Jung's position after his retirement. Jung did not recommend Meier for the position, which angered Meier greatly, but he was appointed to the position without Jung's specific recommendation. Another incident occurred on the Lake of Zürich when Jung and Meier were on a boat and Meier was rowing. Jung was telling Meier how and where to row (Wagner 1983). Meier got angry and said to Jung that he should do the rowing then. Their personal relationship ended, but they continued to work together professionally until Jung's death. Meier became the first president of the Jung Institute, organized the International Association for Analytical Psychology, and followed in Jung's footsteps at the ETH. I was in analysis with Meier during the late 1950s and would never have guessed that this situation existed. Meier continued to practice, teach, and administer as a student of analytical psychology for the remainder of his professional life.

Jung had an earlier assistant, H. G. Baynes, an English physician who came for analysis in 1919 (Jansen 2003). Although Baynes spent much time in Zürich during the 1920s, he lived and practiced as an analyst in London. Baynes was the founder and leader of Analytical Psychology in the UK, which became the second center after Zürich. As Baynes and Jung lived apart from one another, their relationship had a different quality to it. Baynes looked to Jung for advice on a number of personal matters, and he continued to do so until his untimely death in 1943. Baynes was the person who organized the safari to Africa in 1925. He was an extraverted feeling type, gave numerous talks to various professional groups, and was active in promoting Jung's psychology. Although he was often in Jung's shadow, the two men remained close both professionally and personally.

Another very important professional son was Erich Neumann, a German Jewish physician who, with his wife Julia, was in analysis in Zurich from 1933 to 1934. They then emigrated to Palestine where they both practiced until their respective deaths. After the war Neumann returned to Zürich each summer, where Jung made himself readily available. Neumann became a yearly lecturer at the Eranos conferences, and his work on the developmental stages of archetypal development interested Jung greatly. Jung felt that Neumann's work was a continuation of his own pioneering efforts in the field of theory of archetypes. The women around Jung were jealous of the time that Jung spent with Neumann. Jung's physical energy had lessened after his 1944 heart attack, but he often had the energy for Neumann. Neumann died in November 1960 from a rare form of cancer.

Other men in this first generation of professional Jungian analysts include Gerhard Adler, James Kirsch, Joseph Henderson, Jo Wheelwright, and Michael Fordham. All of the above mentioned – except Fordham – had their primary analysis with Jung and based their own analytic practice on their experience with Jung. Fordham, a child psychiatrist and someone who did not have his analysis with Jung, was heavily influenced by the theories and practices of Melanie Klein and Donald Winnicott. He became the founder of a Jungian developmental model heavily influenced by psychoanalysis.

On the family level Jung had one son, Franz, and four daughters. Franz became an architect, and he had many of the physical features of his father. Franz helped his father with the design and building of the tower at Bollingen. I had a chance to have many conversations with Franz late in his life. He bemoaned the fact that his father had not encouraged him more to become an analyst. Instead, his father left him alone with his career choices, which was not really what he wanted. It was extremely hard to be the son of such a famous man. One day he took us out to Bollingen for a visit. He complained lightly that almost every day there were visitors, mainly Americans, who came out looking for the Bollingen Tower. He, or whichever members of the family were there, would have to tell the visitors that the Tower was private property and could not be visited. Shortly after telling the story, a middle-aged American couple came looking for Bollingen, and they asked Franz where it was. He had to tell them that it was a private house and could not be visited. I am sure they did not realize that they were talking to the son of Jung. After Jung's death Franz moved into his father's house, and he became the executor of the Jung estate. This turned out to be a very big job, and it included dealing with translation rights, publishing issues, the use of Jung's name in the theater, access to unpublished material, and miscellaneous other issues. It kept Franz quite busy. I think that it also helped him to work out some of his earlier disappointment with his father.

A foundation was formed in 1981, named the Erbengemeinschaft C. G. Jung, to adapt to the growing size of the Jung family and to deal with the continuing issues related to the Jung estate (Hoerni 2007). An executive committee was formed consisting of one member from each family of the five Jung children. Ulrich Hoerni, an architect by training, had been the president of this trust until its dissolution in 2007. Two other important members are Peter Jung, a psychiatrist, and Andreas Jung, an architect, who has been living in his grandfather's house since 1975 and has been the archivist and librarian. The Erbengemeinschaft had outlived its usefulness, and so a new foundation specifically relating to the ongoing publishing interests, which are many, was formed. Ulrich Hoerni is the chairperson of the new foundation, and both Peter and Andreas have withdrawn. They both had spent considerable time and energy in the past, and it was time for the next generation to take responsibility for the present and future. This new generation no longer has a personal relationship to Jung, so this marks a real transition.

One can see from this brief description of Jung's relationship to his male followers, his father, and to his only son, that he had difficulties in this area of his life.

Moreover, I have only lightly touched on the Freud–Jung relationship which definitely had a father–son quality to it. So much has been written about the Freud–Jung relationship, whereas these other male-to-male relationships are less well known. It does appear that Jung was more comfortable with women. It must have been very difficult for a man to find his independent authority in relationship to Jung. Jung was brilliant and charismatic, but he also had quite a temper which could hamper relationships. We see a glimpse of that in Jung's relationship to Meier. If one lived in Zürich, it would have been especially difficult to live under Jung's shadow. Those men who lived away from Zürich had an easier time with Jung's authority, but even there the transference to Jung was extremely powerful. In my experience, the one member of that first generation around Jung who seemed to have negotiated this issue the best was Joe Henderson. Henderson was one of those who terminated his analysis normally and did not have it truncated either by the war, or running out of money, or for any other external reason. He finished his analysis in 1938 and returned to practice first in New York, and then for so many decades in San Francisco. So many others left Zürich for external reasons before they were ready and were left with unresolved issues with regard to Jung. This was true for both men and women.

Jung was not an easy person to be around, especially for men. He was not comfortable in the role of father, and it showed in his complex relationship to many of the men who were significant in his life. Although Jung had difficulties with men, he had male-to-male relationship which lasted many years. He was in a father role in many of these relationships, and although he had a complex relationship to being a father, he never-theless accepted this responsibility throughout his life.

Bibliography

Freud, S. (1994) *The Interpretation of Dreams*, New York: Random House, originally published in German on November 4, 1899.

Hoerni, U. (2007) personal communication.

Jansen, D. B. (2003) *Jung's Apprentice*, Einsiedeln, Switzerland: Daimon Verlag.

Jung, C. G. (1963) *Memories, Dreams, Reflections*, A. Jaffé (ed.), R. and C. Winston (trans.), New York: Random House.

Jung, C. G. (1967) "The Transformation of Libido," in *Symbols of Transformation*, 2nd edn, *Collected Works*, vol. 5, Princeton: Princeton University Press.

Wagner, S. and G. (1983) *Matter of Heart*, DVD, Los Angeles: C. G. Jung Institute of Los Angeles.

Chapter 21

Citizenship and subjectivity

Lynne Layton

It is impossible to measure the influence that Andrew Samuels' work and person have had on my own thinking, so I must content myself here to focus on just a few points of influence. While I have been politically 'conscious' since my college years, which coincided with resistance to the Vietnam War and with the beginnings of what came to be known as second wave feminism, once I turned from an academic career to clinical practice, it was not always very clear to me how I might bring my politically and my psychodynamically informed selves together. Many colleagues who are politically left argued with me that the clinic simply isn't the place for politics, that what we do is of a different order, but my academic training had made all too clear the many ways that mainstream politics parade as the 'non-political.' So it has been with great relief and admiration that I have followed Andrew's writings over the years. Andrew has not only taught us that therapists deal constantly with political material in sessions, but he has pried open for us the multiple ways one can think about the political. Equally important, he always teaches us new ways to access the political lives of our selves and our patients (most recently in his online discussion of Muriel Dimen's paper on how money functions in the clinical setting, June 2008). Andrew is not afraid to say, look, here's how you do it, here are the kinds of questions you can ask to learn about the political psyche and its development within relational matrices. This directness about how to access the political is an invaluable gift he has given to clinicians.

I think that perhaps the greatest influence has been the way Andrew's work has deepened my awareness that loving well and working well, those Freud-approved indicators of mental health, need to be supplemented with some kind of acknowledgement of our relationship to our fellow beings and the common space we inhabit, a sense of mutual interdependence that reaches beyond the familial sphere to the broader social sphere of citizenship. I have long had the uneasy feeling that clinicians' collusion with the culturally fostered split between the psychic and the social might produce healthier versions of narcissism rather than deeper engagements with the ways we construct our 'selves' in hierarchical relation to other social selves and thereby become implicated in the suffering of others in ways we know little about and perhaps want to continue to know little about (see Layton 1998, 2005, 2009).

Clinical work unravels these constructions within the realms of intimacy and work, but it too often sustains the split between the private and the public sphere by not picking up on patients' attachments to relational matrices that lie beyond their intimate sphere. In this contribution to the Festschrift, I would like to offer some of the work that I have done on this theme. In this work, I have tried to extend Andrew's thinking about how the political enters the clinic by focusing on the moment-to-moment interactions between conscious and unconscious minds that have each been shaped by hierarchical cultural norms of sexism, racism, classism, etc. In what follows, I explore the way a dominant US norm that insists on the separation of individuals from their 'political psyche' generates unconscious conflict and how this shared conflict plays out in unconscious collusions between therapist and patient that shore up the very social reality that has engendered pain in the first place (see also Layton 2002, 2006a).

Clinical vignette: work and love and the passion for civic life

In 'Attacks on Linking: The Unconscious Pull to Dissociate Individuals from their Social Context' (Layton 2006b), I wrote about a dream a patient had just after the Senate vote to go or not to go to war against Iraq. In the dream, she wondered whether or not to tell her state senator her views on what is currently going on politically in American life. In exploring the dream with her, I found myself struggling throughout the session against the urge to close off this inquiry with an interpretation that would reduce what she was saying to the kind of psychological insight that separates the psychic from the social. This experience revealed to me my own resistance to linking the psychic and the social, a resistance of which I was largely unaware. Fighting my urge to interpret enabled the two of us to discover that there are realms beyond those of work and love that are clinically relevant.

Here are the dreams:

> *Dream #1*: She is in the back seat of a car with someone else. John Kerry is outside the car and he's in a wheelchair. She lets him into the car and wonders if she should use the opportunity to tell him what she thinks about what's going on politically.

> *Dream #2*: She's with a group of people and they have to flee. She's supposed to make a fire by rubbing things together and it works. She's

very surprised that it worked and feels good about herself. But the fire is going to burn everything up and she's anxious that it will all burn before she and the others figure out what they need to take with them to start over.

I asked for her associations to the first dream and asked what she would want to tell the senator, who had recently declared his interest in running for President. She began to talk about her political opinions, that she doesn't like what's going on and that she's been annoyed with Kerry because he wasn't sufficiently critical of the Iraq war. Her wondering about whether or not she should say something to him made me associate to what we'd recently been talking about: that it is difficult for her to make herself accountable for things. A psychic dilemma we've long looked at involves her tendency either to give everything over to another, to make that other all-powerful, or to take it all on herself and be unable to ask for help. Often she feels that she's not accountable for things such as the upkeep of her house or her business; she puts herself in a child position, hoping the adults will get the job done. I said something about this dilemma, but I also thought to myself that I'd like to hear more about what she wants to tell Kerry, and when I allowed for that she began to go more deeply into what she feels about the state of the country, evincing a level of passion and a state of conviction that I rarely have glimpsed in her.

Passionlessness, an unlived life, has been her chief complaint. As she began to get more passionate, she pulled her legs up on the couch and sat cross-legged. She looked at me and hesitantly asked: can I really talk about this? I asked her why not. She wasn't sure if it was a proper therapy topic. I assured her that it is certainly a legitimate topic. I told her that I want to know what she's passionate about, and I could see that she feels deeply about this. As I said that, I realized I should just let her talk without jumping in with psychological interpretations, that jumping in and inter-rupting her experience of passion would in fact repeat her original wounds. For, in childhood, her spontaneous passions of all kinds were often found wanting and even mocked. But also, I realized that I in fact was struggling with the same question she asked: is this a therapy topic? In the moment, I didn't think that we might have explored her question further and perhaps understood more about her doubt. At that moment, I was wondering more about my own doubt. I know her politics are left of center, as are mine, and it is perhaps knowing this that made me mistakenly feel that what she was going to say was known territory, that I was just indulging my own wish to hear her bash the Bush regime and the Iraq War. She broke into my reverie when she asked if it was all right to have her feet up on the couch like that – she said she was thinking about that on the way over: is there a couch etiquette? I wasn't sure what to make of this sudden concern, but in retro-spect I wonder about the meaning of the associative sequence. Does speaking about one's political convictions in therapy carry the same kind of taboo of impurity or of being uncivilized as does putting one's feet on the furniture? Was there a connection between her child-like attitude toward political responsibility and her child-like feelings about putting her feet on mommy's couch? Was she simply doing all in her power to interrupt her *own* experience of passion?

She went on to say that she would tell Kerry that she feels that everything she grew up believing about America was being taken away from her, all the values she learned, like doing unto others. She began to cry and I asked what was upsetting her. Crying more intensely, she wailed that she feels betrayed. This is a woman who rarely is able to cry in another's presence, who, in fact, has spoken many times about her longing to be able to express feelings while with me in the room.

She then brought in the second dream, associating to what she called a Jewish theme, 'maybe like there was a pogrom.' Her association to the fire burning was that something very bad was happening and it will be too late by the time we realize what it is. Again, I thought about what was happening to her business, which was falling apart, and felt pulled to interject something about that; but I had the sense that while her passion about what is happening politically may have had multiple psychic sources and motivations, it would be a mistake to understand what she was saying as mere displacement. In part, I did not interpret in this other frame because I share her feelings that what the country stands for is being rapidly dismantled; her passionate feelings of betrayal are clearly valid in their own right. I also just wanted to see where she would go next.

Still crying, she repeated, with more intensity, that everything she feels America stands for is being betrayed and she feels helpless to do anything about it. I asked her to say more about her feelings of helplessness. She said that she supposes she could write letters but she doesn't. I asked her why not. She answered: last night she got home and her partner wanted to watch the baseball game and she didn't. She wanted to sit outside and read the newspaper (the day before she had told me she stopped reading the newspaper because it was too depressing). And then she talked about her partner, who is very left-wing and very voluble about it. Apparently *she's* been writing letters. At this point, a link between the psychic and the social became clearer – in the face of her partner's very big passion, my patient's passion drains away and she detaches, letting the partner carry the political feelings and political activity. My patient doesn't feel quite the same as her partner on these issues, but her feeling of helplessness seems to come from a sense that the partner owns this realm because her passion and anger are so much bigger. I thought about Bush's 70 per cent approval rating (in that period, 2003) and wondered if she might be allowing the other side to own civic life because the other side is louder and so deaf to dissent. Again, a part of me was thinking that, like all other roads, this political road led us back to a particular psychic conflict, the one that gets in the way of her feeling like an autonomous and passionate being. Her parents were also louder, and also deaf to dissent. My first association, the one about accountability, fit into this larger repetition scenario, for she long ago had made a conscious and unconscious pact with her parents that went something like this: 'I'll do as you say but then you're in charge: I refuse to take any responsibility myself for my life.' And yet, again, I felt that we were both discovering something new that day, which I stated at the end: that her passion for a certain kind of America is not a lesser passion than the ones we had been exploring, the passion to work well and to love well. Indeed, the parental interference with her autonomy and passion had led to a kind of isolationist machoism, which coexisted with smolderingly resentful feelings of helpless passivity. All too frequently the resentment issued in acts of passive aggression. Her character style perhaps well illustrates one typical way that American ideology's unlinking of the individual and the social is psychically enacted.

The session ended with what I consider to be an enactment worth thinking about, one I'm a bit embarrassed to admit to: I told her about some political letter-writing activities on the Internet of which I was aware. She smiled and left. I think that through the session she was consistently inviting me to be larger and louder, as when she asked me about whether it was okay to talk about this, okay to put her feet up on the couch. Each time I resisted making an interpretation, I think I was resisting that pull to be larger – although I *did* give permission rather than ask why she sought it. And then at the end, in suggesting something she might do, I went large, and I am not sure why.

The next day she told me how good the day before had felt to her. She was quite surprised and a little embarrassed that her political feelings had made her cry – she doesn't think that most people take these political things so personally. She'd have to describe herself as in some way an innocent, she said, and that is embarrassing. And when I asked what about the session had made her feel so good, she told me that it was because she allowed herself to follow my questions without resistance, that there was something about my encouraging her to keep speaking about it that had put her in touch with her feelings and enabled her to go on expressing them without shame. My sense is that what enabled the passion to emerge, enabled her resistance to recede, was precisely my capacity to put a muzzle on my interpretive impulse. Here was the anti-enactment: shutting up made me less large which enabled her to come forward.

Again, what was striking to me about this hour was how hard I had to struggle to stay out of her way and simply let her feelings develop. I do not generally find myself having irresistible urges to cut in and interpret in my sessions with her. My guess is that this urgency reflected at least two things: (1) my anxiety that because I did not explore what Andrew (1993) calls the symbolic/intrapsychic/transferential aspects of my patient's speech, I wasn't being a proper analyst. Had I expressed the doubts I had at the point when the patient asked if it was a proper therapy topic, we might both have unconsciously colluded with the social norm that keeps the psychic and the social separate; and (2) the sense of urgency about jumping in may well have come from an unconscious pull (hers? mine? ours?) to re-enact this patient's repetition compulsion – to quash her spontaneous gestures by finding them not quite right, to play the larger one and make her small.

Some months after the reported vignette, this patient, who is gay, became terrifically excited by politics and made the first political gesture of her life: she sent out an email to friends and acquaintances with a copy of an article a straight woman had written about gay marriage. The writer, who was about to be married, had a gay brother, and the article revolved around her conflicted feelings about her own right to marry and the state's attempts to limit the rights of her brother. My patient noted that in the past she might have sent the article around with an introduction such as, 'Here's an article you might find interesting.' But this time she wrote a preamble in which she urged people to call their representatives and senators or just to intervene when they hear homophobic conversations. She spoke in that session of feeling alive, and ended the session with the statement, 'I'm pumped.'

In splitting the individual from the social, bourgeois ideology brings about an impoverishment of individuality in which dependence is repudiated and difference not tolerated. This dynamic leaves so many of us vulnerable to manipulation by media, government, advertising, public relations – even as we desperately try to assert our individuality and autonomy. Rather than enable people to live happier lives as 'free individuals,' I, like Andrew, feel strongly that clinical theory and practice have to figure out how to reestablish the links between the psychic and the social that dominant ideologies work tirelessly to unlink.

I have always loved Andrew's oft-repeated sentiment that today's 'bad' practice can become tomorrow's cutting-edge practice. We have seen this happen time and again in the history of psychoanalysis. Andrew's work helps all of us withstand the slings and arrows of those who condescendingly dismiss our project by suggesting that it sullies psychoanalysis. As the foregoing vignette suggests, it seems to me that we expand our and our patients' vitality when we find ways to allow the passion for civic life to take its rightful place beside work and love in the clinic.

Bibliography

IARPP (June 2008) Online colloquium discussion of Dimen, M. (1994) "Money, love and hate. Contradiction and paradox in psychoanalysis," *Psychoanalytic Dialogues* 4, 1: 69–100.

Layton, L. (1998; reprinted 2004) *Who's That Girl? Who's That Boy? Clinical Practice Meets Postmodern Gender Theory*, Hillsdale, NJ: Analytic Press.

—— (2002) "Cultural hierarchies, splitting, and the heterosexist unconscious," in S. Fairfield, L. Layton, and C. Stack (eds), *Bringing the Plague. Toward a Postmodern Psychoanalysis*, New York: Other Press, pp. 195–223.

—— (2005) "Notes toward a non-conformist clinical practice," *Contemporary Psychoanalysis* 41: 419–429.

—— (2006a) "Racial identities, racial enactments, and normative unconscious processes," *Psychoanalytic Quarterly* LXVV, 1: 237–269.

—— (2006b) "Attacks on linking: the unconscious pull to dissociate individuals from their social context," in L. Layton, N.C. Hollander, and S. Gutwill (eds.), *Psychoanalysis, Class and Politics: Encounters in the Clinical Setting*, London: Routledge, pp. 107–117.

—— (2009) "Who's responsible? Our mutual implication in each other's suffering," *Psychoanalytic Dialogues* 19, 2: 105–120.

Samuels, A. (1993) *The Political Psyche*, New York and London: Routledge.

Chapter 22

Jung as a modern esotericist[1]

Roderick Main

Jung as scholar and practitioner of esotericism

C. G. Jung (1875–1961) was deeply interested in and influenced by the western esoteric tradition throughout his long professional life. At various times he wrote substantially about mystery religions (Jung 1911–12/1952; Noll 1992), astrology (Hyde 1992; Main 2004: 75–6), Gnosticism (Segal 1992), Kabbalah (see Drob 2000), and, most extensively of all, alchemy (Jung 1929–54, 1944, 1946, 1955–6; Marlan 2006). His work in each of these areas demonstrates an impressive breadth of reading, usually including primary sources and often in the original languages (especially where these are Latin or ancient Greek). His personal library of books on alchemy was probably among the best in the world, and towards the end of his life his familiarity with at least some periods of European alchemy (especially the seventeenth and eighteenth centuries) could have vied with that of professional historians of the topic. Indeed, Jung has sometimes received credit from historians of science for helping to rescue the subject of alchemy from obscurity (Holt 1987–8).

However, Jung's engagement with alchemy and other esoteric traditions, if it is to be considered scholarship, is scholarship of a particular kind. His aim is not to understand his subject matter for its own sake but to enrich the theory and method of analytical psychology: to provide a cultural amplification of his theories of archetypes, the collective unconscious, individuation, and the self, and a resource for the individual amplification of images arising in particular psychotherapeutic cases (cf. Clarke 1994: 51). If he provides illumination for the historian, this is almost a by-product of his primary psychological concern.

Is, then, Jung's engagement with the western esoteric tradition more that of an esoteric practitioner? There is certainly a sense in which he was a practitioner. He not only knew about astrology but from his early days as an analyst right through to his later days practised astrology, frequently casting horoscopes for patients in order to gain additional insights into their psychic situation (Jung 1973: 24, 475–6). He was not only familiar with techniques of visualisation used by alchemists and other esotericists but developed his own version of such techniques in the form of what he called 'active imagination' in which the subject concentrates on an image until the unconscious spontaneously produces a series of further images that unfold as a story (Jung 1935: par. 398). And he not only discussed the transformative process obscurely described by the alchemists but promoted an analogous process described both in imagery borrowed from the alchemists and in his own terminology as individuation (Jung 1944, 1946, 1955–6). In view of these activities, it is not surprising that Jung should have acquired in his lifetime the popular image of being a magician (Jaffé 1971: 123) or that he should even have seemed to some to be promoting an esoteric cult (Noll 1994).

The influence of Jung's interest in esotericism on the reception of his work

The perception of Jung as deeply involved in esotericism, whether as a scholar or as a practitioner, has greatly influenced the clinical, academic, popular, and esoteric reception of his psychological work. In clinical circles, Jung's interest in esotericism, with its implied move away from obviously scientific principles, has, since the time of Freud (1914), been one of the main reasons for the rejection of Jung's ideas. It is also a fault-line along which different categories of Jungians distinguish themselves or can be distinguished by others. For instance, Jung's esoteric interests figure more in classical traditions of Jungian thought, which stick close to Jung's own theoretical and practical orientation, than in developmental traditions, which have attempted to integrate Jungian ideas with post-Freudian psychoanalytic thought, such at the work of Klein and Bion (Samuels 1985).

At the academic level, Jung's esoteric interests are in principle an acceptable object of investigation for students of religion or historians of psychology, since Jungian psychology would there be scrutinised using the established methodologies of other disciplines. However, wherever Jungian psychology purports to provide the methodological or theoretical framework for a study, other academics easily become alienated. The Jungian esoteric emphases on correspondences, living nature, mediations between a seen and an unseen world, transmutation, and so on, which I shall discuss below, do not sit comfortably with the naturalistic, secular assumptions underlying most mainstream academic disciplines (cf. Main 2007). Nor does Jung's own 'scholarship' on esoteric topics, impressive though it is in its own ways, necessarily provide a sound basis for other scholars of esotericism. As already noted, Jung's scholarship is invariably informed by his own theoretical and psychotherapeutic aims rather than the aim of understanding esoteric traditions in their own terms.

At the popular level, the esoteric dimension of Jung's thought is a major factor contributing to its appeal. This is especially the case among those involved in New Age or alternative spiritualities who are interested in Jung's thought (Tacey 2001). Some explanation for this is provided by Wouter Hanegraaff's research demonstrating the essential continuity between western esotericism and the New Age movement (1998).

Finally, at the esoteric level itself, Jung's approach to esotericism has caused his work to be received in various ways. By some the work has been respected for its serious contributions to and inspirations for esoteric thought (Keane 2007). By others it has been perhaps rather cavalierly co-opted, because of Jung's wider cultural integration as a psychologist and psychotherapist and founder of an influential therapeutic tradition, in order to lend relatively mainstream respectability to traditions that are even more marginal (see Keane 2007: 9–11). By others again he has been rejected for psychologising traditions and practices that are concerned with divine and spiritual realities or for failing to recognise adequately the perennial truth behind diverse religious traditions (e.g., Burckhardt 2003). And by others yet again Jung's engagement with esotericism is acknowledged to be of some significance but that significance is considered to be limited. For instance, Jung is restrained by his psychological orientation and claimed empiricism from fully engaging in the interface between metaphysics and cosmology, which has been one of the main preoccupations of esotericists (Faivre 1994: 8).

Jung as an esotericist

Jung is, then, with good reason, perceived as deeply involved in esotericism, and this perception variously affects responses to his work. But does this amount to a case for seeing him as an esotericist in a sense that would be recognised by scholars of esotericism? The French scholar Antoine Faivre, in his classic formulation of esotericism (1994), identifies four essential and two non-essential characteristics. Jung's psychology evinces clear and substantial parallels with each one. The first essential characteristic is a worldview based on correspondences (Faivre 1994: 10). Jung's concept of synchronicity, which postulates that events that are not connected causally may nevertheless be connected through the meaning they jointly express, is by Jung's own account 'an updating of the obsolete concept of correspondence' (1951b: par. 995). Indeed, he names as forerunners of the idea of synchronicity several of the most influential figures of western esotericism – Hippocrates, Philo Judaeus, Plotinus, Pico della Mirandola, Agrippa von Nettesheim, Paracelsus – each of whom wrote either explicitly about correspondence theory or about related notions such as the 'sympathy of all things' and the relationship between microcosm and macrocosm (1952: pars. 924–35). Furthermore, Faivre himself invokes the Jungian notion of synchronicity when he writes that, in a worldview based on correspondences, 'The principles of noncontradiction and excluded middle of linear causality are replaced by those of the included middle and synchronicity' (1994: 10).

The second essential characteristic of esotericism is an account of nature as living: 'Multilayered, rich in potential revelations of every kind, [Nature] must be read like a book', writes Faivre (1994: 11). This assumption pervades Jung's work, from his early championing of vitalism over materialism in lectures to his student fraternity (1896–9: pars. 1–142) to his late work on synchronicity (1952: par. 864) and his appropriation of the alchemical metaphor of the *anima mundi* (the soul of the world) (for example, 1952: par. 931; 1955–6: par. 748).

The third essential characteristic of esotericism is the importance of imagination and mediations between a seen and an unseen world (Faivre 1994: 12–13). Relevant to this, Jung attaches central importance to the processes he terms active imagination and the transcendent function as well as to the symbolic and mythic content generated by those processes, all of which mediate between consciousness and the unconscious, the known and the unknown, the seen and the unseen (Jung [1916]/1957).

The fourth of the essential characteristics of esotericism is the experience of transmutation (Faivre 1994: 13–14). The parallel here is provided by Jung's core developmental process of individuation (1928b: pars. 266–406), as well as by his discussion of 'rebirth' (1940/1950), which describes the experience of a particular turning point within the process of individuation. Again, Faivre himself makes the connection between esoteric transmutation and Jungian individuation (1994: 107).

The first of the two non-essential characteristics of esotericism according to Faivre is 'the praxis of concordance' – the attempt to establish common denominators among different traditions in the hope of obtaining a superior illumination (Faivre 1994: 14). Jung, while never going as far as perennialist thinkers in asserting the existence of a primordial tradition, certainly sought in his investigations of non-western, pre-modern, and indeed esoteric traditions for common elements that would help him to articulate more clearly the archetypal core of human religious experience (see, for example, 1911–12/1952; 1944).

The second non-essential characteristic of esotericism is transmission – the passing on of knowledge from teacher to disciple, often by means of initiations (Faivre 1994: 14–15). The parallel here is that in Jungian psychology it is axiomatic that one cannot adequately analyse oneself; only those who have undergone a prescribed period of analysis with an already qualified analyst are eligible to become candidates for training to be analysts themselves (Jung 1951a: par. 237; 1946: 366).

Jung as a modern esotericist

On the basis of all these parallels, it is clear that Jung should qualify as an esotericist according to not just popular repute but a precise, scholarly definition. However, Jung's esotericism can be yet more narrowly defined.

The Dutch scholar of religions, Wouter Hanegraaff, has suggested that by the end of the nineteenth century western esotericism, as defined by Faivre, had been transformed by its reflection in what he calls the 'four "mirrors of secular thought": the new worldview of "causality", the new study of religions, the new evolutionism, and the new psychologies' (1998: 518). Hanegraaff's immediate concern is to explain New Age religion as a form of modern, secular esotericism. But his analysis applies equally well, if not more clearly, to Jung. Indeed, Hanegraaff discusses Jung at length as a modern esotericist and a direct link between western esotericism and the New Age movement (1998: 496–513). Most conspicuously, Jung's thought has been shaped by the new psychologies, which indeed constitute Jung's disciplinary base and of which his own work is an eminent instance. The new evolutionism has left its mark on Jung's psychology in his assumption that consciousness develops both phylogenetically (moderns are more developed than ancients who are more developed than primitives) and ontogenetically (individuating adults are more developed than non-individuating adults who are none the less more developed than children) (for example, 1911–12/1952: pars. 17, 21–7). Jung also made abundant use of the resources provided by the new study of religions, drawing on Hinduism, Buddhism, Taoism, Judaism, and Islam, as well as ancient Mediterranean religions and indigenous traditions of Europe, Africa, and North America, both to relativise the Christian context of his thought and to amplify many of his particular psychological concepts, such as archetypes, the self, individuation, synchronicity, opposites, and psychic reality (1928–54; 1963). Finally, the new worldview of 'causality' also deeply shaped Jung's psychology. On the one hand, he certainly acknowledged, in accord with Freud, that many psychic events and symptoms can be explained in terms of their causal history, often leading back to early childhood experiences, especially relating to sexuality. On the other hand, he considered, in disagreement with Freud, that many psychic events can alternatively or additionally be explained teleologically in terms of what they are developing towards (Jung 1928a) or synchronistically in terms of the pattern of meaning they exhibit in the present (Jung 1952). In developing his teleological and synchronistic viewpoints Jung had to struggle with the dominant worldview of causality, and this struggle is evident particularly in some of his writing where his esoteric interests are most in focus (Jung 1952).

Jung as a unique figure in the history of western esotericism

By Hanegraaff's criteria, Jung's work can reasonably be seen as that of not just an esotericist but a distinctively modern esotericist. Even more, Jung is not, according to Hanegraaff, simply one among many modern esotericists broadly similar in their outlooks, but is a unique figure in the history of western esotericism (1998: 505). Hanegraaff distinguishes between two forms of secularised esotericism. Both try to update esotericism in order to make it appear scientific and therefore acceptable within an increasingly secularised culture, but they do so in different ways. One way tries to incorporate the principle of causality, perceived to be the key to the successes of science. The principle of correspondences is retained but in a form blended with causal thinking. A prime example is Theosophy, which attaches special importance to the notion of *karma* because this notion on the one hand applies across all domains of reality, including the spiritual, and on the other hand translates into western terms as a principle of cause and effect. Other examples include Spiritualism and the occultism of such organisations as the Hermetic Order of the Golden Dawn. The other way of updating esotericism, exemplified by Jung, draws implicitly on German romantic *Naturphilosophie*. In this the notion of correspondences is retained without attempting to synthesise it with the principle of causality. Writes Hanegraaff:

> The significance of [Jung's] approach to esotericism is that it enabled him to appear 'scientific' while *avoiding* the necessity of compromising with the worldview of 'causality.' It is by building his psychology on a concept of science derived from Romantic *Naturphilosophie* (and opposed [better: complementary] to modern 'causality') that Jung may have succeeded in finding a way to 'update' traditional esotericism without disrupting its inner consistency. From the perspective of the historical study of esotericism, this makes him a unique figure.
>
> (1998: 505)

If Hanegraaff's distinction is correct, Jung's psychology and in particular his concept of synchronicity provide an intellectual framework for understanding how esoteric practices can be revived without having to be distorted in an attempt at accommodation with mainstream causal science. There are, indeed, indications of this move away from causal thinking in some recent work on astrology and other forms of divination specifically influenced by Jung's theories (see Hyde 1992; Cornelius 1994; Karcher 2003; Tarnas 2006).

Jung's multiple identity

There are, then, grounds for considering Jung to be, as Hanegraaff argues, a modern esotericist with a unique contribution to make to the ongoing tradition of western esotericism. However, Hanegraaff overstates his case when he asserts not just that Jung is a modern esotericist but that he is '*essentially* a modern esotericist' (1998: 497, emphasis added). Hanegraaff argues that the widespread image of Jung paradoxically both as 'essentially a doctor and an empirical scientist' and as 'a sort of modern shaman or an initiate into numinous mysteries', and hence as someone who 'seems to exemplify, in his own person, the possibility of unifying science and religion by means of psychology' (1998: 496–7) is an 'ideal image' that 'does not stand up to historical scrutiny' (1998: 497). To anyone familiar with the diversity of Jung's interests and engagements, this argument must seem implausible. Hanegraaff, like so many who encounter Jung from the perspective of a particular preoccupation, finds evidence to support a characterisation of Jung's identity that, though plausible and helpful up to a point, is ultimately partial. And indeed a major portion of the evidence that Hanegraaff does invoke is of questionable validity. For example, the historical scrutiny on which he almost exclusively relies for his account of Jung stems from Richard Noll's book *The Jung Cult* (1994), much of the scholarship of which has been discredited for its tendentiousness, implausible reconstructions, and outright errors (see, for example, Shamdasani 1995, Segal 1995). In contrast, Peter Homans in his book *Jung in Context* more carefully argues that Jung has a complex threefold identity as originative psychologist, prophet, and social critic (1979/1995: 161). This account of Jung's multiple identity is, I think, closer to the truth – though one could easily extend the number of facets beyond three. Underlying the multiple identity in Homans's account is above all the tension Jung experienced between the conflicting claims of tradition (especially religion) and modernity (especially science) (Homans 1979/1995: 157). Rather than see Jung's identity as a modern esotericist as primary, it is more plausible to view his interests and identity in this area as secondary and as but one of many mediatory attempts to remain true to his dual commitments to the domains of religious tradition and scientific modernity, with analytical psychology itself being the overarching mediatory model for Jung (see Main 2004). Hanegraaff has certainly enriched the picture of Jung's multiple identity by drawing out in a scholarly way the sense in which he can also seriously be considered a modern esotericist. But pushed to nominate an 'essential' identity of Jung, I think the strongest case, bland as it sounds, would have to be for seeing him as first and foremost a psychologist and psychotherapist (see Shamdasani 2003).

Bibliography

Burckhardt, T. (2003) 'Modern Psychology', in W. Stoddart (ed.) *The Essential Titus Burckhardt: Reflections on Sacred Art, Faiths, and Civilizations*, Bloomington, IN: World Wisdom.

Clarke, J. J. (1994) *Jung and Eastern Thought*, London and New York: Routledge.

Cornelius, G. (1994) *The Moment of Astrology: Origins in Divination*, London: Penguin.

Drob, S. (2000) *Symbols of the Kabbalah: Philosophical and Psychological Perspectives*, Northvale, NJ: Jason Aronson.

Faivre, A. (1994) *Access to Western Esotericism*, Albany, NY: State University of New York Press.

Freud, S. (1914) 'A History of the Psychoanalytic Movement', in *The Standard Edition of the Complete Psychological Works of Sigmund Freud*, vol. 14, London: Hogarth.

Hanegraaff, W. (1998) *New Age Religion and Western Culture: Esotericism in the Mirror of Secular Thought*, Albany, NY: State University of New York Press.

Holt, D. (1987–8) 'Alchemy: Jung and the Historians of Science', *Harvest*: 40–60.

Homans, P. (1979/1995) *Jung in Context: Modernity and the Making of a Psychology*, Chicago: The University of Chicago Press.

Hyde, M. (1992) *Jung and Astrology*, London: Aquarian Press.

Jaffé, A. (1971) *From the Life and Work of C. G. Jung*, London: Hodder & Stoughton.

Jung, C. G. (1896–9) *The Collected Works of C. G. Jung*, vol. A, *The Zofingia Lectures*, Princeton, NJ: Princeton University Press, 1983.

Jung, C. G. (1911–12/1952) *Collected Works*, vol. 5, *Symbols of Transformation*, 2d ed., London: Routledge & Kegan Paul, 1967.

Jung, C. G. ([1916]/1957) 'The Transcendent Function', in *Collected Works*, vol. 8, *The Structure and Dynamics of the Psyche*, 2d ed., London: Routledge & Kegan Paul, 1969.

Jung, C. G. (1928a) 'On Psychic Energy', in *Collected Works*, vol. 8, *The Structure and Dynamics of the Psyche*, 2d ed., London: Routledge & Kegan Paul, 1969.

Jung, C. G. (1928b) 'The Relations Between the Ego and the Unconscious', in *Collected Works*, vol. 7, *Two Essays on Analytical Psychology*, 2d ed., London: Routledge & Kegan Paul, 1966.

Jung, C. G. (1928–54) *Collected Works*, vol. 11, *Psychology and Religion: West and East*, 2d ed., London: Routledge & Kegan Paul, 1969.

Jung, C. G. (1929–54) *Collected Works*, vol. 13, *Alchemical Studies*, London: Routledge & Kegan Paul, 1968.

Jung, C. G. (1935) 'The Tavistock Lectures', in *Collected Works*, vol. 18, *The Symbolic Life*, London: Routledge & Kegan Paul, 1977.

Jung, C. G. (1940/1950) 'Concerning Rebirth', in *Collected Works*, vol. 9i, *The Archetypes and the Collective Unconscious*, 2d ed., London: Routledge & Kegan Paul, 1968.

Jung, C. G. (1944) *Collected Works*, vol. 12, *Psychology and Alchemy*, 2d ed., London: Routledge & Kegan Paul, 1968.

Jung, C. G. (1946) 'The Psychology of the Transference', in *Collected Works*, vol. 16, *The Practice of Psychotherapy*, 2d ed., London: Routledge & Kegan Paul, 1966.

Jung, C. G. (1951a) 'Fundamental Questions of Psychotherapy', in *Collected Works*, vol. 16, *The Practice of Psychotherapy*, 2d ed., London: Routledge & Kegan Paul, 1966.

Jung, C. G. (1951b) 'On Synchronicity', in *Collected Works*, vol. 8, *The Structure and Dynamics of the Psyche*, 2d ed., London: Routledge & Kegan Paul, 1969.

Jung, C. G. (1952) 'Synchronicity: An Acausal Connecting Principle', in *Collected*

Works, vol. 8, *The Structure and Dynamics of the Psyche*, 2d ed., London: Routledge & Kegan Paul, 1969.

Jung, C. G. (1955–6) *Collected Works*, vol. 14, *Mysterium Coniunctionis: An Inquiry into the Separation and Synthesis of Psychic Opposites in Alchemy*, 2d ed., London: Routledge & Kegan Paul, 1970.

Jung, C. G. (1963) *Memories, Dreams, Reflections*, recorded and edited by A. Jaffé, trans. R. and C. Winston, London: Collins and Routledge & Kegan Paul.

Jung, C. G. (1973) *Letters 1: 1906–1950*, selected and edited by G. Adler in collaboration with A. Jaffé, trans. R. F. C. Hull, London: Routledge & Kegan Paul.

Karcher, S. (2003) *Total I Ching: Myths for Change*, London: TimeWarner Books.

Keane, L. (2007) 'Routes of Wholeness: Jungian and Post-Jungian Dialogues with the Western Esoteric Tree of Life', PhD thesis, University of Essex, UK.

Main, R. (2004) *The Rupture of Time: Synchronicity and Jung's Critique of Modern Western Culture*, Hove and New York: Brunner-Routledge.

Main, R. (2007) 'Ruptured Time and the Re-enchantment of Modernity', in A. Casement (ed.) *Who Owns Jung?* London: Karnac.

Marlan, S. (2006) 'Alchemy', in R. Papadopoulos (ed.) *The Handbook of Jungian Psychology: Theory, Practice and Applications*, London and New York: Routledge.

Noll, R. (1992) 'Jung the *Leontocephalus*', in P. Bishop (ed.) *Jung in Contexts: A Reader*, London and New York: Routledge, 1999.

Noll, R. (1994) *The Jung Cult: Origins of a Charismatic Movement*, Princeton, NJ: Princeton University Press.

Samuels, A. (1985) *Jung and the Post-Jungians*, London and New York: Routledge.

Segal, R. (ed.) (1992) *The Gnostic Jung*, Princeton, NJ: Princeton University Press; London: Routledge.

Segal, R. (1995) 'Critical Notice', *Journal of Analytical Psychology* 40, no. 4: 597–608.

Shamdasani, S. (1995) *Cult Fictions: C. G. Jung and the Founding of Analytical Psychology*, London and New York: Routledge.

Shamdasani, S. (2003) *Jung and the Making of Modern Psychology: The Dream of a Science*, Cambridge: Cambridge University Press.

Tacey, D. (2001) *Jung and the New Age*, Hove and Philadelphia: Brunner-Routledge.

Tarnas, R. (2006) *Cosmos and Psyche: Intimations of a New World View*, New York: Viking.

Note

1 This chapter was first presented as an invited paper at the Cambridge Centre for Western Esotericism conference on 'Practitioners and Scholars in Dialogue', Cambridge, 21 July 2007. Some of the material was earlier published in *The Rupture of Time: Synchronicity and Jung's Critique of Modern Western Culture* (Main 2004).

Chapter 23

The last desire

A clinical experience of working with a dying man

Konoyu Nakamura

Death, our contemporary society and Jungian psychology

Hayao Kawai, the first Japanese Jungian analyst, whose death in 2007 is a great loss to us, said in his book, 'I can say that I became a psychotherapist and especially belong to the Jungian school because of my own fear of death. . . . As a Jungian analyst, I learned that people more often deal with death in Jungian circles than in other schools' (2006: 27). Also, Rosemary Gordon, a Jungian analyst in the UK, has said, 'Jung was in fact very interested in man's relationship to death and in the symbols that the psyche evolves around this theme' (1978: 29). Certainly they are right, Jungian psychology more directly deals not only with death, but also with spirituality and religion than other schools. Of course, many of Jung's works deal with these matters (Jung: 1938, 1953) and his followers are actively involved in developing his groundbreaking insights in various ways (Hillman 1964, Gordon 1978, von Franz 1986, Rosen 2002).

Gordon has said that the theme of death was the most taboo subject in the Western world during the first half of the twentieth century. She pointed out three reasons for this: (1) the rapid and miraculous development of the physical sciences, (2) the fact of the dramatic reduction of the family unit, (3) the decline and the erosion of the religions and traditional faiths (1978: 8–9).

How, in turn, do contemporary Japanese, who bear Eastern traditions, treat the theme of death? Kawai (2006) said that the view of life and death has become a great problem in Japan due to the rapid progress of modern medicine. It is not easy to sort thing out, but there is little discussion regarding the 'difficulty of dying' in Japan. Tadaharu Nakao, who focuses on medical problems as a sociologist, has said, 'We tend to value youth, health and activity in modern Japanese society, and to look down on and hate the opposite. . . . As a result, people lose opportunities to learn about both death and life through seeing people die.' (1991: 288) So, it is very interesting to discuss whether Japan, like the Western world, has lost its religious traditions, and how Japanese treat the theme of death in their society.

In this chapter, I will report on clinical work with a dying man whom I was involved with as a counselor through the firm where he worked. My client, a man in his forties, was longing to see me, his firm's counselor, rather than a counsellor at the hospital, even though he had never met me. There are two reasons why I took the case. First, it is very interesting that I met him as a firm's counselor, because although companies do sometimes pay attention to the mental health of their employees and may hire counselors, like myself, such counsellors are rarely asked to deal directly with death itself. So, this is a rare case. Secondly, the firm, a most worldly organization, pursues both profits and happiness in this world, though its ultimate purpose is earning money.

For example, in the past, we Japanese were called 'economic animals' and Japanese salaried men are often called 'corporate soldiers'. Such expressions imply that we generally focus on matters far from spirituality or religion. I would like to discuss what happened in my work with one corporate soldier who had to face his sudden and unexpected death. I will also explore the meaning of Jungian psychology in relation to the views of life and death in Japan.

Before the interview

One day I received a call from a manager. He asked me to see his subordinate, Mr. M, a man in his forties who was in the hospital with terminal gall bladder cancer, and who had not been informed of his diagnosis. Honestly, I was troubled at this request, because the hospital was far from my office, my schedule was always full of appointments with other clients, and I had little experience with terminal care. I was wondering why Mr. M was eager to see me, even though we had never worked together before. I reluctantly told the manager to ask Mrs. M to contact me. She called me soon afterwards, and by talking with her, I learned that Mr. M had fallen ill a couple of months previously and had had an operation at once, but it was too late to help him. It appeared that he would live for only one or two months. His doctor, his wife, and his colleagues together made a decision not to tell him the truth. Then he started to be suspicious about his condition and wanted to consult someone. However, he refused to see a caseworker or a counselor working at the hospital and was longing to see a counselor from his firm, myself. Learning these things, I was moved so much that I decided to visit him.

On the day that I visited the hospital, I found myself getting very nervous. I could not choose my clothes and I hurt my finger before leaving. During my two-hour trip from my office to an unknown small town, I was once again asking myself what I could do for him and why I had been urged so to see an unknown man. Arriving at the hospital, I first met his wife. She calmly gave me a brief explanation about his state and took me to his room. The room was full of dull orange sunshine in the late evening. Entering the room, she ran to his bedside and whispered in his ear, 'Ah! Darling! At last, Ms. Nakamura has come!' The man replied simply by nodding. Their short conversation touched my heart deeply. How long they had been waiting for me. The wife seemed very composed and went out the room, leaving me alone with him. In turn, I almost started to cry.

The first and last interview

I approached Mr. M slowly and sat down on the bedside chair. Though he was seriously jaundiced, he seemed so clean, thin, rather like a small boy. I introduced myself to him. He turned his face to me and said clearly, 'Thank you very much for your long trip for me.' 'How are you?' I asked. After a brief silence he answered, 'I have been so bored since I came here.' Bored! I was really surprised at this unexpected word. Rather than focusing on pain or anxiety, he was simply bored. 'I have never had any counseling,' he said. 'Don't you talk, with your wife?' I asked. 'She visits me every day but we do not have anything to talk about,' he replied. I understood at once. I could imagine how his wife visited him every day and devoted herself to taking care of him but turning her back on him to avoid talking with him. I answered, 'I know.' With a heavy sigh he said, 'I, I really wanted someone to talk with me. My wife talks with my doctor, and she is always busy doing something, leaving me.' 'Your wife is so busy, isn't she?' I responded 'She, she . . .' He trailed off. Then he was silent.

After a long time, he groaned, 'I do not know anything about my illness. I don't know what is happening to me! I have never experienced such a thing. I am scared!' I could find no words of my own to respond to his deep suffering. Instead, a phrase from *The Tibetan Book of the Dead* came to mind:

> There may be even those who have made themselves familiar with teaching, yet who, because of the violence of the disease causing death, may be mentally unable to withstand illusions. For such, also, this instruction is absolutely necessary.
>
> (Evans-Wentz 1960: 100)

Remembering this phrase, I understood his deep confusion and extra-ordinary fear. In fact I did not reply to him but I said to myself, 'Oh, yes. Death is always unknown to everyone and no one should know it. You must be scared.' I continued to listen to him carefully. He changed the subject, 'If, if I could work more . . .' I asked, 'What do you do in the firm?' He explained about his job and, finally, he said, 'Something in the firm is not in order. It doesn't work.' Then he fell unconscious, but his vital signs did not seem so bad. So I was watching him and waiting for what would happen next. Since it was very quiet in the room, still filled with orange-red sunshine, I could hear the faint ticktack of an old wrist watch, which suggested to me that he had little his time left. Probably seven or eight minutes later, he woke up again and said, 'Did I sleep? Sorry.' 'Don't worry. No problem. You must be tired of talking. I will be here in the meantime. You can talk with me whenever you want,' I responded. He seemed to feel relieved and he again fell into a sleep. Frankly, I wanted to run away at once, but I thought that I should stay by him. I waited and waited. It was excruciating. After about ten minutes, I asked him, 'Mr. M, don't you have anything else to tell me?' 'No, it's enough,' he murmured. 'That's fine. Shall we stop now? If you want me, call me any time. I will come back,' I said. 'Thank you so much,' he answered. I left the room. That night he died.

Discussion

I would like to discuss this impressive, even shocking, experience from two viewpoints: first, to examine death and transformation from a Jungian perspective, and second, to explore the meaning of Jungian theory and practice in Japan as they relate to views of life and death in Japan.

Gordon said, 'The modern doctor has rarely been willing to assume a task that has up to now been shouldered by the priest' (1978: 9). Not only doctors, but most psychotherapists as well, tend to avoid this difficult task. I am no exception. The ultimate reason that I tried to escape in this case is related to the question: 'Why me? Why am I, not anyone else, suddenly chosen for this difficult and painful duty?' Feelings of confusion, embarrassment, anger and fear are, of course, found in everybody who suddenly has to encounter an unknown situation, often caused by a tragic event, in which ordinary bearings, social skills or personas do not work. In my case, my persona as a psychotherapist was not helpful. This is evident from the fact that I could not choose my clothes on that day. According to Gordon,

> This search for the meaning of life and the meaning of death is, however, inevitably closely tied up with the search for one's own true self. No wonder that many should at first have shied away from such an awesome venture. . . . Ultimately it demands the courage to 'go it alone'.
>
> (1978: 12)

I needed to gather all my courage to take such a step.

Did Mr. M experience the same difficulties? If transformation, to be genuine and thorough, always affects the body, as Hillman (1964) said, drastic physical changes must have forced him to work for his psychic transformation. He was not told the truth about his disease, but, even in deep confusion, he realized he had to enter an unknown area in which 'it doesn't work', as he put it. It is also obvious that Mr. M bravely and actively wrestled with this difficult task, because he was eager to see someone to whom he could confide his suffering. Hillman continues, 'By telling a secret one lets another into the sacred preserve of one's individuality. One keeps one's secrets until one feels that the other person with whom one is about to share a secret also views it as sacred' (1964: 173). When I visited him, he immediately intuited why I was there. Hence he started his disclosures, 'I do not at all understand anything. I don't know. I am scared.' Marie-Louise von Franz has said, 'The great difficulty we have in imagining our own life after death. . . . may well be accounted for by the fact that while still living we identify almost completely with the body' (1986: 1). There is no answer to ultimate questions. Therapists can only carefully watch a patient 'going it alone' in quiet. In such cases, as Kübler-Ross said (1970: 113), silence is the most significant communication.

For Hillman, to face an unknown and unknowable mystery alone, religion perhaps serves best (1964: 176). Therefore, I realized it was so natural or necessary that a phrase from *The Tibetan Book of the Dead* had come to me. Mr. M seemed to have already been reborn as a sinless, pure and sacred little child. The red sunshine strongly contributed to my impression of his rebirth or transformation because, of course, red is the symbol of transformation in alchemy. Indeed, a therapist can assume a role as a kind of shaman initiating people into another world by keeping their secrets and by sharing a religious mystery.

The views on life and death in Japan

Next, I would like to talk about the meaning of Jungian theory and practice as they relate to views on life and death in Japan. When Jung mentioned in his Psychological Commentary on *The Tibetan Book of the Dead*, 'The background of this unusual book is not the niggardly European "either-or", but a magnificently affirmative "both–and". This statement may appear objectionable to the Western philosopher, for the West loves clarity and unambiguity' (1953: 511). For Jung, Western thought about the soul seems 'niggardly', while the East accepts the supratemporality of the soul as a self-evident fact. However, of course, we can not discuss the East as a whole. Here I will stick to that part of it which I know, namely Japan.

In the early myths in *Kojiki* (The Records of Ancient Matters), and in Japanese original religion, Shinto, the fear of death and of the dangers that may come from spirits of the dead are expressed strongly (Reader, Andreason, Stefánsson: 1993: 72). Also, there is the idea in Japan that the spirits of those who suffer sudden, premature or violent deaths will continue to exist in a relationship with this world in an unhappy and angry way. So people have to perform some memorial services and rituals for dead people to escape from the unhappy effects of the dead (ibid.: 57).

Later, Japan, for centuries, introduced various religions – Buddhism, Taoism, Confucianism and Christianity – and these all influenced Japanese views of life and death. So, before discussing Japanese views generally, it is necessary to briefly touch on modern Japanese attitudes to religions. The noted scholar, Edwin Reischauer, in *The Japanese Today*, said,

> If this book were about a South Asian or Middle Eastern people, it would be unthinkable to have delayed a discussion of religion so long . . . Religion in fact might well have been the starting point for these Islamic, Hindu, or Buddhist lands . . . but in modern Japan it plays a lesser and more peripheral role . . . the trend toward secularism dated back at least three centuries in Japan.
>
> (1995: 203)

Ian Reader and his colleagues have also touched on some significant issues in *Japanese Religions Past & Present*. Here, I would like to introduce two important features which are related to the theme of this chapter. The first is the mutual interaction of various religions, and the second is the religious significance of the family and ancestors: 'Unlike the Western world . . . religious practice in Japan is largely centered on the family as a unit. This can be traced to the clan structure of ancient society and also Confucianism' (Reader *et al.* 1993: 40).

Both the secularism mentioned by Reischauer and the religious significance of the family appear extraordinarily important to me in discussing Japanese views of life and death. In a work co-authored by the American and Japanese scholars Shuichi Kato, Michael Reich and Robert Lifton, *Six Lives/Six Deaths: Portraits of Modern Japan* (1979), six case studies of representative modern, intelligent men, lead to the conclusion that identification with and loyalty to a group are crucial. They also say that most modern Japanese have a very secular world view and that no values transcend the groups to which they belong. The fact that individuals in Japan do not have internalized or absolute senses of value leads them to be subject to the value systems of their groups.

Mr. M in this case is a typical Japanese salaried man. Keiko Funahashi, a Japanese sociologist, has said the relationship between an individual and a Japanese firm is not only a form of labor contract but also a familial association. Most men work, gain joy and experience self-actualization only as members of the firm, an extended family which includes men's private families. Therefore, the most important thing in Mr. M's life was his bond to this large family. He was working and living as a loyal member of this family and was eager to die in the same way. Thus his early death was not only a private matter but also a serious problem for his extended family. Probably you have already grasped the reason for his last desire to see me, since I am a counselor at his firm, and thus, in his view, a respectable family member.

His choice was, therefore, completely natural. As I said before, there is an intense primary fear of death in the Japanese mind, as well as the idea that the spirits of those who suffer sudden, premature or violent deaths will continue to exist in a relationship with this world in an unhappy and angry way. Without a ritual or service for premature death, Mr. M must have feared his unhappy spirit would bring something evil to the family members he was leaving. So, all the other family members, his manager, his colleagues and his wife, made efforts to get me to visit him. They devoted themselves to fulfilling his last desire, the notion that he would be satisfied at meeting their counselor and could die in peace. Thus, they could return to their ordinary lives without concern.

In other words, the counselor or the psychotherapist in Japan has to take responsibility for the psyche of an individual and of all the other members of his extended family, like a shaman in a primitive society. It is a heavy load for someone like me, who has no specific faith. However, the counselor cannot avoid this hard task, because the counselor, too, is a member of the extended family, and the one best equipped to deal with the psychic problems of individuals and the larger family as a whole. Honestly, I have never felt happier about my being a Jungian than in the moment of my working with Mr. M, since Jungian theory and training had led me to *The Tibetan Book of the Dead*.

As Gordon said (1978: 9), the decline and erosion of religions and traditional faiths make it difficult for people to deal with the issue of death. The dominant secularism in Japan may make it even more difficult. However, as Reader said (1993: 40), Japanese can introduce many religions or faiths into their lives without exclusion, and these still play a role in Japanese lives. Here, I find the crucial significance of Jungian psychology in contemporary Japan.

References

Canmberlain, B.H. (trans.) (1981) *The Kojiki*. Tokyo, Rutland, Vermont, Singapore: Tottle Publishing.

Evans-Wentz, W.Y. (1960) *The Tibetan Book of the Dead*. London: Oxford University Press.

Gordon, R. (1978) *Dying and Creating: A Search for Meaning*. London: The Society of Analytical Psychology Ltd.

Hillman, J. (1964) *Suicide and The Soul*. London: Hodder and Stoughton.

Jung, C.G (1938) *Psychology and Religion*. New Haven: Yale University Press.

—— (1953) Psychological Commentary on *The Tibetan Book of the Dead*, in *CW 16*, 509–526.

Kawai, H. (2006) *Taiwa suru Sei to Shi Jung Shinrigaku no Shiten* [Dialogue of Life and Death from a Jungian perspective]. Tokyo: Daiwashobo.

Kübler-Ross, E. (1970) *On Death and Dying*. New York: Simon & Schuster.

Lifton, R.J., Kato, S., Reich, M.R. (1979) *Six Lives/Six Deaths: Portraits from Modern Japan*. New Haven and London: Yale University Press.

Nakao, T. (1991) Shi no Shakaigaku-Gendai Shakai ni okeru Shi no Iryoka wo Megutte [The Sociology of Death: The Medicalization of Death in Contemporary Society] In Kono, T. (ed.) *Terminal Care no tameno Shinshinigaku* [Psychosomatic medicine for terminal care] Tokyo: Asakura Shoten.

Reischauer, E.D., Jansen, M.B. (1995) *The Japanese Today: Change and Continuity*. Cambridge, MA: Harvard University Press.

Reader, I., Anderson E., Stefánsson, F. (1993): *Japanese Religions: Past and Present*. Sandgate, Folkestone, Kent: Japan Library.

Rosen, D.H. (2002) *Transforming Depression: Healing the Soul through Creativity*. Lake Worth: Nicolas Hays.

von Franz, M. L. (1986) *On Dreams and Death: A Jungian Interpretation*. Boston and London: Shambhala.

Chapter 24

Unpicking

Susie Orbach

Andrew tells me that we first met when he came to be interviewed for a job at The Women's Therapy Centre in 1976. Those were heady days when political activists had the capacity to challenge conventional institutions and bodies of knowledge and set up alternative sites of excellence to explore social and scientific issues from a different basis. Within psychoanalysis, psychotherapy, counseling and psychiatry, new ideas about the mad and the sad were proposed. The asylums were closed and psychotherapy was being appropriated for its progressive potential. For a brief period radical therapy flourished in Latin America, in North America and in various European countries. Always situating the individual in their social class, gender, age, sexual identity and ethnic contexts, it insisted that psycho-analytic and psychological knowledge was insufficient if it failed to locate the particulars of each individual or each group's experience. People could not be extracted from their history as it was constitutive of self, and that history included the psychological and social trajectories. Reformulating psychoanalysis for the 1968 generation became a quest for which Andrew, with his wide intellectual curiosities, was admirably suited. Andrew once told me he became a Jungian analyst somewhat by accident in that the Jungians were the only group who would interview such a young person with a background in theatre and politics. He had not been a long-standing student of Jung's writings but came across a book on the social meaning of Jung's psychology. It was a felicitous meeting which allowed him to develop and rewrite much of the Jungian canon for a new generation.

Of course you can't rewrite – because no one will listen to you – unless you serve your time, becoming adept in the master theory. And this Andrew did. But where Andrew differed and differs from many of the people who entered the psychoanalytic enterprise is in his commitment to creating theory which was relevant and he extended the endeavour rather than fitting or twisting what he was observing into a pre-existing and increasingly narrow canonical range.

Many who were drawn to psychotherapy, particularly the psychoanalytic wing, found the process of learning problematic. Psychoanalytic training in the UK has the unfortunate habit of analyzing resistance to its ideas in the training context as pathological. Discourse occurs in a limited form in which an apprenticeship system of master–learner implies that the learners must imbibe rather than question what they are offered. The generation of '68 from which Andrew springs brought about a revolution in education from primary school on, in which questioning and opinion are encouraged. Not so, however, in most UK psychoanalytic training institutions. Questioning is or can be considered immature and indicative of unresolved problems with authority and it takes a particularly intellectually secure and, yes, bolshie, character to dare to contest or extend the canon. Many radicals seeking training found that they had buckled under becoming faction fighters for psychoanalytic orthodoxies every bit as rigid, funda-mentalist and replete with correct line-ism as the narcissism of small differences which had plagued the left. One would meet former progressive activists who could not hear what was being said psychoanalytically unless it encoded the key referents of the psychoanalytic school that had reared them.

Not so Andrew. He was and remains an exemplar of a praxis that believes that there is always much to learn from within and without one's narrow or particular psycho faction and that the aim is to open up what we have learned to one another. He does not seek to sequester it and prize it as hidden knowledge only for the initiates who demonstrate their membership of the club by speaking in codes about those they 'treat'. Andrew seeks to meet not only the individual but also the political system, the corporation, the group, and to understand who they believe themselves to be and what he can bring to them.

He is not a pussycat pluralist either. He is trickster and mischievous. He likes to provoke. He can converse in several psychological languages without collapsing what each might have to offer, but more importantly, he is a fighter and when the stakes matter, as with the struggle over challenging hetero-normative sexuality, his clarity of purpose and tireless energy put him out front as an ally one wishes on one's side.

Andrew and I have cooperated inside psychoanalysis and outside in the explicitly political sphere. It is an odd cooperation. We rarely plan or agree on what we will do and yet from our different backgrounds and milieux we end up thinking along pretty similar lines and are often involved in the same actions. The ideas that I am bringing forth are ones that dovetail with Andrew's interests and his desire to bring a psychoanalytic understanding into government thinking.

Psychoanalysis has veered between an excessive modesty about what it knows and an unwarranted arrogance that its mode of analysis is *the* answer to issues within and without its purview. I would like to take a stance that suggests that what psychoanalysis has to offer can enhance our understanding of seemingly incomprehensible or intractable issues by working alongside economic, historical and sociological analyses. There are six key ways that psychoanalysis has a contribution to make, outside its very real value as a clinical treatment, and these are as follows:

1   Psychoanalysis hears what cannot be said in other places. It bears witness to society's secrets. It reveals feelings, attitudes and desires which are often against the grain of social propriety, yet which are endemic to our psychological lives and thus influence our actions.
2   Psychoanalysis of individuals, families, couples and mother and baby pairs is an unparalleled source of research data. Its in-depth methodology is unique.
3   Psychoanalysis's study of child development, of interpersonal relationships, of the relationships between men and women, children and parents, and of group dynamics, is an extremely rich knowledge base which can be used to underpin or guide future social policy.
4   Psychoanalysis details how emotional states can transform from one kind of thing to another when there is no channel for the acceptance of the original emotion. For example, if disappointment is not given expression, it may turn to anger, resulting in possible destructive behaviour and actions.
5   Psychoanalysis provides deeper understandings with which to approach undesirable social phenomena that appear intractable, by detailing the transformations in the internal life of the individual and the group.
6   Psychoanalysis's approach to the issues of meaning and motivation provides a way into understanding particular behaviours as an expression of the individual or group's sense of personal agency. By adding this approach to the more usual assessment of the rational responses of people and groups, it provides an understanding of how, for example, violent and destructive behaviour may be an expression of a complex inner world where bad feeling must be expelled into the environment.

If we turn now to a specific example of how psychoanalytic ideas can be applied, we can consider the issue of violence, in particular domestic violence. Over the last two decades we have witnessed a shift from the invisibility of violence perpetrated by men against women and an attitude which ran "there's not much wrong with women being pushed about a bit" or "it's unfortunate but it happens" to a position in which it is now visible and redefined as a violent crime: domestic violence. We now embrace the notion that domestic violence is unacceptable to us *as a society* not just to the individual woman.

Where psychoanalysis can be valuable is in enabling us to understand: why a woman might feel compelled to stay within a violent relationship when other factors, such as economic and social support, are potentially available to her; why men can be violent; why women can be violent or provoke violent responses in others; and the interpersonal nature of much violent behaviour.

Psychoanalysis problematises the violent relationship. It has a curiosity towards understanding the phenomenon and it attempts to pose questions which exempt the phenomenon from a kind of moralism by asking instead: why does it occur? What keeps it going? What function does the violence have for the relationship as well as for the individuals involved? What keeps the woman in the relationship? Why is a woman who finds herself in a violent relationship unable to extricate herself from it?

Psychoanalysis does this first by enabling us to understand something about the experience of being in a violent relationship. It listens and it asks: does the *experience* of being in a violent relationship transform the individual woman's sense of self? It answers the question by visiting some of the emotional territory of the woman in such circumstances in order to explicate the psychological mechanisms that enable her to tolerate this violation.

If we look at the experience of being on the receiving end of violence there is a deep sense of helplessness and defeat. If a woman has stayed in such a relationship beyond three or four incidents, one can observe in her an erosion of or a lack of the mechanisms of self protection that we rely on to get us out of dangerous situations. Next to the sense of helplessness and defeat may be some anger but this is often overshadowed by an equally strong sense that while she is not at all at fault for engendering the violence, she *feels herself to be responsible* for transforming the conditions under which the violence occurs.

One way in which she manages her feelings of helplessness is by taking on some culpability for it by imagining that it is *she* who could shift the brutal behaviour of the other. Thus, if only she could love him better she could repair the damaged man who turns violent. Thus she protects herself from the feelings of helplessness and defeat by turning them into their opposite in her mind. Instead of the woman feeling sunk by hopelessness she feels some hope that she could *by her own actions* shift the violence. A great deal of her mental ruminations may then be spent in her trying to rework the situation. By relocating the problem – or at least the solution to the problem – from the perpetrator to herself, she becomes occupied with how she can reposition herself and her actions to prevent the violence from occurring. We may judge that this is inaccurate, an example of false consciousness, and so we may say it isn't logical, it doesn't make sense. We may hope that a dose of corrective thinking will set the woman right. But in fact unless we address this turn that the psyche makes when it encounters persistent or repetitive unwarranted violence, our desires and our understandings will be inadequate for we will have failed to take sufficient account of a woman's sense of her own agency within this. And this is one of psychoanalysis's great contributions: its use as a way into understanding the vicissitudes of human agency.

At the same time as the psyche recasts the problem of the man's violence in terms of a solution the woman must find, the woman has the psychological problem of digesting what has actually happened to her. Much of her psychic energy is invested in trying to fend off their re-occurrences. But another part of her episodically dissociates from what has transpired as though it never happened.

In dissociation, which is one of the mechanisms that takes over when the psyche can't find a way to process difficult things, the disturbing event along with the feelings that it provokes are split off from the conscious mind of the individual. The woman "forgets" the violence that has occurred and normalises the relationship. Her man's violence is temporarily effaced and any conception of how, given who he is, he is likely to behave, based on her experience of him, is lost. The woman may go further. She may unconsciously create for herself a man who is caring (as many violent men can be) so that when her man acts like himself, that's to say turns nasty, she is in shock and unable to summon whatever she imagines she might use to stop him or prevent him from hurting her or their children. She has psychically disarmed herself and is therefore deeply unequipped to find whatever new form of engagement, whatever key she fantasised about finding, that will persuade him to desist. Her behaviour then, in the next violent incident, becomes not only a reflection of him in her mind but one of her own failure – she is at one and the same moment trapped. She reassures herself that it is within her potential capacity to master and transform the situation.

Of course this is not the only set of responses that can occur although it is a very frequently observed one. It provides us with a psychological explanation of the adhesive nature of violent relationships. We can see the way in which the woman *believes* herself to be an active participant with something *to do*, not simply a victim or even a survivor of an abusive relationship.

If we observe the range of experiences of women who stay in relationships that they are aware are damaging to them, we can see that for some, the experience of the violence has been so rapidly corrosive that it stimulates feelings of unentitlement to anything better. The violent behaviour seems to signify and encapsulate for the woman something essential about *her*. Feelings of personal value are so diminished that her being hit becomes not a signal to exit from the relationship, nor an outrage, but a plausible comment on who she is. To say this is not to blame the victim and I want to be very clear about this. Unconscious psychic processes which are an attempt to reverse for an individual deep feelings of powerlessness by retranslating them into plausible outcomes is not equivalent with deserving one's status as a victim. It is merely to describe certain operations the psyche engages in, in order to manage profound distress. If we can get hold of this thread, we are some of the way towards understanding the particularly unique contribution psychoanalytic ways of thinking can bring to such knotty phenomena.

The loss of personal value may of course play into a history for the individual woman in which she has not felt well regarded in her upbringing and therefore feels unable to take for granted, within herself, that she is a person of value. The ambiguity that many women have towards themselves and their entitlements is not a function simply of violent relationships per se, although it is an expression of the psychic violence that conditions of inequality can produce. For adult women today, a sense of self which embodies hesitancy, insecurity, feelings of fraudulence, and a confusion about their own entitlements is not unusual. Patriarchal social arrangements have not just intra-psychic consequences, they have depended upon the development of a particular psychology of femininity which makes the reception of inequality possible and sustainable.

The patriarchal requirements of femininity have meant that girls have been raised until very recently to occupy the social and psychological role of mother and carer and develop an identity through being attached to others as wives and mothers and to provide for the needs of those others. Even though the social conditions of women have changed greatly in the last thirty years, the psychological mandates to respond to others, to provide for them emotionally and domestically, to offer relationships on which others can depend while not expecting reciprocal emotional responsiveness in return, means that adult women today can feel quite threatened at the idea of exiting from or breaking up relationships even if those relationships hurt them. They can fear a loss of a sense of self known through attachments. To sever an attachment is to lose a central component of the making of their personal identity.

Further, in being schooled to recognise and take account of the needs of others, a woman can experience extreme confusion in relation to her own needs, especially since the needs of others are primary and overriding. Thus a husband's needs, even those of a violent husband, may predominate. Or the woman may judge that the needs of children to have a father are more important than their own needs for physical safety. *Indeed the woman's personal needs may be a trouble to her.* There may be a hesitancy in relation to them so that at that same time as they arise, they are questioned by the woman herself. She may not *hear or recognise* needs when they originate in her for she is attuned to responding to needs that emerge from others.

This isn't to say that a woman doesn't know that she is angry in the face of violence. Of course she does. But the anger may not be enough to impel her out of the relationship. Curiously it may entrap her. And here we face another problem. The woman's anger can appear to be an expression of her strength and the basis for a sense of self that refuses to be brutalised. Her ability to recognise this anger and yet not act on it becomes a safety valve that makes for homeostatis. She expresses and expels some angry feelings as a means of survival which then allows her to endure the horrendous situation she finds herself in. But here's the rub, if her anger cannot be acted upon and yet is seen by therapists as a good thing, the emotional stepping stone to her making different choices, it can come to obscure other needs and sensibilities that exist in her, such as her fears of taking action, which are harder for her to address.

Paradoxically her expressed anger can bind her to the situation because it occludes more problematic feelings; feelings of vulnerability, fears of being on her own, and her ambivalence. She may want out of the relationship but she is scared to be detached. The capacity to make and maintain affiliative bonds is the hallmark of femininity and to reject this can feel paramount to rejecting the known self. Her socialisation works to make her feel that for her to leave the man would be an act of aggression *on her part*. It is *she* who would be doing the violence by instigating separation. If we can recognise women's ambivalence and their fears and understand their anger both as a means of survival and as a defence, we can think about a future in which such entrenched patterns have a chance of being dislodged and a new energy unleashed.

In addition to the ways in which I have suggested we can approach women's anger, there are two others ways in which a depth psychological understanding can aid our thinking. The first of these concerns the way in which the battered woman in becoming the recipient of violence then takes on the bad feelings that the man who has beaten her has towards himself. His violence is itself the manifestation of his inability to manage distress. This inability then inclines his feelings to become siphoned off into the direction of violence towards another. When the woman is beaten she isn't just physically hurt, she is also the recipient of a set of his angry emotions which then invade her psychic space so that she feels angry and rageful herself. She now has feelings which are not quite hers but have been evoked in her and sit inside her, which feel uncomfortable and alien. The batterer, having expelled and transferred his feelings, gets some relief, in fact he is even able to feel some remorse, sorrow and genuine love for he is now no longer burdened by feelings that he couldn't process except through violent expulsion. There is then a devilish process by which the violence the man is endeavouring to rid himself of is induced in his partner. He feels differently for having released it while she is swamped with a rage she doesn't quite understand.

The situation may be somewhat different for those women who have come from a history of violence or from some kind of systematically abusive situation. Whatever the circumstances of our growing, we seek to repeat aspects of the emotional temperature of the relationships which form the templates for our emotional lives. If we have felt loved and secure we find ourselves in relationships that tend to confirm that. We will anticipate and believe that intimate relationships mean love. If we have been insecure as children we tend to find insecurity in our adult relationships and we will anticipate and believe that intimate relationships are insecure. If one grows up in relationships in which violence is the means by which attachment or strong feelings are shown, violence, however much hated and feared, may resonate as *the* expression or proof of true connection – violence equals love. Although adults who suffered continued or continuous violence in their early relationship may seek to avoid it in their adult life, violence can become a currency in a relationship with deep resonance. It demonstrates that one really counts, has got under the skin of the other, can move them to act in ways that they and oneself may not wish. Violence while consciously rejected may, because it equates with deep feeling, represent relationship. The enactment of violence brings a certain relief. While it may not be actively sought (although of course it can be) it may nevertheless be the only way that a relationship can be felt to have meaning. The adult who knew violence as a child thus has a receptivity for violence at an intrapsychic level which may perplex outsiders who cannot understand why the woman does not take the opportunity to get away from a violent relationship.

Having raised the issue of what makes it possible for a woman to endure a violent relationship we are then in a position to ask: is there anything from this understanding which we can bring to the future about what is required to enable a woman to extricate herself and not endure it? Are there any measures we should put in place that will provide more far-reaching support to enable women to make a different choice? I think we can unequivocally say yes. We need to propagate psychoanalytic ideas so that they don't only live within the psychoanalytic community. We can endeavour to influence the programmes that are on offer for battered women so that they offer a response that addresses women's ambivalence, fears and difficulties with leaving violent relationships. We can try to elevate the public discussion of the dynamics of violent relationships so that we see not just the dynamics within the couple but also the woman's sense of agency within her stance.

What I hope I've shown in this rather encapsulated "case study" of applied psychoanalysis is what it is that psychoanalysis has to offer to social policy. But to do that we need to be clear that we are only one form of understanding. Not *the* form of understanding. This is where Andrew's and my ideas intersect. We know that psychoanalytic ideas have something special to offer if we can do the hard work to clarify what exactly that is, put it into concepts that others can grasp, and not be arrogant about our knowledge, nor too humble. Andrew has been an exemplar of this kind of praxis by marrying his vast psychoanalytic knowledge with his indefatigable political energy. On the occasion of his sixtieth birthday, one is bound to say to him: carry on, carry on.

Chapter 25

Extending Jungian psychology
Working with survivors of political upheavals

Renos Papadopoulos

At the outset, I wish to salute Andrew Samuels, my friend and colleague of more than thirty years, for the breath of fresh air he brought into the world of Jungian psychology. His considerable contribution includes theoretical systematisation and innovation and organisational development (as an officer of the International Association for Analytical Psychology and a founding member of the International Association of Jungian Studies), as well as extension of Jungian psychology in academic/University contexts. His overall presence in Analytical Psychology has been substantial, assisting significantly its upgrading in the world today.

Andrew was responsible for strengthening the presence of the social and political dimensions in the Jungian mainstream (e.g. 1993, 1996, 1997, 1999, 2001, 2002). He did this over the years, always emphasising that in parallel to our analytical practice it is important to address the plight of those outside our consulting rooms. Characteristically, he pleaded that 'Today's Jungians, and other Western therapists as well, need . . . to stand alongside the materially disadvantaged and the socially frightened, as well as sit down with their educated analysands. To do this, they must open their hearts and minds to that which is "foreign"' (2002: 479). It is this very parallel direction that my work has also been addressing.

Considering my own position of being both 'foreigner' and 'local' in the four countries where I spent large chunks of my life, it is not surprising that my work had to also include the dimension Andrew refers to in this plea. Throughout my professional life I maintained a clinical/analytical practice parallel to my academic positions in universities; then, my clinical work always included another parallel involvement – working in the public sector as well as in private practice. Finally, in the last twenty years or so another direction developed more explicitly when I began working as consultant to international organisations in many countries with reference to refugees and other survivors of political upheavals. It is this last direction that this chapter will now address.

Jungian insights

Although I am never employed as a 'Jungian' consultant and my work is never seen as exclusively 'Jungian' (because it is also informed by other approaches, mainly systemic, e.g. Papadopoulos 2008), I have nevertheless found that certain Jungian theories have been extremely useful in comprehending the phenomena I have been working with. However, it is important to emphasise that these ideas have to be extended and adapted to fit in with the realm that they are applied to. Andrew's approach was always sensitive to the need for such an adaptation (e.g. Samuels 2007).

To begin with, it is important to note that the political upheavals that give rise to conflict of the magnitude that causes human casualties are phenomena that are highly *polarised*. These are situations where two factions (e.g. racial, ideological, ethnic–cultural or religious) reach the point that their differences become more important than their similarities and, moreover, the differences acquire a critical and defining significance (e.g. Papadopoulos 2000, 2005a, 2005b, 2006). This oppositionality quickly extends to cover areas well beyond the initial fields of dispute, causing each faction to genuinely believe that the other side is not only wrong in their political positions but, throughout history, they have behaved in a reprehensible way and have no respect for basic human values etc., as opposed to their own side that has always been good, reconciliatory and civilised.

Such sharp *polarisation* at this acute level tends to seep quickly through into every facet of individual and collective realms, affecting at least three distinct and yet inter-related areas: *epistemology, positioning* and *action*.

Each particular group's discourses construct their own clusters of perceiving, knowing and believing that are unique to that group and, under polarised conditions, these clusters acquire their own independence and autonomy, shaping everything around them according to their own logic. If a group feels victimised by another group, its selective perception will be geared towards focusing on incidents that can be interpreted in a way that strengthens the polarised beliefs.

The notion of *positioning* (Davis and Harré 1990, Harré and Van Langenhove 1999) refers to the active effect that discourses have in locating individuals and communities in certain positions. *Action*, then, can only be the consequence of a certain *positioning* given the specifics of the dominant *epistemology* that informs it; in this way, the epistemology, positioning and action keep strengthening and reproducing each other in mutually reciprocal ways.

This means that interventions that ignore the dynamics of epistemology formation and positioning and address only the level of action are not likely to be effective. What is important to remember is that the polarisation tends to continue long after the actual violent conflict comes to an end and it permeates the epistemology, positioning and actions not only of members

of the implicated parties but also of members of the services and organisations that reach out to render assistance.

Polarisation, unipolar archetype and complexity

It is with reference to phenomena of such overwhelming polarisation that
Jungian psychology can be particularly useful, especially by extending
Jung's ideas about the bipolar nature of archetypes. Simply put, the polarisation phenomena in such situations can be appreciated as manifestations
of a state where one pole of the archetype reigns supreme and suppresses
almost totally any elements that belong to the other pole (Papadopoulos
1998a, 1998b, 2000, 2002c, 2005a, 2005b, 2006).

Once we adopt this perspective, then our understanding of other associated phenomena can be enriched.

Usually we experience archetypes in diluted forms that combine not only
the two polarities (positive and negative) but also both collective and
personal dimensions. In occurrences of such acute political polarisation
that escalate into violent factional conflict, what dominate are archetypal
manifestations that are not only unipolar but also saturated by collective
material, thus subjugating personal dimensions. This means that under the
blinding brightness of the unipolar archetype, all other differences and
conflicts (interpersonal or intrapsychic) tend to fade away. Such expressions
of pure archetypal dazzling energy can exert an irresistible fascination,
often of a numinous nature, and individuals and groups tend to become
totally gripped by their power. 'The purity of a unipolar archetypal image,
uncontaminated by any personal dimensions has irresistible powers' (Papadopoulos 1997: 24). In order to convey the overpowering effects of unipolar
archetypal manifestations, I introduced the expressions 'archetypal dazzle',
'archetypal radiation' and 'archetypal whirlpool' (Papadopoulos 1998a,
1998b, 2000, 2002c, 2005a, 2005b, 2006). Indeed, it is as if the purity of the
unipolar archetype emits radiation that, although it is imperceptible, can be
harmful once a certain quantity of it is accumulated in our organisms. The
image of the whirlpool is another apt way to express the irresistible force
that sucks people into set clusters of epistemologies, positioning and
actions, dictated exclusively by the one pole of an archetype.

One of the main effects of being exposed to the archetypal radiation of
unipolarity is to be levelled by blanket oversimplification that lacks complexity, e.g. 'we are only good' and 'they are only bad'. Polarisation implies
simplistic perceptions – black or white, good or bad. Hence, it could be said
that 'the first casualty' of exposure to unipolar archetypes and their resulting
polarised situations 'is complexity' (Papadopoulos 2009). Unipolarity has no
complexity as everything is either on the positive pole or the negative pole of
the archetype. Yet the 'richness of [life] and internal psychological states is

based on the complexity . . . [that is] generated by the various conflictual antitheses and dilemmas' (Papadopoulos 2005a: 37).

The tendency for over-simplification spreads to most areas of functioning. Simplistic becomes the perception of the causes and effects of the conflict as well as what is perceived to be an appropriate response to the conflict. Moreover, the accounts people give about the conflict also become simplistic in order to fit in with the polarised set of clusters of stereotypical formulations (e.g. 'what we did was good' and 'what they did was bad'). It should not be forgotten that this oversimplification tends to overflow beyond the implicated warring factions and also engulfs those who reach out to assist the casualties of the conflict. Staff of the various services and organisations that offer their assistance tend also to get sucked into this whirlpool of over-simplification into sterile and mono-dimensional epistemologies, positioning and actions.

> Thus, paradoxically, in working with refugees, by increasing the level of complexity, despite the pressure to keep things 'simple', new patterns can emerge that can produce not only epistemological clarity but also free both therapists and refugees from falling into fixed, sterile and polarised positions.
>
> (Papadopoulos 2001b: 418)

Increasing the level of complexity can, therefore, reduce the grip of the tyrannical hegemony of the unipolar archetype. This can be achieved (a) by restoring its bipolarity, when positive and negative elements are introduced, and (b) by inflicting cracks on the monolithic collective, when personal dimensions are added.

'Humanising the archetype' – survivors and helpers

In essence, the process of counteracting the effects of a unipolar archetype amounts to what could be called a 'humanisation of the archetype'. I first introduced this term in my paper 'Individual identity and collective narratives of conflict' to describe the 'endeavour to "humanise" the purity of the unipolar archetype' (Papadopoulos 1997: 24) in the context of my work with medical evacuees during the Bosnian war. During that long and arduous work, I became painfully aware of the dehumanising effects collective narratives had on individuals; and those narratives clearly emanated from blatantly unipolar archetypal constellations ('we are only good' and 'they are only bad') devoid of any personal experiences that did not fit in with the extreme polarised formulation. Thus, 'humanising the archetype' refers to the introduction of human dimensions to the inhuman purity of a unipolar archetype, allowing the rich diversity of human and individual experiences to inject it with the messiness of real and actual life. Then the archetype begins to lose its abstract, pure and absolute status and, consequently, its fascinating dazzle. In this way, individuals are enabled to experience their individuality outside the confines of the asphyxiating limits of polarised collective impositions and are enabled to admit exceptions to what they were convinced to be 'the truth', e.g. 'to be honest, I was there when some of us also did terrible things to them', or 'some of them were in fact not that bad to me'. However, often, such complexity is not welcome because the resulting ambiguities and lack of clarity can be unsettling and painful. The simplistic nature of polarisation offers many superficially comforting benefits.

The corresponding polarisation in humanitarian and aid organisations can take various forms; the most obvious one is taking sides, perceiving one faction to be 'right' and the other 'wrong'. Usually, these sympathies follow the same socio-political divisions that gave rise to violent confrontation between the two sides in the first place (e.g. pro- vs anti-American, religious fundamentalism vs secular materialism). In this way, the polarisation that governs the helpers entrenches the original conflict and fuels it further.

However, the polarisation and resulting over-simplification can also affect other dimensions that are not so apparent. Humanitarian organisations and mental health professionals can be equally polarised and their epistemology, positioning and actions can be dictated by over-simplification and lack of complexity in the way they perceive the survivors, the nature and causes of their difficulties and the way help should be offered to them. As the investigations on these matters are carried out by helpers and not by the survivors themselves, the effects of polarisation on the helpers is a neglected area. The usual way that the theory of trauma is used by helpers is one example of how the over-simplification and polarisation can affect helpers (Papadopoulos 2001a, 2001b, 2002a, 2002b).

Field work in a refugee camp

The first time I was invited (in 2006) to consult to the Dadaab refugee camp in Kenya, near the Somali border, was mainly to review the psychological services to refugees and offer appropriate training to staff. The United Nations established the camp in 1991 to offer temporary shelter to 800,000 Somalis who fled their war-torn country. Over the years, the population of the Dadaab camp was reduced to 200,000 but the sub-standard living conditions did not improve. During my visits to Dadaab, I led teams from the 'Centre for Trauma, Asylum and Refugees' (CTAR) of the University of Essex, which included a Jungian analyst, Professor Stefano Carta from Italy.

My work in Dadaab involves consulting to the management team of the camps, consultation to and training of staff (mainly of the counselling services) as well as direct therapeutic contact with refugees. The camp has a handful of trained counsellors and several teams of 'para-counsellors' – young camp residents/refugees who were given brief training to assist the counsellors.

Consultation to the management team

It is always very important to have access to the overall management team of any organisation where one works and it is very fortunate that the Dadaab inter-agency management team always welcomes CTAR input and is very receptive to collaborating with us. Here is one example: during our March–April 2008 visit, there was the issue of a predicted huge new influx of refugees (almost doubling the camp's population) due to the deterioration of the political situation in Somalia. The camp authorities started planning to address the multiplicity of needs of such an influx (e.g. shelter, sanitation, water and food, etc.) and they had all the required expertise to deal effectively with such an emergency. Our input was to help them to consider the complex implications of such a substantial change to the relative stability of the camp. We suggested that, in effect, they were going to have two distinct groups of refugees – the old and the new – and pointed out that it was likely that this division could create three possible outcomes: that the two groups get on well together, become antagonistic to each other to varying degrees, or join together against a third 'other', most likely to be the staff group. In considering various ways of addressing this anticipated polarisation, we suggested that they could seek the assistance of the old group of refugees, acknowledging that they (the refugees) have unique expertise that the staff do not have (i.e. the experience of surviving in the camp for so long). We emphasised the need for staff and old refugees to collaborate to find appropriate ways to share with the new group of refugees their positive and negative experiences of living in the camp, not focusing only on the content of the information but also the best possible medium to convey these experiences, e.g. by enacted narrative stories, information sharing, dance events.

This example illustrates the various realms of polarisation and the type of input that can be offered to counteract its destructive over-simplification. Long after the actual armed conflict that drove those refugees away from their homes, the whole camp milieu still reverberates from its polarised effects in many ways. Refugees are seen as helpless and traumatised and staff are seen as their rescuers and full of endless resources. Many consultation interventions addressed that sharp division with a considerable degree of effectiveness (Papadopoulos 2008, Papadopoulos, Ljubinkovic and Warner 2007). In this particular consultation, we anticipated a possible source of another potentially destructive polarisation which could have then become associated with the existing polarised tendencies. Our suggestions were geared towards increasing complexity, acknowledging the reality of the actual expertise of the old refugees and enabling them to express it in their own way, and increasing the collaboration between all the implicated parties (staff, old and new groups of refugees).

Mother and daughter from Mogadishu

During one of my visits to Dadaab, I was asked to see a mother and daughter who had just succeeded in fleeing the fighting in Mogadishu, found their way to the border (about 800 kilometres away), crossed it and came to the camp where they were found sleeping under a tree. Both were exhausted but in remarkably good physical condition, given their ordeal. The daughter was in her late teens and looked disoriented and frightened. The mother was composed and calm and told me that they had a harrowing escape and that all the male members of her family had been killed.

This is a typical situation where mental health professionals almost automatically would view these two women as traumatised victims and would proceed to treat them as such. In itself, this would not be wrong but it would be inappropriate if this was the only way the two women were viewed and related to. The 'Trauma Grid' (Papadopoulos 2004, 2005c, 2007, 2008) provides a systematic framework that enables the introduction of complexity in such situations and facilitates the identification of different types of responses to adversity; undeniably, the negative effects can be present (e.g. Post Traumatic Stress Disorder) but, in addition, these responses can also include *resilience* (referring to the continuation of existing positive qualities that are maintained despite adversity), and *Adversity-Activated Development* (referring to new positive qualities that are generated as a result of one's exposure to adversity). Consequently, allowing the polarised and over-simplified view to flood one's epistemology, positioning and actions can be limiting and, indeed, dehumanising.

Without going into details about my work with them (due to lack of space), it is important to note that, first, I had to become aware of the grip I felt by the forceful need to help them, save them, make them feel better. Seeing them as victims of such an awful series of tragedies and losses, I was positioned to act based on the assumption that they were just traumatised and totally helpless and I was their rescuer. This is a direct consequence of the dazzling nature of the unipolar archetype. Being aware of this pull, I did my utmost to open up space for the mother to convey the wide range of her experiences and feelings and not only those that fitted within the monolithic image of a helpless victim. Once I created the space within me to view this person in a multidimensional way, the mother was enabled to convey the complexity of her situation and existence. Understandably, she was deva-stated that she had lost her husband and sons, her home and neighbours and her whole life, but at the same time, she clearly conveyed her immense relief of having survived with her daughter. More specifically, her whole being was grateful to Allah for the miracle that saved her and her daughter who, one day, with her own children, would continue their family. The mother was not just a victim but also had a remarkable resilience, was not just fixed in a painful past but was also looking to the future, was not just broken by her grief but was also full of gratitude. Her dignity and humanity were just extraordinary. Hence, I was not just the polarised helper who was assisting a helpless victim but felt grateful for her inspiring humanity. This is a way of humanising the archetype that reduces us to pawns of a levelling unipolar archetypal scenario. Jung was fully aware of this complexity. His following statement, although it became a cliché, still conveys this awareness: 'A psychology of neurosis that sees only the negative elements empties out the baby with the bath water' (Jung 1934, para 355).

Bibliography

Davis, B. and Harré, R. (1990). Positioning: The discursive production of selves. *Journal for the Theory of Social Behaviour*, 20/1: 43–64.

Harré, R. and Van Langenhove, L. (eds.) (1999). *Positioning Theory*. Oxford: Blackwell.

Jung, C.G. (1934). The state of psychotherapy today. In *CW 10: Civilization in Transition*.

Papadopoulos, R.K. (1997). Individual identity and collective narratives of conflict. *Harvest*, vol. 43, 2: 7–26.

—— (1998a). Destructiveness, atrocities and healing: epistemological and clinical reflections. *The Journal of Analytical Psychology*, vol. 43, 4: 455–477.

—— (1998b) Jungian Perspectives In New Contexts. In *The Jungians Today*, ed. A. Casement. London and New York: Routledge.

—— (2000). Factionalism and interethnic conflict: narratives in myth and politics. In *The Vision Thing. Myth, Politics and Psyche in the World*, ed. T. Singer. London and New York: Routledge.

—— (2001a). Refugees, therapists and trauma: systemic reflections. *Context*, No. 54: 5–8.

—— (2001b). Refugee families: issues of systemic supervision. *Journal of Family Therapy*, vol. 23, No. 4: 405–422.

—— (2002a). Refugees, home and trauma. In *Therapeutic Care for Refugees. No Place Like Home*, ed. R. K. Papadopoulos. London: Karnac.

—— (2002b). 'But how can I help if I don't know?' Supervising work with refugee families. In *Perspectives on Supervision*, eds. D. Campbell and B. Mason. London: Karnac.

—— (2002c). The other other: when the exotic other subjugates the familiar other. *Journal of Analytical Psychology*, vol. 47, 2: 163–188.

—— (2004) Trauma in a systemic perspective: Theoretical, organisational and clinical dimensions. Paper presented at the XIV Congress of the International Family Therapy Association in Istanbul.

—— (2005a). Political violence, trauma and mental health interventions. In *Art*

Therapy and Political Violence, eds. D. Kalmanowitz and B. Lloyd. London: Brunner-Routledge.

—— (2005b) Mythical dimensions of storied communities in political conflict and war. In *Balkan Currents: Essays in Honour of Kjell Magnusson*, eds. T. Dulic, R. Kostic, I. Macek and J. Trtak. Uppsala: Centre for Multiethnic Research, Uppsala University.

—— (2005c). Terrorism and psychological trauma. Psychosocial perspectives. *The Journal of Psychological Foundations*, New Delhi, Vol. VII (2): 6–15.

—— (2006). Terrorism and panic. *Psychotherapy and Politics International*, Vol. 4, No. 2: 90–100.

—— (2007) Refugees, Trauma and adversity-activated development. *European Journal of Psychotherapy and Counselling*, 9 (3): 301–312.

—— (2008) Systemic challenges in a refugee camp. *Context*, 16–19.

—— (2009) L'Umwelt, Jung e le reti di immagin; archetipiche. In *Rivista di Psicologia Analitica*, Nuova series no. 26, vol. 78/2008, pp. 93–128.

Papadopoulos, R.K., Ljubinkovic, A., and Warner, S. (2007). Report on assessment of psychosocial needs at the Dadaab refugee camps. Colchester: Centre for Trauma, Asylum and Refugees: University of Essex.

Samuels, A. (1993). *The Political Psyche*. London: Routledge.

—— (1996). From sexual misconduct to social justice. *Psychoanalytic Dialogues*, 6: 295–321.

—— (1997). The political psyche: A challenge to therapists and clients to politicize what they do. In J. Reppen, ed., *More Analysts at Work*. Northvale, NJ: Aronson: 155–82.

—— (1999). Working directly with political, social and cultural material in the therapy session. In J. Lees, ed., *Clinical Counselling in Context*. London: Routledge.

—— (2001). *Politics on the Couch: Citizenship and the Internal Life*. London: Profile.

—— (2002). The hidden politics of healing: Foreign dimensions of domestic practice. *American Imago*, Vol. 59, No. 4: 459–481.

—— (2007). Gender and psyche: Developments in analytical psychology. *British Journal of Psychotherapy*, Vol. 1, No. 1: 31–49.

Chapter 26

Critical looks

The psychodynamics of body hatred

Rozsika Parker

An adolescent girl sent to Winnicott for an assessment constantly touched her face and hid her chin with her hand. Recounting the session some thirty years later she recalled only one remark of Winnicott's. He asked her, 'Is your face lonely?' (personal communication). The question immediately establishes the body as an expression of intrapsychic and interpersonal meanings. My aim with this chapter is to pursue a relational approach to Body Dysmorphic Disorder (BDD): a psychiatric term for the condition of body image disparagement, involving preoccupation with a perceived defect in appearance. If a slight anomaly is present, the person's concern is excessive.

Disparagement of the body, with specific parts selected for particular dislike, seems to be reaching epidemic proportions. Appearance anxiety is afflicting ever younger and younger children. While not precisely causing BDD, contemporary Western culture is providing a matrix within which it can flourish. For bodies are both relationally and culturally constructed by the context in which they live. Susie Orbach, who has written extensively on the role of cultural imagery in eating disorders, points out that the profits of the 'diet/fashion/cosmetic/beauty industry . . . are sustained on the enormity of the body insecurity that they both identify and allege to ameliorate while simultaneously re-inforcing and amplifying this very insecurity' (Orbach 2001: 52).

Here I intend to explore the interpersonal and intrapsychic narcissistic conflicts and desires that sustain the beauty industry, analysing the work-ings of pride and shame in the lived experience of both mild and severe BDD. The affects termed 'the self conscious emotions' (shame, pride, humiliation) are developmentally the earliest human social feelings. All are constructed by an observing other. The myth of the Judgement of Paris conveys the hidden dynamics and purposes involved in submitting the body to assessment, decoration and manipulation. Three goddesses, Athena, Hera and Aphrodite, presented themselves to Paris for him to judge who was the most beautiful. Aware that victory depended not on beauty alone, they all bribed Paris. Athena offered him military prowess, Hera offered him civic power and Aphrodite promised him Helen of Troy if he voted for her. The myth depicts a beauty contest as the desire to 'win over' the other in a struggle for the affirmation of agency, for the confirmation of desirability – and, in a word, to be the most loved.

When the self or other submits the body to judgement, an important aspect of the desire to be loved is the pleasure of pride. Despite polemical reclamation by political movements (gay pride, for example), pride has a bad name, shading as it can do into grandiosity and fuelling shame. The preferred word, self-esteem, nevertheless fails to capture the power of pride: the experience of plenitude, joy, social expansiveness, success, popularity, and agency. The obverse of pride is shame: a sense of failure, inadequacy, helplessness, weakness, defectiveness and humiliation dominated by a fear of loss of the object and the object's love and desire.

The need for pride and the fear of shame drive the Internet social networking sites, where men and women alike post millions of photographs of themselves, suffering severely when others maliciously post unflattering photographs of them. But while the goddesses knew that 'victory' depended not on beauty alone, today 'the judged' experience power, pride and shame as determined overwhelmingly by their bodies. John Berger famously coined the phrase 'men act and women appear' (Berger 1972). Today we all 'appear' regardless (almost) of gender. Managing our appearance, decorating ourselves and selecting the signals our body sends out are integral to our sense of agency in relationships and to experiencing ourselves as actors in our own story. Yet, paradoxically, preoccupation with the body can seal us into the position of the passive object of sight.

Two different experiences of the self are involved in the relational experience of the body; a subjective sense of self and an objective sense of self. In utilizing the idea of different representations of the self I am drawing on two major sources: the theory of mentalization developed by Peter Fonagy *et al.* and the American relational tradition in psychoanalysis with its concept of self reflexivity. Both are inspired by the work of the philosopher William James. He made a distinction between the Me and the I. The Me refers to everything a person feels about themselves through their own observation or through feedback from outside, in other words the set of characteristics we believe to be true of ourselves inferred from the reaction of our social environment. While the I is the experience of self as agent or self as knower – the solid sense of ourselves as people with rights and beliefs. Ideally we are able to move flexibly back and forth between the two different experiences of the self – between experiencing the self as subject with agency, judgement and desire and experiencing the self as an object in the eyes of others (Aron and Sommer Anderson 1998, Fonagy *et al.* 2002).

The myth of the Judgement of Paris and the posting of pictures on the Internet both constitute an attempt to affirm self-as-subject via the experience of self-as-object. I have coined the term 'pathology of judgement' for the state of affairs that pertains when flexibility between experiences of the self is stalled and judgement is placed overwhelmingly in the assumed harsh hands, or rather eyes, of the other, in either severe or mild BDD. Pride may then be sought, but what's found is shame.

Within a psychoanalytic framework we can think about the dialectic in terms of narcissism. When self-as-subject dominates we encounter not healthy pride but grandiosity and an impaired ability to experience self-as-object among other selves. When self-as-object dominates we encounter not a constructive, responsive sensitivity to the other but a lack of sense of agency and vitality. The dialectic takes place both interpersonally and intrapsychically. Thomas Ogden expresses this rather neatly: 'Self-reflective thought occurs when I (as subject) looks at Me (as object)' (in Aron and Sommer Anderson 1998: 9).

Self-as-object dominates in the experience of shame. This is because the capacity to experience shame first appears in connection with the realization that the self can be seen from outside. In shame there is always an awareness of an observer, a possible observer, a past observer, an approving or condemnatory observer (Yorke 2008). The mental capacity to move back and forth and to maintain the tension between a view of self as object and view of self as subject becomes stalled and the imagined gaze of the other defines the self as weak, ugly, defective, abnormal, a failure, helpless and unable to exert self-control.

An intense sense of shame is common to all sufferers from BDD. Shame generates the condition and shame maintains the secrecy that surrounds it (Gilbert and Miles 2002). The preoccupation with appearance – the constant consultation of the mirror, the endless appeal for external judgement ('does my bum look big in this?') manifested by the sufferer from BDD is evidence of the painful dominance of the objective-sense-of-self and the desire for a more secure, positive subjective sense of self. The question asked of the mirror is not 'Who am I?' but 'Am I successfully controlling and concealing the person I fear myself to be. Am I making my shamefully unlovable self lovable?'

Acute cases of BDD are unlikely to reach the psychotherapist's consulting room because shame institutes hiding and concealment. People suffering from acute BDD are frequently totally housebound by their condition, sometimes suicidal, and if they manage to leave home, more often than not it is to seek help from cosmetic surgeons or dermatologists. However, elsewhere I have argued that we need to extend the definition of BDD to cover the mild and fluctuating as well as the constant and disabling (Parker 2003). Without suggesting that the degree of distress between a bad hair day and acute BDD is remotely comparable, there are connections. There is a continuum.

Any part of the body can become the focus for self-hatred. Surveys of the frequency with which body parts are selected for hatred in the USA found skin to be the most common, followed in frequency by hair, nose, eyes, legs/knees, chin/jaw, breast/nipples, stomach/waist, lips, penis, weight, cheeks. A great deal of work has been done on the meaning of skin as a psychic container (Anzieu 1990, Bick 1968, Pines 1993) However, a British survey identified nose and hair to be more frequently a site of concern than skin (Veale *et al.* 1996). Hatred of a body part can signify a defence against total immersion or suffusion in shame. Through splitting, there is an identification with the shaming Other while the object of shame is encapsulated in the perceived defect.

The desire driving the selection of the body part for hatred is not consciously for beauty but for normality, often understood as symmetricality. The homogenous, symmetrical body can be read as a symptom of the desire for an internal sense of unity – a defence against conflicting divergent forces and desires which are experienced as shameful by the shame-prone. Central to the experience of shame is a sense of incongruity or inappropriateness. We need also to bear in mind Western culture's preoccupation with a symmetrical, homogenized body. Current airbrushed representations of the body deny physical diversity, as Western culture becomes more and more ethnically diverse and longevity increases. Elsewhere I have suggested that, amongst current preoccupations with the body, fear and avoidance of difference is primary (Parker 2003). The following, telling, typical quotation is from a patient of Katherine Phillips, an American psychiatrist who has written extensively on BDD:

> I'm the one who looks ugly. It started with my nose, one of my nostrils stuck out more than the other. I remember catching a view of myself in the mirror one day and panicking. I thought, is that what you look like? You look a terrible freak . . . My nostrils don't bother my any more, my skin took over from them. Now all I can think about is how bad my skin looks. I think about it most of the day.
>
> (Phillips 1986: 10)

The onset of BDD is frequently at adolescence, when the pervasive sense of not being good enough crystallizes into a concrete conviction of 'not measuring up' (Laufer 1995). Turning against the body is, of course, a common response to puberty and the changes set in train. The body is experienced as the enemy responsible for the sense of abnormality and worthlessness that dogs the adolescent. The body is the badge of acceptance or rejection by a peer group once appearances are selected as a focus of group cohesion and integration. In particular, a longing for gender certainty becomes a conviction that the body is too male or too female, too small or too big. There is, however, a continuum. While one adolescent with acne may react with awkwardness, another may withdraw from the world, convinced that their face condemns them to ridicule and rejection. Everything depends on how severely shame-prone the individual is.

Two developmental lines have been identified in the growth of shame: one involving narcissism and the other concerning instincts and control (Miller 1985). Sigmund Freud viewed shame as a servant of morality (Freud 1909). He considered shame to be a reaction formation designed to maintain the repression of forbidden exhibitionistic instincts. It's a line of thinking useful in understanding BDD, but within the confines of this short chapter, I am focussing on the work of later theorists who have understood shame as failure of the ego to achieve a narcissistic ideal. Shame emerges in response to an awareness of a discrepancy between the ego ideal and the perceived self when goals and images represented by the ego ideal are not achieved. In an appearance-driven culture, it is hardly surprising that failure to achieve the ego ideal should be experienced as a failure to look 'good'.

Shame provokes hiding. Concealing clothing – baggy or padded – hats and make-up are all employed in BDD to hide the hated body part. Grooming provides a similar function. When hair, for example, is seen as too thin, too plentiful, too flat or too asymmetrical, hours and hours are spent grooming, snipping, flattening or fluffing and a great deal of money is devoted to acquiring hair products which seem briefly to offer solution and solace. Preoccupation with skin can precipitate one of the compulsive rituals associated with BDD: picking. People pick their skin for hours, drawing blood and leaving scars. As in other forms of self-harm, the perpetrator feels powerless to stop the struggle to control the surface of the body, obsessively eliminating any discernible imperfection. A patient of mine, reflecting on a particularly painful and scarring picking session, said, 'At least I was doing something about myself.' A comment that foxed me at the time but later I understood that she was describing the struggle to expunge shame and achieve both a sense of personal agency and accept-ability in the eyes of the other, isolating a sense of badness and self-blame in the hated body part.

For someone in the grip of self-as-object, and hence overwhelmingly defined from without by the other, the mirror is experienced as judge and final arbiter. A sufferer from BDD compulsively checks himself or herself in the mirror. Compared with ordinary mirror use, mirror checking is exces-sive and time-consuming. Literally hours can be spent at the mirror and visits are repeated many, many times a day. Looking in the mirror people experience themselves as judged by the mirror no matter that this is actually their own projected harsh self-judgement. On the other hand, for those who feel concealment is impossible, mirrors exacerbate the sense of helplessness and worthlessness, and are hence avoided.

Inevitably the other is engaged as a mirror and many times a day is besieged with pleas for reassurance. Mollon (2002) cites Sartre's observation that the vision of one's self that the other sees is essentially unknowable to us. To a person preoccupied with the concealment of feared ugliness, this is unbearable. Reassurance is, however, received as patronizing, trivializing or dishonest, while reassurance withheld is interpreted as an unspoken condemnation, and any attempt at an honest or measured response is heard as criticism. Given that the person with BDD usually appears unblemished and even beautiful to the eye of the beholder, the search for reassurance, for protection against the vicious inner judge, often provokes ridicule and exasperation, driving the sufferer into ever-greater isolation.

A major problem with identifying non-acute BDD within psychotherapy is that patients are often hesitant to disclose BDD. As Clifford Yorke writes, 'guilt brings material into analysis while shame keeps it out' (2008: 37). Sometimes patients can spend years in psychotherapy without 'owning up' to the grinding, limiting preoccupation. Because shame as the driving force behind BDD is so primitive and unspeakable, countertransference often alerts the psychotherapist to the presence of BDD before the patient discloses the suffering. Take, for example, a 30-year-old man who sought psychotherapy following the breakdown of a relationship and the collapse of his career. I noticed that each time he came to see me, I would have a fleeting sense that my consulting room was shabby, sparse and in need of a 'face lift'. I began to understand the experience six months into our work together when he admitted that he was continually, painfully preoccupied with his face: 'It's so washed out and tired.' He turned a harsh, measuring gaze both on himself and on the outside world. Pathological shame states had been triggered at adolescence when he was teased for being a late developer and he became preoccupied with his face. But not surprisingly the propensity for shame had deep roots in his family of origin.

The aetiology of shame-proneness in the psychoanalytic literature is understood to lie with early mirroring. Infant observation has identified shame in babies. The 'still face' experience demonstrates the manner in which babies avert their eyes when mothers do not respond as expected. Shame develops in response to an empathic break between the mirroring object and the self.

Amongst theories of mirroring Alessandra Lemma (2009) has usefully distinguished two modes determining BDD, leading to a deficit in symbolic thinking and making it more likely that undigested projections become concretely located in the body. Peter Fonagy's concept of mentalization is also helpful in thinking about the aetiology of BDD in that he seeks to explain the factors that inhibit the development of a strong sense of self as subject which is so central to the evolution of shame and body hatred. The child finds in the caregiver's mind an image of herself/himself motivated by beliefs, feelings and intentions. When psychic reality is poorly integrated through inadequate mirroring the self tends to be experienced as a physical being without psychological meaning. Hence physical attributes come to reflect states such as internal well-being, control, and self-worth. And not having a clear sense of themselves from within means an individual needs other people to react to them, leading to the overwhelming importance of appearance (Fonagy et al. 2002).

Of course, it may not so much be the actual childhood experience that makes for shame-proneness, but how it was understood. A mismatch of attunement, with the emergence of shame, is inevitable and a necessary aspect of development. It is through the mirroring look of the mother, and the equally necessary shifting away of her gaze, that the awareness of self is brought into being (Pajaczkowska and Ward 2008). Shame is a 'normal' and potentially creative affect, establishing boundaries and indicating concern and interest. As Lynd writes, 'experiences of shame confronted full in the face may throw an unexpected light on who one is and point the way to who one may become' (1958: 20). But 'unexpected light' is intolerable for someone suffering from body disparagement.

Ana-Maria Rizzuto (2008) refers to the body of the pathologically ashamed as a shame metaphor. The ashamed person believes him/herself to be repulsive in bodily appearance, foul smelling, monstrously horrifying. The fantasy of the hideous body is an unconscious organizer of painful experience for patients suffering from a pathological disposition to feelings of shame. The physical reality used for shame metaphors is not that of the actual body as a physical reality but a mental construct of that physical reality as it was experienced in reality and in fantasy in the libidinal, aggressive and communicative experiences with the parental objects.

An understanding of relational shame and body hatred requires a social and political contextualisation. Racism, sexism, immigration, class shifts and the condition of parenthood all have to be taken into account. While at a cultural level, the intensity of disgust mobilized by a perceived defect is, I suggest, driven by the dynamics of pollution and taboo which are maintained by threats of contempt and shaming. This is the complex raw material on which the beauty industry goes to work – and has its part in creating.

Bibliography

Anzieu, D. (1990) A Skin for Thought. London: Karnac.
Aron, L. and F. Sommer Anderson (eds.) (1998) Relational Perspectives on The Body. Hillsdale and London: The Analytic Press.
Berger, J. (1972) Ways of Seeing. London: Penguin.
Bick, E. (1968) The experience of skin in early object-relations. International Journal of Psychoanalysis 49: 484–6.
Fonagy, P., E. Gergely, E.L. Jurist and M. Target (eds.) (2002) Affect Regulation, Mentalization and the Development of the Self. London and New York: Karnac.
Freud, S. (1909) Five Lectures on Psychoanalysis, SE11. London: Hogarth Press.

Gilbert, P. and J. Miles (eds.) (2002) *Body Shame: Conceptualisation, Research and Treatment*. Hove and New York: Brunner-Routledge.

Laufer, M. (ed.) (1995) *The Suicidal Adolescent*. London: Karnac.

Lemma, A. (2009) Being Seen or Being Watched? A Psychoanalytic Perspective on Body Dysmorphia. *International Journal of Psychoanalysis*, 90.

Lynd, H.M. (1958) *On Shame and the Search for Identity*. London: Routledge.

Miller, S. (1985) *The Shame Experience*. Hillsdale and London: Analytic Press.

Mollon, P. (2002) *Shame and Jealousy: The Hidden Turmoils*. London: Karnac.

Orbach, S. (2001) *Hunger Strike: Starving Amidst Plenty*. New York: Other Press.

Pajaczkowska, C. and I. Ward (eds.) (2008) *Shame and Sexuality: Psychoanalysis and Visual Culture*. London and New York: Routledge.

Parker, R. (2003) Body hatred. *British Journal of Psychotherapy*, 19(4).

Phillips, K.A. (1986) *The Broken Mirror: Understanding and Treating Body Dysmorphic Disorder*. Oxford: Oxford University Press.

Pines, D. (1993) *A Woman's Unconscious Use of her Body*. London: Virago.

Rizzuto, A.-M. (2008) Shame in psychoanalysis: The function of unconscious fantasies. In C. Pajaczkowska and I. Ward (eds.) (2008) *Shame and Sexuality: Psychoanalysis and Visual Culture*. London and New York: Routledge.

Veale, D., K. Gournay, W. Dryden, A. Boocock, F. Shah, R. Wilson and J. Walburn (1996) Body Dysmorphic Disorder: a cognitive behavioural model and pilot randomised controlled trial. *Behaviour Research and Therapy*, 39: 1381–93.

Veale, D., K. Gournay, W. Dryden, A. Boocock, F. Shah, R. Wilson and J. Walburn (1996) Body Dysmorphic Disorder: a survey of 50 cases. *British Journal of Psychiatry*, 169: 196–2001

Yorke, C.B. (2008) A psychoanalytic approach to the understanding of shame. In C. Pajaczkowska and I. Ward (eds.) (2008) *Shame and Sexuality: Psychoanalysis and Visual Culture*. London and New York: Routledge.

Note

1 Rozsika Parker is writing a book on body anxiety, *Critical Looks*. The above chapter is based on a longer paper published in *The British Journal of Psychotherapy* 19(4), 2003.

Chapter 27

Where is paradise?
The mapping of a myth[1]

Fred Plaut

I am proud to call Andrew my closest friend. The bonds of friendship could not have been stronger if we had been brothers. We have shared professional interests ever since he came to see me for supervision over thirty years ago when I practiced at Devonshire Place, London W1, and he lived just round the corner in Marylebone High Street. The neighbourliness has continued on all levels that are essential to being fully alive. That it has endured is the more astonishing when one considers the difference in our ages, his 60 years against my ninety-six, of which I have lived abroad for the last twenty with at least annual visits to my family and friends in London.

The number of publications, seven books and journal publications more numerous than I know plus a seemingly endless series of lectures, seminars and workshops at home and all over the globe are evidence of his ingenious and fertile mind. His influence has not only been limited to the profession, it has been widely recognised by the media.

If I am now asked to contribute to a Festschrift, my mind goes back to the 1980s, when Andrew asked me to be a co-editor of his Critical Dictionary of Jungian Analysis *which has seen publication in many editions and languages. I gladly do so with alacrity and yes, with love.*

[Editor's note: Since writing this, sadly, Fred Plaut died in June 2009]

Why should anyone in our day and age be interested in what seems an absurd undertaking: the location of a myth? Well, it is easy to be clever after the event and to forget that the Garden of Eden, the terrestrial Paradise or 'Heaven on Earth' (as the Poles call it) was an indubitable fact for well over fifteen hundred years for most Christian believers. For the knowledge revealed in the Holy Bible, specifically Genesis 2: 8–14, was invested with the same authority and wielded the same influence as a scientifically proven fact does today.

Surprisingly, the interest in maps of Paradise has continued right into modern times as the following books show. Two, which bear exactly the same title, *Where was Paradise?* (Delitzsch, 1881; Hennig, 1949), are concerned with the reconstruction of the site of the terrestrial Paradise or

Garden of Eden, and another (Wendrin 1924) is simply entitled *The Discovery of Paradise* without a question mark. The author alleges that the true Paradise had been situated in what is now East Germany and that the Jews had falsely claimed the Biblical site to be 'eastward in Eden'.

Historically speaking, the mapping of Paradise cannot be isolated from other Christian influences on cartography. Jerusalem was the centre of the known world, usually represented in circular form. This provided a schema with Paradise in the east and on top of the map of Jerusalem at the junction of the horizontal and the vertical lines of the T of the familiar T in O and with the circumfluent ocean forming the periphery. In this way the tripartite Roman world schema was combined with the Biblical division of the world among Noah's sons: Shem inheriting Asia, which was the largest part, Japhet Europe, and Ham, who was of dark complexion, seemed the natural heir to Africa. Amalgamations and modifications with other world schema, including that of Ptolemy (who was unhampered by Biblical authority), are of later date.

Early evidence

There is, of course, the famous family of maps based on the Christian schema but also containing much information, including pagan legends:

1   The 'Psalter' Mappamundi, twelfth century.
2   The Hereford map by Richard de Haldingham, in Hereford Cathedral, c. 1300.
3   The Ebstorf world map, c. 1235, destroyed in World War II.

The continued interest in Paradise is, in part, due to a fusion in our minds. No matter how often we remind ourselves that the terrestrial Paradise or the Garden of Eden was a potentially localizable area on Earth, it becomes amalgamated with the celestial Paradise to which the righteous hope to be admitted after death. Therefore I use 'Paradise' to cover both aspects, the literal and the mythological or symbolic. (Etymologically, the word is derived from the Old Persian *Pairidaeza* meaning enclosure or park.) This fusion spurred on the searchers to discover the site, perhaps because of the other forbidden fruit from the tree of life which would bestow immortality on earth. Maybe they found the admission as a merit award too hard to earn; they may also have been spurred on by the usual greed for precious stones and gold which became associated with Paradise, as in Sir Walter Raleigh's *Eldorado*. On the other hand, the searchers were well aware of the special security devices – angels with flaming swords, walls of fire, castles with moats and unscaleable walls and – above all, a secret location, preferably an island in the ocean. Even if one or more rivers were found this clue could not be followed up since the river would disappear into the ground and thereby foil any nefarious designs. Mapmakers seem to have found themselves in a double bind: on the one hand they had to follow scriptural instruction as to the location of the Garden of Eden 'in the East' and delineate it. On the other hand, they dared not be precise as this might lead travellers into temptation. I intend to use the mapping of Paradise to show what happens to mapmakers or any man who comes to an ideological crossroads.

There are indications that a few mapmakers had realised long before the Renaissance and the Reformation that they were not dealing with something as tangible as the name of a town, say Jerusalem, when it came to showing the Garden of Eden. But even if they suspected this could be fiction they may not have been aware that it was of the special kind we call a myth. Add to this the dangers of heresy and it is easy to understand that great caution was required not to deviate from the divine order of things, nor could it be suggested that the Highest Authority might not have been geographically correct. Map makers may also have had a hunch that without an orientating myth which linked Christian values with an explanation of man's origin and place in the cosmic order, chaos and anarchy would have threatened the very foundations of civilization.

The problems increased in proportion to the discoveries that were being made: how could the small space between Jerusalem in the centre and Paradise on top, taken as radius of the circular world, contain all that was becoming known? There were several options open to the makers of world maps.

The manuscript maps, or rather, their surviving copies in books such as Cosmas Indicopleustes' *Christian Topography*, written between 535 and 547 AD, constitute early evidence of a literal interpretation. Isidore of Seville's major works, *De Natura Rerum* and *Etymologiae*, followed on a hundred years later and Beatus of Liebana wrote his *Commentary on the Apocalypse* in the eighth century. Cosmas was a traveller who had seen a great deal of the world yet invented a cosmographic system which accounted in a highly original way for phenomena at which he looked entirely through the eyes of a Bible scholar. His world was oblong, modelled on the Table in the Tabernacle – much else was his own invention.

By contrast, Isidore's span of mind – he compiled his work quoting a hundred and fifty authors – was all-encompassing. He could cope with a variety of world views including classical concepts.

I would describe Cosmas as a pioneer visionary, Beatus as a single-minded missionary, and Isidore came close to being a scientist. It seems significant that in the oldest known copy of an eighth-century world map in the Vatican Library, an abstract symbol of Paradise rather than a portrayal of Adam and Eve was sufficient for Isidore to mark the location of Paradise.

Later evidence

If Jerusalem could not be budged from its central position, Paradise could: while it coincided with the easternmost point on top of the map, no east-west expansion was possible. As shown by Hanns Rust's late fifteenth-century map produced in Augsburg, popular medieval maps were still saleable although out of date. The notions portrayed were the same as those which had been current two to three hundred years earlier. Andreas Walsperger's map, of 1448, with south on top, shows the Cape of Southern Africa breaking through several of the circles which surround the map.

In the fourteenth century, Ranulf Higden, author of the *Polycronicon*, seemed to have become a little negligent about Paradise and so, by gradual stages, the mixture of faith and doubt resulted in Paradise becoming vagrant. Various compromises were tried to bridge the gulf between old and new orientation. For example, Fra Mauro, in his large wall map of 1459 in the Biblioteca Marciana, Venice, resorted to the ingenious device of confining the whole Paradise story into one of the four circles between the round map and the oblong frame. But the vagrant Paradise did not give up all that easily before becoming relegated to a merely decorative position. After all it had been found on the east coast of South America by Columbus himself.

My thesis of alternating progress and regress and the development from literal to symbolic thought depends on the evolution of both the historical era as well as the individual mapmakers' personal and psychological predisposition. For example, d'Ailly, Bishop of Cambray, postulated a mountain so high as to nearly reach the lunar orbit (Buron 1930). It gathered the waters of a vast lake and the powerful river of Paradise emerged, bearing some resemblance to the cosmic role of Cosmas' mountain. Santarem remarks on the absence of Jerusalem from d'Ailly's map. Paradise is also strangely absent considering he was a cardinal. He seems to have lived in two worlds – one was geographical, the other could best be summed up by his statement, following Aristotle: 'Ce[o]lum non est de natura' (the heavens are not made of natural material).

The vagrancy of Paradise was followed by a period in the making of world maps, particularly of the seventeenth century, which may have started with Fra Mauro's clever device: Paradise was relegated to a mere decorative detail. As many of these maps are collectable, I shall concentrate on a few examples. One of the best is Jan Janssonius' world map, 1632 (cf. Figure 27.1). He finds a neutral solution by putting the idyllic scene into a park-like (European) landscape in the upper empty space between the hemispheres.

In a composite atlas dating from the end of the seventeenth century, James Moxon devotes the first two pages to world maps. The first is a planisphere outline with a conspicuous border, consisting of fourteen Biblical scenes.

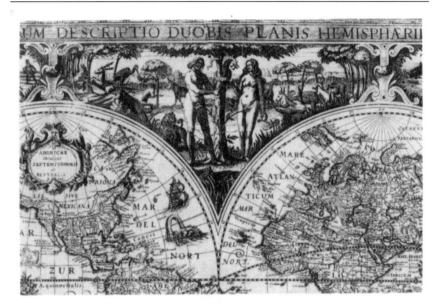

Figure 27.1 Jan Janssonius' world map, 1632.

The seven upper pictures correspond to the seven days of the Creation. The second map concentrates on the Holy Land with the Garden of Eden enlarged and not far from the Tower of Babel. This represents an uncommon mixture of Pagan and Christian mythology. Moxon's emphasis on the marginal vignettes is striking and appears to be of greater importance than the geographical content, which consists of a planisphere world map in outline only. The location of the Garden of Eden is shown rather imprecisely. Moxon's map is a milestone in as much as it stands between Paradise as a decorative detail and a powerful trend towards the rehabilitation of Paradise at its classical site, Mesopotamia.

Among the Defenders of the Faith (meaning the insistence on a definable location, as a reconstruction of the original site of Eden) was Marmaduke Carver. As Rector of Harthill in Yorkshire, after much research, he decided in his old age to publish *A Discourse of the Terrestrial Paradise Aiming at a More Probable Discovery of the True Situation of that Happy Place of Our First Parents' Habitation* (1666). The doubters, according to Carver, had arrived 'at last at the height of superlative insolence (among other Blasphemies) to propound the History of Paradise to scorn and derision, a mere *Utopia*, or Fiction of a place that never was, to the manifest and designed undermining of the Authority and Veracity of the Holy Text.' Indeed he discovered (not by actual travel) *the* place a little further to the north, which truly answered the description of Moses. There it was, at a locality called Eden in Armenia: a river which afterwards branched into four streams.

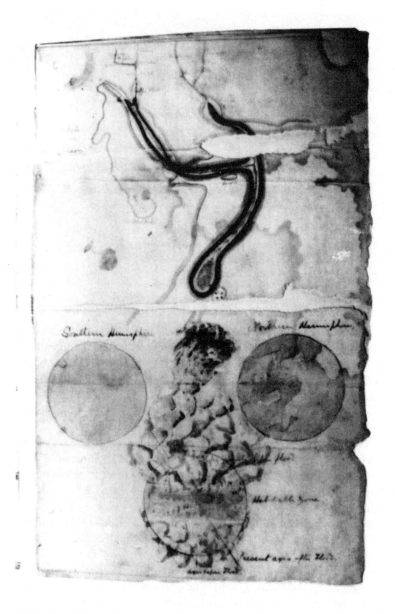

Figure 27.2 General Gordon's manuscript, 1882: Part of East Africa, Arabia and the Red Sea, above a world map.

Salomonis van Til's (1701) book is called *Malachius Illustratus*: Tractatus de situ Paradisi Terrestris. His river of Paradise runs in a straight line between the 34th and 35th parallel, about 400 kilometres east of Damascus, through 'God's Garden', which it waters like a canal running past an orchard, and then branches into four streams, which by a complex network find their way to the Persian Gulf.

Coming up to more modern times, General Gordon's manuscript, signed and dated February 26, 1882, includes maps to support his complex thesis that Paradise had been situated (before the Flood, of course) in the Seychelles, on Praslin (Plaut 1982, cf. Figure 27.2).

Some of those people who desperately wanted to reconstruct the site of Paradise seemed to have been so single-minded and certain of being right that one wonders whether their determination was not close to fanaticism. A few searchers launched into print, including Moritz Engel (1850). His book, *Die Lösung der Paradiesesfrage*, was written in old age. He disclaims that his title, which translated means *The solution of the Paradise problem*, is not as immodest as readers may think since eighty researchers before him tried to find the location and failed! His aim, we are told, was partly to serve science and partly to focus the utmost energy onto the smallest points (of the Scriptures). Both on the title page and in the text of his tract Engel quotes 'The stone which the builders rejected has become the chief corner-stone' (Psalms 118, 22).

My last example of a Paradise reconstruction is the most bizarre, as well as one of the youngest, for it was published in 1924. I am referring to Franz von Wendrin's book *The Discovery of Paradise* (1924). The author claims that he managed to decode some prehistoric ideograms carved in rocks in Sweden which had been regarded as of no significance. He then sets about demolishing all previous theories of location, above all of Biblical sites. Von Wendrin connects his discovery with a racial hierarchy: Paradise belongs to the Germanic races. He demolishes the existing evidence on the grounds that the Hebrews had laid false claim to it. The author ends by expressing the hope that the Lord will liberate us from inferior races! On the other hand, it is surprising that none of the numerous Scripture maps and atlases of the nineteenth century mention the Holy Land with reference to the location of Paradise.

Conclusion

Finally, I return to my point about the need for a myth by which man finds a preliminary explanation for many observed phenomena. As it gives an explanation, so it also attributes meaning to life. Graphic illustrations which become maps serve also as a guide in moral and educational matters and do not require literacy: they evoke, like music, an immediate response. But while some people have to cling to the literal facts which are either true or false, others see the symbolic meaning without the literal fact, for example, treating a precise location on a map as evidence. But why did Pierre d'Ailly of whom Columbus thought so highly, leave both Jerusalem and Paradise off his map although they are mentioned in the text? I suggest that like many great men he was able to live on two planes. Beazley puts it well: 'The terrestrial Eden had one existence under two conditions, visible and invisible, corporeal and incorporeal, sensual and intellectual. As pertaining to this world, it existed [. . .] in a land which was on, but not of, the earth that we inhabit. For it lay on higher ground; it breathed a purer air; and though many of the saints had fixed it in the East, it was really beyond our ken (Beazley, 1897–1906, I, 323).

So perhaps the truth of the matter is that the myth of Paradise, like any symbol, connects two worlds which our minds can perceive and synthesise with the two hemispheres of our brains.

Bibliography

Beazley, C. R. (1897–1906) *The Dawn of Modern Geography*, 3 vols. London: Henry Frowde.

Buron, E. (1930) *Ymago Mundi de Pierre d'Ailly*, 3 vols. Paris: Maisoneuve.

Carver, M. (1666) *A Discourse of the Terrestrial Paradise Aiming at a More Probable Discovery of the True Situation of that Happy Place of Our First Parents' Habitation*. London: James Flesher.

Delitzsch, F. (1881) *Wo lag das Paradies?* Leipzig: W. De Gruyter.

Engel, M. (1850) *Die Lösung der Paradiesfrage*. Leipzig: O. Schilze.

Hennig, R. (1949) *Wo lag das Paradies?* Berlin: Verlag.

Plaut, F. (1982) General Gordon's map of paradise. *Encounter*, June/July: 20–32.

van Til, S. (1701) *Malachius Illustratus: Tractatus de situ Paradisi Terrestris*. Amsterdam: Apid S et J. Luchtmans.

von Wendrin, F. (1924) *Die Entdeckung des Paradieses*. Braunschweig: Georg Westermann.

Note

1 A different version of this text was published in *The Map Collector*, 29: 2–7, Dec 1984.

Chapter 28

Post-Jungians and in praise of multiplicity

Marcus Quintaes and Henrique Pereira

Andrew Samuels is probably the Jungian analyst and thinker from overseas who has visited Brazil the most often in the last twenty years. Since the early 1990s, Samuels has come to our country on numerous occasions to share his psychological experience and knowledge with the Brazilian Jungian community. Rio de Janeiro, São Paulo, Salvador, Belo Horizonte, Canela were among the cities that received this British analyst – and, given his concern for politics, we could say British citizen. During his long journey through our tropical lands, Samuels presented very many contemporary topics and themes. Amongst themes of theoretical and clinical interest, he referred to the relationship of depth psychology and political transformation, the fascination of fundamentalism, the question of the father's body, the relationship between personal anguish and social despair, the notion of the 'good-enough leader', the experience of love and its pains. His most recent lecture, given in São Paulo in November 2008, was on the theme of transforming aggression in personal and cultural contexts.

Most of Samuels' books have by now been translated into Portuguese. However, it was undoubtedly the translation and publication of his 1985 volume *Jung and the Post-Jungians* in 1989 (1989b) that made him a fundamental point of reference for the Brazilian Jungian field. This book is now a Jungian classic both above and below the equator. In it, Samuels presented the main ideas and concepts of the theory and practice of analytical psychology – archetype, complex, ego, personality development, dreams, analytical process – as they were formulated by Jung, as well as the contributions and revisions by post-Jungian authors. We would like to highlight here two topics that we consider essential to understand the importance and repercussions of this book, particularly in Brazil. The first refers to the use of the term 'post-Jungian'. What does this expression mean? What is the *telos* of this image?

We have observed that Jungian psychology has lost much of its brilliance and interest since Jung's death. It seems that many Jungians are satisfied with repeating the words of the master. Hence, analytical psychology gradually became impervious to exchanges with other bodies of knowledge, avoiding the discussion of ideas differing from its own. After Jung, few original conceptions blossomed in the Jungian field. Does this tendency indicate that Jungians were afraid of putting Jung's ideas to the test? Only by understanding this historical scenario as the starting point can we understand the significance of the post-Jungian movement and counter the illusory fantasy that the 'post' prefix can be interpreted as a statement that Jung's ideas are simply obsolete. Rather, the post-Jungian attitude implies an ethical commitment to take Jung's thinking onwards – that is, the intention is to promote the expansion of the borders of analytical psychology beyond the territories already conquered. But there is more. If we wish to deepen the metaphor, we can describe the post-Jungian attitude as involving also the capacity to leave behind and mourn those lands that proved to be infertile and unproductive (for example, the gender prejudices built into the concepts of anima and animus). People came to see that the post-Jungians are with Jung even when they go beyond Jung.

According to Samuels, then, the post-Jungian attitude means rejecting the inappropriate reverence and passive acceptance of Jung's psychology, avoiding an attitude that could be depicted and defined as *fundamentalist* in psychology. An example, taken from the journal *Spring* (2001), entitled *Jungian Fundamentalism*, can help to elucidate the question:

> Several years ago, as a courtesy, we sent a Jungian analyst (a graduate of Zurich's Jung Institute (in Geneva) a few sample issues of *Spring* when she expressed an interest in what we were publishing. Months went by, and we did not hear anything from her, either a thank you, whether she had received the journals, or what she thought of them. Curious and fearing that perhaps the issues had not arrived, we contacted the analyst and asked her if she had received them. She said she had and apologized for not thanking us for them more promptly. Then, there was an awkward pause. So, even more curious, we asked her what she thought of the journals. She said she liked them well enough but was puzzled. She wondered why we bothered to publish essays on psychology since Jung had written everything that needed to be written about psychology already and nothing more was needed!
>
> (Livernois, 2001: v)

The post-Jungian attitude consists precisely in refusing this position, since it implies both a closeness to and a critical distance from Jung's legacy. It is important to stress the word 'critical' in this scenario. Samuels, in an article entitled 'Will the post-Jungians survive?' (1988), commented that if he were to rewrite *Jung and the Post-Jungians*, its new title would be *Critical Analytical Psychology*. This critical detachment is what allows post-Jungians the necessary freedom of thought to engage fully with Jung's writings. In a necessary sense, the post-Jungian attitude means adopting a pluralist perspective in depth psychology. It is no coincidence that Samuels' next book was called *The Plural Psyche* (1989). In this work, pluralism is described as the interplay between multiplicity and unity, not used as a synonym for multiplicity. The one and the many, not the one or the many. From a pluralistic perspective, theoretical and practical differences are welcome, and so is the consensus, as long as it does not eliminate the specific value of particular points of view. To summarize, no theory is *a priori* better than any other, since all show advantages and disadvantages. The corollary of this in clinical practice is that no material of the patient is considered, on principle, to be more important. So the analysis of the transference–countertransference is not a 'better' thing for the clinician to do than working with images and symbols – and vice-versa. This fits in with how we are as persons. As Samuels (2002a: 16) explains: 'we face the pluralist task of reconciling our many inner voices and images with the desire and need of feeling integrated and being able to speak with a single voice.'

Pluralism, as we know, is rooted in the thought of William James (2006). However, we should not forget how much Jung himself engaged the philosophy of this American thinker (Shamdasani 2003; Pereira 2007). In his preface to his essay 'The Theory of Psychoanalysis', dated 1913, Jung (1967) quotes a passage by James to bolster his putting forward ideas and theories that differed from the psychoanalytical orthodoxy represented by Freud's conceptions:

> You must bring out of each word its practical cash-value, set it at work within the stream of your experience. It appears less a solution, then, than as a program for more work, and particularly as an indication of the ways in which existing realities may be *changed. Theories thus become instruments, not answers to enigmas, in which we can rest.* We don't lie back upon them, we move forward, and, on occasion, make nature over again by their aid.
>
> (James 2006: 26)

Jung's kinship to James' pluralism goes much deeper than the passage quoted above, but this cannot be fully entered into here. However, it would be worth recalling a passage from Jung in which he himself reveals an explicitly pluralistic approach. At a medicine and psychotherapy conference in 1945, he remarked:

> Theories are to be avoided except as mere auxiliars. As soon as a dogma is made of them, it is evident that an inner doubt is being stifled. Very many theories are needed before we can get even a rough picture of the psyche's complexity. It is therefore quite wrong when people accuse psychotherapists of being unable to reach agreement even on their own theories. Agreement could only spell one-sidedness and

desiccation. One could as little catch the psyche in a theory as one could catch the world.

(Jung 1966: para. 198)

Now, Samuels, siding with pluralism as the philosophical or ideological approach perfectly adapted for depth psychology, reveals himself, more than ever, as a 'Jungian'! He steps forward as an heir to the restless, heretical and anti-dogmatic character which marks Jung's psychology – or at least a portion of it. The pluralist temperament embedded in the expression 'post-Jungian' constitutes, by itself, part of the soul of Jung's analytical psychology. Samuels – with others, notably James Hillman– deserves credit for highlighting this aspect of Jungian psychology. In an article written in 2002, 'The hidden politics of healing: Foreign dimensions of domestic practice', he tackles again the discussion about pluralism in depth psychology, showing the risks, but also (and more importantly) the benefits of this approach. The pluralist psychotherapist, he notes, promenades by the different schools because he or she understands that, in *some* cases, a specific theoretical approach or therapeutic method may be more beneficial to the patient. Interested mainly in the practical consequences of his or her theoretical choices, the pluralist psychotherapist is a pragmatist.

The acknowledgment of the diversity of interpretations of Jung's works by the post-Jungians brought with it a need to seriously consider the power dynamics playing out in depth psychology. As on the personal level, where heterogeneous psychic complexes fight each other, the professional reality of the Jungian field is marked by dispute. Indeed, the analytical apparatus itself is suffused by power. Questions of class and ideology, for instance, usually have an important role in psychotherapeutic work – above all when they are neglected, as they so often are, even today. Samuels examined these questions in enormous detail in two very wide-ranging books: *The Political Psyche* (1993) and *Politics on the Couch: Citizenship and the Internal Life* (2001).

All this indicates that the way Samuels writes his post-Jungian texts is on one level an enactment of a pluralist fantasy. Fantasy which, with its emphasis on diversity, and its exchange and – why not? – theft of ideas, can orient us in terms of our consumption and production of post-Jungian literature. In this aspect, Samuels' psychology flies under the flag of Hermes, the god of trade, as he himself recognizes (Samuels 2002b).

The second point we would like to stress arising from Samuels' work is the importance of classifying the Jungian schools according to different theoretical and clinical criteria. Moving beyond previous classifications oriented by geographic and historical aspects, Samuels privileges a new modality of classification, which values certain aspects from both the theoretical corpus and clinical practice. From this new direction, he proposes three Jungian schools: classical, developmental and archetypal. The classical school sits in the tradition inaugurated by Jung concerning the quest for individuation and the realization of the Self. The developmental school works on aspects of infancy and the development of the personality, as well as transference and countertransference dynamics. Finally, the archetypal school emphasizes soul-making and work with images, as proposed by James Hillman. It is interesting to note that this attempt to classify the schools, and, subsequently, re-classify them, was the target not only of many disputes among Jungians, but also of a self-examination made by Samuels. Faithful to Jung's precept that all theory is a subjective confession, he made his own:

> Undoubtedly, a shadow element of my own was present in the book – there was an Olympian syncretistic fantasy perhaps in doing a classification like that. I hope that the usefulness of it has over the years outweighed the shadow features. Actually, I did not write the book out of Olympian clarity; I wrote out of the confusion of being a recently qualified analyst who needed to understand what my elders and betters got so agitated and divided over. If there was a God over the book it was Hermes rather than Zeus.
>
> In the book, and subsequently, I have taken a much less literal stance in relation to the schools. What I would say now is that within each Jungian analyst there is a classical school analyst, a developmental school analyst, and an archetypal school analyst. This means that it is potentially open to any Jungian analyst or candidate, or Jungian-oriented psychotherapist, to access a very broad spectrum of ideas, practices, values and philosophies which constitute the overall field of post-Jungian psychology and analysis. This enables us to salute the emergence of what I call now the 'new model Jungian analyst'. This is somebody who, because of the differentiating work that I and others did, is able to know when they work in any particular way which specific ideas and practices they are drawing on: classical (Self and individuation); developmental (infancy, transference-countertransference); archetypal (soul, particular images). They can draw on all of them, some of them, and, as we will discuss in a moment, none of them. They can vary the mix throughout their practice; they can vary it in the analysis of an individual; and they can vary it within the confines of a single clinical analytical session.
>
> (1998: 20)

In this same text, written thirteen years after the publication of *Jung and the Post-Jungians*, Samuels reviews and proposes a new and even more provocative classification for the post-Jungian analytical psychology schools. He maintains that the classic and developmental schools still exist, but adds what he will call the extreme versions of these two schools: *Jungian Fundamentalism* and *Jungian merger with psychoanalysis*.

The Jungian fundamentalists are characterized by the desire to control thoughts and identities. Jung's text is interpreted as holy scripture, provoking an excessive emphasis on the man Jung or on what could be called the 'Jungian way of life'. The notions of order, standards, balance and integration are privileged, and there is an attempt to exclude experiences outside this fantasy pattern: fragmentation, evanescence, dispersion, inconstancy.

The adherents of the merger with psychoanalysis are those who idealize psychoanalysis as a technique and body of knowledge of greater theoretical and clinical refinement than Jungian analysis. Hence, there is a renunciation of concepts and contributions that Jung considered fundamental to clinical practice: the use of countertransference, the *telos* of the unconscious, the symbolic perspective on the psychic life, dreams as compensation. The challenge for this school (as Samuels sees it) is to discover whether they can use psychoanalytical concepts without losing their identity as Jungian analysts.

Here we return to the beginning of our text to ask ourselves: What is the relationship between these two specific characteristics of Samuels' seminal book – the post-Jungian attitude, and his classification of the schools – and his frequent incursions on our country, Brazil?

It seems to us that Brazil was one of the main countries where the seed of the post-Jungian attitude could germinate and blossom in abundance. This is no coincidence. After all, Brazil is a nation made of diversity and of blending some basic ingredients according to a pluralist recipe. In brief, our nation was formed by Portuguese colonizers who brought African slaves to a vast territory inhabited by indigenous Americans. This encounter – not without exploration and injustice, of course – produced a people essentially cross-bred and 'anthropophagic', that is, able to absorb and transform foreign products, and then export them back to other countries. This is the case, for instance, with *bossa nova*, which was strongly influenced by North American Jazz, and football, originally a British sport. After this short digression, let us return to psychology.

There are in Brazil two official societies linked to the International Association for Analytical Psychology (IAAP): the Sociedade Brasileira de Psicologia Analítica (SBPA) [Brazilian Society of Analytical Psychology] and the Associação Junguiana do Brasil (AJB) [Brazilian Jungian Association]. Besides these two official groups, there is a plurality of non-official and independent associations spread over different states in the country, each studying, practicing, and transmitting Jungian ideas in their own specific way. We want to mention some of these groups here, in part because Samuels has made a special point of seeking out and relating to these less formal organisations, which are composed very often of the younger generation of psychologists and other intellectuals. Here is a brief list: Grupo Himma – Estudos em Psicologia Imaginal (Himma Group – Studies in

Imaginal Psychology) in São Paulo; the Sizígia group in Fortaleza; Núcleo de Estudos Junguianos (Center of Jungian Studies) in Minas Gerais; Rubedo in Rio de Janeiro; Clínica Psiquê in Bahia; the Alteritas group in Espírito Santo.

In Brazil, these groups prove Samuels' intuition that is possible to use Jung's analytical psychology in a critical and creative way. Each one reinvents its own 'Jung' according to its preferences, promoting its favorite texts, valuing certain aspects and criticizing others. Some groups are more openly post-Jungian, others have more affinities with the classic school; many are strongly influenced by the archetypal psychology of James Hillman, such as Himma. Ultimately, we are confronted with a varied and plural range of heterogeneous attitudes to the same name: Jung. Not mentioning the Jungians who, somewhat heroically in their relative solitude, take Jung's ideas to the academic arena in Brazilian universities.

It is important, therefore, to understand and stress the fundamental importance of Andrew Samuels in this process. In those many visits to Brazil during the last two decades, he lent his image and authority, his knowledge and vast experience, not only to the official Jungian psychological societies in the country, but also to many other non-official and independent Jungian groups. Acting this way, Samuels is like a messenger, a Hermes who brings and takes messages to different places and people, wandering the globe carrying proposals to inspire the discussion of Jungian ideas in diverse fora. Thus, personally and professionally, he adds a dimension of ethical credibility to the terms he has coined. And more, he sticks coherently to the idea that was always one of the pillars of his theoretical construction: the idea of plurality. We could conclude that, to Samuels, thinking about the theoretical body called Jungian psychology is to think about multiplicity: psychic multiplicity, multiple visions, styles and ways of working with Jungian psychology.

Bibliography

James, W. (2005) *A Pluralistic Universe*. Stilwell: Digireads.
—— (2006) *Pragmatism: A New Name for an Old Way of Thinking*. West Valley City: Waking Lion Press.
Jung, C. G. (1913) The Theory of Psychoanalysis. In Jung, C. G. (1967) *Freud and Psychoanalysis*. New York: Princeton University Press.
—— (1966) *The Practice of Psychotherapy*. New York: Princeton University Press.
—— (1967) *Freud and the Psychoanalysis*. New York: Princeton University Press.
Pereira, H. de C. (2007) O laboratório analítico: a psicologia de C. G. Jung examinada pela teoria do ator-rede. Tese de doutorado. Rio de Janeiro: UERJ.
Samuels, A. (1985) *Jung and the Post-Jungians*. London: Routledge & Kegan Paul.
—— (1989a) The Plural Psyche: Personality, Morality and the Father. London and New York: Routledge.
—— (1989b) *Jung e os Pós-Junguianos*. Rio de Janeiro: Imago.

—— (1998) Will the Post-Jungians survive? In Casement, A. (ed.) *Post-Jungians Today: Key Papers in Contemporary Analytical Psychology*. London and New York: Routledge.

—— (1992) *A Psique Plural: Personalidade, Moralidade e o Pai*. Rio de Janeiro: Imago.

—— (1993) *The Political Psyche*. London and New York: Routledge.

—— (2001) *Politics on the Couch: Citizenship and the Internal Life*. London: Karnac Books.

—— (2002a) *A Política no Divã*. São Paulo: Summus.

—— (2002b) The hidden politics of healing: Foreign dimensions of domestic practice. http://www.andrewsamuels.com (Accessed 2008).

Shamdasani, S. (2003) *Jung and the Making of Modern Psychology: The Dream of a Science*. Cambridge: Cambridge University Press.

Chapter 29

Andrew Samuels' contributions to analytical psychology in Brazil

Visions and creativity

Denise Gimenez Ramos

I met Andrew Samuels personally just under 20 years ago, when I went to fetch him at his hotel to give his first talk in São Paulo. Because of his prolific intellectual production, I expected to meet an older, more sober man, so I was ever so surprised to be introduced to a humorous young man full of vitality and curiosity.

On the way to the event, we chatted about how to give talks. I was telling him that I always tried to find an original idea, study it in depth and explore it during the whole address, when he interrupted me vehemently. Samuels protested, saying that in his talks he did quite the opposite, he launched many ideas and left it up to the audience to assimilate them according to their capacity. I must confess that at that moment I found his attitude somewhat pretentious: changing someone else's way of thinking is no easy task. But on hearing him later on, I realized that he was right. In his talk, Samuels put forward many new, creative ideas that opened up new perspectives and new solutions to old questions. When I thought that he was about to close by tying up all the facts and analyses, he presented new material, and only drew a conclusion at the very end. I could observe many members of the audience chasing after his words and trying to take notes before they were invaded by other thoughts.

This first impression, many years and many meetings later, still remains today.

Recently, during the Third Academic Conference of the International Association for Jungian Studies (IAJS) and the International Association for Analytical Psychology (IAAP) at the ETH in Zurich (July 2008), I saw once more how his ideas gushed out enthusiastically over the audience. He used the basic principles of analytical psychology in his reflections on the latest political events in England and abroad. The importance of this analysis is not trivial. Despite being indispensable, the tradition begun by C.G. Jung of using depth psychology to understand political phenomena did not attract many followers. I feel that this is in part due to the clinical formation of analysts, who restrict their studies to analysis of the individual, as well as to the difficulty of understanding mass phenomena without reducing them to a single cause.

In this sense, Samuels' book *Politics on the Couch* (2001) made a strong impact by showing how our political attitudes, apparently grounded in ideologies and conscious thoughts, are based on our complexes much more than we realize. Awareness of the emotional factors implicit in choosing our leaders and party affiliation certainly allows us to make a more objective and reflexive choice based on factual reality rather than on transferential ties. Samuels shows how awareness of the collective shadow and its complexes would lighten the high emotional charge that permeates political debates. If ideological differences were made explicit, they would be heard with an objective ear, leading to quicker and more objective solutions to society's problems. His psychological perspective in understanding the phenomena of nationalism, environmentalism and market economics reveal his deep knowledge of the human mind; it is this understanding that allows collective conscience to develop, and with it, greater evolution of society as a whole. What kind of society would we have if at the moment we chose our representatives in administrative and legislative government we left behind our desire for power, our parental and cultural complexes, and their shadows, with the consequent transferences and countertransferences?

Samuels' text is above all else practical and in a certain way premonitory in nature. He seems to have forecast the big, terrible economic changes that would come to affect a good part of the planet, and suggests new types of behavior throughout his text, especially when he refers to 'retraining the psyche':

> No one can any longer assume that they have a job for life; in the course of a working life, each of us is going to have many jobs. This means our employability will be directly dependent on our adaptability and flexibility.
>
> (Samuels 2001: 137)

He offers practical proposals on how we should prepare ourselves for the inevitable imminent changes:

> There is no reason in principle why work should not be a form of self-expression, but we have to make a start by treating it as such. If education becomes too work-oriented, its capacity to release people's potential will be stunted.
>
> (ibid: 139)

We are well aware that in the last few years these questions have bothered a good many analysts who, on seeing their patients preferring short-therapy techniques or drugs that offer quick relief, feel inadequate, threatened and outdated. Some even consider that the profession of analyst is threatened by extinction and I believe that if we fail to adjust our therapeutic approach, this will really be the fate that awaits us.

Despite more optimistic views, I hear complaints from Brazilian, North American and European colleagues about the decline in the number of patients or in the number of candidates to the training institutes in IAPP-member societies. Could we be teaching the new generation a profession that no longer meets the basic needs of human beings of the 21st century or have we failed to update our instruments? Could we be using and teaching instruments that are not good enough to deal with the internal dynamics of our own organizations? Here I repeat the words of Murray Stein (referring to the growth of IAAP) in his Presidential Address at the close of the IMP Congress in Barcelona, 2004:

> I have heard from more than a few fellow analysts a deeply felt questioning about the value of Analytical Psychology for shaping and influencing the professional structures we are evolving at this time. The troubling question is: Are we analysts any better at managing power and politics than the less psychologically minded and trained members of other organizations? The evidence is not in our favor. This is sobering. What can we offer the world if we cannot even manage our own comparatively small institutional affairs?
>
> (Stein 2004)

Nevertheless, his speech ends on quite an optimistic note by saying that new opportunities appear when we free ourselves from the weight of past attitudes and legacies that are of no further use in today's world. Here he refers to the debates of Jungians with psychoanalysts, the birth of the International Association for Jungian Studies, and the expansion of Analytical Psychology in Asia (Singapore, China, India), Eastern Europe (Poland, Lithuania, the Czech Republic, Serbia, Bulgaria, Ukraine, Estonia, Georgia), Latin America (Chile, Argentina, Ecuador, Mexico) and Africa (South Africa, Tunisia), among other factors.

This optimism is confirmed by a quick look at the themes presented at the last national and international Jungian Congresses and Conferences (the second and third Academic IAAP and IAJS Conferences; and the sixteenth and seventeenth International IAAP Congresses), which saw countless works that focus on the analysis of mass phenomena and proposals that promote collective development. New concepts such as the 'cultural complex' (Singer and Kimbles 2004) have been developed, which can be creatively applied to the understanding of collective phenomenon.

Samuels' thought enables us to assert that if analysts in their office cloisters face the threat of extinction, those who expand their knowledge towards analyzing and transforming culture, and make efforts to develop effective techniques, will probably escape this fate.

Here I return to how this author contributes to the view of the analyst as a transforming agent in his *Jungian charter*:

> Post-Jungians should speak up for the link that exists between inner and outer worlds, especially in relation to what look like outer-world issues, such as political or social problems. We should build on the very good start that has been made in Jungian psychology in engaging with pressing issues in the world today.
>
> (Samuels 1998: 28)

> In my own work, in the field of political and social policy, my fantasy image is of a spectrum of experts available to any policy-making group, or politician trying to devise a policy. At one end of the spectrum we will find a statistician or an econometrist, or someone similar. At the other end we would have a depth psychologist, or therapist. One among many specialisms in a task of producing new ideas.
>
> (ibid: 29)

However, what do we have to offer in this area when our training is essentially clinical and directed towards the individual process? If papers with a broader and more social focus are present in conferences, the same cannot be said of the training offered to Jungian analysts, as mentioned before. A study of the training programs of several IAPP-member societies (Ramos and Machado 2004) showed clearly the quasi-absence of disciplines of a more social or anthropological approach, so that analysts generally finish their training without the wherewithal to work in groups, let alone in the social field.

How do you train an analyst? What approach do you choose? Why one master and not another? And once you have chosen a path to follow, what other ramifications does it offer? Are we all Jungians? But what does it mean to be a 'Jungian'?

Although these questions have been debated by many authors (among others Casement (ed.) 2007; Papadopoulos 1998; Young-Eisndrath and Dawson (eds.) 2002), the first mapping of the area was made by Samuels in two of his works published almost simultaneously. My first contact was with *A Critical Dictionary of Jungian Analysis* (Samuels, Shorter and Plaut 1986), translated into Portuguese in 1988. This became a classic consultation and reference book for students as they marked out a territory delimiting analytical psychology from psychoanalysis. With this book, analytical psychology is affirmed as a field of knowledge with a language of its own and specific concepts that are not derived from psychoanalysis. In this sense, Samuels' work *Jung and the Post-Jungians* (1985), followed recently by his article "New Developments in the Post-Jungian Field" (2008), lends continuity to this question by mapping out the field and the ramifications of analytical psychology to allow a clear view of the various tendencies within the Jungian movement. In the 2008 article, he claims that the conventional classification into three schools (classical, developmental and archetypal) should be reformulated to include a fourth, so that we now have the fundamentalist, classical, developmental and psychoanalytic schools of Analytical Psychology. Samuels expresses his concern with extreme positions, fearing both the radicalism of the first and the dissolution of the essence of Jungian thinking in the last, which tends to diminish Jung's contributions to clinical practice.

His other books translated into Portuguese: *A Psique Plural* (1992) (*The Plural Psyche*); *A Psique Política* (1995) (*The Political Psyche*) and *A Política no Divã* (2001) (*Politics on the Couch*) are obligatory reading material in several graduate and training courses in Brazil.

But Samuels' investment in the academic area goes beyond his writing, as when he founded the IAJS in July 2002 together with Renos Papadopoulos after the First International Academic Conference of Analytical Psychology, which was organised by the IAAP at the University of Essex in partnership with the Centre for Psychoanalytic Studies. The success of this entity, and the conferences it has organized, comes in answer to a demand repressed for years by academics from various parts of the world. In his evaluation of the advance of analytical psychology in academia, Samuels points to the advantage of its developing one generation after psychoanalysis, so that we can try to avoid

> some of the damaging gaps between clinical work and academic applications. If this kind of alienation is to be avoided in Jungian studies, then both the academic and the clinical camps will have to better interact with one another.
>
> (Samuels 2008: 23)

During his many visits to Brazil, Samuels developed both classical and highly polemic (but always instigating) themes such as: the trickster in clinic and culture, a new anatomy of spirituality, illness and death in the countertransference, in search of the Brazilian child, the Father, countertransference and the *mundus imaginalis*, plus numerous case seminars and experiential workshops. He also participated in joint and solo meetings with Freudian and Kleinian psychoanalysts, plus consultations with local politicians. His curiosity led him to visit different popular religious and cultural centers, and he even went as far as conducting group therapy during a visit to a slum in the city of Rio de Janeiro! (Just to show that his popularity extends far beyond the circuit of analysts and academic Jungians.)

It should be underscored that his participation was never unilateral. The admiration and respect that he receives from Brazilian students, teachers and analysts is due not only to his academic and humanistic excellence but also to his capacity to transcend his own culture. With his transforming and integrating manner, he showed interest in the work of colleagues from South America and recognized their value by opening doors for them to become known in the international circuits through invitations to give talks and publish. His political vision even helped to foster the international recognition of the scientific contributions of both the Sociedade Brasileira de Psicologia Analítica and the Associação Junguiana do Brasil, the two Brazilian Societies affiliated to the IAAP, to the development of the Jungian movement.

It no longer surprises me when a student comes up to me enthused with the most recent text or talk taken from Samuels' website, already translated and with a pile of copies to distribute.

In conclusion, a fitting motto for Samuels, an author who renews himself and renews us, would be a quotation from his own work: '*It isn't enough just to attain knowledge, it has to be shared*' (Samuels 2000). That defines him as a great master!

Bibliography

Casement, A. (ed.) (2007). *Who owns Jung?* London: Karnac.

Papadopoulos, R. (1998). Jungian perspectives in new contexts, in A. Casement (ed.) *Post-Jungians Today*: 163–183. London and New York: Routledge.

Ramos, D. and Machado, P. (2004). *Comparative Study of Training Programs*. Sixteenth IAAP Congress (unpublished text).

Samuels, A. (1985). *Jung and the Post-Jungians*. London and Boston: Routledge & Kegan Paul.

Samuels, A. (1989). *Jung e os Pós-Junguianos*. Rio de Janeiro: Imago.

Samuels, A. (1992). *A Psique Plural: Personalidade, Moralidade e o Pai*. Rio de Janeiro: Imago.

Samuels, A. (1995). *A Psique Política*. Rio de Janeiro: Imago.

Samuels, A. (1998). Will the post-Jungians survive?, in A. Casement (ed.) *Post-Jungians Today*: 15–32. London and New York: Routledge.

Samuels, A. (2000). Interview to Rubedo. http://www.rubedo.psc.br/Entrevis/entsamue.htm. (Accessed 31 June 2008).

Samuels, A. (2001). *Politics on the Couch: Citizenship and the Internal Life*. London: Profile.

Samuels, A. (2008). New Developments in the Post-Jungian Field. *Junguiana*, 26.

Samuels, A., Shorter, B. and Plaut, F. (1986). *A Critical Dictionary of Jungian analysis*. London: Routledge & Kegan Paul.

Samuels, A., Shorter, B. and Plaut, F. (1988). *Dicionário Crítico de Análise Junguiana*. Rio de Janeiro: Imago.

Singer, T. and Kimbles, S. (eds.) (2004). *The Cultural Complex: Contemporary*

Jungian Perspectives on Psyche and Society. Hove and New York: Brunner-Routledge.

Stein, M. (2004). President's Address: The IAAP In Midlife: Where Are We Now? Where Are We Going? IAAP Barcelona Congress, August 29–September 3, http://iaap.org (Accessed July 15 2008).

Young-Eisndrath, P. and Dawson, T. (2002). *Manual de Cambridge para Estudos Junguianos*. Porto Alegre: Artmed.

Chapter 30

Andrew, me and the AHP

John Rowan

I don't know where I saw the advertisement, but it looked interesting. A group where psychology would be explored in an experiential way. It all sounded very new and interesting, and it didn't cost much. So I made my way to the Foresters Hall in Kentish Town, London, and paid my money, and went in. It was a large group, about fifty people, led by Anne Elphick and Hans Lobstein. It was 1970.

It was an enlivening experience, and I met an interesting man named Caron Kent, author of a book called *The Puzzled Body*, which was one of the early books saying that body and mind were a unity. I picked up a green leaflet about the Association for Humanistic Psychology. Up to that point I had thought that the thing was run by the British Humanist Association, which was quite popular at the time. This is one of the classic mistakes, which took me some time to sort out. There are still many people who have not sorted it out, and who refer to humanistic practitioners as humanists. There are in fact some crucial differences, perhaps the most obvious of which are (a) the BHA is purely intellectual, and has no great use for the body at all, and (b) the BHA has no use for spirituality, which is quite important in the AHP.

At that time I was involved with radical psychology, and was one of the people producing a magazine called *Red Rat*, which was critical of academic psychology as practised at the time. In May 1970 there was a visit to London of several leaders from the Esalen Institute, who put on two big experiential events at the Inn on the Park in St James's Park. *Red Rat* contacted them, and made a case that the prices for this Mayfair event were quite high, and excluded ordinary people who might be interested. So they agreed to put on an extra event in Paddington, priced at five shillings, so that such people could come and sample the goods. I met and spoke to several of the Esalen people, and liked them very much. They had a good energy. And two or three of them I bumped into again and again from time to time over the years, especially Jackie Doyle, Will Schutz and Helen Stephens.

Jackie Doyle especially came back to Britain in 1971, and helped to put on an event in connection with the British Psychological Society conference at Exeter. Ever since then there has been a good AHP presence in the West Country. Later, as Jacqueline Larcombe Doyle, she became President of the AHP in the United States.

In 1972 the AHP again participated in the BPS Conference, but this time officially, not as a fringe event. I was also involved in a fringe event organized by *Red Rat*, called "Beyond Ethics", which featured a 32-page pamphlet on some of the ethical issues in psychology. Sidney Jourard (an AHP member and American Professor) gave a talk on "Psychology for control, and for liberation of humans" to a packed audience, as part of the main conference, and it raised many of the same points. This was marvellous, and confirmed my opinion that humanistic psychology and radical psychology were compatible.

Later that year came the first issue of *Humpty Dumpty*, co-edited by Nigel Armistead and me and a woman whose name I have forgotten, a radical psychology magazine which took the place of *Red Rat*, which had come to the end of its life with the departure of some of the founders. It was much better produced, but shared the policy of *Red Rat* of having pseudonyms for the contributors: mine was O. Void. About then, too, some of us (including Keith Paton) produced a large pamphlet called "Rat, Myth and Magic", which was highly critical of psychology as then being taught, and social psychology in particular.

Also that year John Wren-Lewis, the first Chair of the AHP in Britain, left for the United States (with his wife, Ann Faraday), and I became Chair in his place. In the same year I led my first group, at a centre called Kaleidoscope, with the theme of Creativity. I also joined my first men's group, which met in South London, at the home of Angela Hamblin, a feminist who also saw some merit in humanistic psychology. This was the beginning of my long involvement with the anti-sexist men's movement, which continued until 2000 through my work with *Achilles Heel* magazine.

In March 1973 appeared the first issue of *Self & Society*, with an article and a book review from me. Over the next few months I wrote so many book reviews for this journal that it became quite embarrassing, and Vivian Milroy and I decided that I would use pseudonyms from time to time. Over the next few years I became James Crippledini (a fair-minded group leader), O.Void (a highly critical reader), Brian Rainbow (who always liked the books he reviewed), Jean Starry (a French existential androgyne) and Lucy Biko, who wrote about racism. Later Andrew Samuels joined the editorial board.

At about this time I initiated the University Circus – a five-hour experiential event which a few of us took round various universities up and down the country. It gave a taster of what humanistic psychology was all about, and enabled us to distribute leaflets and books. We usually managed to persuade the University library to take *Self & Society* after the event. I can't remember who the people were who took part in these events: the names of Tricia Scott, Helen Davis, Richard Stevens and John Heron come to mind, but I am not sure of the others. I really enjoyed these trips, and must have done more than a dozen of them. I still think this was some of the best publicity the AHP in Britain ever did.

Sometime during this period we had a real disagreement with the AHP in the USA. Carmi Harari had the title of Member for Foreign Affairs (or some such) and visited us from time to time, keeping us in touch with the international movement generally. He kept on conveying the message that they wanted us to become a properly constituted Chapter and pay $200 a year for the privilege. We resisted this, and in the end a compromise was reached, by which we changed our logo to include a B for Britain. So we stopped being the AHP and became instead the AHP(B). But we never paid the money. We really valued our independence, though we did always try to keep in line with the philosophy which we shared. I went to conferences across the water, in Montreal, Princeton, Snowmass, Vermont, Stanford and elsewhere later, and tried to carry the flag for Britain and what we were doing over here.

In 1977 we had the first European conference in London. This conference, entitled "Self Renewal", was very successful. About 200 people turned up, and seemed determined to make it a high-energy event. Five major presenters failed to turn up, but nobody seemed to mind too much. The schedule of lectures and workshops was in a continual state of flux. But some very important ideas were put forward. My presentation on "A basic qualification in psychotherapy" sparked several efforts in the next year or so to start up training institutes with the humanistic approaches. And another one of mine on "Research in the human sciences" started in motion the formation of the New Paradigm Research Group.

In 1978 a second European Conference was held, this time in Geneva, thanks to the marvellous entrepreneurship of Sabine Kurjo and her centre, Vision Humaniste. As a result of the success of this enterprise – again about 200 participants came – the European Association for Humanistic Psychology (EAHP) was formed, with Arnold Keyserling as its first President, and Sabine Kurjo as Secretary-General. In September a French AHP was formed, with Jacqueline Barbin as the most active moving spirit.

In America Jean Houston was elected President, and initiated a three-year programme of social involvement. Andrew would have been pleased. In Europe we had, for the most part, not gone that far; we were still occupied with spreading the word more generally. The European conference in 1979 was entitled "Reaching Out", and a strong attempt was made to do exactly that. And it was very successful – again in Geneva organized by Sabine Kurjo, and this time under the aegis of the newly formed European AHP. There were 650 participants, and 100 presenters from 14 different countries – the biggest gathering in Europe we had had up to that time. *Self & Society* was inspired by this event into renaming itself the *European Journal of Humanistic Psychology*.

In the following year, the Association of Humanistic Psychology Practitioners (AHPP) was founded, with John Heron as its first Chairperson. This was another groundbreaking effort, because this had never been done in America, and still has not been done there or in any other country. What it does is to set up and maintain standards in all the fields where humanistic psychology is applied. There is a strict accreditation procedure whereby people first of all assess themselves, and then are assessed by their peers. Individuals are accredited in a specific area of practice for five years only, after which they come before the Membership Committee for re-assessment.

Later in the year came the fifth EAHP Congress, this time in Rome. This was an excellent conference, with Laing and Laborit (from France) as the two main protagonists. Five hundred people came to this one, mainly from Italy. The sixth Congress was in Paris, and even more people came to that one, breaking all records with about 800 participants.

It was interesting what was happening at this time. Two quite different movements were both progressing at the same time – one towards an increasing interest in the social aspects of humanistic psychology, and the other towards an increasing interest in spirituality. In 1982 there was a joint conference of the AHP in Britain with the Wrekin Trust – rather New Age type of people at the spiritual end of the spectrum – and a special issue of *Self & Society* around psychology and spirituality.

The two things came together in Joanna Macy, who in 1982 and 1983 began to do far more work on what she called "pain for the world". This is a particular kind of pain, which is not psychological in the sense of being due to early trauma or existential angst, but is both social and spiritual. She ran workshops where people could face and own up to their despair at the state of the world – nuclear threats, ecological devastation, political oppression and the rest – and come out the other side feeling refreshed and empowered. She encouraged further networking. Again Andrew would have been very interested in this. In 1984 the European Association of Humanistic Psychology held its conference in Britain, at Surrey University. The weather was brilliant, and the preparations excellent, Wendy Freebourne doing most of the organization. About 400 people turned up from 21 different countries, and the closing ritual was very moving. The last EAHP conference was in 1988 in Barcelona. At first it looked like it would be a great success. Michele Festa in Rome had found a marvellous organizer, a woman with diplomatic experience and access, who had the ability and the money to travel round and do what was necessary. She got the three Gestalt organizations in Spain to cooperate on the ground, and a good hotel to host the conference, and all seemed to go well. Then she fell ill with cancer, and had to withdraw. Michele Festa tried to carry on without her, and might well have succeeded, except that the Gestalt organizations fell out and could not agree on anything, and handed it all back to him. Consequently the numbers were small, and it was hard to break even. To add to the problems,

Ronnie Laing was up to his usual tricks and insisted on an expensive suite, where he ran up large drinks bills for all his many friends. The result was a disaster, which virtually bankrupted Festa and put the whole organization into a decline from which it never recovered.

In 1989 something remarkable happened in England. Around 1980 there had been rumblings about the dangers of uncontrolled psychotherapy. In response to this there had arisen an organization called the Rugby Conference, which met once a year and tried to draw in all the existing training and accrediting centres in the United Kingdom. In 1989 this resulted in the formation of the UK Standing Conference on Psychotherapy. This was divided into sections, the two biggest of which were the Psychoanalytic and Psychodynamic Psychotherapy Section, generally known as PPP, and the Humanistic and Integrative Psychotherapy Section, generally known as HIP. Other sections were devoted to Analytical Psychology (the Jungians), Behavioural and Cognitive Psychotherapy, Experiential and Constructivist Therapies, Family-Marital-Sexual Therapies, Hypnotherapy and Psychoanalytically Based Therapy with Children. Also included were Institutional Members: The Association of University Teachers of Psychiatry, the Tavistock Clinic, the Universities Psychotherapy Association, the British Psychological Society and the Royal College of Psychiatrists.

The AHPP (mentioned earlier) was one of the founding members, and when the time came for each section to draw up its defining statement, two of the three members who wrote this statement for HIPS were members of the AHPP. Later this became the UK Council for Psychotherapy, and in 1993 it issued the first National Register of psychotherapists, comprising the membership of all the 70 or so organizations which belonged to it. It was thus the umbrella set-up for the whole of British psychotherapy, and when the European Association for Psychotherapy was formed, the UKCP was one of its founding members. This was a remarkable achievement, and it was good to see humanistic psychology take such a prominent part in it. The first President was a psychoanalyst, but the second was Emmy van Deurzen, a leading existential analyst and member of the HIP Section, and one of the foremost people in making the European connection. The AHP in the US went through a strange evolution during this period, losing a number of members and having much smaller conferences than it did in the days when I attended a meeting of 2000 people at Princeton. But in 2000 there was a striking new move: the Old Saybrook 2 conference was held at the State University of West Georgia, in the spirit of renewal and regeneration. Out of this came a number of initiatives which seemed to foster a new spurt of growth, and a major book – *The Handbook of Humanistic Psychology*, with over 700 pages. This seems an encouraging portent for the future.

In 2007 the AHP 'married' the Association for Transpersonal Psychology, in a ceremony where they agreed to share a number of facilities. We all know that Maslow created both, and that therefore there has always been a connection, but now this was confirmed in a serious way. There has always been another connection too – looser and less accepted – this time with the Jungians. There is a huge overlap between Jungian thinking and the work of the transpersonal people. Jorge Ferrer tips his hat to Jung, Andrew Shorrock says: "To my mind no study of the transpersonal in psychotherapeutic practice would be complete without mentioning his work"; Brant Cortright speaks of Jung's version of the unconscious being "a transpersonal and spiritual unconscious"; and Ken Wilber's recent work mentions the Shadow quite often.

I am not sure when I first met Andrew, but each meeting, whether in public or private, has been stimulating and rewarding. I get a lot out of knowing him, and value very highly our friendship. Congratulations on hitting 60!

Chapter 31

Writing after Andrew Samuels

Political forms and literary symbols in Shakespeare's *Macbeth*

Susan Rowland

The inspiration of extraordinary connections

I am delighted to contribute to this special volume for Andrew Samuels because it gives me the opportunity to reflect upon his unique achievements. Professor Samuels has been important to the development of scholarship and to its deepening social functions. In addition to a formidable research career, he has done what none other could do, in creating powerful groups of clinicians and academics. Some of these groups take the work of therapy into the sickness of the social and political world. Some groups bring together therapists and academics (and those who are both), in order to foster new research, to challenge the parameters of Jungian practice, and, crucially, from my own point of view, to try to heal what is arid in conventional university disciplines. Samuels's coining of the term Post-Jungian to indicate not only 'after Jung', but also the ability to criticize and revise, is a testimony to the liberatory effect of his work so far (Samuels 1985). Andrew Samuels has been inspirational in creating the possibility of a multi-disciplinary Jungian Studies.

Making groups is about making connections, sometimes counterintuitive ones. I am not qualified to comment on the richness of the full range of Samuels's scholarship. What I want to do in this chapter is to celebrate Samuels's special capacity to inspire the field of Jungian studies. He does this by making original imaginative connections, in branches of knowledge as well as in bringing different professions together. One of the gifts that Samuels has given those around him is the creation of new epistemological space. He has achieved this remarkable feat by making extraordinary connections between political ideas and family dynamics, for example. It means that his intuitive creativity has provided a research area or method for others to follow. This chapter will demonstrate the capacity of Samuels's political psychology to inspire, by taking it further into literary theory.

From reductionism to holism: Literary theory needs help!

Samuels's inspiration of extraordinary connections is important because of the larger framework it responds to. As C.G. Jung himself was well aware, the discipline of psychology is, arguably, itself a response to a larger revolution in knowledge. Since the Enlightenment, knowledge disciplines have partly been formed by, and measured themselves against, the version of 'science' constructed according to principles enunciated by Francis Bacon (1561–1626) and Isaac Newton (1642–1727). Bacon promoted 'scientific method' of repeatable experiments (1620), while Newton's work completed the development begun with the Ancient Greeks of detaching psyche (and the divine) from material reality. God had stepped back from 'his' creation and universe was inanimate (1687).

Newton also advocated reductionism and specialisation. By looking at the smallest possible unit (for him, the atom) and by developing expertise in studying one area as discrete, eventually all the specialisations could be put together to make a complete picture of the truth.

By the early twentieth century, these principles of materialist science had been undermined. Jung's own work on the unconscious insisted that all knowledge was provisional because rooted in its unknowable protean creativity. Hence Jung was in parallel with the new science of quantum physics in asserting that the observer always affects what is observed. Moreover, although Jung largely remained with the older science's sense of the division between the human subject and the objective world, much of his later writing on synchronicity, for example, assumed a *holistic* version of reality (Jung 1960, CW8: paras 843–65). Here, reductionism is reversed with the principle that it is the interpenetration of mind, matter, life and cosmos that is key to their essential being.

So it is possible to see Samuels's work as part of the new holism of the twenty-first century. For now, we know nature not to consist of separate organisms, minerals and units of being. Rather, nature is an eco*system* and our culture's assumption that humans are not an intrinsic part of it is our problem, not our privilege. What Jung implicitly showed, and what Samuels has brought out for the new century, is that the ecosystem extends into humanity as, on the one hand, psychology and spirituality, and on the other, culture and politics. Today, we need to take an attitude of holism to our so-called separate (and hence Newtonian reductionist) academic disciplines. Psychotherapy is not isolated from politics and ecology, and indeed these very definitions need challenging, as Samuels has demonstrated (1993, 2001).

Literary studies as a university discipline has, however, followed a similar epistemological path to Jung from separation to something approaching holism. An apparently holistic attitude dawned with texts considered as material forms of power and gender relations. The recent addition of eco-criticism would appear to confirm the re-definition of literature as potent works in the making of human culture, extending into our treatment of the non-human.

However, insofar as literary theory is based on materialist principles, it still remains reductionist. For materialism claims that matter and power are at the root of reality and so brackets off the sacred and other forms of spiritual and sexual energy as merely derivative. The divine is still a mode by which power is manifest in materialist theory. So Jung, whose one founding principle is the partly unknowable and creative unconscious as the most important factor, offers a way into a holistic literary theory by removing an a priori assumption about reality. Andrew Samuels's theory of *political forms*, which allows for material forces but is not limited to them, provides a new holistic way of looking at literature as a political and social practice.

Andrew Samuels's political forms

Political forms is a way of understanding the transmission of political ideas that are more than just intellectual constructs. Samuels develops this in his book, *Politics on the Couch* (2001: 64–74). Indeed, political forms indicate the way political ideas become emotional narratives of identity and being. Eventually they may become the structure of social groups. Political forms encompass the notion of 'vitalism', suggesting that living things are innately structured as having intention or purpose; something mind-like drives them. By taking vitalism and applying it to political mutations in culture, Samuels succeeds in adding a non-reductionist psychology to materialist versions of political change. Most valuably, Samuels's political forms provide a holistic framework for studying politics for they open the closed field of materialism to issues such as spirituality, eco-theory and creativity without prejudging their ultimate realities.

Moreover, Samuels's political forms suggest a particular dynamic as significant (but not determining) in kinship libido. Could incest fantasy, which Freud reductively always linked to sexuality and Jung (holistically), allowed to have plural meanings, be a means of keeping some political forms together? Indeed, kinship libido itself needs to be understood as capable of many manifestations. It is not limited to Oedipal political forms of dominant patriarchal fathers.

Samuels suggests that sibling libido might be emerging in some radical kinds of politics. He makes the extraordinary inspiring connection of link-ing the transgressive nature of incestuous fantasy with political subversion (2001: 68). So unlike conservative political readings of incestuous desire as locked into patriarchal fathering, Samuels claims incest fantasy for radical and new forms of political leadership.

He ends this chapter on political forms with a very interesting example of sibling leadership in the context of Shakespeare's *Macbeth*: witchcraft.

> One example of leadership in a sibling vein occurs at meetings of witches covens – Wiccan groups . . . When a speaker had finished, she or he passed a staff to the person they had chosen to speak next. This replaced the more adversarial pattern of conventional political meetings.
>
> (2001: 74)

It is time to look at the political forms of a play intimately bound up with regime change in England. Three years before 'the Scottish Play', the new Scottish King James took over from the old feminine magic of Queen Elizabeth.

Macbeth (1606) and the great transgression against nature

At first glance, *Macbeth* is both a testimony to kinship libido as a political structure and a horrified witness to the breakdown of society when it fails. Macbeth himself is a great war leader, beloved of his king, Duncan. After defeating the king's traitorous enemies, two fateful events occur. Travelling home, Macbeth and his friend, Banquo, meet three mysterious witch-like women who prophesy that Macbeth will be king and Banquo's descendants will eventually succeed to the throne. Secondly, Duncan decides to honour the Macbeths by visiting their home.

Despite Macbeth's real reluctance to become a killer, his wife persuades him to murder Duncan, and so become king. Unfortunately the throne acquired by violence is unstable in the mind of the usurper. Insecure, haunted by nightmares, Macbeth has Banquo killed and is horrified when his friend's silent ghost returns to his victory feast.

There follows a disintegration of society as Macbeth eliminates any possible opposition. In particular, he punishes rival Macduff, who has fled to England, by slaughtering his wife and children. Returning to the witches, Macbeth hears more prophecies that he interprets as meaning his invincibility. Meanwhile Malcolm, elder son and true heir of Duncan, seeks out Macduff in England and tests his loyalty. It takes the terrible news of the atrocity against the Macduff family to completely banish distrust. They raise an army and finally defeat Macbeth by fulfilling the prophecies that Birnam Wood will come to Dunsinane (as soldiers carry branches to disguise numbers) and Macbeth is killed by one not born of woman. Macduff, it seems, was born by Cesarean. Lady Macbeth, maddened by horror, has already killed herself.

It is Lady Macbeth who first registers the effectiveness of kinship libido as *king*ship libido. After she succeeds in stiffening Macbeth to the deed (using her sexuality to do so), she says that she herself would murder the king had the sleeping Duncan not resembled her father. Moreover, she infamously violates assumptions about the feminine and maternity when she says that she would have smashed the head of her own breast-feeding child rather than break a vow to become king as Macbeth seems about to do. This is a terrible and fascinating dramatic moment. The metaphorical child was summoned previously in Macbeth's horror at his potential regicide when he speaks of:

> And pity, like a naked newborn babe
> Striding the blast . . .
>   (Act 1, sc. 7. 1. 21–2)

Lady Macbeth is in a masculine position of aggression against the father. She is also in the Oedipal myth as the parent who is prepared to kill a baby, part of the story little considered by Freud. What Macbeth seems to anticipate here is the play's contention that kinship libido may fail if it is bound in a waning political form, but it cannot be driven out. The baby Macbeth invokes is a terrifying figure of conquest *despite or because* of its vulnerability, in kinship libido.

Macbeth shows that kinship libido will not sustain the old politics of the sacred king, but will find a new political form in the sibling-trickster of Malcolm. It is the figure of the murdered child, first as simile for the Macbeths, then in the horrifying scene of the killing of Macduff's children, rather than the father/king that accrues enough kinship libido to re-make this state. Malcolm is, of course, the avenging 'child' of Duncan.

Macbeth's effectiveness as a political argument rests on making the potential for social breakdown within the Oedipus myth concentrate on aggression towards the child, more than the father. So it is unsurprising that what is on the one had a misogynist portrayal of sheer horror of the feminine in any political role is, on the other, a serious warning about how the Stuart state needs to modify its kingship to include less absolute forms of nurture and kinship.

To the Stuart mind, this is an age of patriarchy with the king as divinely sanctioned Father of the nation. When James I watched *Macbeth* in 1606, he could not know that his son, *his child*, would be executed because he could not relinquish the political form of divine fatherhood. Both the play and the later Civil War show incest libido between fathers and sons as a political form that must change.

To put it another way, both play and political history dispute the primacy of the Oedipus complex as defined by Freud, if considered not as sexuality but as power. They confirm Samuels argument that a (Jungian) more flexible interpretation of the Oedipus myth shows the crucial *evolution* of political forms. More precisely, I am arguing that public performances of Shakespeare's plays *are themselves acts of social and political evolution.*

Macbeth could be considered as a political reaction to the long reign of Queen Elizabeth in 1603. For the play stigmatises feminine power as perverted – in the witches – or against maternity – seen as 'against nature' in Lady Macbeth's ferocious child-killing words. The only 'good' woman is safely loyal to the father when safely dead – Lady Macduff. In themselves, the witches may well be a possible example of sibling kinship libido. However their disturbing *otherness* to the patriarchal social order is reinforced by their dark invocations to both nature as destructive of man (storms at sea, etc.) and in their disintegration of the human body and implicit child-killing in their horrifying conjuring spell.

Later, the witches are deprived of sibling political energy by revealing that they have 'masters'. Yet this opening to further levels of diabolic power extends their domain into the future. As well as the near-term prophecies of Macbeth's apparent invincibility, they *stage a play*, or a dumb show of Banquo's royal descendants (his son, Fleance, escaped), which include the king in the first audience, James I. At this pregnant moment, the king in the audience was included *within the parameters of the play* by use of a mirror held up to incorporate his reflection into the dumb show. Hence the radical injection of libido into politics by means of abolishing the flimsy distinction between 'acting' and 'political action'. The witches' magic is *acting/drama* that is directly treading on the realm of Stuart kingship. It is a warning that the sacred king Duncan is dead, and his son has to find different ways of acting/ruling if he is to survive.

Three political forms are discernible in *Macbeth*: the old order of the sacred father king, which lingers in the aged holy king of England; ruthless tyranny; and the witches' (demonised) seeming equality.

One could read the play as radical in the very existence and potency of the witches. After all, their sisterly energy seems to be the crucial factor in Macbeth carrying out a deep desire. The witches' magic 'lies' in psychology and prediction. We see their prophecies fulfilled on stage, up to making King James *part of the performance*. Hence we see the seamless join between play acting and politics. The witches conjure Macbeth's dark desires out of him by the play fulfilling their predictions. Unfortunately for him, he does not realize that he is in the play as well, so when Banquo's ghost appears at his celebration, *he cannot act the king*.

We see Macbeth fail to find the role of king, fail to develop the self-consciousness of 'acting' that Shakespeare's political plays require of a successful monarch. It is not enough, we learn in Duncan, for the king in the Stuart age to sink into the archetype of divine father. That is to possess too little consciousness for the growing complexity of seventeenth-century government. Conversely, *Macbeth* shows the failure of raw hunger for power if unstabilised by kinship libido within and across generations.

Ultimately, Macbeth only learns to act like a king at the end of the play when he realizes that he has been tricked by the witches. Consciousness of trickster energy from the despised *other* enables him to find a shard of nobility. Finally there is a division in him between the desire to be ruler and his understanding of performing a role. The only role left to him is to die as a king by leading his men in battle. His victor, Malcolm, interestingly combines something of all possible political forms struggling in the play. He has sacred legitimacy as Duncan's son, the drive to power through war, and is something of the trickster-actor in spying out enemies. Lastly, there is something of sibling kinship libido in his tackling of Macduff in England on more equal terms.

The end of the play even more emphatically excludes the feminine and nature in cutting down the forest and finding a hero not of woman born. Yet the final scene of conquest produces an unsustainable land and government; both are barren. Fortunately, Malcolm's last speech speaks of 'planting' a new state (Act 5, sc. 9, 1. 32). He assumes authority over the natural and feminine *other*, that he can *cultivate* power. Yet the power of the witches as political theatre lives on. Not heeding the warning of the play, the family watching in 1606 were to meet the witches' brothers thirty years later.

Bibliography

Bacon, Francis (1620/2004) *Novum Organum: True Directions Concerning The Interpretation Of Nature*, Whitefish, MT: Kessinger.

Jung, C. G. (1960) *The Structure and Dynamics of the Psyche* (CW8), in Jung, C. G. (1953–1991) *The Collected Works of C.G. Jung* (CW), London: Routledge, Princeton NJ: Princeton University Press.

Newton, Isaac (1687/1999) *Philosophiae Naturalis Principia Mathematica*, Whitefish, MT: Kessinger.

Samuels, A. (1985) *Jung and the Post-Jungians*, London: Routledge & Kegan Paul.

Samuels, A. (1993) *The Political Psyche*, London and New York: Routledge.

Samuels, A. (2001) *Politics on the Couch: Citizenship and the Internal Life*, London: Profile.

Shakespeare, W. (1603/1977) *Macbeth*, Oxford: Oxford University Press.

Chapter 32

The interface between Jung and humanistic psychology

A tribute to the influence of Andrew Samuels

Christine Shearman and Maria Gilbert

Introduction

It is a privilege for us to be included in this Festschrift in honour of Andrew Samuels and his contributions to psychology. When we refer directly to the work of Andrew Samuels, we will indicate this clearly and the honour is his; where we refer to our understanding of Jung, any preferences, biases and misunderstandings are ours alone.

Andrew Samuels has made a significant contribution to the movement towards integration in humanistic psychology, in his writing, in supervision, in keynote addresses, and in personal communications (Lapworth 2008). Firstly we will look at references to humanistic psychology under the title 'unknowing Jungians' in his seminal book *Jung and the Post-Jungians* (Samuels 1985: 10) and examine their significance in the light of our theme. Next, we propose to highlight some significant areas in humanistic psychology and in the field of integration which, in our view, have some 'unknown roots' in Jungian thinking.

Unknowing Jungians

In *Jung and the Post Jungians*, Samuels states that 'much of modern analysis and psychotherapy has a pronounced Jungian flavour' (1985:10). He points out that the unconscious in Jung's view has 'a creative, purposive, non-destructive aspect' (ibid.).

Jung himself said in his autobiography, when talking of the unconscious as a process, that 'the psyche is transformed or developed by the relationship of the ego to the contents of the unconscious', thus stressing the healing aspect of this process (Jung 1961: 235). In this context Samuels refers to Maslow, whose concept of a human being's drive towards self actualization lies at the heart of humanistic psychology. Growth was also at the heart of the person-centred tradition, with its emphasis on the fully functioning person; in gestalt, with its focus on organismic self-regulation; and in transactional analysis, with its focus on 'physis', defined as 'the growth force of nature which makes organisms evolve into higher forms' (Berne 1957: 369). In discussing creativity we cannot avoid talking about physis, as defined by Berne and further elaborated by Clarkson (1995). They have taken Heraclitus' view of physis as the positive force in nature and seen it as instrumental in change for the better. This has, however, avoided dealing with the destructive side of nature, and the shadow, until recently (see below).

Creativity is central to gestalt therapy in practice. Laura Perls herself used dance and drama in her work, and Joseph Zinker expanded upon and extended Perls' use of creative ways of working in his focus on experimentation in gestalt (Zinker 1978). Although the humanistic emphasis on self actualization has a feeling tone quality which echoes Jung's view of the unconscious as having a creative aspect, there is a major difference in how creativity is approached in the therapy.

Yalom in contrasting humanistic approaches to European existentialism summarizes the position succinctly in the following comment:

> The humanistic psychologists . . . speak less of limits and contingency than of development of potential, less of acceptance than of awareness, less of anxiety than of peak experiences and oceanic oneness, less of life meaning than of self-realization, less of apartness and basic isolation than of the I-Thou encounter.
>
> (1931: 19)

However, in the current field of humanistic integrative psychotherapy it is interesting to note that the 'optimistic' stance has been tempered by the acceptance of the Jungian shadow; for example, in recent years a TA conference was devoted exclusively to this topic.

Samuels makes other points of interest when examining 'unknown Jungians'. He says that 'symptoms should not be looked at solely in a causal reductive manner but in terms of their meaning for the patient' (1985: 10). Although he does not mention gestalt therapy in this regard, a gestaltist would certainly agree with this perspective since gestalt places particular emphasis on the uniqueness of the 'field conditions' that surround each client's presentation and on the uniqueness of each co-created relationship in the therapeutic context. Samuels raises other points here of relevance to humanists. He states that 'the analyst's personality and his experience of the analysis are of central importance' (ibid.). This focus on the person of the therapist and his/her experience of the relationship with the client would be recognisable to a gestaltist in the experience of the dialogic relationship and to a transactional analyst with the emphasis on the two-way nature of all transactions and games.

Samuels mentions 'regression in analysis' as being 'possibly helpful and useful' (ibid.), which is particularly familiar to a transactional analyst's view of working with the 'inner child' of the client. He also reflects here that many psychotherapists now place emphasis on the clinical use of the countertransference, as Jung did, which is an important factor in current humanistic integrative psychotherapy.

Lastly, in this section we note Samuels' recognition that gestalt therapy and transactional analysis think in terms of 'subdivisions of personality with which an analyst may work' (ibid), easily recognized in the two-chair work that is a hallmark of earlier gestalt therapy and the dialogues between ego states in TA therapy.

So how do we understand the avoidance of these 'unknowing Jungians' in acknowledging their debt to Jung? Why did they shun this recognition of his influence? In his book *The Political Psyche* (1993), Samuels examines Jung's political gaffes, his political naivety, and his undoubted racism, drawing close to multiple answers that seem likely. His arguments are too thorough in scholarship and detail to be summarized here without distortion. Suffice it to say they make no attempt to excuse Jung. On the contrary, this work is an act of reparation. Moreover it is written by a Jewish man. There were and continue to be, however, vituperative attacks on Jung which devalue the whole of his opus. In acknowledging Jung's influence in humanistic psychology we may go some way to making reparation of our own.

Unknown roots: The transpersonal

What should be remembered in what follows is that Jung is using his archetypal theory to speak of the self, that central organizing principle in the psyche.

> Symbols of the self not only *express* potential integration or order, they also *contribute to it*, and also to the psyche's self-healing capacities. Symbolic experiences are often stated by Jung to be *numinous* . . . This is similar to Maslow's idea of 'peak experiences'.
>
> (Samuels 1985: 96–97)

First we shall go to Samuels' division of Jungian thinking into three parts: The God-Image, Self and Others, and The Unus Mundus (Samuels 1985; see also Shearman 2006).

The first of these refers to 'the God-image in man as a symbol of the self,' the archetype of wholeness (Samuels 1985: 98). Jung, the son of a Protestant pastor, let us not forget, discusses Christ as representative of this psychological idea, a desire for wholeness. It should be remembered too that there is a real danger for either client or therapist to become inflated with the God-image, a dangerous state.

The second is, in Samuels' view, the transpersonal self in relation with others. As he points out 'the self is the primary source of phenomena such as empathy' (Samuels 1985: 99). Of course to have a reliable self we must come to terms with the internal 'Other' (see Papadopoulos 1991). This will necessarily mean facing the shadow.

The third of Samuels' divisions refers to the holistic view that 'every stratum of existence is intimately linked with all other strata' (Samuels 1985: 185).

In his exposition of transference and countertransference, Samuels says that Jung's particular contribution may be found in the ways in which he combines a one-person psychology with a two-person psychology and so focuses on the relational dimension that is 'larger' than the purely personal relationship (ibid.). All clinicians will resonate with moments in their work when words fall silent and it may be possible to 'hear the voice of God'. Samuels' view is that this is the transpersonal aspect of the relationship: 'a reprise of a relation to the divine' (ibid.: 193). It is interesting that dialogical gestalt therapy based in the work of Buber (1923/1996) was reaching out in a similar way. Hycner in this tradition of gestalt dialogical therapy points out that in every I-Thou encounter 'those moments of deep interpersonal meeting take us to the edge of the sacred' (Hycner 1991: 91). An I-Thou relationship expands our consciousness and takes us out of the realms of the ego to gain a sense of our place in the universe.

Unknown roots: Field theory and politics

There was a move away from the emphasis on purely rational thinking in the twentieth century. Jung's thinking was central to this move in providing a methodology which celebrates 'two kinds of thinking' (Jung 1956: 7), both the rational and 'the language of acausal coherence' (Papadopoulous: personal communication). Samuels (1989) postulates that reductionism inevitably leads us away from multiplicity, diversity and difference, towards an either/or unipolar position. His book *The Political Psyche* (1993) amplifies and elaborates upon Jung's own insistence that psychotherapy is not an isolated endeavour, concerned only with the therapeutic dyad, but that society and the world at large, of necessity, enter the consulting room: 'the psyche is not only a personal but a world problem, and the psychiatrist has to deal with an entire world' (Jung 1963: 154).

One of the ways in which Samuels has taken account of this dimension and taken it outside the consulting room is in being a founder member of Psychotherapists and Counsellors for Social Responsibility (linked with UKCP), a group which is actively involved in looking at the contribution of psychotherapy to the wider domain. He has supported those practitioners amongst us who viewed psychotherapy as inevitably a political and social process and were exploring with clients the implications of political and social issues in their lives, without a rationale in the field to support this work.

Gestaltists unaware of their Jungian roots have always included social issues in their approach. Paul Goodman was a committed and ardent socialist who led the way for subsequent practitioners. Gestalt practice has also drawn on Kurt Lewin's field theory; this has been elaborated by Parlett (1993) in his articles on field theory in Gestalt journals. Parlett has discussed the significance of field theory for psychotherapy practice.

We also at this point wish to acknowledge the contribution of Eric Berne (1957), the founder of Transactional Analysis. When he worked in a psychiatric ward, he insisted that his patients work in a group, first observed by the staff and then moving outside themselves to observing the staff in a group. In this way he ensured transparency in all discussions related to patients. Radical indeed, and from this process the School of Radical Psychiatry was born in the USA. Perhaps it was from his belief in the co-creation of reality that Berne named his theory Transactional Analysis, a system based on the interactivity of all human communication. Berne's focus was on the responsibility of both people in any transaction for the subsequent communication or miscommunication.

Unknown roots: Change and therapy as dialogue

Samuels challenged certain humanistic psychologists to review their attitudes to change, just as they were actually beginning to move away from their goal-oriented, 'fix-the-problem' view. Transactional Analysts have now examined the concept of the change process in a number of ways. Traditionally TA viewed change as focused on specific changes in thinking, feeling and behaviour, agreed between therapist and client, which informed the 'contract'. The ground-breaking exposition of Relational Transactional Analysis has come closer to Jungian thinking about the fourth stage of analysis in viewing change as a transformation resulting from the analytic relationship itself (Samuels 1985: 177ff). However, there are still significant differences. The Jungian notion of change as transformation results from the journey towards the self, which is the centre around which other aspects of the personality cohere. 'The centre is the goal, and everything is directed towards that centre. . . . I [understand] that the self is the principle and the archetype of orientation and meaning. Therein lies its healing function' (Jung 1963: 224). There is thus 'no linear evolution; there is only circumambulation of the self' (ibid.: 222). This idea is relational but somewhat distant from TA and Gestalt's conceptions of relational change.

Although the book from which these quotations were taken was written late in Jung's life, the eye-to-eye position was one of his major deviations from Freud in the early days of their differences. The point for him here was that he regarded analysis as needing a 'social' attitude, as opposed to the formality of the psychoanalytic doctor/patient relationship with all the associations of the doctor 'doing' the curing, and the patient being the passive recipient.

Jung saw alchemy as a precursor to later studies of the unconscious and to those therapeutic endeavours involved in the transformation of personality. Samuels posits that Jung's use of alchemy is essentially a metaphor 'by which to manage [the] combination of the interpersonal and the intrapsychic aspects of therapy' (in Papadopoulos 2002: 186). He points out that coniunctio

> refers metaphorically to the deep and pervasive intermingling of the two personalities involved in therapy. At the same time the image of coniunctio depicts in dramatic form the movements between the parts of the unconscious psyche of both therapist and client.
>
> (ibid.)

Whereas humanists would not use this language, none would dispute that both parties in the therapeutic endeavour are changed through their relating.

An emphasis on the co-created relationship is central to gestalt and other humanistic integrative psychotherapies. Many of these rely on the work of Buber: 'Being gets to know itself deepest in the dialogue between humans' (in Hycner 1991: 86). Yontef also stresses the importance of the 'presence' of the therapist, 'being present as a person meeting the person of the other' (Yontef 1993: 24). This focus on the immediacy of meeting the other in the present moment is at the heart of authentic encounter, which underpins gestalt psychotherapy.

Hycner, when talking about the emphasis in gestalt on dialogue, distinguishes between the 'intrapsychic dialectic' and the 'interpersonal dialogic' aspects of therapy, both of which he sees as central to the process (Hycner 1991: 64). It is interesting to note that Hycner acknowledges his reliance on the work of Hans Trüb, a Jungian analyst. Perhaps not so 'unknown roots'!

Conclusion

Samuels has consistently shown us 'unknowing Jungians' how to become more knowing, and to integrate Jungian thought more overtly into our own core models. We owe him a great debt of gratitude not only for showing us how in his writings, but also in his modelling in the many lectures, keynote addresses, supervisions and personal communications we have been privy to. Thank you very much Andrew for acting as a guide and an inspiration.

Bibliography

Berne, E. (1957) *A Layman's Guide to Psychiatry and Psychoanalysis*. New York: Grove.

Buber, M. (1923/1996) *I and Thou*. New York: Touchstone.

Clarkson, P. (1995) *The Therapeutic Relationship in Psychoanalysis, Counselling Psychology and Psychotherapy*. London: Whurr.

Hycner, R. H. (1991) *Between Person and Person: Towards a Dialogical Psychotherapy*. Highland, NY: Gestalt Journal Press.

Jung, C.G. (1956) Two Kinds of Thinking. In *Symbols of Transformation*. London: Routledge & Kegan Paul.

Jung, C.G. (1963) *Memories, Dreams, Reflections*. London: Fontana.

Lapworth, P. (2008) Personal communication.

Lapworth P., Sills, C. and Fish, S. (2001) *Integration in Counselling and Psychotherapy*. London: Sage.

Maslow, A. (1968) *Toward a Psychology of Being*. New York: Van Nostrand Reinhold.

Maslow, A. (1971) *The Farther Reaches of Human Nature*. New York: Viking.

Parlett, M. (1991) Reflections on Field Theory. *The British Gestalt Journal*, 1: 69–81.

Parlett, M. (1993) Towards a More Lewinian Gestalt Therapy. *The British Gestalt Journal*, 2: 115–120.

Papadopoulos, R. (1991) Jung and the Concept of the Other, in R. Papadopoulos and G. Saayman (eds.) *Jung in Modern Perspective*: Bridport: Prism.

Papadopoulos, R. (2002) The Other Other: *Journal of Analytic Psychology*, 47: 163–188.

Papadopoulos, R. (ed.) (2006) *Handbook of Jungian Psychology*. London: Routledge.

Samuels, A. (1979) Diagnosis and Power. *The Jung Symposium*. London: Group for the Advancement of Psychotherapy in Social Work: 194.

Samuels, A. (1985) *Jung and the Post-Jungians*. London: Routledge.

Samuels, A. (1989) *The Plural Psyche*. London: Routledge.

Samuels, A. (1993) *The Political Psyche*. London: Routledge.

Shearman, C. (2006) A Raid on the Inarticulate. *Journal of the United Kingdom for the Advancement of Psychotherapy Integration*. London: Vukani.

Yalom, I. D. (1931) *Existential Psychotherapy*. New York: Basic Books.

Yontef, G. (1993) *Awareness, Dialogue and Process. Essays on Gestalt Therapy*. Highland, NJ: Gestalt Journal Press.

Zinker, J. (1978) *Creative Process in Gestalt Therapy*. New York: Vintage Books.

Chapter 33

Playing the race card

A cultural complex in action

Thomas Singer

Dedication

This essay would never have been written without many years of support from my friend, colleague, and editor, Andrew Samuels. Andrew's psychological, polymorphous diversity allowed many of us to open up to the diversity of our own psyches, including deep engagement and consideration of politics as part of being 'Jungian.' Without Andrew's passion and encouragement, I know that my own vision would not have found expression.

Introduction

Can we find a way to bring together passionate partisanship and psychological objectivity in a discourse on the forces that propel groups of people to align themselves into sharply differing positions on social, economic and spiritual issues? Put another way – can we find a psychological attitude that allows us to talk about politics in a meaningful way that does not just give us license to be one more species of political 'talking head,' expressing endlessly biased political opinions in the name of a professional persona?

I do not pretend to have the answers to these difficult questions, but I would like to offer one psychological way of considering these matters that allows us to take into account the deep and unpredictable emotional currents in the group and individual psyche – unconscious as well as conscious – without too quickly identifying with one side or another in a polarizing conflict. I believe that the concept of 'the cultural complex' (Singer and Kimbles 2004) is a notion that allows us to speak both to the passions of political conflict (and to one's own subjective passion) and to a search for objectivity in understanding what underlies specific political conflicts. The recently concluded Democratic primaries in the USA and the various ways in which 'the race card' were played illustrate how the concept of 'the cultural complex' can be useful in shedding light on the relationship between deeply conflicted emotional undercurrents of the collective psyche and political process.

Attitudes, behaviors and emotions around race form one of the most potent cultural complexes in the psyche of all Americans – Whites, Blacks, Asians, Latinos, and every hybrid in between. To get a visceral feel for what I mean by the cultural complex of race living in the psyche of every American, listen to Toni Morrison's description of a house haunted by the spirits of black ancestors from her novel, *Beloved*:

> he believed the undecipherable language clamoring around the house was the mumbling of the black and angry dead. Very few had died in bed . . . and none that he knew of . . . had lived a livable life. Even the educated colored: the long-school people, the doctors, the teachers, the paper-writers and businessmen had a hard row to hoe. In addition to having to use their heads to get ahead, they had the weight of the whole race sitting there. You needed two heads for that.
>
> Whitepeople believed that whatever the manners, under every dark skin was a jungle. Swift unnavigable waters, swinging screaming baboons, sleeping snakes, red gums ready for their sweet white blood. In a way, he thought, they were right. The more coloredpeople spent their strength trying to convince them how gentle they were, how clever and loving, how human, the more they used themselves up to persuade whites of something Negroes believed could not be questioned, the deeper and more tangled the jungle grew inside.
>
> But it wasn't the jungle blacks brought with them to this place from the other (livable) place. It was the jungle whitefolks planted in them. And it grew. It spread. In, through and after life, it spread, until it invaded the whites who had made it. Touched them every one. Changed and altered them. Made them bloody, silly, worse than even they wanted to be, so scared were they of the jungle they had made. The screaming baboon lived under their own white skin; the red gums were their own.
>
> (Morrison 1987: 234)

The cultural complex of race, with its mumbling voices of 'the black and angry dead' and the 'screaming baboon . . . under their own white skin' became central voices in the Democratic primaries of the first half of 2008 and continued during the general election on the occasion of a black man becoming the nominee of the Democratic party for President of the United States for the first time in American history. Long-simmering fear, rage and hatred lurk just beneath the surface of the collective psyche on both sides of the nation's intractable racial divide.

The political landscape can be soiled instantaneously when the emotional and ideological toxins of the cultural complex of race are released into the environment by engaging in the time-honored political poker of 'playing the race card.' It takes very little for a politician to trigger the roiling emotions of the race cultural complex. A single, coded word or short phrase such as 'white, working-class Americans' can become a trigger for activating virulent emotions in what amounts to a word association test of the collective psyche.

Playing the race card is an idiomatic phrase referring to an allegation raised against a person or group who has brought the issue of race or racism into a debate, perhaps to obfuscate the matter. . . . It refers to someone exploiting prejudice against another race for political or some other advantage.[1]

In the language of the cultural complex, 'playing the race card' detonates the landmine of one group's most powerful negative emotions and collective memories against another group's very existence.

I want to offer a brief synopsis of how 'playing the race card' came alive in the 2008 presidential elections in America. Many different groups and sub-groups have had different 'cards' to play to achieve varying political purposes, but most are motivated by the desire to speak to and manipulate the powerful, non-rational affects of cultural complexes to get various groups to feel, think and vote in one way or another based on the deep-seated feelings and memories of each particular group's experience. Race stirs up very primitive reactions that become more stereotypical the closer they get to the archetypal core of cultural complexes. This rough sketch of some of the cards that have been played reveals a cultural complex in action:

Card One: 'The race card will not be played'

During all of 2007, Barack Obama framed his campaign's stance to the 'race card' as not wanting to play it at all. He advocated a post-racial politics in which he insisted that the color of his skin should not be a primary issue in the campaign. He was attractive to many because he presented himself as a new generation of black leader for whom race was no longer the defining issue and he offered a new way of being that transcended racial differences. That very post-racial posture, the refusal to play the race card as perhaps a new way to play the race card, made many blacks suspicious of Obama for not being black enough. Black aides within his own campaign urged him to give his wife, Michelle, a more active role as a way of affirming his black identity. In view of what subsequently unfolded in the Democratic primaries, Obama's initial post-racial posture can be described as a good-faith attempt to do an 'end-run' on the cultural complex level of group experience.

Card Two: 'The race card will be played – but you played it first!'

Obama's post-racial politics worked quite well until his stunning surprise victory in the January 5, 2008, Iowa caucus. In other words, it was not until

Obama's candidacy became a real threat to the established Democratic and Republican leadership that race began to insert itself into the elections. This new phase of the race card game was inaugurated by Bill Clinton in late January 2008 when he suggested just prior to the South Carolina primary that Obama might win that state because of its large black vote. This was the first time race was overtly introduced into the Democratic primaries as a significant factor.

After Obama won South Carolina, Bill Clinton further compounded the race issue by seeming to dismiss Obama's victory by comparing it to Jesse Jackson's strong showing in the state in 1984 and 1988, basically saying that South Carolina is an easy state for blacks to win but it is of no broader significance. Clinton later went on to say that he was not the one to introduce the 'race card' in South Carolina. He would claim that the Obama campaign had in fact stacked the deck so that any mention of race at all was going to be seen as 'playing the race card' and that it was in fact the Obama team that first played the race card.[2]

Card Three: 'The angry black preacher appears on Fox News'

In March 2008, an even more inflammatory racial card was introduced – not by the Clintons, but by the right-wing Fox News Network, which uncovered and continuously played video tape of incendiary racial rhetoric from Obama's own minister, Reverend Wright. The 'race card' now seemed to spring full-blown from Obama's own religious community, where Wright was shown accusing the United States Government of infecting black people with the AIDS virus and welcoming the 9/11 attack as the 'chickens coming home to roost,' i.e., as punishment of the US for its own international 'terrorist' activity. The images of an angry black minister playing the 'race card' was the very cultural complex 'bomb' that both the Republicans and the Clintons had been hoping might come out of nowhere, explode, and cause Obama's apparently unstoppable momentum to implode. The irony is that it was Obama's close affiliation with Wright that handed his rivals the 'race card' they had been waiting to play – and they didn't even have to play it themselves other than to show it endlessly on TV.[3]

Card Four: The trump card: 'If the race card is going to be played, we are going to play it in a totally new way'

The Reverend Wright tapes ushered in another new phase in the 'race card' poker game in which Obama had to modify his post-racial politics to include the realities of the divisiveness that festers in the deeply entrenched cultural complexes of both black and white people. Obama chose to energetically probe the emotional and psychic realities of the cultural complex of race in his Philadelphia speech of March 18, 2008. In the language of psychology, Obama chose to make the cultural complex itself more conscious rather than to project 'its screaming baboons, sleeping snakes, and red gums' on to a rival group or manipulating its potent affect to further intensify the fear and hate of one group for another.[4]

Political expediency and Obama's own integrity demanded that he no longer do an 'end-run' on race in his post-racial candidacy. In my mind, this was the moment when Obama truly emerged as presidential, because he showed his capacity to deal directly with a cultural complex in a psychologically insightful way. He chose to make the complex itself more conscious rather than to use the unconsciousness of the complex for his own purposes.[5]

Using the criteria I have laid down elsewhere to define a cultural complex (see Singer and Kimbles 2004), let's look at elements of Obama's Philadelphia speech to see how he spoke to the complex in a psychological way that opened up the festering wound of race for dialogue rather than manipulating it to poison one part of the population against another. Obama began by locating the cultural complex of racial division within his own psyche, as well as the collective psyche of the nation as a whole:

> I am the son of a black man from Kenya and a white woman from Kansas. I was raised with the help of a white grandfather who survived a Depression to serve in Patton's Army during World War II and a white grandmother who worked on a bomber assembly line at Fort Leavenworth while he was overseas. I've gone to some of the best schools in America and lived in one of the world's poorest nations. I am married to a black American who carries within her the blood of slaves and slave owners – an inheritance we pass on to our two precious daughters. I have brothers, sisters, nieces, nephews, uncles and cousins, of every race and every hue, scattered across three continents, and for as long as I live, I will never forget that in no other country on Earth is my story even possible.[6]

After locating the cultural complex in his own experience and psyche, Obama then goes on to define how this has played out in the American collective psyche for centuries. I will link his descriptions and language to the criteria I have outlined for defining and identifying a cultural complex:

1. A cultural complex expresses itself in powerful moods and repetitive behaviors – both in a group as a whole and in its individual members. Highly charged emotional or affective reactivity is the calling card of a cultural complex:

[A] legacy of defeat was passed on to future generations [of blacks] – those young men and increasingly young women who we see standing on street corners or languishing in our prisons, without hope or prospects for the future. . . . For the men and women of Reverend Wright's generation, the memories of humiliation and doubt and fear have not gone away; nor has the anger and the bitterness of those years. . . . In fact, a similar anger exists within segments of the white community. Most working and middle-class white Americans don't feel that they have been particularly privileged by their race. . . . They are anxious about their futures and feel their dreams slipping away. So when they are told to bus their children to a school across town; when they hear that an African American is getting an advantage in landing a good job or a spot in a good college because of an injustice they themselves never committed; when they're told that their fears about crime in urban neighborhoods are somehow prejudiced, resentment builds over time.

2. A cultural complex resists our most heroic efforts at consciousness and remains, for the most part, unconscious:

The fact is that the comments that have been made and the issues that have surfaced over the last few weeks reflect the complexities of race in this country that we've never really worked through – a part of our unions that we have yet to perfect. And if we walk away now, if we simply retreat into our respective corners, we will never be able to come together and solve challenges like health care, or education, or the need to find good jobs in America.

3. A cultural complex accumulates experiences that validate its point of view and creates a store-house of self-affirming, ancestral memories:

As William Faulkner once wrote, 'The past isn't dead and buried. In fact, it isn't even past.' We do not need to recite here the history of racial injustice in this country. But we do need to remind ourselves that so many of the disparities that exist in the African-American community today can be directly traced to inequalities passed on from an earlier generation that suffered under the brutal legacy of slavery and Jim Crow.

4. Cultural complexes function in an involuntary, autonomous fashion and tend to affirm a simplistic point of view that replaces more everyday ambiguity and uncertainty with fixed, often self-righteous attitudes to the world:

Race is an issue that I believe this country cannot afford to ignore right now. We would be making the same mistake that Reverend Wright made in his offending sermons about America – to simplify and stereotype and amplify the negative to the point that it distorts reality.

5. Cultural complexes have archetypal cores; that is, they express typically human attitudes and are rooted in primordial ideas about what is meaningful, making them very hard to resist, reflect upon, and discriminate:

The Declaration of Independence was stained by this nation's original sin of slavery, a question that divided the colonies and brought the convention to a stalemate until the founders chose to allow the slave trade to continue for at least twenty more years, and to leave any final resolution to future generations. . . . I chose to run for the presidency at this moment in history because I believe deeply that we cannot solve the challenges of our time unless we solve them together – unless we perfect our union by understanding that we may have different stories, but we hold common hopes; that we may not look the same and we may not have come from the same place, but we all want to move in the same direction – towards a better future for of children and our grandchildren.

Card Five: 'The angry black man won't go away'

Obama's Philadelphia speech was groundbreaking and went a long way to quieting some of the racial concerns that surfaced in many groups until Revered Wright caused a further uproar with an appearance at the National Press Club on April 28, 2008. Wright repeated some of his more inflammatory opinions in the Question and Answer session which threatened to lethally embroil Obama's candidacy in its identification with Reverend Wright. As a result, Obama more definitively distanced himself from Wright, which in turn drew this 'race card' reaction from Glen Ford on the online journal Black Agenda Report, where he played the 'race card' from a more militant black point of view:

It was the masterful preacher and seasoned political creature Wright . . . who forced Obama to choose in the push and pull of Black and white American worldviews. Obama was made to register his preference for the white racist version of truth over Rev. Wright's, whose rejection of Euro-American mythology reflects prevailing African American perceptions, past and present. Rev. Jeremiah Wright laid bare the contradictions of Obama's hopeless racial 'neutrality.'[7]

Card Six: 'The resentful white man won't go away'

In the meantime, the Clinton camp was becoming angrier and more frustrated as it became clear that Obama had strategically outflanked and out-campaigned them in almost every way. Their only and last hope was twofold – to claim that it was in fact Obama who had played the race card and to further play the 'race card' themselves by mobilizing the poor, white people of Appalachia (southern Ohio and all of Kentucky and West Virginia) to vote based on widespread racial fear and hatred of black people in that region. Pundits speculated that the goal of the Clinton campaign was to convince the still relatively large number of uncommitted super-delegates that racism was endemic among the less educated, white working class throughout America and that Obama would not be able to win that vote in many parts of the country. The argument of the Clinton camp suggested that Obama would not do as well as Hillary Clinton in a general election because he was black. By the time the Democratic primaries had reached West Virginia and Kentucky in May 2008, it felt as though the political process had sunk into the dregs of the 350-year-old, deeply entrenched American cultural complex of racism. To put it in the crudest terms of the cultural complex, the presidential primary now seemed to be pitting 'the niggers' against 'the poor white trash' – a condition that Bill and Hillary Clinton of Arkansas were as familiar with as any political poker player in the United States. It is in that context that Hillary Clinton introduced into the West Virginia primary the coded phrase about 'hard-working white Americans' which to many observers seemed calculated to stir up the most negative racial feelings in a timely playing of the race card:

> Senator Obama's support among working, hard-working Americans, white Americans, is weakening again . . . whites in both states who have not completed college [are] supporting me. There's a pattern emerging here.[8]

Conclusion

The race cards I have outlined are just a few of the more notable ones that were played during the 2008 presidential election. The point of this brief outline of how they were played is that the cultural complex of race in America is far too potent to have not become a major – if not *the* major – issue in the presidential elections. The American psyche has hardly finished with its long history of racial conflict and, although post-racial politics are a worthy goal, they are not yet an emotional reality in the American collective conscious or unconscious. The Reverend Wright, Geraldine Ferraro, West Virginia, North Carolina, Fox News Network, the Clintons and many, many others have made that abundantly clear. Retrospectively, there is no way that the cultural complex of race could not have raised its Medusa-like head during this campaign and threatened to turn to stone even the most modest hope for a change in racial politics. An end run on the cultural complex of race will not bring our country's dream of a more perfect union into being.

At the same time, what is truly encouraging in the face of the monstrously resistant and regressive forces that playing the race card invariably mobilizes is how much Obama has already accomplished. The way in which he has personally carried in his being as well as in his words the polarizing opposites of black and white, the hateful demons of 'screaming baboons, sleeping snakes, and red gums,' suggests that Obama may be among those rare leaders who have the capacity to carry in their psyches the cultural complexes that usually divide groups into warring factions. Many are able to experience in him and through him a transcendent force that shows us as individuals, as groups, even as a nation, a way to digest and metabolize the bitter racial legacy that has threatened to destroy us throughout our history.

Bibliography

Morrison, T. (1987) *Beloved.* New York: Vintage.
Singer, T. and Kimbles, S. L. (2004) The emerging theory of cultural complexes. In Singer, T. and Kimbles, S. L. (eds.) *The Cultural Complex: Contemporary Jungian Perspectives on Psyche and Society.* Hove, New York: Brunner-Routledge.

Notes

1 http://en.wikipedia.org/wiki/Playing_the_race_card
2 http://www.salon.com/opinion/greenwald/2008/01/27/clinton/
3 http://abcnews.go.com/Politics/wireStory?id=4180815 [January 24, 2008]
4 http://blogs.abcnews.com/politicalpunch/2008/01/bubba-obama-is.html [January 26, 2008]
5 http://video.yahoo.com/watch/2422917/7513742 [2008]
6 http://www.nytimes.com/2008/03/18/us/politics/18text-obama.html
7 http://www.blackagendareport.com/index.php?option=com_content&task=view &id=603&Itemid=1 [April 30, 2008]
8 http://www.salon.com/opinion/conason/2008/05/09/clinton_remarks/

Chapter 34

In praise of wild analysis

Martin Stanton

It is widely assumed that psychoanalysis is a form of psychotherapy, and, like all therapies, is centrally involved with the accurate diagnosis of mental disorders and the provision of effective treatment for them. In this context, like all mental health professions, psychoanalysis aims to identify and explore the presenting pathology and enable the patient to work productively with their symptoms. Its clinical journey is therefore clearly signposted from sickness to health, though there are some acceptable alternative therapeutic routes, such as social adaptation, work-life balance (well-being), or learning to live 'well' between others and your symptom.

Psychoanalysis in this therapeutic format is both reductive (as it focuses primarily on mental health issues) and normative (as it aims to promote all that it associates with being *well*). Its pre/proscribed paths therefore transport the patient through the thicket of the symptoms towards self-empowerment (ego strength) and effective social functioning (integration to social norms). The therapeutic travels in this kind of psychoanalysis – including their written and interpretative record – therefore follow a classic *bildungsroman* format, in which the central character (the patient) both *matures* through struggling with adversity and visibly gets *better*.

Psychoanalysis which does not prioritize the clinical practice of psychotherapy in this way is now often labeled *wild analysis*. Freud's celebrated founding text on the subject emphatically asserts that psychoanalysis is a 'medical technique' (1910: 226), based on an accurate diagnosis (ibid.: 224), whose procedures derive exclusively from clinical work with resistance and transference (ibid.: 225). All reference to psychoanalysis outside this therapeutic context is declared irretrievably *wild*, and potentially dangerous to the mental health of both the patient and the general public. Above all, the accuracy and effectiveness of the scientific theories operating within psychoanalysis depend entirely on their formal containment within this medical/therapeutic practice. Any knowledge associated with psychoanalysis that operates outside this restricted zone is inevitably corrupt and contaminated with non-specialist misperception, if indeed it is not fundamentally toxic:

> If knowledge about the unconscious were as important for the patient
> as people inexperienced in psychoanalysis imagine, listening to lectures
> or reading books would be enough to cure him. Such measures,
> however, have as much influence on the symptoms of nervous illness as
> a distribution of menu cards in a time of famine has on hunger. (ibid.)

Freud's solution to the supposed corruption and contamination imposed
by wild psychoanalysis was significantly a *political* one:

> in the face of dangers to patients and to the cause of psychoanalysis
> which are inherent in the practice . . . of a 'wild' psychoanalysis . . . we
> founded an International Psychoanalytic Association (IPA) . . . in order
> to be able to repudiate responsibility for what is done by those who do
> not belong to us and yet call their medical procedure 'psychoanalysis'.
> (ibid.: 226–227)

This political gesture served both to consolidate the notion of scientific and
theoretical uniformity housed exclusively in a family of therapeutic special-
ists, and to promote the formal exclusion of all those whose journeys led
them elsewhere to arrive at different conclusions. So, following the foundation of the IPA in March 1910, it is hardly surprising that some analysts
came to slot in to the 'wild' bill, not least because their scientific/theoretical
practices significantly differed and led them elsewhere. As they were 'wild',
they clearly did not 'belong', so their work was either formally declared a
public health hazard (Jung's *active imagination* supposedly promoted
psychosis, and Reich's *Sex-Pol* supposedly unleashed promiscuity and
'degenerate' sexual practice) or their theories themselves were formally
diagnosed as the product of a mental disorder (Ferenczi's later discoveries
were attributed by Ernest Jones to a personal 'collapse into psychosis'
[Jones 1957: 165]). In all cases, the 'wild' element – the theoretical
difference/deviance and its supposed potential detrimental/subversive effect
on the mental health of the patient – needed to be formally displayed in
public. All this was conducted in the name of science, following the imposed
internal politics of clinical efficacy, and the protection of the mental health
of the patient, leading ultimately to the promotion of the well-being of
society as a whole.

Furthermore, Freud's choice of the epithet 'wild' has itself generated a
whole range of unforeseen resonances. The very fact that he puts the word
'wild' in inverted commas in his title 'Über "wilde" psychoanalyse' formally
marks out the common spoken currency of the term: 'wild' for him is
patently a buzzword with popular current associations. Paradoxically, this
assumed common spoken currency – and set associative range – is significantly different in (the original) German and English. In particular, the
whole associative line in German linking 'wild' to 'illegality' is lost in

translation into English – such as in *wildes Parken* (to park illegally), *wilde Taxis* (unlicensed taxicabs), or *in wilder Ehe leben* (to live in sin). In English, the unrestrained, unknown, and profuse associations of 'wild' are not formally balanced against, or mediated by the law, though a 'wild' person may be vaguely or very generally associated with 'unruly' or 'anti-authority' attitudes and behaviour. Also the 'wild' place in English – the *wilderness* – is firmly associated with journeys in which the subject (the patient) confronts the raw, profuse and unrestrained in nature to arrive at self-discovery. In German, this place has a different name – *die Wüste* – which means a 'desert', 'waste' or 'wasteland'. This is a negative, empty, and inhospitable place – '*in die Wüste schicken*' poignantly means 'to give someone the push'. So 'wild' analysts in German have definitely broken the law and been given the push; whereas 'wild' analysts in English may be unruly and anti-authoritarian, but also potentially heading out on journeys of self-discovery.

Let us try now to recover imaginatively what is lost in this translation. Two very different potential spaces seem to be cleared for wild analysis. One involves a negative vortex provoked by certain supposed theoretical/clinical *detours* that transgress scientific and natural law (health and well-being). Another is a process of radical living discovery (*das wilde Erlebnis*) – provoked during an analytic journey into the unrestrained and rich profusion of the wilds. May indeed these two potential spaces themselves be linked, if not by some direct main highway (formal legal/scientific procedure), then by some common core assumptions (contained in some virtual highway code or GPS navigation system)? Is indeed the negative vortex space now so clearly signposted in psychoanalysis that it is not only explicitly *known* – its trigger-points are identified and located – but also positively *exploited*? Is there clear exploitative mileage here for radical journeys to steer straight into the negative vortex, both to expose the normative and reductionist dynamic of 'belonging' (to the family, society or science), and to promote their own outsider status? Are in fact both potential 'wild' spaces equally corrupt(ed) because they mutually exploit the differences generated between them?

Over the last two decades, Andrew Samuels has been an inveterate and irrepressible aficionado of the trigger-points embedded in wild analysis. First of all, he has cogently and provocatively explored the tensions generated by pluralism and theoretical diversity for classic clinical psychoanalysis (Samuels 1989). Samuels has illustrated both the epistemological conceit of singular visions of clinical work – in particular the object relations tradition of assuming an exclusive co-extensiveness with psychic 'reality' (Samuels 1993). For Samuels, the psyche is irrepressibly plural, so to attempt to regulate, impose laws, or repress different ways of looking at it will simply foment revolt amongst those quarters declared out of order or un-scientific. For Samuels, pluralism and theoretical/clinical difference is to be celebrated not repressed. There are inevitably many therapeutic paths up the spiritual mountains encountered in life, and many basic factors that determine which path you choose and how you muster your energies actually to get up it. You may opt for the quickest, safest therapeutic route, or perhaps for the most aesthetic, or the one which most challenged your ancestors. You may start with a solo therapeutic route, or prefer to sign up for the group or art option. You may even rely on your own knowledge, or you may hire a Sherpa to help negotiate the rock outbreaks. But, following Samuels, when you all arrive together at the summit, or re-assemble after the climb at the base camp, it would be unproductively omnipotent to argue for the exclusive rights or your particular vision of the reality of the mountain over the numerous others. If you do, all the others will inevitably speculate why you choose in the first place to claim such authority. Perhaps to maintain the high fee-structure of an exclusive group of Sherpas? Or to promote the rosette evaluation system for the Michelin Guide to the Soul and Psyche?

In Samuels' pluralism, the mountain itself naturally confers a basic wild consensus. However diverse the mountain pursuits, however complex or circuitous they may be, all journeys head somewhere in relation to the summit, irrespective of whether the travelers actually reach any pinnacle or not. So, for Samuels, it is vital always to hold on to the bigger collective picture, and then work with all emergent differences as revelatory of the raw plural nature of the psyche itself. At precisely the point where different perspectives attempt to divide and rule (psychic) reality, the Samuelsian wild analyst will install a debate. This is nowhere more important than in clinical training in psychoanalysis, where all singular visions need to be re-engaged in a big-picture debate – which is Samuels' view of the pluralistic radical mission of psychoanalytic studies (Samuels 1996). With hardly surprising but ingenuous irony, the critical response to Samuels' notion of pluralism from orthodox psychoanalysis has involved the unmodified re-play of the 'wild analysis' card: the 'theoretical trends are viewed as potentially harmful clinically'; there is supposed conceptual rogue-trading, or a

> tendency to import, often uncritically, ideas from other theoretical systems into his fundamentally Jungian framework'; and the overall focus on diversity is disintegrative (rather than integrative), in so far as it predominantly employs the polyvalent dimensions of metaphor and imagery – rather than the 'literality of developmental events' – as the 'quasi-autonomous prime mover of mental life'.
>
> (Stolorow and Atwood 1991: 99–100)

No doubt even the mountain analogy employed here could ultimately be dismissed in this perspective as a covert and unauthorized bid to globalize a particular Swiss alpine outlook!

A more appropriate mountain to visit in this critical context is Thomas Mann's (1924) 'Magic Mountain' (*Der Zauberberg*), because it involves a prolonged imaginative exploration of the place and treatment of sickness and health in battle-torn and alienated society. In this novel, the protagonist, Hans Castorp, visits his sick cousin, Joachim Ziemsten, fairly clear that all the sickness (definitively diagnosed as tuberculosis) is neatly contained on the magic mountain in the sanatorium. Everywhere else around on the mountain is supposedly sublime and healthy wild nature, untrammeled by humans, and accompanied by unpolluted fresh air – a certain recipe for *cure*. In fact, in a protracted surprise journey, Castorp discovers not only that the sickness equally lies within him – he is soon diagnosed with tuberculosis – but also that the *malaise* lies far deeper and is much more widespread than he originally thought. The sickness even becomes reflected in the ever-retreating promise of cure – whose 'reality' becomes transformed into a psychological *placebo* to ward off the grim truths of suffering unto death. Worse, the various philosophical and psychological 'solutions' to the world's ills – extensively aired and debated between fellow inmates – lead not to some shared understanding and appreciation of difference, but rather to a fierce gridlock of prejudice, which is seemingly only resolvable through an act of violence. Seven years later, finally declared 'cured', Castorp re-enters the 'normal' world with a 'healthy' surfeit of *Weltschmerz*, and immediately becomes conscripted to fight as one of anonymous millions for the hallowed principles of Good, Truth and Justice.

Castorp's mountain tour prompts vital 'wild' questions about the place of the primary aligned sites of pathology and therapy (the clinic) in the orthodox *Weltanschauung* of psychoanalysis. If indeed the 'normal' world out there is 'sick' and operates through manipulation, exploitation and violence, is it then justifiable to propose a therapeutic aim of 'healthy' adjustment to it? Does the implicit *Bildungsroman* form of this clinical journey – in which the patient supposedly *matures* through triumph over adversity (the symptom) – therefore actually lead everyone principally to *learn* to compromise, or to *know* how to live 'well' with alienation? Or does the Castorpian alternative – the *Gegenbildungsroman* – rather question the very status and function of sickness and health in the sanatorium in this analytic journey? What indeed would such a 'wild analysis' alternative then entail?

Quite clearly, this wild alternative would have to be political – and formally question the social construction of sickness and health, in particular the role of hierarchies of mental health professionals in marketing and exploiting a notion of cure. In this context, 'wild analysis' assumes a radical if not revolutionary place – and formally comes to question the core social norms that both purportedly drive individual 'well-being', and furnish the curative destinations in the classic psychoanalytic clinical journey. The site generated for wild analytic critique then inevitably shifts out to the mountain edges and becomes increasingly militant, as the 'normal' world out there becomes visibly more deeply mired in war, violence, prejudice and exploitation. *In extremis*, like Castorp discovering the true spread of his *malaise*, wild analysis might even come to believe itself an essential *prophylaxis* against the contaminations of the political world. As Adorno poignantly remarked: 'they (revisionist psychoanalysts) come ultimately to act as if the antagonism between the private and the social being can actually be "cured" by therapy' (Adorno 1972: 38).

In this context, it is significant that Samuels' own conception of the political challenge to orthodox analysis is minimalist – he simply asserts that political discourse is as integral to therapy as any other discourse (Samuels 1993); and he argues entirely from within therapy itself – his radical focus centers principally on what therapists can offer politicians and political institutions (Samuels 2001). In this way, the internal politics of clinical psychoanalysis feed both from and into the political realm as a whole. For Samuels, this is nowhere clearer than in family and sexual politics. He regards promiscuity, for example, as a complex 'political act' that both exploits the potential plural dimensions of sexual experience, and directly challenges the *status quo* of family life (based on marriage vows, monogamy, and fidelity). The open prominence and acceptance of promiscuity in some gay circles therefore stands as a direct political challenge to the sole-owner assumptions of heterosexual coupledom. For Samuels, the therapist cannot possibly brush off such a political challenge, not least when working directly with a promiscuous patient. To pathologize that patient – to declare their promiscuity 'deviant' or 'sick' – equally constitutes a political statement, even if it might trade as a neutral scientific or clinical diagnosis, and the patient consequently has the right to engage in direct (political) debate with it, either inside or outside the session. Finally, for Samuels, there is a *meta*-political level of theoretical promiscuity – or pluralism – which inevitably comes into play in therapy, principally around the practical issue of how to distinguish between, and work with, the patient's burgeoning diversity of desire and concomitant pleasure. *Homo therapeutens* – to paraphrase Marcuse (1964) – inevitably finds it ever more difficult to fit such profusion into a one-dimensional *cure*, particularly in the new political/pathological context of virtual-reality-assisted magic mountaineering (otherwise known as pornography).

In all cases, Samuels' prime political task is to re-vision the clinic: to open all its doors and windows, re-locate it, and launch sub-venues, but not close it or declare it out of order. If, following the anarchic (anti-law) dimension of wild analysis, the clinic installs a false authority within psychoanalysis, then the analytical process itself needs to be de-pathologized and disentangled from *cure*. The very dichotomy around which Freud constructed his 'wild' category – the dichotomy between clinical and applied psychoanalysis – becomes a false one (Stanton 1995). Psychoanalytic procedures like free association and dream interpretation are then not governed and judged exclusively by cure, or their clinical effectiveness. They may indeed serve to make the patient worse. They are rather integral to the exploration of the unconscious – an open-ended voyage of discovery to encounter the raw, the wild and the unforeseen, rather than a proscribed clinical tour, bordered throughout by health and well-being. In this wild German terrain, psychoanalysis rather forms part of broad cultural and experiential education (*Bildung*). It remains fundamentally heterodox (unbound by any external law), consistently unbinding all that appears complex (*Lösung*), and irrepressibly improvisational in exploring ways forward. As Laplanche succinctly puts it: 'Psychoanalysis has to put all socially adaptive aims in brackets. That is why it can never be a profession' (Laplanche 1992: 6).

In conclusion, wild analysis not only merits praise, but also needs to be protected as a threatened species from the legislative excesses of health professional registration bodies. Freud's polemical category has generated a vital critical space to question normative theoretical elaborations and scientific pretensions in psychoanalysis. It has also promoted important discussion of wider political and social issues that impact on psychoanalysis above and beyond so-called medical or scientific impartiality. Finally, it has enabled open and enthusiastic debate and collaboration with various academic disciplines and creative pursuits, housed notably in the alpine muster-points pitched by Psychoanalytic Studies. If these wild spaces are allowed to fall into disuse, psychoanalysis will lose its place for radical questioning, and its royal ways to the unconscious will be declared forever closed.

Bibliography

Adorno, T. W. (1972) *La psychanalyse "revisee"*. Paris: Olivier.

Freud, S. (1910 [1957]) '"Wild" Analysis', *SE*, Vol. 11, London: Hogarth.

Jones, E. (1957) *Sigmund Freud: Life and Work*, Vol. 3, London: Hogarth.

Laplanche, J. (1992) 'Jean Laplanche talks to Martin Stanton', in *Jean Laplanche: Seduction, Translation. Drives*, Fletcher, J. and Stanton, M. (eds.). London: ICA.

Mann, T. (1924 [1972]) *The Magic Mountain*. Harmondsworth: Penguin.

Marcuse, H. (1964) *One-Dimensional Man*. Boston: Beacon.

Samuels, A. (1989) *The Plural Psyche*. London: Routledge.

—— (1993) *The Political Psyche*. London: Routledge.

—— (1996) 'The Future of Jungian Studies', in *Teaching Transference*, Stanton, M. and Reason, D. (eds.). London: Rebus.

—— (2001) *Politics on the Couch*. London: Profile.

Stanton, M. (1995) 'The False Dichotomy between Applied and Clinical Psychoanalysis', in *Confronting the Challenges to Psychoanalysis*, Friedlander, S. R. (ed.). San Francisco: IFPE.

Stolorow, R.D. and Atwood, G. E. (1991) 'The Plural Psyche', in *International Review of Psychoanalysis*, vol. 18.

Chapter 35

City men, mobile phones, and initial engagement in the therapeutic process

Martin Stone

For Andrew. In recognition of many years of cooperation, friendship and fun. Martin.

Paolo walked into my consulting room, threw three mobile phones onto the couch, took off his jacket, and sat down. 'What a load of arseholes!' he said, referring to his boss and colleagues. The difference between this and our first meeting was that this time he had turned off the phones before throwing them down; later in our work he turned them off before coming into the room.

During our first meeting two of the phones had gone off in the session, his Hong Kong one and his London one (the third one had a German SIM card in it, as he worked as a fund manager for a German bank in the City).

This chapter explores difficulties encountered when beginning therapeutic work with financially successful men with relationship problems. Typically they might be described as being out of touch with their feelings, emotionally cut off and lacking empathy. The question arises whether the nature of their work has led them to behave in this way, whether they were attracted to it because of their personality, or a combination of the two. For men to succeed in this environment is there an advantage in not feeling and in being cut off? If they do have a well-developed feeling function, can it survive, or do they need to suppress it to survive? If the City attracts those with very good thinking and poor feeling functions, does life there reinforce this to an almost pathological degree?

Paolo was in many ways typical of a number of successful, highly motivated men with whom I have worked. Their careers are within the financial and legal sectors in the City: in investment banking, fund management, financial advice, accountancy, commercial law and IT. Their arena is in global organisations. They frequently have to travel, often at short notice, and they may suddenly be asked to relocate to another country. In general their loyalties are only to their work, to fulfilment of their ambitions, and to personal success. As James, a public school-educated investment banker, said to me, 'All investment bankers are out to get as much money as they can, as quickly as possible, and they cheat their customers and colleagues if they can.'

They often work 100 hours a week, in the office and entertaining clients. A call in the afternoon means leaving early next day for mainland Europe or further afield. A rare evening at home is interrupted by conference calls. The two weeks' annual holiday has to be called off at the last minute. Even when the holiday takes place, they can't escape the Blackberry. Home is like a hotel.

The financial rewards for this life are enormous, in terms of salary, bonuses, pensions, medical care. The downsides are equally obvious. How can a long-term relationship be sustained when you are physically, emotionally and psychologically so unavailable? This is the usual presenting problem that brings them into therapy, often at the behest of their partner.

Paolo, James and Steven came from very different backgrounds, but reveal a pattern that is reflected in their difficulties and behaviour.

Paolo was brought up in New York by hard-working parents of Italian origin, determined that their son should escape from poverty and succeed in the world. He learnt to meet their expectations by working hard at school, and in the family shop at weekends. From his father encouragement came more as criticism than praise. His mother was quick-tempered and sharp-tongued, and Paolo knew that her love was conditional on excellent school work and helping in the store.

After graduating from a prestigious New York university he went first to Hong Kong, and was currently a fund manager in the City with a major investment bank. His social life revolved around drinking and drugs during the week, weekends in the country, flying visits abroad, or slumped in front of his TV or computer.

During his twenties he had kept his relationships casual, relying on singles' bars, a network of easy girls in Hong Kong, and wine bars and clubs in London. Having recently met a girlfriend who he felt genuinely cared for him, he was shocked when she told him she couldn't carry on any longer with his drinking and drugs, thoughtlessness, unreliability, and apparent lack of emotional attachment.

James' early childhood was spent overseas. His father was successful and emotionally remote, and when James was eight he was sent to boarding school in England, visiting his parents overseas during the holidays. His mother was physically beautiful, but more interested in herself than her children. He described her as demanding, critical and self-centred.

James also worked in the City, and was married with two children under ten. The initial excitement and glamour of a lifestyle with no money worries, weekends in Paris or skiing had faded to the reality of seeing each other infrequently in the evenings, of cancelled theatre and dinner dates, interrupted weekends and disrupted holidays. The fun of recreational drugs, clubbing all night, dinners out and champagne had been replaced by James with drinking with colleagues after work, taking cocaine, and coming home late, often drunk. Although she was dependent on the huge sums of money James provided, his wife was bored and frustrated, and exhausted from essentially being a single parent. She missed the interest and challenge of her previous work, she could never rely on him, and there was no intimacy or even good sex any longer. James told me that she was threatening to leave if he didn't see someone to talk about his part in the situation.

When we first discussed his childhood, he told me it was happy. His parents satisfied all his material needs, he went to exotic places to visit them on holiday, and he 'loved' his public school and Oxbridge. As we explored how little affection or love his mother had ever shown him, his anger emerged. Any physical contact felt like a demand to appreciate her. He remembered how critical and uninterested she was in him, and then became aware of his own apparent lack of feeling or empathy and cold, split-off behaviour.

Paolo also told me how loving and supportive his parents had been, interested in how he did at school, helping him when they could. He was unaware of needing more from life, or that his deep feelings of emptiness and worthlessness might be connected with what he lacked as a child and still needed. Until he met his recent girlfriend, he had scorned people who showed love or affection for being weak, looked down on women, and used sex as a substitute for intimacy. His sense of loss, destructiveness, anger and despair led him in turn to blame his girlfriend, the bank, his parents and himself. As long as he continued to blame someone he could avoid taking real responsibility.

Steven's father came to England with his parents just before the Second World War; they were refugees from Nazi Germany. At the end of the war his father remained in the army and had a successful career as an engineer. Discipline, straight speaking, and a no-nonsense approach to life were his priorities; feelings were irrelevant, although when he had had a few drinks he could become sentimental or morose.

Steven's mother was mouse-like and self-effacing, and he learned at an early age that he had to be happy to prevent her being depressed. In this way he carried her depression, and continued to bear this burden into adult life. Stephen studied hard, got a good science degree at university, and worked in design and sales for a chemical engineering company. He frequently travelled overseas during the week, returning home to his wife and children each weekend.

Before going to university he was in a relationship with a beautiful depressed girl, but even for a young man used to satisfying his mother's deeply depressed needs, he found her demands too much and wanted to end the relationship. When she tragically drowned, he blamed himself for her death. Stephen's father behaved as usual in the face of strong emotion and said he would just have to forget about her and concentrate on his studies.

His mother identified with the girlfriend, and removed all the photos and letters Steven had of her, rationalising her actions as not wanting him to be hurt by constant reminders of her.

Steven's response was to cut off his feelings, try to bury his guilt, work hard, and have a number of short-term relationships. The guilt he suffered from childhood, firstly in response to his mother's depression, and exacerbated by his girlfriend's death, was now transferred to his abandonment of his wife and family each week. His repressed anger manifested as a compliant passive-aggressive attitude to try and avoid his guilt and his wife's envy.

All three men had parents who were dysfunctional in the way they related to each other and their children. The model they grew up with was based on an expectation of intellectual and academic achievement and success measured by status and money. Feelings were devalued and perceived as weaknesses. We could summarise their difficulties as being split off from their feelings; lacking empathy; and apparently not thinking about their partners, family, or colleagues (except in a self-interested way).

Samuels (1985), in his introduction to *The Father* comments that the effect on children of having an actually or emotionally absent father may be similar to that of a tyrannical and domineering one. 'Being dominated is not a relationship at all. [It is] another facet of the emotionally missing father' (Samuels 1985: 37). Seligman (1982) notes the schizoid traits in men whose fathers were violent and destructive, or subsumed in an overbearing mother: 'Outside his [successful] professional life [he] was totally passive and unrelated. Clinically he might be described as schizoid' (Seligman 1982: 85). Many of my patients described their mothers as being cold and critical. There is an overvaluation of academic achievement, a devaluation of feeling, and a denigration of emotional response. Art and culture are valued for collective not personal reasons. Creativity is encouraged if it fits the parents' expectations and values, but not when it is for the sake of the child. The sense of being loved and valued for what and who one is, rather than for what one does, is absent; and there is therefore no feeling of being loving and valuable. The innate core validity is non-existent, and there is a sense of emptiness and inner despair.

Some difficulties immediately present themselves in therapy. On an inner level, these men are emotionally distant. This can manifest as restlessness, lack of eye contact, switching from one subject to another, and avoiding feelings from fear of being emotionally touched. On an outer level, they frequently travel and are literally up in the air. Collective work expectations are of constant availability, including weekends and holidays, with mobile phones switched on.

If the therapy is to last beyond a few sessions, I have found I need to make concessions to my normal working practice. Coming to a session is more important than maintaining a rigid weekly frame. Attending at a set time or more than once a week on a regular basis is an unrealistic expectation until the therapy is established. The method that works most effectively for me is to contract for a regular session time each week, and be willing to move this within the week if need be. On this basis I charge for one session each week, whether attended or not, and if the frequency is increased, I attempt to fit in another session. I believe that being flexible encourages the therapeutic relationship, and the patient gradually plans his travel round the fixed therapy sessions in order to attend. Adjusting to their needs, rather than being rigid, is something their mothers did not do, and facilitates engagement with the part of them that wants to come, whereas rigidity activates the desire to cut off.

Mobile phones provide an interesting indication of the progression of the therapy. Invariably they are switched on during the first session, and if they ring, the patient stops in mid-sentence to answer it. We talk about the interruptions, and the internal and external effect of them, and then phones are turned off in the room at the beginning of the session. The initial engagement has parallels with the mother–baby relationship. At first the baby cannot think and mother does this for him. When the patient switches off the phone before arriving at the session, it is as if the baby can think on his own. Implicit in the process is a sense of emerging consciousness of the requirements of an intimate relationship.

The fear of intimacy, and the inner desire to cut off and take flight, is expressed physically in their private lives, and in therapy, through absence at weekends, overseas travel, and premature endings. From experience I now know that these patients will want to end prematurely, and my increasing awareness of this has contributed to adjusting the way I work. The high salaries and bonuses they earn lead them to expect to get what they want – from their partners and from their therapist. The level of fee I charge is not a real problem, but they may well quibble and try to bargain. The arrogance of being able to buy what they want means they demand instant answers and a quick fix. There is no more engagement in the process or intention of long-term relationship, than in the quick fix of alcohol, cocaine or casual sex.

The underlying anger and lack of trust are experienced in other ways in the transference and my countertransference. What I say is ignored or talked over. There can be a demand for intellectual knowledge, or to know if the therapy will work and how long it will take, made in a way that precludes any reflection or responsibility on the part of the patient. This attitude is hidden under a compliance and desire to please, whether in giving the 'right' answer to a question I ask, or in quickly (and unreflectively) agreeing to an interpretation. My countertransference is to feel shut out, unseen, intellectually inadequate, frustrated, and sleepy; or charmed, put on a pedestal – and sleepy! My help is being sought, but I am being kept firmly out of the way.

There are powerful defences at work to frustrate any breakthrough into relating to the 'true self' (Winnicott 1960). The different patterns of behaviour described above may obscure a fear of confrontation, dominating (compensatory) aggression, passive aggression; the devalued inner world must be protected at any cost, or compensated for by a high-achieving job and financial reward. If feelings are allowed, or real intimacy experienced, there is a fear of being overwhelmed by all the other repressed feelings, and of eventual breakdown. The price of this defence is loss of real creativity, and a constant feeling of being unloved and unlovable.

Panic at the potential loss of a wife or partner, on whom they depend like a son on his mother, may bring them to therapy, but what really frightens them is the potential loss of their children. The loss of wife/surrogate mother resonates with the separation from their own mothers and abandonment by them, literal or emotional. These devastating childhood feelings and fears are then projected onto their own children, and the possible loss of their children is felt to be unbearable, as it threatens the core of their personality.

Patients displaying these character traits function typically through the construction of what Winnicott (1960) describes as a 'false self'. Men with strong, well-polished personas can survive abandonment by wife/mother on an ego level, and if they operate in an environment of clubby peer bonding, reminiscent of public boarding school, they can appear strong and independent. This false independence will grow through casual relating in the early years of marriage, cushioned by lack of financial worry.

'City life' has in recent years attracted a higher proportion of the brightest Oxbridge graduates than any other career, as the financial rewards are so high (Anderson 2008: 270). Typically they have strong thinking functions and weak feeling functions. 'The one-sided emphasis on thinking is always accompanied by an inferiority of feeling' (Jung 1923: para. 955). This may be an advantage, as to succeed in this highly competitive world it undoubtedly helps to cut off from feelings and empathy. Drugs, alcohol and casual sex anaesthetise feelings and block their emergence into consciousness. The inferior feeling function is carried by the man's anima and projected onto his wife, partner or girlfriend. Where these feelings are discouraged from emerging and devalued, the recipients of them (the women in their lives) will correspondingly be taken for granted, devalued and denigrated (Jung 1923: paras. 588–590, 634–5).

In his exposé of life in London's financial centre, *Cityboy*, Anderson (2008) gives examples of how to survive and compete effectively: learn from your boss, steal his ideas and clients, and form your own team. Never talk about your feelings (it's worse than being interested in art, theatre or literature), but either hide them or pretend. Don't expect to find friends from among your colleagues (they are for socialising and talking about sport, money or sex), but pretend to be friends with customers. Never show weakness or uncertainty, but pretend to be knowledgeable and confident.

Anderson notes (2008: 224–8) several possible reasons to explain the behaviour of City workers. They relate to areas of insecurity, competitiveness and avoidance (or denial) of life and reality in their childhood and upbringing. Feeling unloved can lead to pursuit of wealth and greed. A strong, obsessional work ethic may be related to a Protestant upbringing, or to the determination of immigrants from the Far East or the Indian subcontinent to succeed. Being bullied at school can lead to a desperate desire never to be beaten or put down again, while masochistically suffering ruthless working conditions and insecurity. The painful reality of life can be avoided or denied by drink and drugs.

Although he does not directly address the question of whether the problems and behaviour of his work colleagues were pre-existing or the consequence of their working environment, Anderson makes two interesting, contradictory observations about them: 'Firstly, [his behaviour] is probably not [his] fault but rather it's his job that's destroyed his personality. Secondly, he needs to be an arrogant buffoon to carry out his job properly' (ibid.: 148). On the other hand, Anderson asserts, 'I would say that the majority of great City analysts whom I've met are borderline autistic or at least sufferers of Asperger's Syndrome. These guys who live in peculiar formulaic unemotional worlds have a distinct advantage over us 'normal' types when dealing with something as abstract as shares or derivatives' (ibid.: 132).

Anderson's anecdotal comments match well Fairbairn's description of the schizoid personality. Fairbairn writes, 'To overcome difficulties involved . . . in emotionally giving, individuals with a schizoid propensity avail themselves of [two] techniques. These are: (a) the technique of playing roles, and (b) the technique of exhibitionism' (1940: 16). A later paper discussing the psychopathology of these patients looks at their problems in relating, and at their narcissism, both of which were evident in all my patients.

> It is the great tragedy of the schizoid individual that his love seems to destroy; and it is because his love seems so destructive that he experiences such difficulty in directing libido towards objects in outer reality. He becomes afraid to love; and therefore erects a barrier between his object and himself . . . [his] narcissism is specially characteristic of the schizoid individual. Accompanying it we invariably find an attitude of superiority . . . based upon an orientation towards internalized objects. In relation to . . . outer reality the basic attitude . . . is essentially one of inferiority [which] may be masked by a façade of superiority.
>
> (1941: 50)

Fairbairn notes the connection between introversion and schizoid states (ibid.: 29, 50). Men with superior introverted thinking are likely to be attracted to work in the City, and their weak extraverted feeling leads them to becoming enslaved in their work and caught in the collective behaviour of colleagues (Jung 1923: paras. 634–5, 146). The financial rewards of work that bolster their narcissistic egos generally discourage them from trying to leave their gilded prisons, even to escape the painful treadmill. Jumping off a fast-moving treadmill cannot be done without damage. Fear of – or actual – breakdown, abandonment, or loss of job lead these men to seek help.

This chapter suggests how a working relationship can be nurtured to enable these 'City men' to begin the long psychological journey towards finding their individual identities and their souls. Building a relationship of intimacy and trust, and an understanding of empathy, is the first step on this journey so they can separate from the collective, and find a positive connection to and valuation of the inferior feeling function.

Bibliography

Anderson, G. (2008). *Cityboy: Beer and Loathing in the Square Mile*. London: Headline.

Fairbairn, W. R. D. (1940). Schizoid factors in the personality. *Psychoanalytic Studies of the Personality*. London: Routledge & Kegan Paul (1952).

Fairbairn, W. R. D. (1941). A revised psychopathology of the psychoses and psychoneuroses. *Psychoanalytic Studies of the Personality*. London: Routledge & Kegan Paul (1952).

Jung, C. G. (1923). General description of the types. *Psychological Types. CW 6*. London: Routledge & Kegan Paul.

Samuels, A. (1985). *The Father: Contemporary Jungian Perspectives*. London: Free Association.

Seligman, E. (1982). The half-alive ones. *The Father: Contemporary Jungian Perspectives*, Samuels, A. (ed.). London: Free Association (1985).

Winnicott, D. W. (1960). Ego distortion in terms of true and false self. *The Maturational Processes and the Facilitating Environment*. London: Hogarth and Institute of Psycho-Analysis (1965).

Chapter 36

Extraversion, with soul

David Tacey

There are several debts I owe to Andrew Samuels, and this is about the intellectual ones. Almost single-handedly, he created the field of Jungian Studies by getting all the separate and split-off strands of Jungian thought talking to each other, or at least aware of each other's existence. Prior to Andrew Samuels, the field was fragmented and thin, with competing interest groups 'doing their own thing' without even so much as looking sideways at each other. Samuels urged, perhaps even forced, us to start thinking about where we all stood in terms of his critical and taxonomical model put forward in *Jung and the Post-Jungians* (1985). This work impacted on everyone and made us all think more clearly about our indebtedness to Jung and where we departed from him. It also helped many of us to separate ourselves from the widespread devotionalism and subservience to Jung, which had stifled debate and intellectual vitality in the Jung field for a generation, with certain important exceptions. Samuels' clear thinking enabled us to differentiate Jung's thought from his prejudices and opinions, to disentangle what was authentic and enduring about his work from what was merely ephemeral and a product of his time and conditioning.

Some evidently did not like what Samuels was doing, as they felt he was being too critical of the Jungian enterprise and disturbing too many cosy nests. But here, at last, was a true intellectual in our midst, a man of vision and considerable breadth. And here was a writer who was not afraid to *think*, whereas so much of Jungian discourse seems to operate primarily through feeling. Samuels was introducing into Jungian discourse a 'function' of consciousness that had almost been banned by the overemphasis on feeling in the past. One of my university colleagues once referred to Jungian writing as a 'cult of feeling', and in a sense, this was not wide of the mark. Even the work of Erich Neumann, with its strong emphasis on art, culture and history, was primarily a product of feeling rather than thinking. Jungians believed they were compensating for the *lack* of feeling in the modern Western world, and that may be true. But in the process of addressing this imbalance in scholarly and clinical writings, they had gone too far in the opposite direction. Jungians had gone so far into feeling and introverted intuition that it was almost impossible for me, as a scholar in the university system, to find much Jungian writing that I could proudly set before my colleagues and invite them to read.

A great many Jungian books, for instance Edward Whitmont's *Return of the Goddess* (1982), or Marie-Louise von Franz's *The Problem of the Puer Aeternus* (1970), were written by Jungians for other Jungians. But when Samuels' *The Plural Psyche* was published in 1989, I was able to give this to my academic colleagues as an example of strong work being done in the Jungian and post-Jungian field. And I did notice that my colleagues began to adopt a different attitude from that point. Since so much 'Jungian' writing had gone pop or 'new age', and was constantly appearing in prominent places in the bookshops, it was a considerable relief to be able to point to writings which had intellectual substance rather than sugary spirituality. The pop or new age Jungians seemed to imagine that archetypes emerged fully grown and able-bodied out of the minds of gods and goddesses, but Samuels was able to show that the 'archetype' was as much a construct of culture and society as it was a thought in the mind of God. Even James Hillman's early work, which was intellectual, had too much about it of a 'surfeit of soul' for my academic colleagues to be able to stomach. Samuels was probably the first writer since Jung to be academically respectable, and that, in turn, had a positive effect on my own academic ambitions and the locating of my own work in the academic milieu. We build our own careers on the shoulders of those who have gone before.

Although popular or new age Jungians make a lot of money out of their writings, and sell to large and ever-increasing audiences, the commercial success of their works has a detrimental effect on the field. The richer such writers become, the poorer is the reputation of the field. The biggest problem is in presenting the archetypes in an impossibly nostalgic and cosmic light. Popular writers deliberately distort Jung's writings, because the wider reading public is always keen to be told (or rather, cajoled) that there is some kind of fairyland parallel to this reality, and that we can simply 'tune in' to this fairy world in times of crisis, to find guidance, assurance and support. We are suckers for delusion, especially when we are down and feeling vulnerable. It is a kind of psychological version of the cargo cult, or a new version of the elixir that solves all our problems. Samuels did not discount the theory of archetypes, but he returned our knowledge of archetypes to their original meaning. That is, he pointed out, time and again, that the archetype in itself (*an sich*) is unknowable and without content, and that it is only social conditions, history and culture that fill the 'empty' archetype with content. Therefore, the world creates the archetypes, as much as the archetypes create the world. The new age wants this two-way traffic to be one-way, so that we feel nurtured and held by an omnipotent source. Too many of us today are keen to relinquish responsibility, and hand everything over to a god or goddess.

Samuels reminded us of the Kantian underpinning of Jung's theory of archetypes, which had become so thoroughly distorted by years of sentimental writing, in which archetypes were confused with archetypal images. All we can know, Jung said, are the archetypal *images*, and these images are subject to history and constructed by society as much as any other aspect of culture. There is no such thing as fully fledged 'archetypes' which are eternally the same and which, as Joseph Campbell (1949) falsely reports, are found everywhere at all times. Robert Johnson's (1983) version of Jung might be balm to fragmented nerves, but it is intellectually wrong and academically unsound. Campbell and Johnson are good storytellers, but they are not good exponents of Jungian theory. Jung would turn in his grave if he felt that such readings of his work had become almost 'standard', at least in the United States. Although Samuels is often seen as an exemplar of the post-Jungian position, his approach to archetypes is fully and classically Jungian, and it is only because we have lost the original distinction between archetype and image that his work looks 'different' from that of some other writers. If he is different at this level, it is because we have lost the understanding that made Jung's work intellectually viable and scientifically credible.

Samuels taught us in several of his books, and not just in his original classic, that we could have Jung's archetypes without his stereotypes, that we could have depth psychology without Jung's sexism, or Eurocentrism, or racial biases (I don't want to call it racism). Prior to Samuels, many felt that we had to embrace the whole of Jung, warts and all, or reject the lot. Samuels taught us how to be discriminating Jungians, which often meant that we did not become 'Jungians' at all, or groupies or followers, but rather discerning readers of his complex and voluminous works. He taught us how to think critically about Jung and how to differentiate working with Jung's ideas from adherence or uncritical devotion. If it were not for Samuels, we would not be where we are today, that is, a relatively sophisticated, if still somewhat starry-eyed, intellectual and clinical community that is able to be critical about our field and each other without having incessant rows or flying into a rage as soon as someone makes a critical remark. Samuels taught us how to be plural, namely, how to value and respect difference rather than defend against it and insist that everyone should be of like mind. Even if some Jungians did not like the 'box' in which Samuels had put them in his taxonomy, whether developmental, classical or archetypal, at least even arguing about this brought consciousness to the field, and made us more aware of who we are and what we are doing. Samuels also, at his best, showed us where we might be going.

When I first read his classic work in 1985, I was firmly in the 'archetypal' tradition after having spent a number of years working with James Hillman in the United States. As an 'archetypalist', I not only carried the strengths of this position but also some of its weaknesses. For instance, I had already decided, by prejudice rather than knowledge, that I did not like the developmentalists. They were not profound or deep enough for me, and did not engage Jung's numinous dimension, and did not seek to cultivate *psyche* as a Neoplatonic vision and an aspect of reality. However, on reading Samuels' account, I softened my resistance, began to read the developmentalists instead of ignoring them, and found much to admire in their writings and points of view. To engage psyche was not merely an act of vision, bequeathed by the gods, and enjoyed by those privileged enough to have an aesthetically cultivated mind, but it was also a developmental process available to everyone and not merely to those who had the gift of *mythopoesis* or deep seeing. The archetypalist position was in danger of becoming a form of aestheticism and a cult of the beautiful, and the developmental position was at times closer to the tortured rhythms of 'soul' that the archetypalists claimed to champion.

At a more personal level, the book that affected me most profoundly was *The Political Psyche* (1993). I liked very much Samuels' 'centrifugal vision', that is, his ability to start with the insights of the clinical world and apply these to a whole range of social and political phenomena, including patriarchy, race, gender, party politics, social and sexual morality and the psychology of nations. But what impacted on me in particular was Samuels' idea of *resacralization*. In a world which thought it was modern and secular, and getting more secular by the day, Samuels had the courage to call for a project of resacralization. Some might have seen this initially as too churchy or religious, but Samuels pointed out that resacralization could be seen as a response to hidden currents in postmodernity, and not as a reaction to it:

> The resacralizing perspective recovers a sense of the religious verities but these are played through a changing world view less dependent on religious organization. The resacralizing ethic may be plebeian in its roots, but it is sublime in its aspirations.
>
> (1993: 12)

In other words, resacralization was not about those gifted with vision, intelligence or grace, but it was a possibility found in everything and everyone. Samuels' vision of religion was postmodern and democratic. All things, no matter how secular, banal or mundane, could be read as containing psyche and therefore as containing something numinous or spiritual. In *The Political Psyche* he explored 'Numinous Experience and Sociopolitical Criticism', bringing together seemingly incommensurable things – a religious vision and a radically leftist social conscience. It is little wonder that, in recent years, Samuels has been involved in the work of Rabbi

Michael Lerner, and his magazine, *Tikkun*, which bears the descriptive subheading: 'politics, spirituality, culture'. Those three areas, so often kept apart and seen as incompatible, are naturally fused in the mind and work of Andrew Samuels.

Meanwhile, if any priests or rabbis were getting a bit too excited about Samuels' seeming conversion to religion, he would put them straight with disclaimers such as these:

> I doubt that contemporary resacralization will ultimately glorify God or lead to a new religion. But, along the way, most aspects of human culture will be touched by this attempt to connect to a feeling level that we sense once existed but we find has vanished from the modern world (hence *re*sacralization).
>
> (1993: 12)

Samuels was proposing a fusion state or a union of opposites: a secular religiousness, or a religious awareness as a way of being in the social and political world. This was Jung's *religious attitude* as distinct from what he called *creedal religion* (1932: 509), but applied by Samuels to the world of social experience rather than merely to subjective realities such as dreams, fantasies and introverted feelings. Some say that Samuels' vision is 'extraverted', and I would heartily support that notion, if it were not for the sense that this is sometimes used in a derogatory way, as if to suggest lack of depth or meaning. Samuels gives us extraversion, perhaps, but with soul, depth and interiority. His work does not respect the dualisms that some Jungians invent as a defence against the reality of the world.

Analytical psychology and Jungian studies has been a magnet for introverts and unworldly people, and as such the field's social, political and academic potential has been curtailed by those who construct a false dualism between 'the world' and 'the psychic interior'. However this is doing Jung a disservice, because a neglected element in Jung's work is that which is concerned with the state of the world, the condition of religion and the relations between inner and outer reality. Indeed, Jung's late work on synchronicity argued that there was no hard distinction between interior and exterior reality, and that this dualism is a product of wrong thinking. The form of introversion that does not want to live in or engage the world should be regarded as a form of narcissistic woundedness rather than be glorified by the term 'Jungian'. Even introverts have to live in the world, take part in political reality, and participate in the social system, and Samuels shows us how to do this in such a way that psyche is brought to the world and revealed as an 'always already' dimension of the world.

What Samuels shows us, in theological terms, is that God is now doing something new in the world. The old way of separating chosen from unchosen, devout from fallen, saved from unsaved – all that is finished.

Jung himself had experienced the collapse of the old religious order when he suffered his childhood vision of God defecating on 'his' cathedral. There was to be a new dispensation, a new way of doing and being religious. The old religious container has been smashed and this crisis indicates that the religious must now be in and of the secular order, or it will not exist at all. Samuels puts it eloquently: 'The contemporary desire to render the secular holy [is] a creative response to the fate of God' (1993: 13). Yes, and it is a creative response to the death of God. God 'dies' but only to be reborn in a new place.

This was the clue I needed, and it kick-started my own career as a writer and a public intellectual. Before meeting Samuels, my academic career was firmly established but I had not yet found my place in the wider world, or my voice to speak to the wider world. I knew I was 'religious', but I was not religious in the old, churchy, devout or moralistic way. The old religious dispensation repelled me, and I did not want much to do with it. But in separating myself from 'creedal religion', I had also isolated myself from religion in society, and felt something missing in my life and work. I did not want to be a narrow academic, but wanted to take part in public dis-cussions and political forums. Like Samuels, I have a worldly interest and a worldly soul. I cannot be locked up in any confined space, whether it be the clinical room or the academic office.

After reading *The Political Psyche* in 1993, I found the confidence and voice to write my own book *Edge of the Sacred* in 1995. It was motivated by Samuels' resacralizing project, by 'the contemporary desire to render the secular holy' (1993: 13). This book explored all the things that were near and dear to me: the situation of Aboriginal Australians (with whom I had grown up, in childhood), the possibility of 'reconciliation' between white and black Australia (as distinct from the 'assimilation' of Aboriginals), the state of the natural environment, and the possibility of resacralizing our relations with nature, earth, body and sexuality. To my utter dismay, this book became a national best-seller, and it didn't even present a false view of archetypal theory! From 1995 onward, I was placed in the public domain and brought into many religious, ecological, political and social forums. Ironically, the only forum I was not involved in was a Jungian one, because what I had done was 'worldly' and not clinical enough. I had gone into an extraverted mode that many Jungians were not interested in. I wrote other books in this vein, books on men, gender and social change. Then I wrote *ReEnchantment* (2000), which was almost entirely focused on race relations, and most recently *The Spirituality Revolution* (2004), about what has become of God after the death of God.

I have known Andrew Samuels for about twenty years, and when I first met him I was no one in particular, not a public figure and entirely unknown. But I had a yearning inside me; I knew there was a new show to explore and I wanted to be part of it. Andrew always gave me his time and respect, and he did so without even a hint of being patronising. He lived at the centre of things, London, and I lived at the edge, Melbourne, Australia. But from the edge, I feel I may have been able to contribute something that is of concern to everyone, and that is the resacralization of daily life. In coming into conversation with Andrew, and his international circle, I have felt less isolated at the edge, less 'on edge' about my identity and myself. Through the resacralization project in which we are mutually engaged, I feel myself to be part of the centre of things. With Paul Eluard, I can almost say:

> Le centre du monde est partout et chez nous.
> (The centre of the world is everywhere and with us.)
>
> (Eluard 1929: 25)

Bibliography

Eluard, P. (1929) Saisons. *Last Love Poems of Paul Eluard*. Baton Rouge: Louisiana State University Press (1980).

Campbell, J. (1949) *The Hero with a Thousand Faces*. New York: Meridian.

Johnson, R. A. (1983) *The Psychology of Romantic Love*. London: Penguin.

Jung, C. G. (1932) Psychotherapists or the Clergy. *The Collected Works of C. G. Jung*. Princeton: Princeton University Press, Vol. 11 (1969).

Samuels, A. (1985) *Jung and the Post-Jungians*. London and New York: Routledge.

Samuels, A. (1989) *The Plural Psyche*. London and New York: Routledge.

Samuels, A. (1993) *The Political Psyche*. London and New York: Routledge.

Tacey, D. (1995) *Edge of the Sacred*. Sydney: Harper Collins.

Tacey, D. (2000) *ReEnchantment*. Sydney: Harper Collins.

Tacey, D. (2004) *The Spirituality Revolution*. London and New York: Routledge.

von Franz, M.-L. (1970) *The Problem of the Puer Aeternus*. Zurich: Spring Publications.

Whitmont, E. (1982) *Return of the Goddess*. New York: Crossroads.

Chapter 37

'The actual clash'

Analytic arguments and the plural psyche

Nick Totton

My starting point is a pair of quotations from Andrew Samuels' book *The Plural Psyche*, published in 1989:

> When analysts argue, the plural psyche is speaking. Differing points of view reflect the multiplicity of the psyche itself.
>
> (Samuels 1989: 5)

> Just as the alchemists projected the workings of the unconscious into chemical elements and processes . . . so the texts of the depth psychologist, taken as a whole, may unwittingly provide us with documents of the soul. What was intended to be *about* psyche is *of* psyche. The conscious aim may be to plumb the past for its truths, or to connect past and present, or to reveal the workings of cumulative psychopathology. But what gets revealed, however, are the central characteristics of psyche itself. . . . The warring theories and the specific points of conflict speak directly of what is at war in the psyche.
>
> (Samuels 1989: 217)

These two passages, at opposite ends of the book, struck me very powerfully when I first read them, and still do. When I first met Andrew, and more than once subsequently, I urged him to develop these ideas. After twenty years, though, I doubt that this is going to happen! So in what follows I shall try to develop my own interpretation, almost certainly different from what Andrew's would have been, and very probably not as profound, but serving at least as a celebration of the way in which he proceeds by throwing off extraordinary *aperçus* to either side of the main track of his interests.

One way in which the importance of the central notion expressed in these passages is brought home to me is through the sheer difficulty I have in keeping their meaning clear in my mind, as it constantly tries to slip away and become unconscious. This is after all a mark of important concepts in depth psychology: they are slippery silver fishes that tend constantly to escape the net and return to the dark waters. 'What was intended to be *about* psyche is *of* psyche'. That is, analytic theory can be treated as its own object, as a massive projection *onto* the unconscious *by* the unconscious. And presumably our interpretation of this process is in turn an example of itself, and so on – a recursive structure of the kind we know to be typical of unconscious material.

Freud's whole initial version of psychoanalysis was a real bouillabaisse of fishes drawn out of the psyche, a welter of fantastic concepts (see Freud's letters to Fliess in Masson 1985) about noses, periodicity, hysteria, sexual substances, dreams, paralysis, blood, smells, childhood – some of which have attained respectability as part of analytic theory, but many of which have sunk back into the unconscious. It is only retrospectively that the first group of ideas can be distinguished from the second; or that Freud and his little band of Jewish eccentrics can be distinguished from any other cult or clique with peculiar notions of one sort or another, all of which – as psychoanalysis helps us to understand – reflect authentic aspects of psychological reality.

(At this point I need to interpolate a note on terminology. I generally use 'unconscious' rather than 'psyche' in my writing – a reflection of my greater connection with Freudian than with Jungian thinking. Writing this chapter, however, has brought home to me the advantages of a compendious term like 'psyche': without it, I would need to pause every few sentences to define exactly where on the map I am locating the phenomena I am discussing – preconscious, repressed unconscious, creative unconscious, unconscious ego . . . This sort of discussion is fascinating, but it would be a major distraction from what I want to do here. So with a grand insouciance I shall use 'psyche' and 'unconscious' fairly indiscriminately.)

Samuels' suggestion takes us back to the old heroic days when analytic Titans strode the earth, interpreting everything they encountered, turning all the works of humanity back into libido. Machines, for example, Ferenczi argues (1919: 389), are 'organ projections', deriving from children's libidinal enjoyment of 'kneading, boring, drawing water, squirting, etc'; and in a supplementary note (1920: 393–6) he discovers in the book by Ernst Mach on which he bases his interpretation an unconscious 'crypt-amnesic recovery' of Freud's theories. Certainly there was a simultaneously both trivial and grandiose aspect to this approach to culture; but it did have the great virtue of taking depth psychology *seriously*, as something with implications beyond the consulting room.

Christopher Bollas, another writer who takes depth psychology seriously, has recently made some similar points to Samuels. In particular, he takes a strong stand for pluralism: 'the question is not whether one is a pluralist or not. The question is whether one is a pluralist or a totalitarian' (Bollas, 2007: 7). Like Samuels, he argues that we cannot hope for anything like an adequate view of depth psychological material without having available to us multiple and conflicting theoretical viewpoints.

If one has more ways of seeing mental life and human behaviour then, in my view, it follows on logically that one is going to be more effective in working with the analysand. If your preconscious stores multiple models of the mind and behaviour to be activated by work with a particular patient in a particular moment, then you will find that you are either consciously or unconsciously envisioning the patient through one or other of these lenses.

(Bollas 2007: 7)

I often use the image of the optician's tool, with multiple lenses that can be swung in and out in various combinations to achieve the best focus for the task in hand. Bollas' pluralism, though, unlike Samuels', is – in the ideal – non-conflictual: all must have prizes, all theoretical models have their unique virtues (although Bollas does make his own likes and dislikes abundantly clear). In contrast to Samuels, there is an anti-political assumption: 'Theory is very important, but when it is used for purposes of –K, when we use ideas as heralds of political positions, then psychoanalytical ideas are reduced to things: to weapons in the psychoanalytic wars' (Bollas, 2007: 3).

Andrew Samuels' position, I suggest, includes two very crucial and original elements. He identifies a creative role for conflict, for struggle, which potentially gives positive value to these psychoanalytic wars with their 'incorrigible competitiveness and argumentativeness' (Samuels 1989: 4); and he does this through arguing that an analytic theory functions, somewhat like an archetype, as *a representation in consciousness of an objective element of unconscious mental life*. Not only the theory, but equally and even especially the *clash* of theories, figures forth something that exists in the psyche itself: 'the actual clash contains the definitive psychic issue' (Samuels 1989: 217).

In a sense, Samuels is suggesting that we treat a theoretical clash as we might treat a conflict in a therapy group: as a nodal point in the group-dynamic network, or what Process Work calls a 'hot spot' (Mindell 1995: 27). This leads us to let go of the question 'Who is right?' and substitute the question 'What is being expressed?' (Samuels 1989: 225). Process Work offers the further concept of 'deep democracy' (Mindell 2002): that for conflicts to be amplified creatively, it is both necessary and sufficient for *every position to be represented*, every voice to be heard from. I think that Samuels would agree with this on both levels, that of the clash of debate and that of the clash in the psyche.

We can connect this line of thinking up with an Hegelian or Marxist dialectic: that it is through, and only through, the conflict of opposing positions that development takes place. In a group-dynamic context, this frequently involves a leap of trust, a willed assumption that *both* or *all* positions have part of the truth. What needs to be avoided, though, is what

Samuels (1989: 222–4) calls 'holism', the assumption that polarised positions can and should be united. 'There is a certain compulsiveness that gets attached to holism. Holism can be an attempt to deny the pain of rupture' (ibid.: 223).

I want to proceed to examples, and to explore one or two theoretical clashes in the field of psychotherapy which, according to Samuels' theory, represent or express clashes in the psyche itself. There are any number of good candidates, and in this chapter I can only look in a very cursory way at even one or two of them; so I will concentrate on trying to discover the beginnings of a *methodology* for such exploration. I am going to further restrict myself to binary clashes of an 'either/or' sort: despite my acute awareness of the dangerous attractiveness of binaries, they present a 'two-body problem' which is a lot easier to get hold of than three-or-more body conflicts. Some of the first examples to occur to me, drawn from very different areas and levels of depth psychology, are:

- Mother vs father
- The creative unconscious vs the repressed unconscious
- The goal of developing the self vs the goal of subverting the self
- Attachment vs drive
- Transference vs free association
- The unconscious as language vs the unconscious as body

These descriptions are sketches only, but I think the debates referred to will all be recognisable (and Andrew Samuels has, I think, contributed to all of them).

My sense is that for each of these clashes, there are a large number of psychotherapists who would immediately say that to choose between the two alternatives is absurd, and that there must somehow be truth in both; while for several, possibly for most or all, a substantial number would insist to a greater or lesser extent on the correctness of one alternative only. This second group would often be justified in challenging the first group to explain exactly *how* there can 'somehow' be truth in both: on the level of bivalent logic, in several of these examples the alternatives seem mutually exclusive, though in other examples this is perhaps less clearly the case.

It plainly *is* so for the last in the list: *either* the unconscious is 'structured like a language' as Lacan famously insisted (Lacan 1979: 149, 203) and as some of Freud's work implies, *or* it is the psychic representation of embodied impulses, as Freud at a certain stage and later Ferenczi and Reich argued. To express it more tightly, the unconscious is either produced by (consists of) language, or it stands in opposition to language. How could it be both? Yet the arguments on both sides are convincing – more to the point, the *visions* of both sides are powerfully compelling. One way out of the problem would be to say that they refer to two different *sorts* of unconscious, or to two different modes in which the unconscious expresses itself (I tried this angle myself in Totton 1999: 232–3). But I think Samuels is right to suggest that such a 'solution' is actually an evasion of the challenge with which such an argument between analysts presents us.

If I understand him correctly, Samuels is saying that the first step in addressing a clash of this kind is to *accept* it: to acknowledge that it is a *real* clash, and that it can be solved neither by supporting one side against the other, nor by somehow making them both true. We need to proceed in a way closer to Claude Lévi-Strauss's analysis of myth, identifying the clash as an irreducible binary which constitutes an element of meaning. Lévi-Strauss's anthropology sees the whole apparatus of myth as a way of trying to resolve the anxiety associated with such binary tensions by weaving a web of concepts which between them can wholly or partially bridge the gap. 'The purpose of myth is to provide a logical model capable of overcoming a contradiction (an impossible achievement if, as it happens, the contradiction is real)' (Lévi-Strauss 1967: 266).

The contradictions listed above, we are stipulating, *are* real, although the psyche, and conscious human thought, try to bridge them with a multitude of conceptual strategies. My purpose right now is not to explore these strategies, fascinating though they are, but to cleave to the bare contradiction itself, which it may be useful to express in Lévi-Straussian style:

unconscious as language: unconscious as body

Perhaps like Lévi-Strauss we can treat this as if it were a mathematical statement, and simplify it further by cancelling the shared element, '*unconscious*', from both sides. This leaves

language: body

We may now have established something about the psyche – that it contains within itself an unresolvable struggle between language and the body.

This is obviously not a wholly novel discovery, but I think it is an enormously important one – and one which, on closer examination, is expressed within *both* the Freudian–Lacanian and the Freudian–Ferenczian–Reichian theories. Bruce Fink, for example – admittedly making an effort to link with other analytic traditions, but still stating Lacanian orthodoxy – says, 'Language is "encrusted upon the living", to borrow Bergson's expression. The body is overwritten/overridden by language' (Fink 1995: 12); and then again:

> The real . . . is the infant's body 'before' it comes under the sway of the symbolic order, before it is subjected to toilet training and instructed in the ways of the world. In the course of socialization the body is

progressively written or overwritten with signifiers; pleasure is located in certain zones, while other zones are neutralized by the word and coaxed into compliance with social, behavioral norms.

(Fink 1995: 24)

(The point of the inverted commas around 'before' is to emphasise that in practice the symbolic order is always already in place.) While one possible conclusion from Lacan's work is that the real is forever beyond our knowing, and therefore irrelevant, he also presents a continual struggle between the real and the symbolic, with the real irrupting periodically in the form of uncanny and unbearable experience. 'The Real is apparently traumatic *in itself* and inaugurates a primal anxiety as a basic affect' (Verhaeghe 1996: 28, original italics). The Freudian–Ferenczian–Reichian approach would in many ways entirely agree with this; all three describe 'universal, typical and innate hysterical attacks' (Freud 1926: 133; 1917: 199), 'traumatic-hysterical' or 'organic-hysterical' crises (Ferenczi 1988: xii), 'reactivation of the infant hysteria' (Reich 1972: 292), which are the irruption of bodily affect into language and thought.

The disagreement between the two traditions is primarily over what attitude the therapist should take towards this core conflict between language and embodiment. From their shared tragic perspective, Lacan and Freud rehearse scripts of irreducible loss and failure. Both of them have a strong tendency to equate the body with death. More pragmatic by nature, Reich gets on with life: 'the intellectual function itself is a vegetative [i.e. bodily] activity . . . It can function correctly in unison with the most lively affect, and it can also take a critical stance towards the affect' (1972: 306). As he says elsewhere, 'biological energy governs the psychic as well as the somatic. A functional unity prevails' (1973: 265).

However, Reich also describes how, while expressive movement in the face, head and upper body is 'immediately intelligible' and translatable into language, once body psychotherapy addresses the diaphragm and below 'we are no longer in a position to translate the language of movement into word language' (Reich 1972: 385). In fact, he emphasises through capitalisation that 'THE EXPRESSION OF THE CONVULSIONS IN THE ORGASM REFLEX CANNOT BE TRANSLATED INTO WORD LANGUAGE' (ibid: 386). This exactly parallels Lacan's opposition between the Real and the Symbolic – except that Reich aligns the unconscious with the former rather than with the latter!

I have been struggling through twenty-five years of working as a body psychotherapist to make sense of these issues, which often get expressed in terms of body and *mind* rather than body and *language*. For some time I more or less accepted the body psychotherapy orthodoxy that 'the mind–body split' is a wholly undesirable artefact of our particular culture. I have come to see that this won't do: that while it seems right that 'mind' and 'body' are not objectively split, it also seems right that the psyche experiences an irreducible clash between them, or perhaps better, several clashes in this same area of experience. After all, many of the other clashes on my original list are clearly linked to this one: attachment vs drive, for example, or even mother vs father. With both of these clashes, though, the first term relates more closely to the Lacanian imaginary than to either the real or the symbolic; so that attachment vs drive aligns with imaginary vs real, and mother vs father aligns (as Lacan makes very clear in his ongoing critique of Klein) with imaginary vs symbolic.

One of Lacan's great contributions was to move definitely from the binary formulations which dominate Freud's work to a trinary structure – in fact, a structure conceived of as a 'Borromean knot' of three rings, linked only so long as all three elements are present (Thurston 1998). This raises complex questions about the role of duality in the psyche. There certainly appears to be a powerful attraction towards dualistic formulations, often structured in parallel to male:female or masculine:feminine, which gives these formulations a falsely naturalistic appearance; the question is not in what ways men and women form a dualistic pair, but why in the face of so much contrary evidence (e.g. Bem 1993) we *want* to think of them as a dualistic pair. Like Samuels, I am generally drawn to pluralities, to the many rather than the One or the Two; but something needs to be grasped about the profound role of dualism and of dualistic conflicts. Whether the conflict is two-way or many-ways, though – and conflicts in the psychotherapy world certainly tend to be many ways! – Samuels' key point here is that we should not be seeking a synthesis or transcendence of the conflict (though partial synthesis is certainly possible and often creative, certainly far preferable to choosing between the alternatives) but *a recognition that the conflict is intrinsic.*

In Lévi-Strauss's vision referred to above, a function of creative thought, both conscious and unconscious, is to address the polarised contradictions which we experience as wounds in the fabric of being – to bandage them in a webwork of myth and metaphor. These wounds seem rather like black holes exerting a powerful gravitational pull on the psyche, sucking the richness of existence into themselves. Samuels' view, I think, is the opposite: that clashes in the psyche are more like white holes from which energy streams into the universe, energy with which we can align ourselves by welcoming and processing conflict – for instance, in the form of analytic arguments.

Bibliography

Bem, S. L. (1993) *The Lenses of Gender: Transforming the Debate on Sexual Inequality*, London: Yale University Press.
Bollas, C. (2007) *The Freudian Moment*, London: Karnac.

Ferenczi, S. (1919) The psychogenesis of mechanism, in *Further Contributions to the Theory and Technique of Psychoanalysis*, New York: Brunner/Mazel, 1980.

Ferenczi, S. (1920) Supplement to "The psychogenesis of mechanism", in *Further Contributions to the Theory and Technique of Psychoanalysis*, New York: Brunner/Mazel, 1980.

Ferenczi, S. (1988) *The Clinical Diary*, London: Harvard University.

Fink, B. (1995) *The Lacanian Subject: Between Language and Jouissance*, Princeton, NJ: Princeton University.

Freud, S. (1917) Mourning and melancholia, *Standard Edition*, Vol. XIV, London: Hogarth.

Freud, S. (1926) *Inhibitions, Symptoms and Anxiety*, *Standard Edition*, Vol. XX, London: Hogarth.

Lacan, J. (1979) *The Four Fundamental Concepts of Psycho-Analysis*, London: Penguin.

Lévi-Strauss, C. (1967) *Structural Anthropology*, New York: Doubleday Anchor.

Masson, J. (ed.) (1985) *The Complete Letters of Sigmund Freud to Wilhelm Fliess*, London, Belknap.

Mindell, A. (1995) *Sitting in the Fire: Large Group Transformation Using Conflict and Diversity*, Portland: Lao Tse Press.

Mindell, A. (2002) *The Deep Democracy of Open Forums*, Charlottesville, VA: Hampton Roads.

Reich, W. (1972 [1945]) *Character Analysis*, New York: Touchstone.

Reich, W. (1973 [1942]) *The Function of the Orgasm*, London: Souvenir.

Samuels, A. (1989) *The Plural Psyche*, London: Routledge.

Thurston, L. (1998) Ineluctable nodalities: On the Borromean knot, *Key Concepts of Lacanian Psychoanalysis*, D. Nobus (ed.), London: Rebus.

Totton, N. (1999) *The Water in the Glass: Body and Mind in Psychoanalysis*, London: Rebus.

Verhaeghe, P. (1996). *Does The Woman Exist? From Freud's Hysteric to Lacan's Feminine*, London: Rebus.

Chapter 38

Politics and hypocrisy

Liliana Liviano Wahba

Hypocrisy

Hypocrisy, from *hypokrisia* (Greek) means a reply; acting a part, feigning to be what one is not; a deception as to the real character and feeling, especially in regard to morals and religion. *Hypokrités*: the actor.

Silveira (2000) uses a philosophical perspective to make a realistic analysis of politics and the nature of power, postulating that hypocrisy is a key element and effective instrument in power relations. The author quotes Habermas, who called this premise 'instrumental reason', which is risky because it acts in accordance with the presupposition that the means justify the ends, and considered it an operation of narcissistic logic of those in power for their own interests, arrogance and private gain. This thinker opposes 'communicative reason' to instrumental reason, which is tied to mutual understanding, an ethical reason. However, as Silveira sees it, the political scientists who use ethics as a basis for criticizing hypocritical recourses are dealing with imaginal rather than real politics.

A century after Machiavelli, Cardinal Mazarin succeeds Richelieu in 1642 and writes *The Politicians' Breviary* (1997) to advise politicians on how to obtain and maintain power. This extremely cynical book conveys the maxim that efficacy is what matters and that self-knowledge serves to cultivate the most pleasant and seductive image: 'The ancients said: contain yourself and abstain. We say: simulate and dissimulate' (Mazarin 1997: 35). Eco (1997) finds *The Politicians' Breviary* surprising in its calculated theoretical rigor and very human pettiness.

While Machiavelli and Mazarin unmask the eternal perversity of politics, Lamounier (1997) ponders whether this manipulation, malice and evil is inherent and necessary to politics, and concludes that trickery in the democratic state, though it does exist, is less intense. In this light, Mazarin formulated the rules so as to distance the exercise of power from violence, and in so doing democratizes power, showing that it is not the fruit of transcendental or supra-individual causes. Amid maxims on advice on how to recognize people, he teaches how to obtain power by manipulating consensus.

The discourse

The Peruvian writer Vargas Llosa claims that political language has lost its power of persuasion and uses a dead language made up of conventional formulas (Maia 2008). The same view is shared by Samuels (2002), who refers to the lack of integrity, imagination and new ideas among today's politicians.

Foucault (2008) makes an analysis of the instances of discursive control through history and proposes a critical analysis of discourse and its political use. His starting point is the presupposition that words and discourse possess a power that comes from the institutions in which they are inserted, and that they exercise a sort of pressure and power of coercion over other discourses. There are procedures that favor controlling discourse, among which is one that is relevant to our theme: the use of exclusion and interdiction by means of the opposition between true and false. That is to say, 'truths' are sustained by the institutional systems that impose them, which implies 'the wish for the truth'.

Foucault draws closer to the sophists in his criticism of truth, but also proposes an 'ideal truth' as an ethics of knowledge that 'only promises the truth to the very wish for truth and only to the power to think it' (2008: 45). To achieve such an understanding of truth born of discourse, one has to face the fear of all that is violent, discontinuous, combative and disorderly in it: 'That great buzzing of discourse, so endless and disorderly' (ibid.: 50).

In short, Foucault's proposal is to make a critical analysis in order to understand the power of coercion in discourse and the reflexive attempt to liberate it. The objective is to reclaim its original and non-categorizing phenomenological truth by questioning the 'wish for the truth' and restituting the characteristic of a happening, a suspension of the sovereignty of the significant. In this way, the polarities *truth* and *lie* meet in the conciliation of opposites, which seems healthy, but it remains to be known whether it can be applied to relations of power.

Truth and power

Hannah Arendt (2007) ponders over the relation between truth and power and its deceitful nature, as history shows the conflict between morals and politics. She questions the presupposition that it would be a lesser evil to sacrifice the truth if this precluded acts of greater violence. She establishes a difference between the truth of philosophers and the truth of politicians. According to the author, politics is vital for individuals and society, deals with the co-existence of differences, and is based on consent and rational persuasion. The process of opinion formation requires a genuine encounter with different opinions, and representative opinions need to enlarge personal opinions to incorporate those of others. Here, opinion differs from the solitude of philosophical thinking. Opinion should not be measured by the standard of truth. Truth would be anti-political, since by eliminating debate and diversity it eliminates the very principle of political life.

Although she stresses the negative consequences of rational truth when applied to the sphere of politics and collective deliberation, she also defends the importance of factual truth for the preservation of an accurate account of the past. Freedom of opinion is a farce unless factual information is guaranteed. She reasserts the value of political discourse of deliberation and persuasion, of a politics that acknowledges differences and the plurality of opinions.

Politicians need to mold the facts to the expectations of the audience and to the use of image and propaganda as a means of transmitting the desired messages. A modern aggravating factor has been added to the art of lying, because nowadays manipulating the facts is accompanied by self-deceit: 'self-illusion has become an indispensable instrument in the need to make images' (ibid.: 313). The continuous re-creation of image, which tends to fade, favors a kind of cynicism and disbelief. In a world of falsity there is nothing to lean on, so sticking to lies and distorting facts removes from the sphere of politics its main stabilizing force as a starting point for change, for beginning something new.

So, Arendt concludes that organized lying is contrary to political life, whose principles are freedom, equality, justice, solidarity.

Once it is realized that political action is in practice closely linked to hypocrisy, which is justified as an effective recourse to stay in power, the debates go on multiplying.

The psychological question posed by hypocrisy is to know to what extent this is a manipulating action motivated more or less consciously. The question is whether the grandiose narcissistic self and the defensive persona would engage in political lies, as well as psychopathy and cynicism.

Narcissism

The term *narcissism* is understood partially as self-admiration, but also as feelings of hatred and inferiority towards oneself, which are compensated for by insistence on the perfection of beauty, intelligence and power (Jacoby 1990). These are the demands of an unrealistic 'grandiose self'. Narcissism as self-centeredness is a defense against underlying unpleasurable linkages, based on the overcompensation of inferiority complexes and the accompanying fear of self-depreciating life situations. Feelings of grandiosity or of inferiority may also be produced by identification of the ego with transpersonal contents.

The persona is on the top, but the self-esteem must be grounded in genuine individuality where the social role is only a part. The risk of over-identification with the persona is a state of self-alienation and depersonalization.

Although we need several characteristics to diagnose a narcissistic personality disorder, some common features that are of interest to our topic are: pathological lying, lack of empathy to the feelings of others and the inability to form significant relationships, in addition to occasional delinquent activities. 'Delinquent activities may be found, together with attacks of uncontrolled rage and pathological lying' (Jacoby 1990: 156).

The extreme need for recognition, and susceptibility to narcissistic injury and the feeling of being hurt, threaten the cohesion of the ego and manifest as an indiscriminate permeability or as a defensive armor. Seductive charm is also a defensive attitude that guarantees admiration, but narcissistically disturbed people defend against empathizing, as closeness with the other would involve the risk of fusing and dissolving an already weak ego identity.

For Whitmont (1985), the false self is stimulated in our culture and provokes feelings of emptiness, alienation, impotence, depression, and absence of feeling in relationships and the imagination. A dominant syndrome in patients with borderline narcissistic pathology is described as: 'Ego pride, hate, greed, envy, and fanaticism repressed, denied and projected, are the real social ills that threaten to unleash disaster (Whitmont 1985: 47).

Politics and alienation

Although we find in the above description characteristics that can easily be applied to politicians, it would be rash to claim that this class gathers together narcissistic personalities, since a distinction should be made between what is performed consciously as a maneuver and what is repressed and defensive, as well as other disorders or neuroses that are occasionally present, including psychopathy. Samuels (2002) criticizes interpretative reductionism and speculations on the psychological motivations of politicians instead of focusing on understanding this power game.

The alienating character of the politics of lying and mystification is nevertheless confirmed by humanist thinkers. Psychiatrist and writer Ronald Laing denounced the alienation of experience and influenced post-modern thinkers. 'It is not enough to destroy one's own experience and that of others: this destruction must also be covered with a false conscience hardened, as Marcuse says, against its own falsity' (Laing 1969: 45).

Laing speaks about the experience and roles of social representation; experience is based on the authentic self. Human alienation is seen as normal in society, but self-alienation makes us lose the feeling of being, as well as making encounter impossible. Experience of the other is negated through techniques accepted as natural. Coercion and exploitation are disguised as amorous benevolence, which begins with education.

One of the effective modes of negation is mystification, as Laing exemplifies: if Jack wants to forget something, it bothers him that Jill reminds him of it; the best way is not to ask her to be quiet, but to incite her to forget it too. Negation is a constant in human relations and mystification is an effective way to exercise it, as the author brilliantly puts it: 'you have to be paranoid to think that' (Laing 1969: 31); in other words, doubt what you perceive, what you feel, what you think.

The parallel with revisionism of history for political ends, the repetition of lies until they become a plausible truth, censorship or punishment for whoever denounces it, all this denotes how current Laing's observations are.

In keeping with this line of reasoning, Baumann (2000), a sociologist and analyst of post-modern society, quotes Arendt (1973) in *The Origins of Totalitarianism*, explaining that the totalitarian tendency is to make human beings superfluous, redundant and dispensable as individuals. Since the subject cannot be prevented from thinking, his thinking is made impotent, irrelevant and without any influence on the success or failure of power.

Returning to Arendt's ideas, one wonders where and how to find the space for shared opinion in today's society.

Baumann (op. cit.) describes the insecurity of modern life and its political repercussions, an insecurity that does not encourage union and solidarity as mitigating factors. In an age of uncertainties, the defenses against insecurity have been dismantled; the author claims that the market thrives on uncertainty and stimulates competitiveness, deregulation and mobility to the detriment of support and solidarity. What is lacking is a common cause with the quality of joint action, and the politicians tend to deviate the deeper cause of anxiety – the experience of uncertainty and insecurity – to generalized concerns about threats to security, mainly directed at the other, for example the immigrant. For Baumann, rather than alienation, which presupposes a totalizing world and people, there is instability or disadaptation. The contemporary human being is becoming a 'lonely collector of sensations' (ibid.: 48).

As Baumann (2005) sees it, the global world has become a deposit of human waste, of outcasts, of superfluous populations. The present key to the political crisis is the absence of an effective agent to legitimize, promote and serve any set of values or any agenda of consistent and coherent options (Baumann 2000). The author proposes rescuing in the public political space the interrupted discourse of the common good, and criticizes the supposed neo-liberal ideology with its emphasis on productivity and competitiveness, on the cult of the victorious and on promoting ethical cynicism. He also differentiates political authenticity, which in essence contains critical reflection, from the merely 'political' exercise of power.

We can infer from this author that in the mere exercise of power, critical reflection is replaced by camouflaged action and subjugation via subterfuge.

From what has been outlined above, it can be concluded that the scope of lies is linked to the way that power is exercised. The possibility of incorporating love of truth would only occur were control and domination to be replaced by consensus and reflection. The Greek ideal, according to Plato and Aristotle, was to gather the whole population together inside the *agora*, that is to say, the population could not grow beyond a certain limit. Such an ideal could hardly be applied nowadays, except perhaps by adapting it, for example by gathering small groups together.

In moral terms, maintaining coercion only causes repression, which psychoanalysis has shown to contain, but not to transform, as can be seen in various explosions of violence throughout the world.

In *Answer to Job*, written in 1952, Jung warned about the scope of the power of destruction given to man and the necessity to 'temper his will with the spirit of love and wisdom' (Jung 1977: par. 745).

> The only thing that really matters now is whether man can climb up to a higher moral level, to a higher plane of consciousness, in order to be equal to the superhuman powers which the fallen angels have played into his hands.
>
> (ibid.: par. 46)

According to Bernstein (1985), the mature hero resembles the politician who recognizes the limits of power and the moral and ethical issues of life; he does not identify with power. This hero is contrasted with the warrior who lives on glory, pride, the supremacy of force, even though there are moments when one or the other needs to be put to action. He quotes Jimmy Carter's speech of 1977: '[. . .] power as a quiet strength based not merely on the size of an arsenal, but on the nobility of ideas' (Bernstein 1985: 19). The author concludes that power gets out of control when the thinking function cannot contain it: 'The feeling function carries the moral imperative of a society, and the thinking function carries the moral idea' (ibid.: 29).

Samuels (2002) claims that politics embodies the psyche of a people, and perceives in the experience of the politics of differences a path where psychotherapy can contribute with its knowledge, as applied to the problems of the real world. The author refers to an occult politics which allows us to address the theme of the game of truths, half-truths and lies, whether or not associated with repression. He also advocates the need to change relations, based on alliances instead of rivalries.

To this end, a change in the power structures would be inevitable, and he points to the leader who can afford the art of failure, and the *trickster*, in the sense of breaking rules and being spontaneous, which is only possible in the meetings of small political groups. This type of irreverence is different from the dishonesty and hypocritical solemnity of many politicians in the large parties.

Samuels proposes a dialogue of diversities – in addition to Arendt's harmonious co-existence of the different, and Baumann's postulated universalism – a polycultural society that embraces differences and the capacity to communicate and reach mutual understanding, 'a communion of meanings' (ibid.: 204), in order to find out how to carry on (as Wittgenstein put it).

It is important to have a sense of perspective and to be able to endorse *Tikkun Olam*, the Hebrew words for the repair and restoration of the world (Samuels 2008).

> A new approach to spirituality is necessary so that transforming politics can achieve its potential. This includes understanding spirituality as the expression of a deep democratic commitment to equality – equality in God's eyes – which means equality in society.
>
> (Samuels 2002: 219)

Conclusion

'While you talk, the world is being destroyed', said a little boy aged four to the adult he was playing with. A wise political counselor; in the context, he was referring to preventing the adult from chatting with the others in a room, because the child and the adult were in the garden playing at combating alien creatures.

This declaration shows in the real world to what extent we talk so much and do so little. And also, how often we make empty speeches. We need to reclaim the sense of talking and associate it with action, which is no easy task.

Accepting hypocrisy as a legitimate means to avoid a greater violence implies the risk of cheating the conscience, which is necessary for an ethical stance, which in turn constitutes the path of our freedom, our harmony and inclusion in the world.

With all this in mind, the problem posed by political hypocrisy is less that of knowing whether it would be licit to use subterfuges to affirm power, particularly if the objective is some common good. The relevant question is the manipulation that stifles the conscience and the iatrogenics inherent to this procedure: loss of the capacity of moral judgment, the ethical discernment that leads us to the discovery of possible answers to our dilemmas and challenges. Recognizing the personalities that rely on manipulation, whether conscious or narcissistic or else the result of some other personality disorder, would be an instrument against alienation and accommodation, against the skidding of these hyper-modern times on the deafening and bewildering race-track to the void.

Bibliography

Arendt, H. (1973) *The Origins of Totalitarianism*. London: André Deutsch.

Arendt, H. (2007) Verdade e Política. *Entre o Passado e o futuro (Between Past and Future)*. São Paulo: Perspectiva: 282–325.

Baumann, Z. (2000) *Em Busca da Política (In Search of Politics)*. Rio de Janeiro: Zahar.

Baumann, Z. (2005) *Vidas Desperdiçadas (Wasted Lives: Modernity and Outcasts)*. Rio de Janeiro: Zahar.

Bernstein, J. (1985) Power and Politics in the Thermonuclear Age. *Quadrant*, 18 (2): 11–34.

Eco, H. (1997) Os sinais do poder. *Breviário dos Políticos*. São Paulo: Editora 34: 23–31.

Foucault, M. (2008) A Ordem do Discurso (*L' Ordre du Discours*). São Paulo: Loyola.

Jacoby, M. (1990) *Individuation and Narcissism*. London: Routledge.

Jung, C. G. (1977) Answer to Job. *CW 11*, Princeton: Princeton University.

Laing, R. D. (1969) *La Politique de l' Expérience (Politics of Experience)*. Paris: Stock.

Lamounier, B. (1997) O poder e seus micromecanismos. *Breviário dos Políticos*. São Paulo: Editora 34: pp. 9–23.

Maia, E. C. (2008) Entrevista Vargas Llosa. www.cafecolombo.com.br (accessed September 2008).

Mazarin, J. (1997) *Breviário dos Políticos (Bréviaire des Politiciens)*. São Paulo: Editora 34.

Samuels, A. (2002) *A Política no Divã (Politics on the Couch)*. São Paulo: Summus.

Samuels, A. (2008) Can Psychotherapy and Psychology Offer Anything to the Political World? *Contemporary Symbols of Personal, Cultural and National Identity*. Zürich: ETH.

Silveira, F. E. (2000) Reflexões sobre a natureza do poder político: o problema da hipocrisia. *Civitas – Revista de Ciências Sociais*, 1 (1).

Whitmont, Edward. (1985) Individual Transformation and Personal Responsibility. *Quadrant*, 18 (2): 45–56.

Chapter 39

A thank-you note to Andrew Samuels

Polly Young-Eisendrath

It seems that I've known Andrew Samuels since I came of age in the Jungian world in my late twenties. Probably that's not true, but it feels that way to me because it seems now that I've always considered him to be my friend and fellow traveler. I recall that when I first encountered Andrew's ideas, they opened my eyes to the possibility that I was not alone in my 'post-Jungian' strivings and views, even though he probably hadn't come up with that term yet.

As a training candidate in the analytical psychology of the late 1970s and early 1980s, I felt burdened and sharply offended by some nineteenth-century stereotypes – then in wide circulation – that foisted upon us as fact such culturally laden assumptions as the 'animus-possessed woman' with inferior thinking; the notion that black peoples in our dreams always represent the 'shadow'; and the view that the collective unconscious is racially layered from most primitive to most evolved, with white gentile Europeans at the top. I wrestled hard with Jung's theory of 'contra-sexuality' because I thought it was both original and important, and also troubling and narrow in its gender categories. I wanted open dialogue on these and other matters that I took to be critical to the future of analytical psychology. I found little of this kind of dialogue in those early years. At the same time, I did my best to learn the history of Jung and his followers, and to master the major concepts of the theory and practice of analytical psychology without swallowing anything whole.

Two of my own long-term adaptations have, I believe, always served me well: being a good and disciplined student, and speaking out directly when I feel that something is unfair, confused or foolish. And it didn't take me long, even as a training candidate, to object to what I took to be elitist prejudices in analytical psychology, in regard to race, anti-semitism and gender in our practices of that period. These objections were paired with a serious dedication to the discipline which I thought held insights and ideas that no other depth psychology offered.

By 1987, I had published an essay called 'The Absence of Black Americans as Jungian Analysts' (1987a) and another entitled 'The Female

Person and How We Talk About Her' (1987b). I was beginning to be influenced by Andrew's writing – especially his seminal study, *Jung and the Post-Jungians* (1985). I think I must have met Andrew around this time. I recall being thrilled to hear him speak about the ideas that eventually became his next groundbreaking work, *The Plural Psyche* (1989). Now that I am thinking about it, I believe that we met when he came to Philadelphia to speak about this second book.

What first struck me about Andrew, in person, was that he was refreshing. He showed a genuine intellectual curiosity in both his wit and his open-mindedness. I had not found this mix among many of my Jungian colleagues and associates up until then. In Philadelphia – where I moved in 1982 – there were some archetypal colleagues, 'Hillmanians,' who displayed sharp wit, but they were not open-minded in their inquiry. Instead, they applied the same rhetorical methods to any and every topic they analyzed, leaving me feeling that they were working from a formula without a true and deep openness to what might emerge from dialogue and engagement.

When Andrew appeared, probably in Philadelphia, I heaved a great sigh of relief. He was clearly open-hearted and open-minded. He was not a dyed-in-the-wool proponent of a particular point of view, but wanted to sharpen our points of view, embracing what was deeply valuable in analytical psychology while jettisoning what was not. Quite quickly I could see that Andrew was going to change our field because he was thorough, thoughtful, honest, and engaged. And he has done just that and continues to do so.

That is why, when Terence Dawson and I were editing *The Cambridge Companion to Jung* (1997), we invited Andrew to write the introduction. There was no one else who had so thoroughly mastered an overview of the different approaches to our field while sharpening our critical inquiry about the value of our ideas and methods. Andrew still maintains a broad mastery and a sharp criticism of what is emerging in the different branches of the Jungian world. In his new introduction to the revised 2008 edition of *The Cambridge Companion to Jung*, Andrew gives us a wake-up call about the extremes of what is happening in our field. At the same time, his account of what is valuable, original and definitive in our discipline could not be more apt, sincere or thoughtful. It seems to me that Andrew is an excellent representative of the best of contemporary Jungian thought in both clinical and cultural applications.

Of course, Andrew's contribution to an in-depth view of politics and psychoanalysis, *The Political Psyche* (1993), took him and us in another new direction that continues to produce fruit. Andrew's challenge to us was to bring the couch to politics and politics to the couch and we still benefit from this challenge as we move into an increasingly complex and nuanced political environment. Andrew has wanted us to be honest about our political intentions and views, and to consider how they also fit with the dark ranges of our unconscious motivations.

As a personal friend, Andrew has been always been sincere, transparent, smart, engaged – and really funny in a moving, human way. In the past five years or so, my own interests have turned increasingly toward the dialogue between Buddhism and analytical psychology – especially in regard to the self and no-self. What do these concepts point to in our subjective lives? Why do we need them, and what do they actually discriminate? If we take the self to mean something that is individual, particular and constrained by the embodiment of a certain person, then we can assume that the no-self is the absence of that: that it refers to the kind of interbeing or interdependence that arises from engagement, encounter, and embeddedness. In this way the no-self is born freshly in each new context and depends on being open to what is arising from moment to moment. The no-self expresses an attunement to one's experience and a willingness to jump into the fray repeatedly without excessive self-consciousness or neurotic constraints. In my view, Andrew Samuels expresses this style of no-self in much of his work and in his friendship with me. Thank you, Andrew, for being a lifelong friend and a seminal contributor to our beloved field of analytical psychology.

Bibliography

Samuels, A. (1985). *Jung and the Post-Jungians*. London and Boston: Routledge & Kegan Paul.

—— (1989). *The Plural Psyche: Personality, Morality and the Father*. London and New York: Routledge.

—— (1993). *The Political Psyche*. London and New York: Routledge.

Young-Eisendrath, P. (1986a). 'The Absence of Black Americans as Jungian Analysts.' *Quadrant: The New York Journal of Analytical Psychology*, 20: 2.

—— (1987b) 'The Female Person and How We Talk About Her.' In M. Gergen (ed.) *Feminist Thought and The Structure of Knowledge*. New York: New York University Press.

Young-Eisendrath, P. and Dawson, T. (1997). *The Cambridge Companion to Jung (First Edition)*. Cambridge: Cambridge University.

—— (2008). *The Cambridge Companion to Jung (Second Edition)*. Cambridge: Cambridge University.

Chapter 40

For Andrew Samuels on his 60th birthday

Luigi Zoja

Dear friend, we have always confided in each other and told each other everything. Or to put it more extremely yet more accurately, we have never hidden anything from each other because we have always had a degree of understanding that has not required words. Something similar is going to happen in the writing of this piece for your *Festschrift*. I will have to write in words, even though they might not be necessary. Such an active silence has, for us, always constituted a kind of mutual support and recognition. It has been so for almost 40 years. It is not that often you find two people who are friends in this way, both of them knowing that there is a certainty of discovering a complementarity of thinking leading to a deep under-standing. And if, sometimes, we really do not understand one another, we can still reach a high level of discussion and not waste our time – increasingly precious with the passing of the decades – on petty criticisms.

I will now lower my voice, because I am going to speak some scandalous words. I am not so happy where I am. In my country, in my city. I don't feel that at ease even in my profession, which I have not chosen lightly but as an intensely passionate decision and which I continue to love. But, most of all, I am not at ease in our new century, which, pompously, even calls itself a 'new millennium'. I don't believe that we live in an age of decline. No! We live in an age of *decadence*. Of course, decadent ages have always existed, followed by rebirths, reawakenings, renaissances. The present novelty, though, is that decadence has gone global, interwoven with planetary crises that have become so structural as to be by now irreversible. Hence, ours could be the first decadence not to be followed by rebirth or recovery.

I am well aware that my devaluation of the new century is simplistic. In fact, the new times are, no doubt, full of injustice as a kind of inheritance stemming from the years immediately preceding them. And it is by now common knowledge that – contradicting those who saw progress as the defining feature of humanity – the last century was the most criminal epoch in human history. It is not hard to work out that, from the nineteenth to the twentieth century, the progression of carnage has been such that, if it were to continue into this century, even without nuclear war or environmental catastrophe, humanity could easily destroy itself. Would we be justified in claiming that, while science often works cumulatively for the good, this is counterbalanced by a general immorality that is equally exponential, bringing the prevalence of evil to ever greater levels?

Well, the fact is that (and you know that this theme is an obsession of mine) the enormous, extremely rapid progress resting on technology, economic growth and more sophisticated means and media of communication tends to function more and more as a multiplier of evil, only seldom of good. This tragic phenomenon seems simply to intensify with the more recent achievements of technology and economy. If we look beneath the surface of populist and optimistic announcements of progress, we have become adept at noticing the evils the newer age has inherited from the previous one. Yet we are much less observant of the benefits with which it has been endowed by its predecessor.

Therefore, the terrible gifts of the twentieth century darken the clear skies of the twenty-first. But the twentieth, in its turn, was not born in a year zero. What were the manifold inheritances of the twentieth from the nineteenth century? Among the most important, there was the seminal work of intuition of Darwin which, as it spread, became nothing more than a cynical justification – framed as a so-called law – of the rule of the strongest. Similarly, the great linguistic renaissance of Romanticism which, spread in the crudest manner possible, morphed into a literary justification for aggressive nationalism. The two together, blurring the differences between zoological species and cultural process, produced what came to be known a scientific racism. Even the more humanistic ideas of Marx (which can be seen as a clear attempt to align Judaeo-Christian ethics with secular philosophical thinking) soon degenerated, without waiting for Stalin and his horrors to finally and fatally end the dream.

All in all, it is instructive to think that the moral regression of the twenty-first century, which I think we already fear, will be linked to the techno-economical developments of the twentieth, in the same way as we by now see clearly that the horrors of the twentieth have a link with scientific progress, literature and the humanistic progressive politics of the nineteenth. In a sense, this is a perverse replay of the multidisciplinarity of the Renaissance. In that time, knowledge was far less specialized and the well-learned person was, much more than today, scientist and philosopher at the same time.

Are we worried by the paradox that progress is, at the same time, regression? If so, there is no need. For this was the principal message of the first Western authors, the Greek tragedians. From a philosophical perspective, we can call this an *enantiodromia*, the reversal of something into its opposite. It is a form of dynamism which was not discovered, but simply re-defined by Jungian psychoanalysis, according to which unilateral conscious attitudes aid in the repression of other attitudes. These, sooner or later, will take their revenge in the form of unexpected, irrational, explosive compensations.

But if this is such a general and ancient law, could we then go even further back, right to some of the sources of recorded human history? Probably we could, but for our purposes in this short chapter, it might be wise to go only one century further back.

The eighteenth century was also called the century of lights. Enlightenment, *Lumières*, *Aufklärung*, *Lumi* all characterise this century in much the same way – as a source of light. Here we see the beginnings of so-called modernity and this provides a helpful frame to these discussions. My question concerns how it has been possible that, in spite of an undeniable and unprecedented process of 'civilization', the Western world passed so quickly from light into darkness. The eighteenth century remains, in a way, the unmatched climax of the human mind's opening out, of the positive virtues of curiosity, of the growth of tolerance. In the same century, though, we can see corrupting factors already at work. Indeed, precisely when and where (at the end of the century, in France) it produces its highest results, the Enlightenment creates also a particular sub-phase of itself whose name remains one of the most ominous and redolent in all history: the Terror (*Terreur*).

In sum, as we traverse the past, we continually rediscover a kind of human continuity and a central unchanging aspect of our temperament throughout the ages. Humans, alone now, without Gods, perceiving themselves alone and divorced from the sacred, turn their energies to the deployment of new knowledge and the discovery of a new strength that can only be searched for within. I am talking about a reawakening of the mental heroism invented by classic antiquity. But this reawakening, first scattered and shy during the Renaissance, explodes untamed among the European cultivated classes during the Enlightenment. Such a substitution of external authority with a self-reflexive awareness which is humanistic and ethical at the time is, from a psychological perspective, too quick and too self-referential. For, if we know that the world broadly equates to what is inside us, then we experience fear and omnipotence at the same time. We become both God and King and it is very frightening. But it is that sort of psychic intoxication – invisible to the subject, but clear for those who observe it at a distance – which the ancient Greek language (but also modern English) calls *hubris*.

Human subjects were distancing themselves from superstition, and finally opening up to rationality and to the sense of the possibility of the permanent progress I referred to earlier. Yet we paid for it with a feeling of this being an existential exercise in a field of life without borders or clear definition. The superstition we thought we had abolished reappears and resurfaces as a feeling that it is our very modernity that is itself responsible for our bad luck. We learn the hard way that irrationality and a belief in magic cannot so easily be expelled from the psyche.

So, when we achieve Enlightenment, there is nowhere left to go but downwards into the dark. We plummet into cosmic pessimism. Here dwells the secret twin of the Enlightenment. Romanticism was an attempt to ride out the storm by announcing its actual love of the night and the dark shadows playing in the woods. The mystic relation Romanticism established with geography produces the collective and religious captivation of the populace of Western countries by blood-and-earth notions of ethnic identity that may still rip up and dismember Europe. On the one hand, those who can still believe in social utopias continue to praise the rationality of Enlightenment. On the other hand, we see how the capacity of nationalism to foment conflict leads to a further paradox: mass movements that seek to turn back modernity but often end by becoming its servant. These groups become ensnared in the values that accompany the mass communications they seek to use. They become impossibly tainted by the world from which they are fleeing. The growth of 'liberal capitalism' seems to herald the end of ideology but the result is a discourse characterized by triviality and a dearth of ideas let alone ideology. The mass media acts as a container for all of these developments but it is an essentially empty vessel. Yes, the medium is the message.

After the Enlightenment, irrevocably formed by the events I am delineating, Westerners do not believe in substantial progress any more. Instead, they track the useless swings of so-called current affairs, noting their intense destructiveness. Enlightenment may still be possible for it is a part of us. Some are not definitively disappointed or corrupted. Analysts and their more engaged analysands are, in a way, survivors of the Enlightenment, but alive in a different century. To understand the needs of the new century, we should pay attention to its harsh and over-loud proclamations yet listen also to the more subdued soul of humanists in exile. Even analysis runs the risk of reducing itself to something modern – just a profession, not any more a pursuit of an ideal. Can we still promote individuation or should we be content with applying a technique?

I leave this and my other questions with you, Andrew, to mull over in the decades to come. I am certain that they will be as fertile as those during which I have already enjoyed your creativity and our friendship.

A teacher affects eternity;
one can never tell
where his influence ends

Henry Adams

Index

Abraham, K. 114
absence: the absent father 271;
    emptiness 83, 84, 109, 114, 270, 271,
    294; loss *see* loss; the Missing 121–6;
    of parental love 271; of social
    recognition 53; the void 84
abuse 24, 62–3
accountability 162, 164
accusation 53; *see also* blame
Achilles Heel magazine 233
acting out *see* enactment
action, polarised 193, 194–5, 196, 198
active imagination 168, 170, 262
Adams, Henry 307
Adams, M.V. 102, 103
Addison, A. 89–90
adhesive identifications 94
Adler, G. 38, 157
Adorno, T.W. 266
Adversity-Activated Development
    198
Aesculapius 102
ageing 113–19
agency 53; aggressive energies and 28;
    appearance and 202, 205;
    complementary relations and loss of
    53; the 'I' as agent 202
aggression/aggressiveness: aggressive
    energies in relationship 28–30, 32–4;
    aggressive fantasy 28, 30–1;
    amalgam of curiosity and 31;
    Buddhist perspective on aggressive
    energies and breakthrough 31–4;
    compensatory 273; depression and
    70; Lady Macbeth and 242; love and
    30, 34; passive aggression 48, 164,
    271, 273; psychosomatic diseases
    and 70; purpose of aggressive

energies 30–4; as the very stuff of
    relationship 34
Agrippa von Nettesheim, Henricus 169
AHP (Association for Humanistic
    Psychology) 232, 233–7
AHPP (Association of Humanistic
    Psychology Practitioners) 235, 236
Ailly, Pierre d' 212, 216
air 70
AJB (Associação Junguiana do Brasil)
    222, 230
alchemy 99–100, 104, 167, 250; *opus
    circulatorium* 101–2; uroboros 100,
    101–2; and the work of Physis
    102–4
alienation 83, 294–7; self-alienation 294
Alteritas group, Espírito Santo 223
analytic relationship *see* therapeutic/
    analytic relationship
analytical psychology: analysis as pre-
    requirement for training in 170;
    archetypal school 221; classical
    school 220–1; clinical experience of
    working with a dying man 176–82;
    community, *communitas*, and
    147–52; death, contemporary
    society and 176–82; developmental
    school 221; dialogue with Buddhism
    301; extended to working with
    survivors of political upheavals
    193–9; group process seminars in
    analytic training 152–3; IAAP *see*
    International Association for
    Analytical Psychology; multiplicity
    and 218–23; and the post-Jungian
    attitude 217–19; psychoanalysis,
    Jungian thought and 72–7;
    psychoanalysis merger with Jungian